RE CAVANAGH

Lyric Poetry and Modern Politics

RUSSIA, POLAND, AND THE WEST

Yale University Press
New Haven &
London

Set in Sabon type by Integrated Book Technology.
Printed in the United States of America.

Library of Congress Cataloging-in-Publication Data

Cavanagh, Clare.
   Lyric poetry and modern politics : Russia, Poland, and the West / Clare Cavanagh.
        p. cm.
   Includes bibliographical references and index.
   ISBN 978-0-300-15296-8 (pbk. : alk. paper)
   1. Lyric poetry—History and criticism.   2. Russian poetry—20th century—History and criticism.   3. Polish poetry—20th century—History and criticism.   4. Politics and literature—History—20th century.   5. Politics in literature.   I. Title.
   PN1356.C38 2010
   809.1'04—dc22   2009023902

A catalogue record for this book is available from the British Library.

This paper meets the requirements of ANSI/NISO Z39.48-1992 (Permanence of Paper).

10 9 8 7 6 5 4 3 2 1

To Mike, always

Contents

Acknowledgments

The debts I have incurred while writing this book are many. Vladimir
Gippius gave his young students "a house, a home" in Russian literature,
Osip Mandelstam recalls. My dear friends and teachers Anna and Stanisław
Barańczak gave me a home in Polish culture many years ago in Boston, and
in my heart I've never left. Their generosity—intellectual, literary, culinary,
and otherwise—has left its mark throughout this book, and to say I am
grateful is small repayment. My friend and colleague Gary Saul Morson
supported this project from its earliest inception through the long journey
through to its final publication. His enthusiasm kept it afloat and his criti-
cism set me straight at crucial moments. Saul and Jonathan Brent at Yale
University Press proved stalwart champions of a polemical Slavist's defense
of poetry, and I owe them more thanks than word limits permit. Lawrence
Lipking read an early version of the book in its entirety: his erudition and
imagination pointed me in new directions. Adam Zagajewski not only pro-
vided the poetry and criticism that inspired much of my argument. He also
read through more versions of this book than I care to recall; great poets
who are also great critics and friends are few and far between, and I'm
lucky to have begun translating a writer thirteen years ago who proved to
be all of these and then some. Lazar Fleishman brought both his critical
acuity and his unparalleled command of Soviet literary politics to bear on

the manuscript, and it is much the better for his kindness. Irena Grudzińska Gross has lent her erudition, her passion, and her enthusiasm to this project in multiple ways. An unnamed reader for Yale was immensely helpful. Rosanna Warren generously took time to read the penultimate version of my introduction, while the final chapter is very much the better for Christopher Ricks' astute, scrupulous editing of an earlier incarnation. The faults that remain are of course all my own doing.

Other friends and colleagues—Caryl Emerson, Madeline Levine, Victor Erlich—generously supplied me with support, conversation, and yes, the occasional, dreaded letter of recommendation over the many years of this book's gestation. My wonderful colleagues Susan McReynolds, Elisabeth Elliott, and Nina Gourianova have helped in more ways than I can say. I want to thank Jenny Holzer and Kerin Sulock of the Jenny Holzer Studio for extraordinary kindness. As if being inspired by a great poet I happen to translate weren't enough, I've also been privileged to follow the work of a great artist who takes inspiration from the same source in her meditations on the public functions of private art. Nice work if you can get it. Jonathan Galassi, Drenka Willen, Sal Robinson, Krystyna and Ryszard Krynicki, Anna and Stanisław Barańczak, Natalia Woroszylska, and Adam Zagajewski generously assisted with the permissions process. Yale Press's editorial staff—Sarah Miller, Ann-Marie Imbornoni, and Gavin Lewis, copy editor extraordinaire—have been models of patience and persistence. I've been lucky in my graduate help over the years: Jenifer Presto, at the project's early stages, and Katherine Bowers and Kolter Campbell later in the game were both exemplary research assistants and terrific interlocutors.

Chapter 2 first appeared in somewhat different form in *Rereading Russian Poetry,* ed. Stephanie Sandler (New Haven: Yale University Press, 1999). An early version of Chapter 3 was published in *Slavic Review,* vol. 55, no. 1 (Spring, 1996), 125–135. An abbreviated version of Chapter 6 appeared in *Wisława Szymborska: A Stockholm Conference,* ed. Leonard Neuger and Rikard Wennerholm (Stockholm: Royal Academy of Letters, History and Antiquities, 2006). An early version of Chapter 8 was published in *Literary Imagination,* vol. 6, no. 3 (2004), 332–55. I am grateful for permission to reprint them here.

The John Simon Guggenheim Memorial Foundation, the American Council of Learned Societies, and the Social Science Research Council generously provided the fellowship support that made research for the project possible. The University of Wisconsin, Madison, and Northwestern University supported the project with research and travel assistance, and the International Research and Exchanges Board funded a research trip to Poland in the summer of 2002. The Alice Kaplan Institute for the Humanities at Northwestern provided a year's senior fellowship in 2003–4 to pursue my research on Miłosz, some of which found its way into the book's last chapter.

Parents should always use words their children don't understand, Marina Tsvetaeva warns. They should also read their children poetry. Ogden Nash, Robert Frost, "The Wreck of the Hesperus," "The Cremation of Sam McGee"—of these only Frost made his way directly into the book that follows. (I should also mention Shakespeare, particularly with Mickey Rooney as Puck.) But what my father and mother, John and Adele Cavanagh, gave me way back then informs this project in ways they themselves could never have anticipated. I wish I could tell them so today.

Last, but never least, are my nearest relations and best friends, Mike and Martin Lopez. Martin has lived with this project virtually his entire life; and he is what made living with it possible. Mike has been my friend, teacher, editor, advisor, and best support throughout this long, long process. Daily conversations with a superb critic who is also a scholar of British and American Romanticism would be good luck enough. When he also leaves you exactly the right books and bibliographies after those talks; gives you exactly the advice you need, even when you don't know you need it; reads your work; sets you straight; and makes your home the place you do your best thinking and writing, and your best resting after the thinking and writing: then you have more than you could ever ask for. And that's Mike.

Introduction: Acknowledged Legislation

Poets are the unacknowledged legislators of the world.
            —*Percy Bysshe Shelley*, A Defence of Poetry *(1821)*

"*The unacknowledged legislators of the world*" *describes the secret police, not the poets.*
                —*W. H. Auden, "Writing" (1962)*

Do not be elected to the senate of your country.
                —*W. B. Yeats, "To Ezra Pound" (1937)*

The Lyric under Siege, and the Mystery of the Missing Second World

Poetry is power.
            —*Osip Mandelstam, quoted in Nadezhda Mandelstam,*
                        Hope Against Hope *(1970)*

What is poetry which does not save
Nations or people?
                —*Czesław Miłosz, "Dedication" (1945)*

> *If Galileo had said in verse that the world moved, the Inquisition might have let him alone.*
>
> —*Thomas Hardy, from* The Life and Work of
> Thomas Hardy, *ed. Michael Milgate (1985)*

"What would American poets and critics do without the Central Europeans and the Russians to browbeat themselves with?" Maureen McLane asks in a recent review in the *Chicago Tribune.* "Miłosz, Wisława Szymborska, Adam Zagajewski, Zbigniew Herbert, Joseph Brodsky—here we have world-historical seriousness! Weight! Importance! Even their playfulness is weighty, metaphysical, unlike barbaric American noodlings!" McLane takes aim at a critical commonplace now well entrenched among anglophone poets and critics. In anthologies, essays, and poems alike, the great Eastern Europeans of the century just past— Akhmatova, Mandelstam, Brodsky, Miłosz, Herbert, Szymborska, et al.—play the acknowledged, if unofficial, legislators to their unhappily marginalized, conspicuously unoppressed neighbors to the west. "Only here do they really respect poetry—they kill because of it," Osip Mandelstam remarked to his wife at the onset of Stalin's Great Terror. "More people die for poetry here than anywhere else." There are advantages, needless to say, to coming from nations where poets are less highly rated. But to writers reared on the Romantic myth of the poet-Christ, the fate of Eastern Europe's modern bards, besieged by history, persecuted by one repressive regime after another, must seem seductive indeed. Few writers have ever died of benign neglect.[1]

> If dictators still wished
> to read our wrathful, rabid,
> well-wrought rhymes, then poetry
> would surely change the world.
>   (Adam Zagajewski, "Thorns" ["Kolce," 1983])

> If only Russia had been founded
> by Anna Akhmatova, if only
> Mandelstam had made the laws
> and Stalin were just a minor
> figure in some long-lost Georgian
> epic, if only Russia would give up
> its bristling bearskin
> and live within the word and not
> the fist, if only Russia, if only
>   (Adam Zagajewski, "If Only Russia" ["Gdyby Rosja," 1985])

Taken together, Adam Zagajewski's brief lyrics seem to embody what Seamus Heaney calls "the unacknowledged legislator's dream," the dream of the unjustly neglected prophets whose fate Shelley famously laments in his *Defence of Poetry* (1821). Shelley's "unacknowledged legislators" stand unfailingly on the side of "great and free developments of the national will"—but they are spurned by the very nations whose interests they seek to serve. Shelley yearns for "earlier epochs" in which poets were revered as priests and seers, even as he ponders the "circumstances of the age and nation" that might lead once more to the poet's proper valuation. And his poetic offspring have inherited his thwarted longings, or so Heaney's gently self-mocking little poem suggests:

> I sink my crowbar in a chink I know under the masonry
> of state and statute, I swing on a creeper of secrets
> into the Bastille.
> My wronged people cheer from their cages.
> (from "The Unacknowledged Legislator's Dream")

So runs the fantasy of the would-be prophet, who publicly takes his people's suffering upon himself so that his oppressed, applauding nation might be free.[2]

The poets of Eastern Europe are not immune to such dreams: "If only Mandelstam had made the laws," Zagajewski sighs. But they do not dream in isolation. Their vision of the poet's mission is shared in key ways by compatriots raised on traditions demanding, Miłosz notes, that the poet "speak in his poems of subjects of interest to all the citizens." Beware of answered prayers, the saying goes. I will deal elsewhere with the less than enviable historical circumstances—familiar to Slavists, less well known to students of other traditions—that helped to make Shelley's dream a reality for his Russian and Polish contemporaries and their literary descendants. Auden gets it only half-right in his essay "Writing." The secret police may be the true unacknowledged legislators, but it takes the secret police both to make and to break a nation's acknowledged, if unauthorized poet-prophets.[3]

For now, though, I want merely to note the ambivalence that colors both "Thorns" and "If Only Russia" even grammatically. Both poems are carefully couched in the conditional mood: they thus run counter to reality by definition. And that is as it should be, or at any rate, the way it is, Zagajewski implies. Tyrants make the rules, not poets, and dictators' deeds change worlds far more often than artists' words do. Poetic legislation has its limits: "No lyric has ever stopped a tank," Heaney remarks. Indeed, by the mid-eighties, when both poems were written, Zagajewski had challenged his compatriots' preoccupation with poetry as a form of collective resistance. He chose to "dissent from dissent," to break ranks with would-be artist-legislators by setting his lyric "I" against the defiant "we" that had shaped his poetic generation. The "unacknowledged legislator's dream" has a nasty habit of becoming the acknowledged prophet's nightmare, as Zagajewski suggests in his programmatically unprogrammatic *Solidarity, Solitude* (*Solidarność i samotność,* 1985).[4]

In its original context Heaney's poem likewise hints at the poet's ambivalence towards his own nation's bardic tradition, and more specifically, towards the demand, and the temptation, to speak for the oppressed Catholic minority of his native Northern Ireland. His poetic portrait of the artist as would-be martyr forms an ironic coda to the sequence of "bog poems" from *North* (1975) that mark Heaney's most controversial effort to articulate his troubled nation's turmoil in verse. He thus subtly undercuts his own aspirations to serve as poetic spokesman for his wronged nation's woes: "Were those your eyes just now at the hatch?" the would-be poet-savior inquires from his prison cell. Artistic dissidence generally has a dangerous tendency "to lead to a certain theatricalization of intellectual life," Zagajewski notes. Heaney's suffering writer requires both a captive and a captor audience in order to realize his redemptive fantasy.[5]

My project in the pages that follow is threefold. The book is firstly an overview of twentieth-century Eastern European poetry in its Russian and Polish incarnations. It is also a comparative study of modern poetry on both the Eastern and Western side of the great political divide that came to be known mid-century as the "Iron Curtain." Finally, it is a polemic with Western postmodern literary and philosophical theories from French post-structuralism and deconstructionism to American cultural criticism and New Historicism. Part of my task will be to track the splendors and miseries of acknowledged legislation in twentieth-century Russia and Poland, and to examine ways in which postwar Polish poets particularly have sought to wrest themselves free from the burdens of barddom that their Western counterparts have been so eager to embrace. In doing so, I hope to complicate notions of poetry and politics for non-Slavist scholars by testing modern Anglo-American definitions of lyric poetry against cultures in which the rules of poetic engagement are radically different than those prevailing in the West. More than this—the Marxist theory that informs, implicitly or explicitly, so much contemporary Anglo-American critical discourse has yet to be scrutinized through the lens of those literary traditions dominated by avowedly Marxist states during much of the century just past. This book attempts to address that gap.

I do not pretend to anything like exhaustiveness. Modern poetry and politics is a vast topic in any of the cultural contexts I discuss, and the list of Slavic case studies and Western comparisons could be extended indefinitely. I trace only one possible variant of this story, beginning with Aleksandr Blok in the early part of the century, moving through the first few decades of Soviet rule in Russia by way of Mayakovsky, Akhmatova, and Mandelstam, and then crossing, with the victorious Soviet troops, into Poland in the aftermath of World War II. I track two generations of "acknowledged legislation," both official and un-, on Polish soil, first through the work of Wiktor Woroszylski and Wisława Szymborska, and then by way of several members of Poland's so-called "New Wave" or "Generation of '68," most notably, Stanisław Barańczak, Ryszard Krynicki, and Adam Zagajewski. I conclude with Miłosz's Anglo-American reception as a way of tying together several strands of my argument: the translator of Yeats, among many other anglophone poets, and lifelong admirer of Whitman comes to exemplify the quintessential Eastern European poet-witness to his many admirers in the West.

I have mentioned the preeminence of Eastern Europe's poet-bards among their Anglo-American counterparts in recent decades. The Slavist perusing the Anglo-American scholarship on literature and politics of recent years will be struck, though, not by these poets' ubiquity, but by their virtual absence from such discussions. Why is this? I will turn to likely causes among non-Slavists in a moment. One thing is clear, though: we Slavists are partly to blame for this state of affairs. The retrograde Russians "must deliberately hammer into [their] heads things which have become habit and instinct with other peoples," Piotr Chaadaev laments in his "First Philosophical Letter" (1829). Backward Poland is the "parrot of nations," the Romantic poet Juliusz Słowacki charges in *Agamemnon's Grave* (1840).[6] Both Russia and Poland have long been obsessed with their marginal status vis-à-vis the Western culture to which they play country cousins determined to catch up to their more advanced and civilized kin. Anglo-American Slavists still bear traces of this inherited complex today. In our efforts to keep pace with apparently more sophisticated modes of literary and cultural scholarship, we have too frequently adopted Western theoretical models uncritically, without recognizing the sometimes radical divide that separates Eastern European culture from its Western counterparts. Too often we have been content to play the rude mechanicals at Western theory's fête champêtre, without recognizing that we too have something to offer in a conversation claiming to prize difference, otherness, and outsiders.

Recent theory has taught critics to "resist universalizing cultural discourses," as Edward Said writes, by recovering the particular peoples and places such discourses tend to erase. The scholar's task is thus to "reclaim, rename, and reinhabit" the cultural loci left strategically blank in the West's "great legitimizing narratives of emancipation and enlightenment." Said notes, though, that the term "imperialism" itself runs the risk of "mask[ing] with an unacceptable vagueness the interesting heterogeneity of Western metropolitan cultures." What of the no less interesting heterogeneity found slightly to the East of the metropolitan cultures that the Slavic nations, colonies and colonizers alike, envied and longed to emulate? "Nations are themselves narrations," Said remarks. The counternarrative he opposes to the West's self-serving storytelling in *Culture and Imperialism* (1993) takes a revealing shape, one that other postcolonial theorists have followed in mapping their revisionary histories. This master plot traces the rise of the great bourgeois capitalist empires of the nineteenth century—chiefly those of Great Britain and France—and then follows their further fates by way of their latter-day inheritor, the United States.[7]

"Historicize, historicize," the town criers call on the quad. New Historicism and its offshoots, cultural criticism and postcolonial studies, have done much to fill what Conrad called the "blank spaces of the earth," the conspicuous gaps left on the West's map of conquests and colonizations. More precisely, scholars employing these methodologies have worked to show that such lacunae are already, and have long since been, occupied. But every new theoretical paradigm produces its own brands of blindness as well as insight. Whether by oversight or design, the cultural critics have largely turned a blind eye to the historical experience of modern Eastern Europe. "Contemporary theorists," Fredric Jameson explains, are "concerned with the internal dynamics of the relationship between First and Third World countries . . . which is now very precisely what the word 'imperialism' means for us." He is not alone in his strikingly selective geopolitical purview. Jameson merely articulates the parameters that tacitly define cultural studies as practiced in the Anglo-American academy today. Why has the so-called "Second World," the now-defunct Soviet Union and its satellites, been banished so peremptorily from sight? Why should Western theorists turn their backs on the potent mix of literature and politics that has proven so seductive to their poet-contemporaries? The names Bakhtin and Conrad strew the pages of contemporary scholarship. But the empire that, in one incarnation or another, shaped their bearers' lives and thought is conspicuous chiefly by its absence.[8]

"This is not a story of the West of Europe," as Conrad writes in *Under Western Eyes* (1911). And I will be using the notoriously un-narrative genre of lyric poetry to tell my story of literature and politics in Soviet-era Russia and Poland. Such an undertaking may seem doubtful: lyrics and large-scale narrations make for an unstable mix. This is partly my motive in combining them. "I have felt that the problem of my time should be defined as Poetry and History," Miłosz remarks in "A Poet Between East and West." To many contemporary scholars, his comment pairs virtual antonyms. "The poem is a device which produces anti-history," Octavio Paz observes, and the lyrical resistance to history has become a critical commonplace in recent decades, largely to the lyric's detriment.[9]

Predictably, New Historicism has shown little patience with what it sees as modern poetry's suspiciously antihistoricist bent. The common end of all poetry, Coleridge asserts, "is to convert a *series* into a *Whole*, to make those events that in real or Imagined history move on in a *strait* Line, assume to our Understandings a *circular* motion." It is this Romantic "grand illusion" that poetry "can set one free of the ruins of history and culture" with which contemporary criticism must do battle, Jerome McGann argues, since Romantic poetry "typically erases or sets aside its political and historical currencies." For the New Historicists, Nicholas Roe comments, the "escapist poems" of the Romantics and their literary descendants "enact dramas of idealization in which history is . . . variously 'displaced,' 'repressed,' 'erased,' obscured' or 'denied' by the imagination." Their critical task is thus to recuperate the suspect process that converts "history into poetry," Marjorie Levinson explains. Alan Liu frames this conflict explicitly in terms of genre. History, he declares, "is quintessentially narrative," while the "antinarrativistic and antimimetic" lyric seeks chiefly to escape or evade history in its quest for timeless truths.[10]

Angus Fletcher gives a different account of this intergeneric conflict in his *New Theory for American Poetry* (2004). If the lyric "seems to resist narrative," he observes, its "resistance may result from a distrust of the *progressive* implications of storytelling generally" (italics in original). Fletcher does not use the term "progressive" in its political sense. He means simply the forward temporal thrust that gives any narrative its structure. Yet the lyric proved resistant to the large-scale Soviet effort to create a historical narrative intended to be progressive in multiple ways. Time and again, it played havoc with what Stephen Kotkin calls the "supremely confident narrative of the laws of history and all-purpose explanation of the present" (and the future, we might add) that the Soviet rulers adapted from Karl Marx. The modern lyric, as described by McGann, Levinson, and others, is a deeply conservative, even reactionary genre virtually by definition: its rejection of history is tantamount to an endorsement of the bourgeois status quo. Fletcher's remarks suggest, though, ways in which a lyric resistance to history as grand narrative might reveal its subversive potentials in a state consecrated to History with a capital H.[11]

"So long as the poet, East or West, appears before the public only as a lyrist, banking on the irresponsibilities traditionally associated with that role, he will be tolerated by the governing class and allowed to communicate with his readers," Donald Davie asserts in *Czesław Miłosz and the Insufficiencies of Lyric* (1986): "It is only when he oversteps that pariah's privilege that he is in trouble." Lyrical irresponsibilities have sometimes proved less palatable to the powers-that-be than Davie is prepared to admit. Plato famously expelled poets from his ideal state, and the Polish poet Aleksander Wat was quick to see the analogy between Plato's imaginary republic and the Soviet-backed regimes of Eastern Europe. "Plato ordered us cast out / of the City where Wisdom reigns / In a new Ivory Tower made of (human) bones," he laments in his poem "Dark Light" (Ciemne świerczadło). This is not mere Romantic hyperbole, as Wat's own fate and those of his fellow poet-pariahs expelled from one ominous ivory tower or another amply demonstrate. "Our epoch is not lyric," Leon Trotsky proclaimed early on, and the state he helped to create took such distinctions quite seriously.[12]

Why is this? Let us return to the problem of definitions. "What is poetry?" Miłosz asks in his poem "Dedication" (1945). "More than one rickety answer / has tumbled since that question first was raised," his compatriot Wisława Szymborska replies nearly half a century later. "The borderline dividing what is a work of poetry from what is not is less stable than the frontiers of the Chinese empire's territories," Roman Jakobson moans in his essay "What is Poetry" (1933–34). Fletcher locates the shaky structures and unstable boundaries that Szymborska and Jakobson see in poetry's provisional definitions squarely in the thing itself. "In a strict sense, every poem is a state," he writes, and "states live only when they are always changing shape." This shape-shifting state does not exist in isolation. It has a distinctly social significance. The lyric tests the profoundly social issue of "human belonging or not belonging" by continuously tracing and retracing "the boundaries that define inclusion and exclusion," as it "cross[es] back and forth between an inner self and a world out there." It thus must be ranked, Fletcher argues, among Foucault's "approximating discourses," "those approximate, imperfect, and largely spontaneous kinds of knowledge which are brought into play in the construction of the least fragment of discourse or in the daily processes of exchange." Fletcher's lyric poem, the inherently unstable state in miniature, might well prove distasteful to a much larger, better-regulated regime dedicated to what Wat calls the mandatory, inflexible "semantic instrumentalization of everything. Of the world of people and the world of things. Of all human activity, economic, social, spiritual. Of human beings as such. Of their consciousness, thoughts and words. And finally, of the [state] doctrine itself."[13]

Fletcher's provisional definitions provoke a flurry of further questions. "The orthodox view" of the lyric, he comments, sees it chiefly as "an art of formal achievements, achievements of form": "the poem, for reasons of aesthetic pleasure, comprises a deliberately formed linguistic artifact, a grouping and organization of words such that the very form of the poem is an inherent and strongest part of its aesthetic power." It is surprising to realize how many varieties of orthodoxy subscribe to this definition. "A poem should not mean / But be," Archibald MacLeish announces in his Imagist "Ars Poetica"; and the poem's being has been conceived by friends and foes alike in largely formal terms. There are, of course, the New Critics' celebrated well-wrought urns and verbal icons. "Poetry achieves concreteness, particularity, and something like sensuous shape," William Wimsatt observes, through "the interrelational density of words taken in their fullest, most inclusive and symbolic character. A verbal composition . . . [thus] takes on something like the character of a stone statue or a porcelain vase."[14]

As their name attests, the Russian Formalists were no less attentive to questions of aesthetic form, of which poetry was their prime exemplar. "Poetry is language in its aesthetic function," Roman Jakobson explains in an early essay. Viktor Shklovsky elaborates: "Poetic speech is *formed* speech" and "poetic perception" is "that perception in which we experience form" (italics in original). In his later, high structuralist incarnation, Jakobson insists that in the poem "different levels blend, complement each other or combine to give the poem the value of an absolute object." The structuralist's task is thus to ascertain what he calls, rather unnervingly, "the mandatory unity" of this object: "Any unbiased, attentive, exhaustive, total description of the selection, distribution and interrelation of diverse morphological classes and syntactic constructions in a given poem surprises the examiner himself by unexpected, striking symmetries and antisymmetries, balanced structures, efficient accumulation of equivalent forms and salient contrasts, finally by rigid restrictions in the repertory of morphological and syntactic constituents used in the poem, eliminations which, on the other hand, permit us to follow the masterly interplay of the actualized constituents." Exhaustive indeed. Such bristling verbal fortresses might well repel the unwelcome incursions of history, if that is in fact the aim of lyric poetry.[15]

The lyric has long been seen as an effort to stop time, to seize the moment and make it ageless: Keats's notoriously unravished urn provides only the most obvious example. The lyric reprieve from temporality is achieved, in such views, precisely through the artifice of which Keats's vase is the emblem. The Grecian urn embodies the lyric poem's "controlled rejections of the world replaced by artful vision," Sharon Cameron argues in *Lyric Time* (1979): "The lyric is seen as immortal . . . because it is complete/completed in and of itself, transcending mortal/temporal limits in the very structure of its articulation." This transcendence is in turn graphically represented by "the lyric's own presence on a page, surrounded as it is by nothing"; whatever happens in the poem is "arrested, framed, and taken out of the flux of history." The lyric, as Cameron defines it, is a notably antisocial genre. The lyric project consists "of the banishing of the social world" as the poem attends "to no more than one (its own) speaking voice."[16]

"How does the lyric represent division, conflict and multiple points of view? If seeming to defy the social world from which it is set apart, how is it coerced back into relationship with that world?" Cameron is hardly a cultural critic *avant la lettre*—*Lyric Time* is clearly closer to Yale-school deconstruction than to the then-nascent New Historicism. Still, her questions anticipate what Susan Wolfson calls the "formal charges" that ideological critics have filed against both the lyric itself and the critical schools committed to its formal analysis. For such critics, Wolfson comments, "poetic forms became features to be seen through, read beyond, around, or against." Through its use of ostensibly "organic form" to mask its artifice, moreover, the Romantic lyric enters into an unholy compact with its age's reigning ideologies. Its "refusal of life actually conducted in actual society" amounts to a "complicity with class-interested strategies of smoothing over historical conflict and contradictions with claims of natural and innate organization."[17]

Although this is certainly not her intention, Cameron's terms—arrest, framing, banishment, coercion—translate with disconcerting ease into what David Bromwich has called the "police blotter slang" of recent theory, the rhetoric used to sentence suspect genres to Jameson's infamous prison-house of language—or, alternatively, to force them to make amends through punitive public service. The self-absorbed lyric must be coerced back into society by all necessary means. "The recovery of [its] 'excluded' or 'suppressed' historical contexts require[s] vigorous policing" by vigilant critics, Roe comments. Why should this seemingly effete, ineffectual little genre be singled out for such harsh treatment? The ideological critics themselves suggest probable causes. "Cultural studies in English-speaking universities," Vincent Leitch notes, are characterized by "a leftist political orientation rooted variously in Marxist, non-Marxist, and post-Marxist socialist intellectual traditions all critical of the aestheticism, formalism, antihistoricism, and apoliticism common among the dominant postwar methods of academic literary criticism." Aestheticism, formalism, antihistoricism, apoliticism: the lyric in a nutshell, as many New Historicists would have it. The genre thus becomes a convenient stand-in for postwar criticism generally.[18]

More than this—these same traits have specific class associations, as Leitch's remarks suggest. "The construction of the modern notion of the aesthetic artefact," Terry Eagleton asserts, is "inseparable from the construction of the dominant ideological forms of modern class-society, and indeed from a whole new form of human subjectivity appropriate to that social order." Modern aesthetics, with its dubious commitment to liberation from history achieved by way of the quasi-autonomous individual imagination, is thus the "very paradigm of the ideological" in its modern capitalist incarnation. This aesthetics, moreover, has a distinct generic profile. Through its efforts "to transcend, and to make the reader transcend, concrete spatial and temporal circumstances," McGann contends, Romantic poetry embodies "the most fundamental of all bourgeois concepts." The modern lyric, as the aesthetic artifact par excellence, serves as a pocket-sized version of aesthetics as such, and Cameron's little poem stranded on its lonely page assumes a more dubious identity. With its single speaking voice privileging private over public experience, individual autonomy over civic responsibility, and aesthetic independence over social engagement, the lyric becomes a metonym or synechdoche for the bourgeois subject in all its illusory, self-sufficient glory.[19]

Such charges sound oddly familiar to the Slavist. "The lyric—unlike the novel, whose task it is to legislate the conflict between social and personal reality—presents interior reality as if there were no other with which it must regretfully contend." The lyric "must attend to no more than one (its own) speaking voice. This fact makes the self in the lyric unitary, and gives it the illusion of alone holding sway over the universe, there being, for all practical purposes, no one else, nothing else, to inhabit it." "No imaginative fiction is as resistant to the interruption of its interior speech as the lyric." These quotes show Cameron once again anticipating the sins for which the lyric would be taken to task by the cultural critics. More notably, though, she unwittingly points us toward a key source in recent critiques of the lyric: the work of Mikhail Bakhtin.[20]

Cameron herself does not cite Bakhtin's writings, which were largely untranslated when *Lyric Time* first appeared. The distinctions she draws between novel and poem coincide strikingly, though, with the Russian theorist's description of the lamentably "monologic" lyric. Unlike the "heteroglossic" novel, Bakhtin insists, with its "diversity of social speech types (sometimes even diversity of languages) and a diversity of individual voices artistically organized," the ruthlessly efficient lyric "strip[s] all aspects of language of the intentions and accents of other people, destroying all traces of social heteroglossia and diversity of language" in its quest for "a unitary and singular language." The coincidence in Cameron's and Bakhtin's views is apparently just that. It demonstrates only the powerful cultural continuities, bridging nations, traditions, and even political systems, that underlie key critical conceptions of lyric and novel alike. But the convergence between Bakhtin and other recent critics is no accident. "Bakhtin just overthrew my Yale education," McGann remarks (he has in mind presumably his training in New Criticism and old historicism of one stripe or another). He is not alone in placing Bakhtin at the heart of a critical paradigm shift. Bakhtin and his circle have served as a "touchstone," Wolfson comments, in the recent critical "disdain for formalism." Indeed, the current "sociopolitical disparagement of formalism" is itself, she concludes, a continuation of postrevolutionary "Russian polemics" between the formalists and their ideological opponents. Hence perhaps the Slavist's occasional sense of déjà vu amidst recent critical arguments on the lyric.[21]

"All personality (*lichnost'*) aside. Make way for anonymous prose," Mandelstam announces in "Literary Moscow: Birth of the Plot" (1922). Prose's victory coincides quite precisely with the Bolsheviks' success in the Russian Civil War (1918–21), as Jurij Tynianov argues in his essay "Interval" (1924): "Three years ago prose gave poetry the boot. . . . Prose has triumphed." If poetic language was the hero of the Formalists' work by virtue of its singularity and exclusiveness, then it is no surprise to find it cast in a less flattering light by the orchestrators of a revolution waged in the name of the collective, the toiling masses to whom a recherché bourgeois lyricism was superfluous at best.[22]

Bakhtin's ideologically charged descriptions of poetry in "Discourse in the Novel" (1934–35) and elsewhere thus acquire a distinctive double-voicedness from a twenty-first-century perspective. They not only resonate with recent Anglo-American critiques of the lyric. Bakhtin also clearly shares the generic biases of his own revolutionary era. "The social revolution of the nineteenth century cannot draw its poetry from the past, but only from the future," Marx proclaims in *The Eighteenth Brumaire,* and his latter-day Soviet disciples took such pronouncements quite literally. "The poetry of the Revolution is synthetic. It cannot be changed into small coin for the temporary use of the lyric sonnet-makers," Trotsky declares in the early twenties. He grudgingly grants "personal lyrics of the smallest scope" a temporary residence permit on Soviet literary soil—but only until "a new lyric poetry" capable of forging the "new man" emerges to demonstrate "how socially and aesthetically inadequate" the old poetry has proven to its newly assigned tasks. Nikolai Bukharin echoes Trotsky's comments a decade later in a collectively authored, programmatic speech on "Poetry, Poetics, and the Problems of Poetry in the U.S.S.R." given at the First All-Soviet Writers' Congress of 1934. He insists that the newly instituted official doctrine of Socialist Realism "is not anti-lyrical." Like Trotsky, though, he opposes the old lyricism to the nascent "synthetic poetry," which will assist in the engineering of socialist souls that is the proper project of the Soviet artist en masse: "We are not here speaking of an antirealistic form of lyric, seeking for a 'world beyond,' but of a lyric which gives poetic shape to the spiritual experiences of the socialist man who is now coming into being."[23]

"Communist individualism," Bukharin proclaims, "is a contradiction in terms, an 'oxymoron,' a logical solecism." He was more moderate in this than many of his fellow revolutionaries. During the first years of Soviet power, the ideological "attack on the individual self reached the most incredible extremes," Zinovyi Papernyi observes. "The complete absorption of all individuals in a million-headed impersonal mass," and the new "collective man" to be born once the "soul-encumbered individual man" has been "mercilessly exterminated": such were the conversational commonplaces of the time in Soviet Russia, an early visitor to the new state recalls. These notions had obvious generic implications. The new proletarian poetry typically employed "not the lyric of the personal 'I', but the lyric of 'comradeship,' for the creating subject of proletarian poetry was not the "'I'" of the poet' but the 'real, most basic creator of this poetry—the collective," Aleksandr Bogdanov announces in a postrevolutionary manifesto. By the end of the twenties, Boris Eikhenbaum laments, both "personal poetry (the lyric)" and "the lyric 'I'" were "virtually taboo."[24]

In his speech, Bukharin derides the "anti-realistic lyric," with its unsocialist attachment to otherworldly imaginings. Bakhtin was very much Bukharin's comrade-in-arms in this, if little else. In "Discourse in the Novel," he deplores the "private craftsmanship" that "ignores the social life of discourse outside the artist's study." And the lyric is his prime example of such aesthetic isolationism. The lyric poet aspires to the creation of a "unitary and singular Ptolemaic world outside of which nothing else exists." Elsewhere this scientific anachronism appears in an equally outmoded, quasi-religious incarnation: the poet seeks an "'Edenic' world" to be achieved by means of "a purely poetic, extrahistorical language, a language far removed from the petty rounds of everyday life, a language of the gods." Bakhtin's metaphors betray the social and political realities of his day. Language itself, he warns, may resist the poet's encroachments, since "not all words . . . submit equally easily to this appropriation, to this seizure and transformation into private property." And his images in turn call to mind more recent descriptions of the lyric's reactionary tendencies: "What we witness" in Wordsworth's "Tintern Abbey," Marjorie Levinson comments, "is a conversion of public to private property." The bourgeois lyric strikes again. But why this convergence between critics separated by half a century, not to mention continents, languages, and political systems? And why Wordsworth? Again, Bakhtin and his influence on recent scholarship provide clues.[25]

Bakhtin's lyric is an oddly bifurcated genre. It is on the one hand distinguished by its hermeticism; it constitutes a kind of linguistic bell jar, an airtight, "monologically sealed-off utterance." Such a generic recluse would scarcely seem to pose a threat to society at large. But this "aesthetic object" achieves its self-enclosure at a high social cost, or so Bakhtin's imagery suggests. Not only does its poet-maker engage in the illicit appropriation and seizure of linguistic public property by "stripping all aspects of language of the intentions and accents of other people, destroying all traces of social heteroglossia and diversity of language." Preoccupied as he is with achieving "a complete single-personed hegemony over his own language," the poet presents a clear danger to others' language as well. He annihilates his linguistic opposition in utero; he "destroys in embryo [other] social worlds of speech." He is not just a Robin Hood in reverse, plundering the people's speech for the sake of lining his own linguistic coffers. He is also, more ominously, a King Herod of sorts, murdering infant language as it sleeps.[26]

It is no surprise to find that "the language of poetic genres" naturally tends, in Bakhtin's view, to become "authoritarian, dogmatic and conservative." But this is not the worst of its offenses. As his politically charged terms suggest, poetry does not merely mirror the larger evils of the society it works so assiduously to exclude. It actively supports the social structures that share its own hegemonic propensities, Bakhtin implies. At the same time that various proto-novelistic genres were subverting the socio-linguistic status quo in the Middle Ages, he claims, "poetry was accomplishing the task of cultural, national and political centralization of the verbal-ideological world in the higher official socio-ideological levels."[27]

Large-scale centralization, linguistic and otherwise, enacted at the highest socio-ideological levels: it is difficult to read such phrases in a Russian essay of the mid-thirties without thinking of Joseph Stalin and his policies of forcible collectivization at all levels of Soviet life. Perhaps by "poetry," Bakhtin has in mind the kind of court verse being written in his own times, the panegyrics, hymns, and odes composed in the name of the Great Leader whose "words are like iron weights," and whose "decrees" fall "like horseshoes" on the bodies of his hapless subjects, as Mandelstam writes in the poem known as the "Stalin Epigram"(1933). I have suggested that Bakhtin shares his revolutionary era's generic prejudices. In "Discourse and the Novel," though, he may also be tacitly criticizing the newly canonized system of genres to be employed by all members of the recently formed Soviet Writers' Union, that is, by any author hoping to see her or his words in print. His descriptions of the lyric are in any case a far better fit for Stalinist literary politics than they are for the Russian tradition, in place since Romanticism, of poet-rebels who refuse to write their lyrics on what Mandelstam calls government-sanctioned "police" paper and are punished accordingly by an autocratic state. Such an interpretation might explain the disparity between poetry as it appears in "Discourse and the Novel," and Bakhtin's far more sympathetic writings on Pushkin and other poets elsewhere.[28]

Bakhtin's vision of a conservative genre that upholds the political status quo dovetails neatly, though, with the narrative proposed by McGann, Levinson, and others vis-à-vis Romanticism generally and Wordsworth in particular. Recent ideological critics have charged Wordsworth with helping "to invent the autonomous individual" in his early poetry, David Bromwich notes. Their prime exhibit is Wordsworth's "Lines written a few miles above Tintern Abbey" (1798), which marks, so the argument runs, his rejection of a revolutionary politics that engages the world in favor of a subjective, internal transformation that elides it. In his speech at that First All-Soviet Writers' Congress, Karl Radek denounced escapist "Romantic flights, such as those taken by the intelligentsia disappointed in the outcome of the French revolution." This is the same trajectory that recent critics see at work both in "Tintern Abbey" and in Romantic poetry generally. At the poem's end, McGann comments, "we are left only with the initial scene's simplest natural forms": "Everything else has been erased—the abbey, the beggars and displaced vagrants, all that civilized culture creates and destroys, gets and spends. We are not permitted to remember 1793 and the turmoil of the French Revolution, neither its 1793 hopes nor . . . the subsequent ruin of those hopes." "Between 1793 and 1798 Wordsworth lost the world merely to gain his own immortal soul," he concludes. Critics like McGann and Levinson thus locate the true turning point in Wordsworth's politics not in his later, explicitly conservative poetry, but precisely in the closing moments of the ostensibly iconoclastic "Lyrical Ballads." It is just one short step, in other words, from poet-radical to Poet Laureate, from "Tintern Abbey" to Westminster Abbey and a statue in Poets' Corner.[29]

Levinson dubs her method "deconstructive materialism." She calls upon the critic to identify a poem's "ideological subtext" by means of a procedure whose origins she describes as follows: "Freud worked out its psychic economy and Marx produced its political logic." Levinson's approach, like that of McGann and most cultural critics, is explicitly Marxist or "Freudo-Marxist," in Frank Lentricchia's phrase. Revolutions, Marxist dialectics, and lyric poems: once again, some mention of the Russian Revolution, the empire it inaugurated, and that empire's demise less than two decades ago would seem inevitable, if only to point out the catastrophic misapplication, if that is the case, of the theory on which so much recent literary scholarship has relied. "The end of the Cold War and of the Soviet Union has definitively changed the world map," Said concedes in *Culture and Imperialism*. However, these definitive changes, and the history that precipitated them, remain beyond the pale not only of his study, but of cultural criticism generally.[30]

It is no accident that Wordsworth has become the lightning rod in current discussions of poetry and ideology. His rejection of the French Revolution and retreat into lyrical privacy provide ideal exempla of what we ought not to do and be. "We are . . . as Wordsworth (for example) deliberately chose *not* to be—'citizens of the world'" (italics in original), McGann explains, and he reminds us that we now read against a backdrop of "Vietnam, Palestine, Northern Ireland—Bosnia, Kosovo, Cambodia, Chile, Uganda." The "Romantic ideology" was born in the wake of one failed revolution, and McGann attributes its demise to a shift in consciousness following another social trauma closer to home. The "aesthetic positions" of this ideology, he claims, "dominate[d] the theory of poetry for 150, 175 years, more, even to our own day. . . . Up until the Vietnam War, it seems to me that they held perfect and total sway. They do not hold sway anymore." Liu casts his net more widely: he describes the New Historicism as "our latest post–May 1970, post–May 1968, post-1917, . . . post-1789 (and so forth) imagination for an active role for intellect in the renascence of society." 1917 rates at least a mention in passing; but what about its bookend dates of 1989 and 1991?[31]

Soviet Russia was "Europe's last imperial power and "communism turned out to be the last, and perhaps the highest stage of imperialism," the historian Mark Mazower observes; and Mazower places "communism's demise" squarely against the broader backdrop of "European decolonization" generally. Historians and New Historians do not always see eye to eye on such matters, though. "Only those theories of imperialism which acknowledge the Marxist problematic are of concern," Jameson states baldly in "Modernism and Imperialism"—but this problematic addresses only Marxism's theoretical apparatus and not its historical applications. "Marxism is at present enduring the most grievous crisis of its fraught career," Eagleton acknowledges in the introduction to *Marxist Literary Theory* (1996). He pointedly roots this crisis, though, not in "the collapse of neo-Stalinism, or however the political taxonomists choose to label whatever was under way in eastern Europe," but in the capitalist West: "It was not the implosion of the Soviet world, but the quickening contradictions of the Western one, which first began to undermine historical materialism." This implosion has not helped matters, though, as Eagleton admits: "At least Stalinism and its progeny seemed to mean that Marxism of some species was here to stay. . . . It may not have been to one's taste, but one couldn't ignore it."[32]

Ignoring Marxism in its Eastern European variant has in fact proven all too easy for contemporary critics, as I've argued. There are a few notable exceptions. In *The Politics of Nature* (2002), Nicholas Roe notes the irony of "teaching and writing Marxist criticism and theory while McDonalds was opening for business in the former Soviet Union." Thomas McFarland acknowledges what he calls "the permanent importance of the Marxist analysis of culture, history, and human activity" in *Romanticism and the Heritage of Rousseau* (1995)—but he also addresses its large-scale abuses in the latter-day "Jacobinism" of the Russian Revolution and its aftermath, with its toll of "staggering numbers of human beings." "One of the signal failures" of contemporary theorists, Mark Edmundson remarks in *Literature against Philosophy* (1995), "has been their unwillingness to read Marx in the way they have so eagerly read Hegel and Kant": "The question of whether, or to what degree, Marx's commitment to a univocal standard of truth, his truth, inspired his various disciples, from Lenin to Guzmán, to commit their barbarities remains one worth investigating. For Derrida could surely have found in Marx, who is Hegel's most consequential heir, and thus in some sense the major heir of metaphysics, rather than in Heidegger, the culminating move in an intellectual tradition devoted to suppressing different interpretations, and perhaps too to suppressing different people, by whatever means necessary."[33]

Eagleton, predictably, sees things rather differently. "The story which Marxism has to tell" may be "tedious," he explains in *Marxist Literary Theory* (1996), but it is also "more true to the humdrum, vulnerable nature of humanity" than competing modern narratives of the past have proven to be. Miłosz for one would not agree. In *The Captive Mind* (1953) he presents "dialectical materialism, Russian style" as just the kind of oppressive metanarrative that Eagleton seeks to overthrow. "Undoubtably, one comes closer to the truth when one sees history as the expression of the class struggle rather than a series of private quarrels among kings and queens," Miłosz concedes: "But precisely because such an analysis comes closer to the truth, it is more dangerous. It gives the illusion of *full knowledge*; it supplies answers to all questions, answers which merely run around in a circle repeating a few formulas. . . . Centuries of human history, with their thousands upon thousands of human affairs, are reduced to a few, most generalized terms" (italics in original). "Poetry is . . . a more philosophical and higher thing than history: for poetry tends to express the universal, history the particular." In *The Captive Mind* and elsewhere, Miłosz sets Aristotle's famous dictum in reverse. For Miłosz, lyric poetry defends humdrum humanity in all its particularity against History en masse, whether in the Soviet Marxist variant or any of the other master plots that the modern age has proven so adept at generating.[34]

"The true enemy of man is generalization," Miłosz writes in the fourth of his "Six Lectures in Verse": "The true enemy of man, so-called History, / Attracts and terrifies with its plural number." The poet combats History by means of his commitment to recuperating the fragile, particular fates erased by its large-scale narrations:

> Still in my mind [I try] to save Miss Jadwiga,
> A little hunchback, librarian by profession,
> Who perished in the shelter of an apartment house
> That was considered safe but toppled down . . .
> So a name is lost for ages, forever,
> No one will ever know about her last hours . . .
> History is not, as Marx told us, anti-nature,
> And if a goddess, a goddess of blind fate.
> The little skeleton of Miss Jadwiga, the spot
> where her heart was pulsating. This only
> I set against necessity, law, theory.

From wartime Warsaw to the banks of the Wye: what can Miłosz's vanished Miss Jadwiga possibly share with Wordsworth's lonely "wanderer through the woods"? How does the one poet's purported flight from history tally with the other's concerted battle against it?[35]

"The greater Romantic poem" became, in Wordsworth's hands, a rhetorical retreat from social action to aesthetic contemplation, the argument runs, while Miłosz's commitment to a "poetry of witness" led to his works being banned for decades by a repressive state: Can both be said to practice the same art? And what art would that be? The building of bourgeois bell jars? The formation of hegemonic monoliths masquerading as *objets d'art*? The creation of subversive shape-shifters or of reactionary devices containing antihistory? The erasure or the defense of particularity? Let us revisit Wordsworth's controversial lyric in a rather different context by way of addressing these and like questions.

Tintern Abbey versus People's Poland

Is not the marvelous book of history closed with seven seals to our poets?
>   —Nikolai Bukharin, "Poetry, Poetics and the
>   Problems of Poetry in the U.S.S.R"

Even apolitical poetry is political.
>   —Wisława Szymborska, "Children of Our Age"

Under the Communist regime, Miłosz explains in *The Captive Mind,* the poet "is free to describe hills, trees and flowers." "But if he should feel that boundless exaltation in the face of nature that seized Wordsworth on his visit to Tintern Abbey," he warns, "he is at once suspect." Miłosz should know. He himself translated Wordsworth's lyric for an anthology of Anglo-American poetry that he hoped—in vain, as it turned out—to publish in People's Poland at the war's close. Wordsworth's poem was polonized in the wake of a cataclysm that its author would have found difficult to imagine. Miłosz did his translating in 1945 in Krakow, one of the few Polish cities spared from wartime devastation: Warsaw, where he spent much of the war, existed at this point chiefly in name only. And Poland was itself caught up in yet another battle, a civil war being waged between allies and opponents of the Soviet occupiers then in the process of forcibly importing their own revolution westwards.[36]

Like many younger intellectuals, Miłosz sided with the Soviets for ideological reasons. The ostensibly democratic West seemed thoroughly discredited by the war's end. Not only had its states proven fertile breeding grounds for the fascism that precipitated the war in the first place. At its conclusion the Western victors had shown themselves all too eager to hand Poland over to their Soviet allies, despite repeated promises to the contrary. A postwar present under Joseph Stalin looked bleak at best. But communism held at least the hope of a brighter future—and what did the West have to offer?

Miłosz would soon find out firsthand. Shortly after completing the ill-fated anthology, he was posted as the new regime's cultural attaché first to the New York consulate, and then to the Washington embassy, where he remained until 1950. His reaction to the West in its North American incarnation was mixed at best. But his wartime passion for the Anglo-American poetic tradition continued unabated. For all this, though, Miłosz was never a great Wordsworth fan (he much preferred William Blake): "Everything I write, I write *against* nature," he replied when asked about his taste. So why does Wordsworth emerge three times at this key juncture in Miłosz's own adventures with revolution and engagement? "Tintern Abbey" is prominently featured in the projected anthology of 1945, just as Miłosz decides to cast his lot with the new Communist regime. It is singled out yet again in *The Captive Mind,* the book that marked his public break with that regime in 1953 (he had received political asylum in Paris two years earlier).[37]

Miłosz cites Wordsworth in only one other place, so far as I know. The British writer makes a brief, uncredited cameo in a letter sent to the poet Jarosław Iwaszkiewicz from Washington in 1949, at the height of Miłosz's service to the state. "All this extroverted literature is repugnant," Miłosz complains to his friend: "Poetry is 'recollection in tranquillity' (*przypominanie sobie w stanie spokoju*) and there's an end to it. Without that detachment, that disinterestedness, you've got, and will get, nothing." "I'm really struggling," he continues, "I sense that I have to snap the shackles that bind my hands and feet." The shackles he has in mind are both literary and political. The relentlessly extroverted writing Miłosz resists is the Socialist Realist poetry he describes in *The Captive Mind:* "He [the poet] does not speak for himself but for the ideal citizen. His results are reminiscent of songs written to be sung on the march since the aim is the same—the forging of the fetters of collectivity that bind together an advancing column of soldiers." And the antidote to these "mind-forged manacles" is the solitary "emotion recollected in tranquillity" that Wordsworth describes in the "Preface to *Lyrical Ballads*" (1802).[38]

Public and private; collectivity and solitude; history and distance; engagement and detachment: the familiar oppositions emerge once more, but their meanings have changed dramatically. In "Tintern Abbey," Levinson writes, the "persona confesses its divorce from an order of collectivity that might validate poetic achievement, or confirm the poet's social and therefore individual experience." In the People's Republic, though, to embrace collectivity and engagement meant to serve the state, not to subvert it, while to indulge in the bourgeois luxuries of introversion, contemplation, and disinterestedness was to challenge its dictates. "Communism is the enemy of interiorization, of the inner self," Wat observes in his memoirs. This is doubtless why "Tintern Abbey" would have met with a chilly reception in People's Poland, as Miłosz sees it. Raptures and ecstasies were reserved for public occasions and state functions, not private meditations. And the regime would have been no happier than more recent critics with Wordsworth's failure to address the social conditions that had shaped his solitary landscape. The most introspective terms in the "Preface"—"tranquillity," "recollection," "contemplation," and so on—become fighting words when translated into a different language, time, and place. In Miłosz's letter, they presage the break with People's Poland that would lead him to a very different kind of isolation, the decades of exile in the West when his writings reached his compatriots, if at all, chiefly through clandestine channels.[39]

It is precisely the writing produced under such circumstances—whether by poets hounded at home or driven into exile by an oppressive state—that has led Western poets to venerate their Eastern European counterparts in recent decades. In his introduction to *The Faber Book of Political Verse* (1986), the Irish poet Tom Paulin shares his primary targets with his New Historicist contemporaries. He mocks "the ahistorical school of literary criticism"—once again the New Critics and their literary offspring—for finding in poetry "a garden of pure perfect forms which effortlessly 'transcends' that world of compromise, cruelty, dead language." For such critics, "art stands for freedom, while politics is a degrading bondage we must reject and escape from." Paulin likewise identifies such notions with specific geopolitical entities and a large chunk of modern history. "In the Western democracies," he comments, "it is still possible for many readers, students and teachers of literature to share the view that poems exist in a timeless vacuum or a soundproof museum, and that poets are gifted with the ability to hold themselves above history, rather like skylarks." Our ostensibly open society, with its misguided "liberal belief in the separation of the public from the private life," has paradoxically given birth to an airtight, impervious version of art.[40]

So far, so good. But here Paulin parts company with the New Historicists by venturing across what was then the Iron Curtain in search of countermodels. "Poets such as Zbigniew Herbert, Różewicz, Holub remind us," he insists, "that in Eastern Europe, the poet has a responsibility both to art and to society, and that this responsibility is single and indivisible": "In this authoritarian or totalitarian reality there is no private life, no domestic sanctuary, to retire into. Here, any and every action has a political significance which cannot be evaded." Through their commitment, willy-nilly, to public values, the Eastern Europeans create "the most advanced type of political poetry" now being written and their less progressive brethren to the west would do well, he implies, to follow their lead. A key passage from *The Captive Mind* that I have cited earlier apparently lends weight to Paulin's comments, and I will give it here in full: "In Central and Eastern

Europe," Miłosz insists, "the word 'poet' has a somewhat different meaning from that which it has in the West. There a poet does not merely arrange words in beautiful order. Tradition demands that he be a 'bard,' that his songs linger on many lips, that he speak in his poems of subjects of interest to all the citizens." But Miłosz describes both the strength of this tradition and its great danger. It is partly the craving to remain on center stage, speaking for and to the nation, that led so many poets, himself included, into the service of the Soviet "Imperium" following the war, as he argues in *The Captive Mind*. Perhaps this is why he cites in the same work not the poet in revolt, but the poet in retreat, the distanced, disaffected writer—which is to say, Wordsworth and his controversial lyric—as a prime example of what the state cannot tolerate.[41]

Lyricitis

"Good manners, decorum, formality and personal privacy": these are the "reactionary" Western traits to which Eastern European poets provide an antidote in Paulin's essay. The poet Reginald Gibbons sees the same writers quite differently. "In much eastern European poetry," he remarks, "the idea of privacy seems a defiance of state powers of surveillance, an insistence that individual powerlessness imposed by the state will not succeed in eradicating identity. . . . What is wanted by the poet is the right to a thoroughly private life." Perhaps, Gibbon suggests, the lyric's creation of a private space for the individual voice is the best service a poet can render fellow citizens in a state given to monitoring or confiscating what Miłosz calls "private thought-property." The erstwhile poet-dissident Stanisław Barańczak suggests as much in an interview of 1990. "The attempt to save or defend one's own personality and the right to individuality generally is," he insists, "the most subversive public act" a poet can commit.[42]

Such notions might seem close to Theodor Adorno's well-known argument in "Lyric Poetry and Society" (1957). "You experience lyric poetry as something opposed to society, something wholly individual," Adorno explains. "Your feelings insist . . . that lyric expression, having escaped from the weight of material existence, evoke the image of a life free from the coercion of reigning practices, of utility, of the relentless pressures of self-preservation. This demand, however, . . . that the lyric word be virginal, is itself social in nature. It implies a protest against a social situation that every individual experiences as hostile, alien, cold, oppressive." "The 'I' whose voice is heard in the lyric," he continues, "is an 'I' that defines and expresses itself as something opposed to the collective, to objectivity," and "the greatest lyric works" are those "in which no trace of . . . crude materiality remains."[43]

Innate opposition to collectivity and materiality: the defining features of the lyric as Adorno sees it might help to explain the Soviet state's distrust of lyric poets on both sides of the political divide. Postrevolutionary Russia's most famous lyrical antipodes provide a case in point. "It is as though all of Russia is divided today between Akhmatovas and Mayakovskys," Kornei Chukovsky announced in an influential lecture of 1920. "Between the two there are millennia. And they hate each other." According to Chukovsky and others, Akhmatova was the representative of "Old Russia" with its long, distinguished heritage, while Mayakovsky embodied the still inchoate potential of the revolutionary future then unfolding. For all their cultural and ideological differences, though, both poets were diagnosed with variants of the same disease by Soviet critics in the twenties. This illness took the form of incurable lyriticis, though its name varied depending upon the patient. Mayakovsky suffered throughout his brief lifetime from chronic "mayakovskovitis" (*maiakovshchina*), while Akhmatova was apparently plagued for decades by a contagious "akhmatovitis" (*akhmatovshchina*) requiring extended periods of enforced isolation. "Enough of *mayakovshchina*," ran one headline in the state organ *Pravda* as early as 1921. Party officials were still cautioning that "*akhmatovshchina* should be cauterized with a red-hot poker" nearly three decades later. The obdurately individual nature of this ailment appears in the need to personalize its name in each instance. But the symptoms in each case proved remarkably similar.[44]

Mayakovsky speaks boldly for the nation at large in 1922 when he identifies Akhmatova's "indoor intimacy" as the sign of her poetic obsolescence. She will find her "place in the pages of histories of literature," he concedes, "but for us, for our age," she is a "pointless, pathetic and comic anachronism." Mayakovsky's own scope may have been larger than the "narrow, petty, boudoir home-and-family poetry" that Soviet critics found so offensive in his contemporary: "there is nothing in her except love, nothing about labour, about the collective," one reviewer complains. But Mayakovsky's greater ambitions did not save him from similar accusations. The self-proclaimed bard of the proletariat was at heart, Trotsky charged, a mere "Mayakomorphist" who "speaks of the most intimate things, such as love, as if he were speaking about the migration of nations"; he is "profoundly personal and individual" in even his most overtly revolutionary epics.[45]

For Adorno, Mayakovsky's chief problem would have been his desire to step outside his "lyric I" to begin with, no matter how worthy the cause he espoused. "The less the [poetic] work thematizes the relationship of 'I' and society," Adorno argues, the more fully it expresses, paradoxically, "the historical relationship of the subject to objectivity, of the individual to society." "The lyric work of art's withdrawal into itself, its self-absorption, its detachment from the social surface," he insists, "is socially motivated behind the author's back." The total "unself-consciousness" of the author is crucial to the lyric's fulfilling its—unwitting—social function. The critic may be sentimental. But the poet must remain naive in order to create the truly lyrical work of art that constitutes his or her inadvertent contribution to social criticism.[46]

In his 1934 address, Bukharin saw just such a hermetic protest at work in the prerevolutionary poetry of Boris Pasternak. "The bloody hash, the huckstering barter of the bourgeois world were profoundly loathsome to [Pasternak]," he notes, and so the poet "seceded, he shut himself up in the mother-of-pearl shell of individual experiences, delicate and subtle. . . . He is the embodiment of chaste but self-absorbed labour over verbal form . . . profoundly personal—and hence, of necessity, constricted." Certainly the lyric retreat from society may constitute an oblique form of dissent—etymologically the dissident is, after all, one who insists on sitting apart from the rest. And a programmatically collectivist society may give special resonance to this singular mode of resistance, as I have suggested. But what of *self-conscious* lyricism as a form of social protest?[47]

Adorno rules out this possibility—but the later career of Akhmatova challenges his theory. I will deal with her masterworks *Requiem* (1935–40) and the *Poem without a Hero* (1940–66) at some length in my third and fourth chapters. Here, though, I want only to call attention to a distinctive generic form of "double-voicedness" that affects one of *Requiem*'s most moving segments, "The Sentence" (*Prigovor*), the seventh in the sequence of ten lyrics that form the poem's narrative core. *Requiem* was published in its entirety in Russia only long after Akhmatova's death. But "The Sentence" appeared without its compromising title in 1940 both in the Soviet journal *Zvezda* and in Akhmatova's collection *From Six Books* (*Iz shesti knig*)—her first volume to see print in Soviet Russia in nearly twenty years—where she gave it the intentionally misleading date of 1934. (It was in fact composed in the summer of 1939, as *Requiem*'s full text reveals.) The poem reads as follows:

> And the stony word descended
> On my still living breast.
> No matter, I was ready,
> I'll find a way to deal with this.

I've got a lot to do today:
I need to strike my memory dead,
I've got to petrify my soul,
I have to learn to live again.

If not . . . the hot rustling of summer,
like a holiday outside my window.
I foresaw this long ago,
The bright day, the deserted home.

Why should the poem's dating prove crucial to its publication? In August, 1939, Akhmatova's only child, Lev Gumilev, was sentenced to ten years in a Stalinist labor camp chiefly for the crime of being his parents' son. (His father, the poet Nikolai Gumilev, was executed for alleged counterrevolutionary activities in 1921.) That date, along with the incriminating title, would have been more than enough not just to block the poem's publication. It might well have condemned Akhmatova herself to the fate, camp or prison, she had thus far managed to escape.[48]

During what proved to be a brief respite from earlier strictures against publishing her work, Akhmatova succeeded in shepherding this poem, in its strategically abbreviated form, into print under the protective camouflage of old-fashioned bourgeois lyricism. "Akhmatova's poems were written long ago, during the difficult period of the bourgeois family's decline," the Soviet critic V. Pertsov explains in a contemporary review of *From Six Books*. (It is worth noting that the review, like the volume itself, were the products of shifts in official policy, not in public or private taste.) The times have changed—"the seventeen Soviet years" that separate her last two volumes mark "a geological era," he comments—but Akhmatova remains the same: "Her constant theme is strange, tragic love, love as punishment and suffering . . . the woman's amorous self-crucifixion (*samoraspiatie*)." Akhmatova's outmoded charm and strikingly "narrow experience of life" serve chiefly to confirm, he concludes, "our new purpose in life, our orientation towards the general, not the particular or private (*chastnoe*), toward the fate of all mankind," an orientation that eludes the misguided poet who persists in "sacrificing herself for love" time and again.[49]

Memory, loss, unhappy love, a self profoundly at odds with the world beyond its bounds: Akhmatova laid claim to these quintessentially lyric topoi long ago, Pertsov notes. But her lyric boxes sometimes contain trapdoors and false bottoms, she warns in the *Poem without a Hero*.[50] For readers like Pertsov, who knew chiefly the earlier work, the key to this brief poem must have seemed painfully obvious. The first line's "stony word" marks the lover's inevitable rejection. And the second stanza's chilling "to do" list is merely Akhmatova exercising once again her unfortunate tendency to self-punishment following yet another romantic abandonment. The radiant summer holiday outside her door in the poem's final stanza was likely taken by such critics as the joyous Soviet reality—"life keeps getting better and happier," the Stalinist slogan ran—in which the poet willfully refuses to participate.

Any admirer of *Requiem* will instantly see how wrong such a reading would be. This poem about isolation yields one interpretation when read in isolation—that is, outside its assigned position in *Requiem*—and quite another when approached in the company of voices that Akhmatova has assembled for it in her distinctively lyrical epic. "Amorous self-crucifixion": could Akhmatova have had Pertsov's phrase in mind when she called *Requiem*'s climactic tenth poem "Crucifixion" (*Raspiatie)*? The dates she gives for the poem's composition, 1940–43, make this at least a possibility. In any case, "Crucifixion" only underscores what *Requiem*'s readers have known from the start: the suffering "The Sentence" describes is anything but self-inflicted. "Crucifixion" marks the moment in the lyrical sequence when the agonized speaker, who has lost both husband and son to Stalin's purges, is finally able to frame her own sufferings in a richer, more resonant cultural context. The community of bereaved women she commemorates in the epilogue is both suggested and sacralized here through the figure of the Mother who takes center stage in Akhmatova's imaginative recreation of Christ's death: "But no one even dared to glance / There, where the Mother stood silently." To return to the seventh lyric in its larger context: the "stony word" that falls on the speaker's chest is of course no lover's rebuff. It is instead akin to the decrees of the "Stalin Epigram" that rain like iron weights on the bodies of the living. And the spiritual self-annihilation that "The Sentence" presents as a paradoxical preface to new life is merely the continuation of a process already begun by the state: "Stalinism means the killing of the inner self," Wat comments.[51]

What is most lyrical about "The Sentence"—its articulation of intensely private anguish—is exactly what creates its communal value within the framework of the larger poem. Giving voice to mute suffering and shared solitude—"Can you describe this?" a blue-lipped woman asks in the poem's opening—is the first step toward creating the community that Akhmatova evokes in *Requiem*'s closing lines: "For them I have woven a broad shroud / Of their own poor words, which I overheard."[52] *Pace* Adorno, Akhmatova's clear, canny consciousness of "The Sentence"'s dual existence as both solitary lament and social gesture permits her to actualize it in two radically different contexts. "The Sentence" enters Soviet public life by masquerading as that obsolete art form, the purely private lyric, while performing its true public service in private, through illicit manuscripts or clandestine recitations. Pertsov was right to note the persistence of Akhmatova's lyric gifts, though neither he nor the Soviet censors could have imagined the subversive purposes to which they would be put.

Soviet poetry is "a poetry of gladness, profoundly buoyant and optimistic, essentially linked with the triumphant march of the millions and reflecting the tremendous creative impulses, the struggle, the building of a new world," Bukharin announces in "Poetry, Poetics, and the Problems of Poetry": "Here we find no fog of mysticism, no poetry of the blind, no tragic loneliness of a lost personality, no inconsolable grief of individualism . . . [no] elegant bric-à-brac of the boudoir or the drawing-room." If Akhmatova's poem shows how private grief may be turned to social purposes in *Requiem,* then Mandelstam demonstrates the no less subversive functions of bourgeois bric-à-brac in a little poem, "I drink to the military asters" (*Ia p'iu za voennye astry*), composed during what Akhmatova called the "relatively vegetarian" early thirties.[53]

The better-known "Stalin Epigram" derives its defiant force from what James Longenbach calls its "little collection of fanciful metaphors."[54] The bag of lyric tricks Mandelstam draws upon in "I drink to the military asters" consists instead of synechdoches evoking the bourgeois imperial Europe that played the capitalist Antichrist to Soviet Russia's messianic Marx:

> I drink to the military asters, to all that they've scolded me for,
> To a noble fur coat, to asthma, to a bilious Petersburg day,
>
> To the music of Savoy pine trees, to benzine in the Champs-Elysées,
> To the roses inside of Rolls Royces, to Parisian pictures' oil paint.
>
> I drink to the waves of Biscay, to cream in Alpine jugs,
> To British ladies' ruddy grandeur, to quinine from distant colonies,
>
> I drink, but I've not yet decided which of the two I will pick:
> A sparkling Asti Spumante or a Châteauneuf-du-Pape.

"I have strange taste," Mandelstam admits in a 1909 letter to the Symbolist poet Viacheslav Ivanov: "I love the patches of electric light on Lake Leman, the deferential lackeys, the noiseless flight of the elevator, the marble vestibule of the hotel, and the Englishwomen who play Mozart in a half-darkened salon for an audience of two or three official listeners." He himself was guilty of composing what postrevolutionary critics called "chamber poetry"—but as the son of a Jewish tanner, Mandelstam was hardly to the manor born, and the early letter's recherché predilections betray the anxious longings of an outsider with his nose pressed to the window of fin de siècle European culture.[55]

The later poem-toast is a different matter. Soviet Jews had to leave Russia in order to become Russians, or so the joke once ran; their internal passports excluded them from true Russianness by indicating "Jewish" under nationality. It took a proletarian revolution for the Jewish tradesman's son to be branded with what one unsympathetic contemporary called the "mandelstamp" of "bourgeois Western civilization." "This class struggle plays hell with your poetry," John Reed reportedly told his Bolshevik comrades-in-arms. By the thirties, Mandelstam had discovered that poetry can play hell with the class struggle as well. The Soviet *Literary Encyclopedia* of 1932 charged him with the "ideological perpetuation of capitalism and its culture" through his politically dubious oeuvre. But Mandelstam was familiar with such accusations by then, and he had his answer ready in "I drink to the military asters," where he sets avant-garde *épatage* in reverse by way of his bourgeois slap in the face of politically progressive taste.[56]

The toast is of course a public gesture par excellence, though Mandelstam could hardly have expected to see his poetic taunt in Soviet print. (It appeared for the first time in its entirety only in an émigré publication in 1961.) The defiant outsider at a feast from which he had pointedly been excluded still managed to make himself heard, though, to judge by the evidence of the Soviet critic A. Selivansky, who specifically cites Mandelstam's Rolls Royces, Savoy pines, and Parisian paintings as evidence of the poet's ineradicably bourgeois inclinations in an essay on "The Decline of Acmeism" (1934). (Acmeism was the poetic movement to which both Akhmatova and Mandelstam had belonged before the revolution). And at least one Soviet poet apparently felt the affront of this toast so keenly that he rose from the dead to avenge the state's sullied honor. Sergei Esenin had committed suicide in 1925. Still, Esenin "once even tried to beat Mandelstam," the critic Aleksandr Kovalenkov insists. "And with good reason. After all he was the one who wrote: 'I drink to the military asters . . . the benzine of the Champs-Elysées.'"[57]

If the lyric has been pressed into service as "a weapon in the class struggle," as another critic of the Acmeists asserts, then Mandelstam hands his enemies their ammunition himself. "Decadent art," "gastronomic satisfaction," "symbols of the 'high life,'" and "other typical categories of the exploiting class" such as the army (the "military asters" represent imperial epaulets), the nobility, capitalist manufacturers, colonialism (the quinine), even the church (Châteauneuf-du-Pape): he squeezes all these ideological taboos into the space of eight exceptionally efficient lines, Aleksandr Zholkovsky comments. Suspect foreign place names (including a conspicuously anachronistic, un-Soviet Petersburg) stand alongside product placements *avant la lettre* (Rolls Royce, Asti Spumante), and an impressive array of russified foreign borrowings (*benzin, kabina, khinin,* and so on). If Akhmatova uses her alleged bourgeois self-absorption as a form of camouflage in "The Sentence," then Mandelstam takes the opposite tack in this aggressively bourgeois "baring of the device." No need for critical unmasking here. The ideological key to what might seem under other circumstances to be the poet's own quirky personal tastes is self-evident. Mandelstam hands it to his critics on a plate, alongside the quinine and the cream. Even his asthma is ideologically motivated, Igor Chinnov remarks: "The illness evokes the image of Proust, who glorified the French aristocracy." Mandelstam's lyrical tactics may be radically different than Akhmatova's. Like hers, though, his strategies are both highly self-conscious and strikingly effective.[58]

"Probably I'm just an ordinary bourgeois / defender of individual rights, I understand / the word freedom without special class distinctions": the opening lines of Adam Zagajewski's poem "Fire" (1983) constitute both a defense of lyric individuality and a refusal of collectivist class politics mandated from above. They also mark the break with another collectivist ethos, that of mass resistance to state oppression, that I mentioned earlier.[59] Zagajewski's compatriot Zbigniew Herbert embraces his role of chronicler to a nation's woes in his collection *Report from the Besieged City* (1984)—but he too draws upon a discredited bourgeois concept to explain his own and his fellow artists' protests. "It didn't require great character at all / our refusal disagreement and resistance" he insists in "The Power of Taste" (1984):

> we had a shred of necessary courage
> but fundamentally it was a matter of taste
>   Yes, taste
> in which there are fibers of soul the cartilage of conscience . . .

"So aesthetics can be helpful in life," Herbert concludes. "One should not neglect the study of beauty." Militant bourgeois aestheticism and subversive stylistic analysis join forces in the underground army of artists arrayed against the state in Herbert's lines.[60]

Herbert himself laments elsewhere, though, the lyric losses that attend the poet's assumption of collective responsibilities, however noble and necessary: "we took public affairs on our thin shoulders," he complains to a fellow poet-dissident, Ryszard Krynicki, "recording suffering the struggle with tyranny with lying." "But—you have to admit," he concludes, "we had opponents despicably small."

in our poems Ryszard there is so little joy—daughter of the gods
too few luminous dusks mirrors wreaths of rapture
nothing but dark psalmodies stammering of animulae
urns of ashes in the burned garden . . .

what strength of spirit is needed to strike
beating blindly with despair against despair
a spark of light word of reconciliation

so the dancing circle will last forever on the thick grass
so the birth of a child and every beginning is blessed

The spark of light, the endless dancing circle on the grass: such lyric trifles
are abandoned only at a cost, Herbert suggests. But what exactly is this
cost? What good are poems that do not serve the greater good?[61]

"O, reason not the need!" Lear begs his daughters: "Our basest beg-
gars / Are in the poorest thing superfluous." That poorest thing appears to
be poetry itself in Mandelstam's "Verses on the Unknown Soldier" (1937),
where the poet assembles his own ragtag collective of cripples armed with
"wooden crutches" and led by the unlikely duo of Cervantes's mournful
knight and Hašek's Švejk. For and against whom does this haphazard army
fight? Is it pro- or anti-Soviet? Does it constitute a poetic third column of
sorts? I won't address these much-contested questions here. One thing is
clear, though: the poetic economy binding Mandelstam's unprepossessing
warriors is anything but Soviet. "The superfluous alone unites us (*Nam
soiuzno lish' to, chto izbytochno*)," he proclaims in the poem's seventh seg-
ment, and the Russian phrase underscores the perversity of his poetic credo.
The name of the Soviet state itself (*Sovetskii Soiuz*) is conspicuously imbed-
ded in Mandelstam's imagined community ("nam *soiuz*no"). But the unify-
ing force Mandelstam envisions could not be further from the utilitarian
ethos guiding Soviet ideology. His programmatic "superfluity" or "excess"
(*izbytok*) sounds suspiciously close to the parasitic bourgeois aesthetics that
critics saw exemplified in his writing. Certainly the "comradely commu-
nity" (*tovarishchestvo*) Mandelstam imagines "tapping around the age's
outskirts" in the poem's fifth segment hardly seems based on utility, uniting
as it does "Schweik's flattened smile" and Quixote's "bird-like lance" with
a feckless fraternity of prosthetics.[62]

Mandelstam himself spoke of "I drink to the military asters" as a poetic
joke: "They didn't even notice the preposterous wine I chose," he com-
plained to his wife. But its aggressive frivolity provides its social punch,
as I have argued. The tone of his toast is worlds apart from the high seri-
ousness that dominates the "Verses on the Unknown Soldier"—but the

mismatched weapons and unexpected comrades-in-arms of its fifth segment suggest affinities nonetheless. In a relentlessly use-driven society, whatever its guiding ideology, uselessness can have its purposes. "Lyric poetry, however responsible," Seamus Heaney comments, "always has an element of the untrammelled about it": "There is a certain jubilation and truancy at the heart of an inspiration. There is a sensation of liberation and abundance which is the antithesis of every hampered and deprived condition." This in itself is enough to justify what Heaney calls "lyric action" in a "world that is notably hampered and deprived."[63]

What does he mean by "lyric action"? Like other anglophone poets, Heaney has looked to Eastern Europe for inspiration in recent decades. It has been the "tragic destiny," he remarks, of certain Russian and Eastern European poets "to feel [the] 'call to witness' more extremely than others." With his compatriot Tom Paulin, he reveres the "heroic names" of those poets called upon by history to bear witness, to express "poetry's solidarity with the doomed, the deprived, the victimized, the under-privileged." Witness, solidarity, social justice: we apparently find ourselves once more in the land of acknowledged legislation to which Paulin opposes the disengaged art of the West. Indeed, the phrase I have quoted derives from a sentence that seems initially to reinforce this impression: for Mandelstam, Heaney comments, "lyric action constitutes radical witness."[64]

Heaney's notion of witness is more unpredictable than these remarks suggest. Postrevolutionary Russia was profoundly at odds with what Max Eastman calls the "totally impractical exuberance" of lyric poetry. The observation might be taken straight from Heaney's essays on Mandelstam, where he celebrates time and again the verbal energies he sees as the Russian poet's most vital form of lyric testimony. In the late writing, Heaney argues, "the hedonism and jubilation of purely lyric creation develop an intrinsically moral dimension." In *Poetry and Pragmatism* (1992), Richard Poirier speaks of "a human need for superfluousness." Though "the superfluous has to do with excess and luxury and exuberance and uselessness and desire, none of which are usually thought necessary to the rational and moral conduct of life," he explains, the longing for the unnecessary is nonetheless "a need anterior to ideology which can nonetheless create an ideology of freedom." For Heaney, one suspects, the ideological allegiance of the troops assembled in the "Verses on the Unknown Soldier" would be less important than the intricate, exhilarating verbal play that makes the poem's political affiliations so elusive to begin with. Lyricism in and of itself as a deeply ethical stance: this notion, as much as his sense of collective responsibility, brings Heaney close to the Eastern European poets he admires.[65]

The Battle of the Bards

I lived in the plural, we lived
in the plural, among friends
strange to us and friendly enemies,
so rarely on my own, our own, so little
loneliness in such a lonely
land. Even poems said
we, we poems, we lines, we
metaphors, we points. The I
slept like a child beneath the cloth
of a distracted gaze.

—Adam Zagajewski, *"In the Plural"* (1983)

"I hate the builders of dungeons in the air," Emerson protests in one of his lectures. Do lyric poets create such dungeons or help us to escape their fetters? Is the lyric a miniature mockup of Jameson's prison-house or the place where we go to be sprung from such linguistic prisons? I do not see these questions as merely rhetorical. When a genre invites widely divergent definitions, the truth is often to be found somewhere in between, possibly in the shape of an ongoing negotiation between the two extremes. Near the end of *The Government of the Tongue* (1989), Heaney speaks of the "problematic relation between artistic excellence and truth, between Ariel and Prospero, between poetry as impulse and poetry as criticism of life." Criticism of life, or even its wholesale reshaping, he hints elsewhere: how do we reconcile poetry's urge "to be Prospero, harnessed to the rational project of settling mankind into a cosmic security" with the purely lyric verve Heaney celebrates in Mandelstam and others? What happens, in another possible scenario, if Ariel turns his back on his lyrist's calling in order to enlist, voluntarily or otherwise, in Prospero's corps of subordinate spirits?[66]

"We are not prophets, not even precursors," Mandelstam laments in an early lyric. Like so many of his own poetic precursors, contemporaries, and descendants, he longed for the "prophet's staff and ribbons" that would help him lead his persecuted people into the promised land. The whimsical lyrist who empties his sack of linguistic tricks into the "Stalin Epigram" also claims to speak for his silenced nation at large in that poem's opening: "*We* live without feeling the land beneath us" (my italics). The poet says "we"— but his own voice is clearly the exception to the rule he sets forth in the next phrase. "Our speeches can't be heard ten steps away," he roars, and his lines about cowed silence eventually carried, as he apparently intended, to the ears of the "Kremlin mountaineer" himself.[67]

This poet-pariah is a far cry from the willful isolationist described by Bakhtin, Adorno, and others. He sets himself up, improbably enough, as a peer and rival to the Great Teacher himself. The poet who takes dictation from the muse in private may turn around and use his rebellious rhymes to take on dictators. Or even to replace them, at least in overheated poetic imaginations. "We alone are the Government of Planet Earth," Velimir Khlebnikov trumpets in his "Appeal by the Presidents of Planet Earth" (1917), and his self-chosen first name, Velimir, means just that, "world ruler." "We artists who have been so long the despised are about to take over control," Ezra Pound warns in 1914. There is little need to rehearse the dangerous directions that Pound's taste for power took in subsequent decades.[68]

In interwar Europe, Lucy McDiarmid notes, "the poet's wish to create community through the living voice was complicated from the start by the existence of his nightmare doppelgänger, the dictator . . . [By] unifying a large group of people, he seemed to be achieving the poets' own goal, and by their very means." This problem assumed peculiar resonance in the Soviet Union. Like Marx and Engels (who especially admired Shelley), Stalin was drawn to poetry as a young man, and the onetime "versifier" and seminarian proved peculiarly susceptible to the Russian cult of the poet-prophet. In Stalinist Russia, Benedikt Sarnov remarks, the "position of prophet was already occupied." "The greatest genius of all ages and nations, coryphaeus of learning, glorious commander, founding father, creator, originator, dearest friend of physical fitness, etc., etc." also assumed the role, not surprisingly, of "interpreter and prophet" for the nation, and indeed for the globe itself. Other applicants need not apply. And woe to any would-be poetic interlopers.[69]

Sarnov's list of epithets reminds us that Romantic poets were not alone in falling prey to the nineteenth century's penchant for messianic historiosophy with glorious beginnings and preordained conclusions. Another originator and founding father, Karl Marx, acquired early on a taste for the "new Romantic literature" which remained unaltered until his death, Isaiah Berlin comments: hence Marx's own language, not surprisingly, is "that of a herald and a prophet." "A spectre is haunting Europe—the spectre of communism. All the powers of old Europe have entered into a holy alliance to exorcise this spectre: Pope and Tsar, Metternich and Guizot, French Radicals and German police-spies." The famous opening of "The Communist Manifesto' (1848) sounds strangely familiar to readers of another prophetic text written less than two decades earlier. "The

Polish nation did not die" at the hands of the "Satanic trinity" of European empires who sought to erase it, Mickiewicz thunders in his grandiloquent *Books of the Polish Nation and the Polish Pilgrimage* (1832): "Its body lieth in the grave; but its spirit has descended into the abyss, that is into the private lives of people who suffer slavery in their country. . . . But on the third day the soul shall return again to the body, and the Nation shall arise, and free all the peoples of Europe from slavery." We have only to substitute "Proletariat" for "Nation" to translate the passage's last two phrases from Mickiewiczian nationalist messianism into Marxist materialist eschatology.[70]

Even the most ardent champions, or critics, of lyric isolationism agree that the genre enters, knowingly or not, into a variety of relationships with the world beyond its bounds. What are these relationships and how does the lyrist express them? The very nature of the "lyric I," or "lyric speaker," or "lyric hero"—the term varies from critic to critic and country to country—embroils us in problems of definition. "I," "you," and "we": these terms may be the lyric poet's stock in trade, but their meanings are anything but clear. Like all personal pronouns, they are what Jakobson calls "shifters." Their referents are contextually determined, and alter depending on who uses them, and how, and when. My "I" is your "you"; your "we" may or may not include me, just as my "you" may be either inclusive or exclusive in English at least. My "we," finally, may strike you as mere rhetoric, a linguistic trick inadvertently expressing not solidarity, but solipsism. And vice versa.[71]

"I am called Million—since for millions / I love and suffer torments," Mickiewicz's Konrad exults in *Forefather's Eve, Part III* (1832). "We are hordes upon hordes and hordes," Blok boasts of the Bolshevik "Scythians" in his poem by that name. "150,000,000 speak through my lips," Mayakovsky crows in his first postrevolutionary epic. "A nation of a hundred million shrieks" through "my tortured mouth," Akhmatova insists in *Requiem*. What is the function of the lyrist's "I" in traditions and ideologies—be they oppressive or oppositional—that live in the first person plural as a matter of principle? In the chapters that follow, I will trace the relationship of the poet's "I" to the various "we's"—the nation, the people, history's victims or its victors, even humanity at large—that have claimed her or his allegiance in modern Russia and Poland, even as I explore the potential dangers, poetic and otherwise, attendant upon such demands. I will also explore the distinctive "lyric strategies" of twentieth-century Russian and Polish poetry, strategies that challenge accepted notions of lyric engagement in the modern Anglo-American literary and critical tradition.[72]

A Tale of Two Pronouns

For we know in part, and we prophesy in part.
—St. Paul (I Corinthians 13:9)

"All personality (*lichnost'*) aside. Make way for anonymous prose."
Mandelstam's proclamation comes, as I've noted, from an essay on prose's
victory in the literary battles waged and won during Russia's years of war
and revolution. Though poetry surfaces only briefly in "Literary Moscow,"
Mandelstam clearly recognizes both the generic and the social implications
of his statement. A revolution fought in the name of the masses has created
a new mass readership, and this readership, in turn, demands a new kind of
writing en masse. It requires "the pure action of verbal masses, bypassing
the author's personality (*lichnost'*), bypassing everything accidental, per-
sonal (*lichnoe*) and catastrophic (the lyric)." The lyric in parentheses: could
there be a more graphic display of the genre's alleged limitations? It huddles
in its little brackets as History, Narrative, and the Masses pass it by. Cer-
tainly Mandelstam himself feared that he and his age had parted company:
"The revolution stripped me of my 'biography,' my sense of personal (*lich-
noi*) significance. . . . I offer it gifts for which it has no need," he mourns in
a 1928 questionnaire.[73]

But there is another way to read Mandelstam's shorthand definition of the
lyric in retreat. McGann decries the Romantic lyric's tendency to traffic in
the "personal, subjective and local signs" that it works to convert into "cos-
mic" drama. By confining his lyrics to "private, or generally, inconsequen-
tial, unchronicled, and plastic experience," Levinson argues, "Wordsworth
suppresses all those large, recorded events . . . not so obsequious to the imagi-
nation." Mandelstam's accidental poetics apparently lay him open to similar
charges, just as his response to the later questionnaire might well be taken for
a confession of both personal and generic failure. The final adjective in his
little triumvirate challenges such notions though: why should the intimate,
incidental lyric be "catastrophic"? Perhaps it is because, *pace* Levinson, the
dangers of suppression go both ways. Lyric poets may indeed be tempted to
erase or resist history—but this resistance may be motivated by the tendency
of "large recorded events," the action of masses, verbal and otherwise, to
suppress the inconsequential, unchronicled stuff of which both individual
lives and works of art are made. A lyric has never stopped a tank, Heaney
cautions. But tanks can easily crush the fragile forms—be they artifacts,
their creators, or their possessors—that make up our humdrum quotidian,
as Miłosz observes in his exquisite "Song on Porcelain" (1947):

Rose-colored cup and saucer,
Flowery demitasses:
You lie beside the river
Where an armored column passes.
Winds from across the meadow
Sprinkle the banks with down;
A torn apple tree's show
Falls on the muddy path;
The ground everywhere is strewn
With bits of brittle froth—
Of all things broken and lost
Porcelain troubles me most.

Before the first red tones
Begin to warm the sky
The earth wakes up, and moans.
It is the small sad cry
Of cups and saucers cracking,
The masters' precious dream
Of roses, of mowers raking,
And shepherds on the lawn.
The black underground stream
Swallows the frozen swan.
This morning, as I walked past,
The porcelain troubled me most.

The blackened plain spreads out
To where the horizon blurs
In a litter of handle and spout,
A lively pulp that stirs
And crunches under my feet.
Pretty, useless foam:
Your stained colors are sweet
Spattered in dirty waves
Flecking the fresh black loam
In the mounds of these new graves.
In sorrow and pain and cost,
Sir, porcelain troubles me most.
                    (tr. Czeslaw Miłosz and Robert Pinsky)

Bourgeois bric-à-brac once more—but with a difference. Miłosz's shattered crockery is moving precisely because it mediates between daily existence and the realm of art. It demonstrates how easily both worlds fall victim to the forces of history. The broken saucers exemplify both the fragile forms of a vanished quotidian and the no less fragile human beings that once inhabited it, beings now "spattered," like their dishes, "in dirty waves / Flecking the fresh black loam / In the mounds of these new graves." The formal patterns of Miłosz's poem, beautifully sustained in the translation, commemorate the forms, human and otherwise, that have fallen prey to the "armored columns" passing periodically through human history: "Not many works escape the sands and fires of history," Herbert reminds us.[74]

The tacit metaphor that animates Miłosz's poem and provides its unexpected pathos—why should porcelain trouble us most?—suggests another way of construing the relation between the poet-legislator's "I" and the "we" for whom he or she aims to speak. The poet-prophet is ideally larger than life, more powerful than opponents and constituents alike. "The poet remembers," Miłosz thunders in "You Who Wronged" (1950): "The words are written down, the deed, the date. / And you'd have done better with a winter dawn, / A rope, and a branch bowed beneath your weight." His words were in fact inscribed on the monument erected in Gdańsk in 1981 to commemorate shipyard workers killed in strikes against the state. Elsewhere, though, Miłosz insists upon the poet's "private obligations," duties sharing little with the lyrical self-absorption that New Historicists have ascribed to Wordsworth and his descendants. Wordsworth, Bromwich argues, opposes "the abstracting tendency of modernization" with the capacity, cultivated through lyric poetry, "to feel as an individual being rather than as a member of an aggregate being." Miłosz is in this sense very much a Wordsworthian. The lyrist's duty, as he sees it, does not involve fleeing history or society. It demands "defending the privacy of the individual" from the dangers of one collectivizing ideology or another, be it socialist, nationalist, or that of modern mass culture generally.[75]

What matters in this line of lyric thinking is not the poet's power, but his or her vulnerability to the various historical forces that threaten not just poems or porcelain, but the individual lives they exemplify. When Mandelstam speaks of his age "bypassing the author's personality," he has, I suspect, something similar in mind. Indeed his very syntax suggests this possibility: "the pure action of verbal masses, [*in*] bypassing the author's personality [*is also*] bypassing everything accidental, personal, and catastrophic (the lyric)," or so we might emend his phrase to read. The poet's personality is significant, in other words, not because it seeks an exemption from its age, or because it aspires to some realm of transcendent, ahistorical being. Just the opposite. Its very perishability permits it to represent other beings and things that are likewise accidental and personal and thus prone to catastrophic erasure by history. The poet symbolizes, in this vision, not humanity en masse, but humans in particular, the individual beings of which the species is made, and the things that these beings choose to make and keep around them in an effort to imbue the world with what Mandelstam calls "teleological warmth." The poet's task, Szymborska claims, is "to pick up what's been trampled and lost in the triumphal procession of objective laws." And to grant it, Mandelstam might add, a precarious safe haven within the tenuous parentheses of lyric form.[76]

"I liked him as he did not look for an ideal object," Miłosz writes in "Bobo's Metamorphosis":

> When he heard: "Only the object which does not exist
> Is perfect and pure," he blushed and turned away.
>
> In every pocket he carried pencils, pads of paper
> Together with crumbs of bread, the accidents of life.

What happens if we retrieve "Tintern Abbey" from among the world's would-be perfect objects and place it amid the scraps and accidents of life instead, as both Mandelstam's definition and the poem itself invite? Wordsworth's lyric, Levinson charges, is a "fragile affair, artfully assembled by acts of exclusion." Of course it is: the frailty of human making as balanced against "the heavy and the weary weight / Of all this unintelligible world" is one of the poem's great themes. The lyric tests the boundaries of human belonging and exclusion, Fletcher claims. His comments might be made to order for "Tintern Abbey." Human habitation, much like lyric poems, is a matter of considered, provisional exclusions and inclusions, the poem suggests. "Hedge-rows" and "plots of cottage-ground" shaped through agricultural acts of exclusion may vanish as readily as the verses that mimic the farmer's labors (the word *verse* itself derives from the Latin term for the plowman's repeated turnings). Acts of kindness may be overlooked; faint lines of smoke "sent up in silence" may go unrecognized and unread; city and country dwellers alike may find themselves "houseless" in an inhospitable reality.[77]

In this line of reading, Wordsworth's controversial poem helps us to realize not the lyric's limits, but its possibilities. Or rather, we come to see that these limits and possibilities are one and the same. Miłosz picked wisely when he chose "Tintern Abbey" as his emblem of resistance to an ostensibly limitless state. For Edmundson, Wordsworth's poem becomes a paradigmatic modern text not in its willful evasion of reality, but through the ongoing, inconclusive negotiations it conducts between self and society, "I" and "we": "The self that achieves its freedom by skeptically regarding all established beliefs, social and religious, and making a sustaining myth about its own identity, has a vulnerable and tenuous being. Always it is in danger of being shattered by loss or suffering in that it has no generally accredited story to tell about how we'll meet again in a future life, or how later generations will be free thanks to our sacrifice." "Oh, the leaky boundaries of man-made states!" Szymborska exclaims in her poem "Psalm." She has in mind the permeable lines that divide one principality or republic from another. The same might be said, though, of the shaky little poem-states created by Wordsworth and his latter-day descendants in Britain and elsewhere.[78]

Wordsworth's speaker has "no generally accredited story to tell." Is this a strength or a weakness? The answer depends largely on whether you see the lyric as offering its visions chiefly under the sign of completion, or whether you also admit the possibility of a lyric that is tentative both by choice and by necessity. In his study of Miłosz, Davie laments "the insufficiency of the lyric mode for registering, except glancingly, the complexity" of modern experience. As Christopher Ricks comments, though, "even the most capacious of the ancient genres, epic and tragedy, are vantage-points from which certain things—and only certain things—can be seen and shown." Part of the lyric's function is thus to ask if the very "idea of sufficiency—whether sufficiency as achievement or sufficiency to life—is itself insufficient." "Historically, from the Greek Anthology to Palgrave's *Golden Treasury,* lyric has been seen to occupy itself chiefly with the private life," Helen Vendler observes—but such perceptions run the risk, she continues, of overlooking the lyric's function as "provisional symbolic structures": "Since no lyric can be equal to the whole complexity of private and public life at any given moment . . . each poem says, 'Viewed from this angle, at this moment, in this year, with this focus, the subject appears to me in this light." The lyric not only does not seek permanence and impermeability; it questions the very possibility of such notions.[79]

The lyric is thus partial in two senses. It is incomplete, and it is partisan; it represents, by necessity, a particular, provisional point of view. Cameron reads the white boundaries surrounding the lyric on the printed page as pointing to the genre's willed divorce from history. They could just as easily be seen as signaling its self-conscious insufficiency, its built-in limitations. A poem's margins, after all, are scarcely carved in stone; they alter from one printed version to the next. The company each poem keeps in its different printed incarnations is equally varied, ranging from footnotes to want-ads depending upon the venue. And as students of modern Eastern European poetry know, these margins disappear entirely in versions sung or recited by heart: unprinted poems have a special function in cultures where the state controls the means of publication. The soul may select its own society—but the same does not hold true for lyric poems. If the modern lyric does aspire to be context-free, this may simply be wishful thinking, since it has in reality so little say in choosing its neighbors. *War and Peace* or *Buddenbrooks* are unlikely to be memorized in their entirety, reprinted from soup to nuts in an anthology of everybody's favorite novels, or copied from some reader's flawed memory onto one website or another.

In the lyric, Cameron acknowledges, "meaning is consciousness carved out of the recognition of its own limitation." This recognition, though, is born of "despair of the possibility of completed stories, of stories whose conclusions are known, and consequently it is despair of complete knowledge." And this despair, in turn, prompts the lyric to sever "incident from context, as if only isolation could guarantee coherence." But the incomplete stories of lyric poetry may also lead, as Cameron's own exemplary poet suggests, to a sense of liberation, to the openness that creates "a fairer house than prose, / superior of windows, more numerous of doors." "Every beginning / is only a sequel after all, / and the book of events / is always open halfway through," Szymborska observes in "Love at First Sight." Like many of the poets I discuss in the chapters that follow, Szymborska experienced early on the seduction of finished stories as embodied in the large-scale narration of past, present, and future alike offered by Soviet Marxism. Only after her initial passion had passed into disillusionment—shades of "The Prelude"!— did she discover the value of having, like Wordsworth, only unaccredited tales to tell. The unauthorized tales she relays in her mature writing become her way of challenging the human need for official stories generally.[80]

One way of conceiving the story I myself tell here would be as a tale of two pronouns—the lyric "I" and the public "we" that may signify either affiliation with a state that claims to embody the nation, or resistance to that state in the name of an oppressed people. Or it may serve, alternatively, to indicate the *desire* for this collective function: the unacknowledged legislator's dream. I have argued for the lyric as a peculiarly context-driven genre, a genre both invested in and testing the limitations that set it apart from its larger environment, literary and otherwise. Hans Robert Jauss speaks of the shifting "horizon of expectations" that individual literary works generate at different points in their reception history.[81] Genres likewise generate their own culture-bound horizons of expectations. And there are distinct advantages to examining the ostensibly private lyric in the context of cultures where it has traditionally performed public functions: in Russia "every taxi driver can quote Pushkin," the saying goes. The same holds for Poland, where a cab driver asked me to pass on his best wishes to the ailing Miłosz (he recognized the street address I gave), and where I first encountered Miłosz's "Song on Porcelain" sung in a student cabaret at the height of the Solidarity movement in 1981. The poet's desire to take his or her art public is hardly confined to Russia and Poland, though, as the cult of the great Eastern Europeans among recent anglophone poets shows. Hence the comparative focus of my study, ranging as it does from Whitman and Yeats to Tel Quel and its theorists of poetic language (Chapter 7), and finally, to contemporary Anglo-American poetry, with various stops at points between.

My organization is both chronological, running from the earliest years of the last century until poems written very near its close (and even beyond), and geographical, or rather geopolitical: I begin in prerevolutionary Russia, and move to Poland in the wake of the revolution forcibly imported by its neighbor to the east. The first four chapters deal chiefly with the varieties of lyric prophecy, as first Blok and then Mayakovsky struggle to conflate their lyric gifts and personal narratives with that of a revolutionary state in the making. Mandelstam and Akhmatova, in their later work, represent the opposite impulse, or perhaps more precisely, the same impulse taken in an oppositional direction, as the unprintable poet-bard claims to speak for the masses oppressed by his or her pseudo-prophetic adversary in what Nadezhda Mandelstam called Stalin's "pre-Gutenberg era."[82]

Chapter 5 finds Mayakovsky staging an encore appearance as the young Wiktor Woroszylski uses his revolutionary precursor first to write himself into a triumphant Communist "we" in the early years of People's Poland, and then to envision an alternative "we" by way of the same poet. The revolutionary writer who initially signifies acquiescence with the party line gradually becomes an emblem of resistance for his Polish disciple. Szymborska also moves from early work in which poetic lines and party lines converge to a radically different lyric practice. Unlike Woroszylski, though, she finds not a new "we" to replace the old, but addresses instead the quintessentially lyric question of what it means to have an individual viewpoint as she scrutinizes, from first one angle and then another, not so much the Marxist metanarrative in its Soviet redaction, but our need for such master plots generally in the face of the "great numbers" that make up human history, whether past or passing.

I then move from the poets of Poland's "New Wave" of 1968 and their complex relationship to their generation's and their tradition's collective voice of opposition, to the case of Czesław Miłosz, a self-professed "promethean romantic" who also articulates as compellingly as any poet of the past century the obligation, both ethical and aesthetic, to remain faithful to lyric singularity. Miłosz's work is the best possible reminder that the various lyric impulses and strategies I have been discussing can and do coexist within the same poet and even within the same poem. I have quoted from the fourth of his "Six Lectures in Verse," in which he opposes Miss Jadwiga's singular fate to Great History. The resurrection of vanished individual histories is, though, part of a larger project to rehumanize a fallen earth through the true Book that counters false "necessity, law, theory," as the next lecture reminds us:

> The Book is always with us,
> And in it, miraculous signs, counsels, orders.
> Unhygienic, it's true, and contrary to common sense,
> But they exist, and that's enough on the mute earth.

The crippled, forgotten librarian will live on in this ideal Book, for, as Miłosz might exclaim with his beloved Blake, "all that has existed in the space of six thousand years, / Permanent, and not lost, not lost nor vanished. . . . For everything exists, and not one sigh nor smile nor tear, / One hair nor particle of dust, not one can pass away." Prophecy and partiality go hand in hand among us humans, as Paul observes in this section's epigraph.[83]

Let me return in closing to the problem of limits as revealed in lyric form. Lyrics resist "the primacy of the *One,* the Great Idea producing the *Ultimate Theory,*" Fletcher insists, precisely by way of their formal limits: "Poetry, especially lyric verse, focuses larger issues onto limited screens and hence intensifies social issues to the point where individual writers and readers can begin, as individuals, to think these matters through according to their own personal lights" (italics in original). Poetry's "very formality is social," Robert Pinsky remarks, and Fletcher's own imagery—large issues projected onto limited screens—calls attention to the peculiarly modern potentials of lyric form. His language evokes the myriad screens—from Imax to plasma to laptop or cellphone—on which we receive our bulletins from modernity each day. Of course these screens had their precedents in previous eras. Throughout her work, Szymborska calls attention to the framed images and texts—be they ancient or modern, cave paintings, stained glass, film clips, postcards, or classifieds—that we have used to communicate through the ages. One distinctively modern frame surfaces at intervals throughout her work: this is the form that lends its shape to "Snapshot of a Crowd," "Frozen Motion," "Hitler's First Photograph," "Negative," and most recently, "Photograph from September 11."[84]

The affinities between photography and poetry should be obvious: the notion of framed moments fits snapshots as well as lyric poems. But the last lyric in this series calls special attention not just to the limits of photographs or poems, which can only pretend to stop time as a way of calling our attention to time's relentless motion. It also hints at the limits of critics who persist in enforcing the boundaries around artworks in ways that the works themselves resist. By pointing to the limits of her chosen form, Szymborska demonstrates how and why such formal matters matter:

Photograph from September 11
They jumped from the burning floors—
one, two, a few more,
higher, lower.

The photograph halted them in life,
and now keeps them
above the earth toward the earth.

Each is still complete,
with a particular face
and blood well-hidden.

There's enough time
for hair to come loose,
for keys and coins
to fall from pockets.

They're still within the air's reach,
within the compass of places
that have just now opened.

I can do only two things for them—
describe this flight
and not add a last line.

"Is there then a world / where I rule absolutely on fate? / A time I bind with chains of signs? / An existence become endless at my bidding?" Szymborska asks in "The Joy of Writing" (1967) Of course not, and that is writing's sorrow. "Chains of signs" bind for a moment at best. Even then their force holds only in the individual imaginations of readers and writers who are in turn helplessly time-bound themselves.[85]

"Stop all the clocks, cut off the telephone," Auden commands in his "Funeral Blues." But poems can stop neither clocks nor gravity, as both poets know full well, and Szymborska's lyric cannot end open-endedly. The true end of these human stories, with their particular faces and pockets and coins, lies inexorably just beyond the poem's frame. But the poet can resist this foregone conclusion by recuperating a few moments of free fall— "They're still within the air's reach, / within the compass of places / that have just now opened"—for her elegy's subjects. Even then the inevitable conclusion that Szymborska programmatically refuses will itself be short-lived. The species will carry on—"Reality demands / that we also mention this: / Life goes on," she reminds us elsewhere—and the separate beings she mourns here will be subsumed into the large numbers that simultaneously dominate human history and defy human imagination. The singular victims will become "a contribution to statistics," to the history that rounds off its victims "to zero," since for history, "a thousand and one is still only a thousand"—and three thousand and one, or two, or three, is still only three thousand. We know the end of the story that inspires this particular poem as well as the poet does, or the photographer whose work inspired hers. By refusing to provide a final line, or rather, by turning her final line into this refusal, Szymborska urges us to reimagine that ending, to see it as the arbitrary conclusion to a few irrepeatable lives that have, for an instant, been retrieved from history.[86]

, not the extinction, of the artist and his class, but with the decid-
tic revolutionaries who would find in Blok's art, life, and death
for the narrative they were themselves in the process of shaping
iet Russia's formative years.

turn to this distinction between the two poets later in my discus-
t to turn here, though, to an equally telling affinity between these
members of an endangered aristocracy, namely, the paradoxical
heir poetic vocation as they saw it. There is no direct link between
Yeats, although, like so many Modernists, the common cultural
y shared—from medieval alchemy, Rosicrucianism, Swedenborg,
d Schopenhauer to Wagner, Nietzsche, and Madame Blavatsky—
m closer poetic kin than they could possibly have imagined. The
rs were born, for better or for worse, into nations where acknowl-
islation was both a way of life and a mode of political resistance
who chose to follow the poet's calling. Blok and Yeats both took
ulturally prescribed artistic missions with a vengeance. They were
inventive proponents of literary traditions whose poets claimed
r beyond those accorded to their less fortunate brethren trapped in
ere their various prophesies and jeremiads went unheeded.

this, Blok and Yeats both sought to erase the division between lyric
by creating large-scale narrations of self and nation from the pri-
mate stuff that would seem to be lyric poetry's stock-in-trade: love,
sion, marriage, family. Both poets worked to forge through their
ot only the symbolic structure of their own lives—what the Rus-
dernists called "zhiznetvorchestvo," "life-creation"—but the very
f their nation's past and present as they prophesied its apocalyptic
he lyric impulse, writ large, was to bridge the distance between
on, and history.[5]

eats, Declan Kiberd comments, "nation-building can be achieved
imple expedient of writing one's own autobiography." His remark
ually for Blok. Both writers were antipodes to the powerful strain
rnist writing that preached—in its Anglo-American incarnation, at
—a poetics of impersonality in which the poet worked assiduously
all traces of the artist's life from his creation and to achieve "a con-
xtinction of personality," as Eliot famously put it. "Instead of turn-
npersonal philosophy, [the Irish poets] have hardened and deepened
rsonalities," Yeats insists in "Modern Poetry" (1936). "Art, life, and
are inseparable," Blok explains in the introduction to "Retribution"
Finally, both poets found themselves compelled to articulate their
ship to their nation, past and future, by way of a literary tradition,

Courting Disaster: Blok and Yeats

There have been men who loved the future like a mistress
—William Butler Yeats, "William Blake
and the Imagination" (1897)

I remember once telling a seeress to ask one among the gods who, as
she believed, were standing about her in their symbolic bodies what
would become of a charming, but seemingly trivial labor of a friend,
and the form answering, "The devastation of peoples and the over-
whelming of cities."

—Yeats, "The Symbolism of Poetry" (1900)

Oh my Russia! My wife!
—Aleksandr Blok, "On the Field of Kulikovo" (1908)

Bardic Gentlemen

In 1981, the Irish dramatist Thomas Kilroy chose to set a production of
Chekhov's *Seagull* not in fin de siècle England, as British theatrical tradition
would have it, but "on an Anglo-Irish estate in the West of Ireland" in the
late nineteenth century. The Slavist need only substitute "Blok" or "Blokian"

for Kilroy's "Chekhov" and "Chekhovian" in the following passages to see
the affinities linking the Russia of Aleksandr Blok (1880–1921) with the
Ireland of his near-contemporary, William Butler Yeats (1865–1939). "Like
Chekhov's gentry," Kilroy observes, "the Anglo-Irish landowning class no
longer exists, having been swept away in the foundation and later develop-
ment of the new Irish state" in the first decades of the twentieth century.
Both the Russian and Anglo-Irish gentry, he continues, "represented and
enacted imperial authority over a much larger, subservient population. Both
played significant roles in the Crown Civil Service and in military command
which did so much to preserve that power in their respective countries. For
both, the source and symbol of that power was the country estate with its
dependent peasantry or serfs and the instability of this property in the latter
half of the nineteenth century marks the first signs of the disintegration of
the empires themselves." The key difference between the two cultures lies,
Kilroy argues, in the "all-important distinction" of national origins: "The
Anglo-Irish represented a foreign, English power in Ireland," while Russia's
gentry "at least shared a common Russian nationality with those around
and beneath them."[1]

Well, yes and no. As those who study modern Russian culture realize,
this culture was largely a Western import, as was the language that the
gentry used to distinguish themselves from their peasant subordinates.
Tatyana, Pushkin's emblematic embodiment of Russianness, must of course
write the letter in which she bares her very Russian soul in French. Laura
Engelstein observes that "Europeanized Russians" "approached their own
native culture . . . as anthropologists confront an alien society." Yeats him-
self seems to have recognized the resemblance when he announced in 1901
that "all Irish writers have to choose whether they will write as the upper
classes have done, not to express, but to exploit this country; or join the
intellectual movement that was heard in Russia in the 'seventies, the cry
'To the people.'"[2]

The Russian populist tradition he evokes was Blok's own political and
moral legacy by way of his parents and their generation, as he recalls in his
unfinished epic "Retribution" ("Vozmezdie," 1910–21). Foreignness, more-
over, was in many ways Blok's stock-in-trade, however much he resisted it.
His very pronunciation, Kornei Chukovsky notes, was "typical of the gentry,
too elegant and bookish, with recently Russianized words pronounced in the
foreign manner: not 'mebel' [furniture], but 'mebl' [meuble], not 'trotuar'
[sidewalk], but 'trottoir.'" Blok himself worried that the Russian peasantry
he courted so assiduously would dismiss him as a "la-di-da semi-foreigner."
His fears were well-founded according to the peasant poet Nikolai Kluyev,

who informed him that the village gi[r]
verse] as though a young lady from t[h]
suddenly come to join their country re[

"Life is illiterate," Blok insists in [
Europe, he continues, "Russia is life."[
ate. Of his entire generation, he was, C[
possess "the kind of old-gentry educat[
"It seemed as if fate had purposely arr[
father and father-in-law were professo[
who idolized books and thrived on the[
moreover, foreign literally by definitio[
(*belletristika*) did not reach Russia un[
has only to recite the key terms that des[
(*literatura*) in Russian to be reminded o[
both the phenomena themselves and the[
roman, drama, tragediia, komediia, poe[
oda, elegiia, ballada, romans, and so o[
and *liricheskii poet.* Hence perhaps Bl[
gifts: "Hatred for the lyric is the source o[
in an essay of 1908 (2:63).[4]

"Hatred for the lyric"—fighting word[
widely heralded in his lifetime and beyon[
eration. Blok himself does not elaborate. [
not just in his distaste for the foreignness[
ern Russia. New Historicists join forces w[
their suspicion for what they see as the eg[
poetry, I've argued in my introduction. Li[
avant-garde or reactionary, Blok despised [
greater part of his large prerevolutionary au[
sian lyric, were, like Blok's own, both arist[
descended from German émigrés who had[
status in their adopted country.

Blok's hostility towards his chosen genr[
self-hatred. It marks his antipathy towards t[
represents. Lyricism was for Blok finally a [
Practiced properly, the genre should lead in[
And not just its own. It was ideally to be pl[
tion that aimed to eliminate not just the supe[
classes from which its prime exponents and[
Blok shares common ground not with Yeat[

and in Yeats's case even a language, that was alien to the very people they claimed to represent. For both writers this divide between gentry and people is articulated in terms of an endlessly thwarted courtship between the poet and the elusive, beloved nation embodied in feminine form.[6]

These courtships took dramatically different paths through the poets' lives and writing, though. Their divergent careers reflect the schism that divided Modernists into radical leftists calling for a revolutionary transformation of the status quo, and their equally radical right-wing contemporaries, who sought not revolution, but restoration of a an idealized, hierarchical past order. "Pastists" and "futurists" alike relied of course chiefly upon their own poetic imaginations to provide the prototype for the ideal society they hoped to install or reinstate through their writing. Blok envisioned a cosmic leveling by way of the revolution that would annihilate him along with his oppressive class. The "great, universal Revolution," he exults in "Art and Revolution" (1918) "will destroy the age-old lie of civilization and elevate the people (*narod*) to the heights of artistic humanity" (2:230). Once achieved, this artistic nation will have no further need for the bards who helped to herald its ascent or even to bring it into being. Here, at least, he agreed with the revolution's architects, who saw in art chiefly a tool to be discarded once its purpose had been served.

Unlike Blok, Yeats hoped to sustain, or create, the aristocratic traditions to which he laid claim. He aimed to forge a nation in which the Anglo-Irish ascendancy would continue to lend, by violent means if necessary, its shaping force to a people who might otherwise remain confined to inchoate potential alone. "Historic Nations grow / from above to below," he proclaims in a late play. Historic nations that refuse to recognize the natural order of things invite intervention by spurned aristocrats—or aristocrats of the spirit—whose unimpeded view from above leads them to endorse what Yeats approvingly calls "the despotic rule of the educated classes." If Yeats's mission might be defined as "saving civilization," then Blok felt compelled to assist in its demolition.[7]

The poets were alike, though, in seeing the modern world as teetering on the brink of a cataclysm that would lead either to its destruction or its renewal. And like so many of their contemporaries, they perceived this crisis in sexual terms. One need only think here of the ruthless April that persists in breeding new life from dead earth in the opening lines of "The Waste Land." Modern society survives at the price of the sexual instincts it represses to its peril, Yeats's contemporary Sigmund Freud warns in *Civilization and Its Discontents* (1929), and he uses an analogy that seems to speak directly to Yeats's and Blok's shared mission. "Civilization," Freud claims, "behaves towards sexuality as a people or a stratum of a population does which has subjugated another one to exploitation." Yeats and Blok were likewise preoccupied with the vexed relations of sex and civilization. For the poets, though, sexual relations were not the bottom line, but a point of departure, symbols that mirrored, even shaped, the very structure—or destruction—of the world's cosmic order. They were true heirs to a Romantic tradition in which sex, as Mario Praz comments, "[is] the mainspring of works of the imagination." All his symbols, Yeats insists in *A Vision* (1925), "can be thought of as the symbols of the relations of men and women and the birth of children." Courtship, marriage, consummation, progeny: all are key terms in Blok's and Yeats's perception of the crisis facing self, nation, and cosmos alike. They provide the primary narrative thread that yokes, in each case, the poet's life to his work, and the work, so he hopes, to the fate of his nation and the transformative forces it embodies.[8]

Let us turn here to two poems that mark the earliest stages of the poets' troubled wooing of the elusive nation, "I Foreknow You" (*Predchuvstvuiu Tebia*, 1901; 1:37) and "To the Rose Upon the Rood of Time" (1892/95):

> And the heavy sleep of worldly consciousness
> You will cast off, yearning and loving.
> Vladimir Soloviev

I foreknow You. The years pass by—
In one visage alone I foreknow You.

The whole horizon is aflame—and unbearably bright,
And I wait silently—*yearning and loving.*

The whole horizon is aflame, and the apparition is near,
But I'm terrified: You'll change Your visage,

And awaken a bold suspicion,
Having changed at last the accustomed features.

Oh how I'll fall—pitifully, low,
Without mastering mortal dreams!

How bright is the horizon! And radiance is near,
But I'm terrified: You'll change Your visage.
—Aleksandr Blok

> *To the Rose Upon the Rood of Time*
> Red Rose, proud Rose, sad Rose of all my days!
> Come near me, while I sing the ancient ways:
> Cuhoollin battling with the bitter tide,

The Druid, gray, wood nurtured, quiet-eyed,
Who cast round Fergus dreams, and ruin untold,
And thine own sadness, whereof stars, grown old
In dancing silver sandalled on the sea,
Sing in their high and lonely melody.
Come near, that no more blinded by man's fate,
I find under the boughs of love and hate,
In all poor foolish things that live a day,
Eternal Beauty wandering on her way.

Come near, come near, come near—Ah, leave me still
A little space for the rose-breath to fill!
Lest I no more hear common things that crave;
The weak worm hiding down in its small cave,
The field mouse running by me in the grass,
And heavy mortal hopes that toil and pass;
But seek alone to hear the strange things said
By God to the bright hearts of those long dead,
And learn to chaunt a tongue men do not know.
Come near—I would, before my time to go.
Sing of old Eri and the ancient ways:
Red Rose, proud Rose, sad Rose of all my days.
—William Butler Yeats[9]

I have said that the poems mark the early stages of each writer's life story in verse. Both poems are shaped, though, not by narrative progression, but by circularity: each ends where it begins, in a repetition that resists the narrative line set in motion by the opening. They are courtship poems marked by a resistance to consummation, and the symbolic nature of the poet's beloved in each case shapes the indeterminate outcome of the frustrated relationship.

For all its fin de siècle frills and furbelows, Yeats's lyric is clearly intent upon emphasizing the Irish folk traditions that he, along with other members of the Irish Renaissance, hoped to revive in their writing. Cuchoollin (or Cuchulain), Fergus, the Druid, Eri, or Eire, or Erin: all are familiar figures in Yeats's early verse, and are intimately linked here to the poet's muse, the flower he invokes in what is the opening poem of his collection *The Rose* (1892). To the Symbolists, Osip Mandelstam complained, "the rose is a likeness of the sun, the sun is a likeness of a rose, a dove—of a girl, and a girl—of a dove. . . . The rose nods to the girl, the girl nods to the rose." Yeats's Rose (who appears, like Blok's You, exclusively in capitalized form) is no less multivalent. She is, James Pethica notes, not only a symbol of "eternal and spiritual beauty" central to the occult Order of the Golden Dawn in which Yeats was an active participant. She also represents, as Yeats commented in an early edition, both love and Ireland itself.[10]

Blok's lyric does not evoke Russia per se, although the poem's imagery, with its flaming horizons and otherworldly apparitions, makes clear that this is no ordinary sweetheart. Indeed, the capitalized "Ty" (the Russian informal "you") throughout the poem was ordinarily reserved for invocations of God alone, and as such was altered by government censors before the poem went to press. The poem's epigraph would have revealed to initiates, though, that Blok's "You" was none other than the nineteenth-century philosopher Vladimir Soloviev's Divine Sophia, Holy Wisdom, the Eternal Feminine who promises through her imminent return to earth a revelation "of nature as it should be, humanity as it should be, the cosmos potentially redeemed and restored; the 'world soul' within all these things growing gently and inevitably, as the corn in the ear, the child in the womb, towards a new life."[11]

In another early poem, written just a few days before "I Foreknow You," Blok reveals the distinctively Russian nature of the feminine figure he invokes. The very title of "The Divine Cannot Be Measured by the Mind" (*Nebesnoe umom neizmerimo;* 1:36) recalls Fyodor Tiutchev's famous lyric "Russia Cannot Be Comprehended by the Mind" (*Umom Rossiu ne poniat'*); and the Eternal Feminine chooses in fact a distinctively Russian incarnation this time around:

> And I perceived the Russian Venus,
> Swathed in a heavy tunic,
> Impassive in her pureness, joyless beyond measure,
> In her features—a peaceful dream.

This Venus does not emerge naked on the half-shell, à la Botticelli. Unlike her Renaissance precursor, she makes her appearance draped demurely in a thick tunic—perhaps to fend off the Russian cold? And unlike her namesake, she is impervious, passionless, "joyless beyond measure." This distinguishes her from her apocalyptic sister in "I Foreknow You," whose cosmos-shaking passion is suggested by the fiery sunrise ("the horizon is aflame") that prefigures her arrival; by the love, yearning, and terror with which her would-be lover awaits her; and, perhaps most importantly, by her volatility, her capacity for change. The verb that denotes this ability in the poem, *izmenit'*, does double duty in Russian for both sexual and political betrayal: Blok uses it in both senses on a single page in "Retribution" to describe wives deceiving husbands (and vice versa), and the son who betrays the fatherland (*a syn—on izmenil otchizne!*) (1:514).[12]

The "bold suspicion" (*derzkoe podozrenie*) she will arouse (*vozbudish'*) in her hapless lover confirms the verb's dubious double sense: this overwhelming female is both the Woman Clothed with the Sun and the Whore of Babylon. Her capacity for the change and betrayal that will precipitate his own fall from grace ("Oh how I'll fall") terrifies the suitor seeking chaste changelessness from his still-distant object of desire. The speaker's dueling emotions of longing and dread determine the poem's very structure, which comprises a sequence of six couplets whose rhyme-words cross stanzaic boundaries to create quatrains of alternating rhymes. Four of the couplets, moreover, have strongly marked caesuras in each line, and these come equipped in turn with their own set of insistent, if irregular internal rhymes: *v ogne* (l. 3), *v ogne* (l. 5), *mne* (l. 6), *v kontse* (l. 8), *mne* (l. 12) (literally, "on fire," "on fire," "to me," "in the end," "to me"). The poem's would-be couplings are undercut at every turn.

This courtship would not be a mating of equals in any case. The poem's speaker, its "I," is eclipsed even grammatically by a potentially overwhelming "You." This "You" may be capitalized throughout, but the "I," as Jenifer Presto observes, never appears as a subject at all in the original text. Russian's conjugated verb forms permit personal pronouns to be omitted without running the risk of semantic ambiguity—though this is not standard practice—and the "I" is elided throughout the poem. From the start, then, the speaker lays low while his "You" looms larger than life: "Predchuvstvuiu *Tebia*" (my italics). More than this—forms of the first-person pronoun appear only in an oblique case (the dative) and a passive construction (*mne strashno*; literally, it is frightening to me).[13] The "You," on the other hand, is clearly capable of dramatic action: "You'll change Your visage," the speaker frets. The "I" is diminished still further by the percussive end-rhymes that emphasize his beloved's might; fully a third of the poem's twelve lines end either in nominative forms of "Ty" or in echoing rhyme-words ("cher*ty*," "mech*ty*").

Yeats's fussy diction masks a less structurally sophisticated lyric, with its two stanzas built of neatly paired, monosyllabic rhyme words and its infrequent enjambments. Yet his speaker also shrinks from the consummation so devoutly to be wished as the second stanza opens. "Come near, come near, come near," he begs his muse. But just as he seems on the brink of success, he interrupts himself abruptly in mid-line: "—Ah, leave me still / A little space for the rose-breath to fill!" Both the dash and the unexpected enjambment work to create the space he now craves as acutely as the proximity he had urged just moments earlier. The stanza's closing lines hint at the speaker's fears. If she draws too near, he will cease to notice "common things," and "seek to hear alone the strange things said, / By God to the bright hearts of those long dead, / And learn to chaunt a tongue men do not know." "Singing ancient ways" is his self-proclaimed mission, though, and so the courtship dance must resume as the poem closes. He requires her presence if he is to achieve his goal—but too much of a good thing is apparently as fatal to this mission as too little. He'll miss the "foolish things that live a day," he complains, if Eternal Beauty has her—or rather, his—way.

But is this really Yeats's chief concern? The revival of Gaelic as the language of both art and life was very much on the minds of Irish writers at the time this poem was written. Yeats may have wrapped himself in what Kiberd calls "the black cloak of a professional Celt."[14] But an Anglo-Irishman could not claim the Celtic tradition as his birthright, and a thoroughly Gaelicized nation would hold no place for a self-proclaimed bard singing the ancient ways in the oppressor's tongue. To renounce this paradoxical calling, though, would require Yeats to forfeit his Anglo-Irish identity entirely, to be consumed by lovely Erin. Hence his resistance to the seductive Rose who would lure him into learning "to chaunt a tongue men do not know."

For Blok, Pyman notes, an aggressive, even demonic "eternal masculinity" formed the necessary counterweight to the essentially passive principle of the Eternal Feminine. In "I Foreknow You" and "To the Rose," though, the poets find themselves confronted not by some ideally submissive feminine principle, but by a perverse and potent nation well equipped to outwit her timid poet-suitors. Yeats's Helen, we recall, is not the reluctant cause of Troy's fall, but its active instigator: "Was there another Troy for her to burn?" the speaker asks of that latter-day Helen, Maud Gonne, in "No Second Troy" (89). Perhaps this is why both Blok and Yeats feel compelled to enlist a company of fellow worshipers to join in their wary praise of the all-powerful Lady; she is simply too much woman for one poor poet alone.[15]

"Many turn-of-the-century nationalisms imagined national community as a deep emotional bond among men united in the service of a country or cause personified by a woman," Marjorie Howes remarks. Both Blok and Yeats followed suit. "The Rose upon the Rood of Time" opens *The Rose*. In its bookend poem, "To Ireland in the Coming Times," Yeats makes his claim to be accounted "true brother of that company, / Who sang to sweeten Ireland's wrong, / Ballad and story, rann and song" (46–47). The rann is "a verse of a poem in Irish," Pethica notes. The other genres in Yeats's list suggest, though, that he is not concerned with Celtic forms alone. Indeed, the exalted company he keeps in the poem's second stanza—"Davis, Mangan, Ferguson"—consists of three Irish nineteenth-century writers and cultural heroes of whom two were Protestant, while the one Catholic, James Clarence

Mangan, knew no Irish and wrote his poetry, like his fellows, in English. The company of those who would chase Ireland's "red-rose-bordered hem" comprises Protestant and Catholic alike, but they must translate their praise of Erin into a language that reaches far beyond her borders. The ancient ways must be sung in a new tongue for their true meaning to be revealed to the modern age, Yeats suggests. The Lady's real history is not confined to Ireland alone; it began, after all, "before God made the angelic clan." And this, in turn, gives Yeats the necessary distance both to court and resist his version of Irishness.[16]

Blok's tactics are different, but they likewise speak to his dilemma as a semi-foreigner wooing the ostensibly homegrown beauty. In "The Divine Is Not Measured by the Mind," the speaker describes the circle of worshippers who have gathered to greet the "Russian Venus" (*Rossiiskaia Venera*) in her most recent incarnation:

> She has come to earth before,
> But she is encircled for the first time
> By different heroes (*bogatyri*), different warriors (*vitiazi*) . . .
> And the gleam in her deep eyes is strange . . .

The strange gleam in the eyes of this chaste Slavic Venus hints at her capacity to wreak havoc among her suitors for all her seeming modesty. This time, though, the speaker has apparently joined forces with the heroic warriors of ancient Russian sagas and legends, the *bogatyri* and *vitiazi* he evokes in the poem's penultimate line. The Europeanized gentleman bypasses his troublesome Western legacy to become part of a primeval Slavic brotherhood well qualified to pay suit to the ancient nation-goddess Rus'.[17]

Like Yeats's Rose, Blok's Beautiful Lady both embodies and exceeds the nation of which she is the emblem. Like Yeats, Blok sought to fuse ancient Western myths—here his russified Venus—with their indigenous incarnations. "Antiquity," he asserts in an essay of 1905, provides the key that "links us with the truth of religion, the nation, and history." Yeats goes Blok one better. Like the Greeks, he insists in "Ireland and the Arts" (1901), the Irish "have a history fuller than any modern history of imaginative events; and legends which surpass, as I think, all legends but theirs in wild beauty." (Elsewhere he even purports to find a link between the early Irish nation and "Slavonian peasants.") Blok's poetic mythologies proceed, D. Maksimov notes, from "'small-scale,' 'local' historicism to macro-, even metahistoricism." The same holds for Yeats, who calls upon his small nation to reforge ancient myths for a modern age: "I would have Ireland re-create the ancient arts, the arts as they were understood in Judaea, in India, in Scandinavia, in

Greece and Rome, in every ancient land; as they were understood when they moved a whole people and not a few people who have grown up in a leisured class and made this understanding their business."[18]

But it takes a member of a modern leisure class, with the requisite European education, to perceive the larger contexts from which merely local traditions derive their metahistorical significance. The Modernist cult of the primitive proved peculiarly congenial to the Europeanized bards of backward nations. It allowed them to stake a claim in a native past to which their dubious background might otherwise deny them access. And it placed them, as their nations' poet-prophets, at the heart of the cosmic revelations in which their seemingly retrograde peoples would play a leading part. Ireland was "the most belated race in Europe," Joyce complained. For Yeats, Ireland's very "technological and economic backwardness" gave it "the benefit of a spiritual glamour which had faded from the rest of Europe," Seamus Deane observes. The task of the Irish artist, Yeats explains, is "to begin to dig in Ireland the garden of the future, understanding that here in Ireland the spirit of man may be about to wed the soil of the world." His language grows more bombastic elsewhere as he charges Irish artists "to forge in Ireland a new sword on our old traditional anvil for that great battle which must in the end re-establish the old, confident, joyous world."[19]

For Yeats the Irish had "a crucial, redemptive role to play in the recovery of European civilization from barbarism," Deane remarks. Blok plays out this scenario in reverse: Russia's "barbarism" is its best weapon against the "old, exhausted cocotte" of Europe, with her "sacred shopping centers." Like all "wild, barbaric nations," Russia "creates life," Blok insists shortly after the failed revolution of 1905. That "idle, thousand-eyed," gypsy Russia "has given her very flesh to the world," though the shape it takes may look like chaos to jaded Western eyes, he warns (2:45). But "true Russians," the "warriors' descendants" (*potomki bogatyrei*) on whom the world's future rests, will not be daunted by her apparent formlessness. "Blessed beings," these heroes have "voluntarily orphaned themselves," as they wander along "the boundless plains" destined to give birth to the future of both their own nation and the species itself (2:32–34).[20]

The Irish were "barbaric Scythians," Edmund Spenser insists in his *View of the Present State of Ireland* (1596), and as such required speedy extermination. Spenser's lethal insult would become Blok's ideal as he celebrates the imminent barbarian invasion of effete Europe by its neighbors to the east in "The Scythians" (1918; 1:453–454). For all their differences on the uses and abuses of barbarism, Blok and Yeats shared a vision of a primeval nation freed not just from the shackles of an alien culture, but from the religious legacy that had superseded its ancient rites. Nietzsche's notoriously anti-Christian stance—"Christianity has cheated us out of the harvest of ancient culture," he charges in *The Antichrist* (1888)—certainly influenced both writers. But their ambivalence, even antipathy toward Christian culture had deeper roots. The advantages of Nietzschean "anti-Christianity" to Yeats are obvious. A Protestant writer could not possibly play the prophet in an Ireland defined by its Catholicism. His best hope lay in bypassing Christianity completely by laying claim to an ancient folk culture that Ireland herself had half-forgotten. "'I have longed to turn Catholic that I might be nearer to the people.'" Yeats records his friend Lady Gregory as saying. "'But you have taught me that paganism brings me nearer still.'" His preoccupation with the occult springs from the same source; the Anglo-Irish ascendancy developed a modern tradition of occult interests to compensate for its increasing distance from the actual life of its nation, Foster comments.[21]

This fascination with the occult marks yet another trait that the Anglo-Irish shared with their early twentieth-century Russian counterparts. Blok, with his Eternal Feminine, sometimes found himself the unwilling center of a modish mystical coterie inspired by Soloviev's teachings: "Don't convert our quests into mere fashion," he begs in one essay (2:84). And like Yeats, Blok sought to merge his esoteric interests with ancient folklore as a way of circumventing the Christianity that stood, so he felt, between him and his nation. Though they shared in principle the same Orthodox faith, he was deeply ambivalent towards their common heritage and sought to heal the rift between poet and people by reviving "the ancient pre-Christian Slavonic world of myth and legend."[22]

Blok and Yeats could not escape the fascination with the poet-Christ they had inherited from their Romantic precursors, the persecuted Savior who suffers and dies so that his nation, and through it, humanity itself, might be freed from all earthly shackles. In their early poetry, though, the suffering Man-God is supplanted by the Beautiful Lady: hence Yeats's Rose upon the Rood, or Cross, of time. The poet does not embody the transcendent; rather he yearns, and fears, to merge with it. But Yeats's Rose refuses to stay crucified, just as Blok's feminine ideal does not consent to imprisonment within the single visage he has imagined for her. Blok and Yeats both worried—with good reason in the event—that they were not prophets, but only latter-day Pygmalions who shaped the nation in the image of their own confused desires. In "Poetry and the Tradition," Yeats speaks wistfully of the "perhaps imaginary Ireland, in whose service I labour." Blok likewise laments the solipsistic nature of his cosmic yearnings in "On the Current Condition of Russian Symbolism" (1910): "And so it has come to pass: my own enchanted world has become the arena of my private actions, my 'anatomical theater' or puppet-show (*balagan*), in which I myself perform alongside my astonishing dolls (*ecce homo!*)" (2:151). This did not stop either poet from recruiting flesh-and-blood women to play leading parts in their symbolic dramas.[23]

Cosmic Courtship, or Life-Creation and Its Discontents

It is only those things which seem useless or very feeble that have any power and all those things that seem useful or strong, armies, moving wheels, modes of architecture, modes of government, speculations of the reason, would have been a little different if some mind long ago had not given itself to some emotion as a woman gives herself to her lover.
—Yeats, *"The Symbolism of Poetry" (1900)*

It dawned on me how very much we are strangers to each other, how little you understand me. For you look at me as if I were some kind of abstract idea . . . I even gave you a hint about this when I said: "One must translate the abstract into the concrete."
—*Liubov' Mendeleeva-Blok, unsent letter to Aleksandr Blok, from Mendeleeva-Blok, "Facts and Myths about Blok and Myself" (1929)*

Let's admit that although Blok was not the embodiment of my girlish dreams—a Lermontov or a Byron—he was nonetheless a lot better-looking than all my friends.
—*Mendeleeva-Blok, "Facts and Myths about Blok and Myself"*

The Blok of 1901 surrounds his Beautiful Lady with warriors and heroes drawn from ancient legends. A famous photograph of 1904 suggests a somewhat more earthbound scenario. The writers Andrei Belyi and Sergei Soloviev—Blok's colleagues in his mystical endeavors—sit, impeccably dressed, around a small table holding three objects: a bible, a portrait of Vladimir Soloviev, and a photograph of Blok's young wife, the unfortunately named Liubov' ("Love" in Russian) Dmitrievna Mendeleeva-Blok. ("Even my name . . . set me apart from the commonplace," she notes ruefully in her memoirs.) The writers' choice of icons was only half-joking. Blok had known Mendeleeva since childhood; another early photograph shows the two adolescents costumed as Hamlet and Ophelia for a domestic production of Shakespeare's tragedy. Their convoluted courtship reached its apparent climax in 1903, when the two were married at a church located halfway between their families' neighboring estates. But the marriage was, if not doomed from the start—it survived until the poet's death in 1921—then destined for a singularly bumpy trajectory. Blok had long worshiped his lovely neighbor with her "ancient Russian beauty" from both near and far as the modern Russian incarnation of the Divine Sophia. In a 1902 letter to Mendeleeva-Blok, he professes his "faith in you . . . as in the notorious Immaculate Virgin or the Eternal Feminine, if you like." The 1904 photograph demonstrates that he was not alone in his veneration.[24]

But the Eternal Feminine proved to be, unsurprisingly, ill-suited to married life: Beautiful Ladies and bedazzled poets make for uncomfortable bedfellows. Blok's vision of a companion "still a bride and eternally a wife" (1:108) proved more congenial in poetry than in life. "I am destined only to 'live in white,' but not 'to create in white: it may be my lot to test the Whore of Babylon," he confesses, with suitably Symbolist obscurity, in a 1903 letter to Belyi. He apparently took this "living in white" quite seriously, and tested Babylon's Whore by setting up housekeeping with his new bride in what was by all accounts a "white marriage." "Naturally, we were not 'husband and wife,'" Mendeleeva-Blok recalls in her memoirs: "My life with my 'husband' (!) by the spring of 1906 was completely shattered. His brief outburst of sensual interest in me in the winter and summer before the wedding soon (in the two months that followed) had spent itself without having succeeding in dispelling my girlish ignorance. . . . He immediately started theorizing that we did not need physical closeness, that this was 'astartism,' 'darkness,' and God knows what else."[25]

Blok's convictions did not prevent him from experimenting with various forms of astartism elsewhere. "I have not possessed 100, 200, 300 (or more?) women, but only two," he boasts in a journal entry of 1915. "One is Lyuba [Liubov']; the other—all the rest." The marriage was apparently first consummated a year after the actual wedding and all physical relations between the two ceased shortly afterwards, according to Mendeleeva-Blok. She suggests that Blok's squeamishness may have derived from the illnesses contracted in the brothels he had frequented since adolescence: "Physical closeness meant one thing to Blok: paid sex, and the inescapable result was disease." But the metaphor nascent in his venereal ailments proved too tempting, and the couple translated even this sordid detail into the language of legend: "The two Aphrodites—Aphrodite Urania and the Aphrodite of the streets [were] separated by a chasm," Mendeleeva-Blok explains.[26]

Aphrodite Urania, the "heavenly" or "spiritual" Aphrodite versus her sensual sister Aphrodite Pandemos: the opposition evokes the elusive, tunic-swathed Venus of Blok's early lyric, who stands as a tacit rebuke to her more unruly earthbound counterparts. These multiple goddesses raise a peculiar question: what does the poet do when he finally finds "the kind of love it is possible to feel for a mother, a sister or a wife in one person, in Russia," and marries the beloved motherland, or her closest human approximation? Imagine Whitman setting up housekeeping in his final years with Lady Liberty herself. Unlucky Liberty would certainly have suffered: symbolically charged marriages with would-be bards pose challenges unknown to lesser mortals. However much Blok's young bride ("poor Liubov' Dmitrievna," as a colleague of mine used to call her) may have struggled with her unlikely ménage, though, it proved remarkably productive for her poet-spouse.[27]

Yeats cherished "the twin issues of sexuality (the personal crisis) and Ireland (the historically unique culture) . . . as sources of value and of feeling," Deane notes. "The universal, higher mysticism" of politics joins forces with the "lower, personal mysticism" of private life, Blok insists in an autobiographical sketch of 1915. It is, I suspect, no accident that he ceased to identify his wife with Holy Russia during the brief period in 1904 that led to the marriage's long-delayed consummation, which took place, conveniently enough, shortly before the failed revolution of 1905. The two events apparently converged in Blok's poetic imagination: "Hardly had my fiancée become my wife when the lilac worlds of revolution enveloped us and swept us into the whirlpool," he explains in his notebooks. Crises in both lunar and sublunar realms coincide as mystic "brides" and "girls" clad in the "red sarafans" of Russian peasants mingle with "streetwalkers in red skirts" in essays written in the revolution's aftermath (2:30–35). Most famously, the Beautiful Lady of his poetry undergoes a terrifying transformation to become the ambiguous demimondaine known as the Stranger from the poem by that name (1906; 1:76–77). Variations of this fallen woman will henceforth coexist in the poetry with the Holy Wife and Sacred Mother whose image "not forged by human hands" illuminates Russian past and present alike in poems like "On the Field of Kulikovo" (1908; 1:284–288).[28]

The shifting shapes that Blok's real and symbolic beloveds take in Russia's revolutionary year have been thoroughly explored elsewhere, and I won't attempt to summarize them here. But Blok was not alone in perceiving the advent of Russia's revolutionary years in terms of sexual crisis. After 1905, "the language of social commentary relied increasingly on emblems of sexual disorder," Engelstein observes; and satiric journals of the times represented disturbing new social realities "as devilish, vampiric creatures, sometimes ravishing a woman—usually Mother Russia." The immense popularity of Blok and his poetry in the years following 1905—postcards bearing his photograph were widely available, and prostitutes reportedly donned the silks and ostrich feathers made famous by the beautiful Stranger of the poems— suggest that his lyric obsessions had a recognizably public dimension.[29]

He had company as well in his preference for poetic over genetic off-spring. Soloviev's Symbolist disciples opposed in principle and frequently in practice what the master called "the bad infinity of the physical reproduction of organisms." "If I have a child, it would be worse than my poems," Blok comments in his notebooks. The poet Zinaida Gippius went still further, providing, incidentally, a compelling argument in favor of unacknowledged legislation: "The abolition of procreation," she announces, "abolishes the [sex] act, of its own accord—not by any law, but because of its having become . . . an unlawful state." Blok apparently agreed: "The state of prohibition should always remain even in marriage," he commented shortly before his wedding. Poor Liubov' Dmitrievna indeed. But Blok's stake in this antireproductive ethos was also deeply personal. His gentry precursors were, he insists in "The Guardian Angel" (1906), a "generation of slaves," and the "family curse" (*prokliatie sem'i*) he shares with the "angel" who is simultaneously his "sister, bride, and daughter" dooms them to a fate precluding procreation. "Will we rise from the grave? Perish? Die?" he asks in the poem's final line: mundane reproduction is apparently not among their options (1:179–180). And this is as it should be, according to Blok. "We are moneyed, childless people," he writes in his notebooks, and for him the two adjectives were, quite properly, virtual synonyms.[30]

Modernist literature generally demonstrates, Edward Said argues, "the failure of the generative impulse." "Childless couples, orphaned children, aborted childbirths, and unregenerately celibate men and women populate the world of high modernism with remarkable insistence," and their condition "is portrayed in such a way as to stand for a general condition afflicting society and culture together." All happy families are alike, or so the famous opening of *Anna Karenina* would have it, while each unhappy family creates its own private brand of misery. There are striking similarities for all that between the frustrated families that mark Blok's and Yeats's early experiments in life-creation, poetic and otherwise. I have spoken at some length about the real-life prototype for Blok's Beautiful Lady. Yeats's Red Rose, his Eire, his Helen and Cathleen ni Houlihan also found their this-worldly inspiration in a beautiful woman, the "English ex-debutante" turned Irish nationalist Maud Gonne (1866–1953).[31]

Yeats first met Gonne in 1889, and was captivated by the girl who had already "cast herself precisely as the *fatale*, capricious beauty of whom the poet dreamt," Foster comments. She continued to play this role in Yeats's life and art for decades. "There was an element in her beauty," he recalls in his *Autobiographies*, "that moved minds full of old Gaelic stories and poems": "she looked as though she lived in an ancient civilization where all superiorities whether of the mind or of the body were . . . in some way the crowd's creation," while "her whole body seemed" at the same time "a master-work of long labouring thought." She effortlessly embodied the fusion of ancient myth and Irish legend, of individual artistic labors and collective creation, that is his prescription for both national and "super-terrestrial" transformation.[32]

And like the Ireland of his dreams, she kept her distance. Yeats courted Gonne for the better part of three decades, hoping against hope that she would be worn down by his persistence. She steadfastly refused him, though, even using their shared occult preoccupations to justify her continued resistance: she conveniently discovered in a dream that the two had been brother and sister in a past life, hence present-day consummation would be incest. The relationship was consummated in 1908, but its physical dimension was short-lived. When Gonne declined his last proposal in 1916, he promptly turned his attentions to her daughter Iseult, who had the good sense to refuse her mother's rebuffed suitor.[33]

However frustrating Gonne's resistance may have been to Yeats personally—although a man who proposes to the same woman unsuccessfully four or five times over the course of a quarter-century presumably derives some kind of satisfaction from his protracted suffering—it was remarkably fruitful in other respects. His convoluted courtship proved no less productive, both poetically and mythopoetically, than Blok's torturous marriage. I have mentioned Blok's poem "The Guardian Angel." The angel, sister, and daughter who is the poet's bride can promise only some unspecified brand of resurrection beyond the flesh. The heroine of a quatrain written two days later holds out the possibility of more concrete forms of gratification:

> To the Maiden-Revolution
> Oh maiden, I follow you—
> And is it fearful to follow you
> To one who loves your soul,
> To one who loves your body? (1:180)

Blok's revolutionary maiden lures him away from his guardian angel. For Yeats, though, the Beautiful Lady and the Revolutionary Maiden were the same. In his *Autobiographies*, Yeats credits Gonne with igniting the political passions that he hoped would win her favor: "I was sedentary and thoughtful," he recalls, "but Maud Gonne was not sedentary." The mystic had to turn activist in order to woo his revolutionary sweetheart. And this was the inspiration behind "To Ireland in the Coming Times," which "announced [Yeats's] arrival as a frankly political poet" by "fusing occultism and advanced nationalism in a manner calculated to appeal to Maud Gonne, and to irritate nearly everyone else," Foster comments.[34]

A shared "passion for theatre becomes the most distinctive connection between the Anglo-Irish and Russian worlds," Kilroy remarks. Be that as it may, Blok and Yeats clearly shared a flair for self-dramatization, and their preoccupation with enacting national and cosmic dramas in the arena of their private actions lent itself to theatricalization in more public forums as well. Lyric conflicts writ large were the stuff of which their poetry was made; literal stages served as convenient way stations en route to the more expansive, less tangible theaters both poets craved. Blok and Yeats were prolific playwrights, although only Yeats, true to form, set about creating a theater that would serve both as a vessel for national self-definition and, at least initially, as a call for political action. Their respective muses shared their theatrical bent. Mendeleeva-Blok eventually became a professional actress, although not a particularly successful one, while Gonne was actively involved in Yeats's efforts to forge a national theater. Their theatrical collaboration reached its apogee in 1902 when Gonne agreed to perform the title role in the premier of Yeats's drama *Cathleen ni Houlihan* at the Irish National Dramatic Society, of which Yeats was president. Mendeleeva-Blok wisely declined the title role in Blok's drama *The Stranger*, written in the same year as the famous poem; she apparently felt that the line dividing art from life had grown fine enough.[35]

Yeats's play tells the story of a courtship cut short by no less than Ireland herself in the person of the titular Cathleen ni Houlihan, a folk symbol of the nation. The action takes place in 1798, the date of a famous, abortive Irish revolt against the British. It is set, though, not during revolutionary upheaval, but in a prosperous peasant cottage as the parents ready their son Michael for his wedding to a "fine, comely girl," his neighbor Delia. Their minds are fixed, understandably enough, on things other than their country's fate—but the nation would have it otherwise. She appears at their doorstep as an old beggar with "no man of her own": "With all the lovers that brought me their love, I never set out the bed for any," she tells Michael. The family welcomes her and she repays them by recounting in parable and song the nation's history, the tale of the many men who "died for love of me." "It is not a man going to his marriage that I look to for help," she explains. Bewitched by her stories, Michael turns his back on family and bride alike, and follows the mysterious stranger to take his place in the ranks of the doomed rebels. Renewed by the prospect of new lovers and victims, Cathleen appears transformed to Michael's brother Patrick—her next conquest?—as the play closes. "I saw a young girl, and she had the look of a queen," he tells his father in the play's final line.[36]

A fellow Protestant nationalist left the premiere wondering "if such plays should be produced unless one was prepared for people to go out to shoot and be shot." Yeats echoes his fears in a late poem: "Did that play of mine send out / Certain men the English shot?" (353). But the political and personal do not part company in the play. As its original casting suggests, the autobiographical drama of Yeats and his own Cathleen stands close behind the story of Michael and the vampiric goddess-nation who desires bloodshed, not the marriage bed. Under the influence of his own imperious and off-putting muse, Yeats himself could produce only plays and poems, not progeny. "Pardon that for a barren passion's sake, / Although I have come close on forty-nine / I have no child, I have nothing but a book, / Nothing but that to prove your blood and mine," he mourn in the lines that introduce *Responsibilities* (1914; 101).[37]

By that time, Blok was already at work on "Retribution," the extended poem that unapologetically extolled the end of his own "barren" line. "They have no exit," he writes of his kind, "neither in love, nor in children, nor in the formation of new families." And rightly so, as Blok saw it: the death of his own family tree and those like it was the only hope for the emergence of a liberated, truly Russian people. But Yeats viewed the fate of his country as vested in the continuation of its Anglo-Irish aristocracy, and he hoped for a happier ending to his own symbolic tale. He had long been convinced "that his natal horoscope presented inherent problems for his romantic life," Brenda Maddox notes. Experts had assured him, though, "that he could never expect a better time to overcome the liability of his stars than late in 1917 when the number of favorable planetary conjunctions would be quite extraordinary." According to expert predictions, "if 1917 was the year for his marriage, October was the month."[38]

Killing a House

Blok was preoccupied with his ancestry, both as a man and as a poet. He was the last of the poet-gentlemen, the last of the Russian poets who could adorn his house with portraits of his fathers and forefathers.
> —*Kornei Chukovsky,* Alexander Blok as Man and Poet *(1924)*

But he killed the house; to kill a house
Where great men grew up, married, died,
I here declare a capital offence.
> —*Yeats,* Purgatory *(1939)*

The historian F. S. L. Lyons speaks of an Irish "revolutionary decade" that ran from 1912, or the year of the British Third Home Rule bill, to 1922, the year in which the Anglo-Irish Treaty granting Southern Ireland dominion status was ratified by the Dáil, the Irish Parliament. Russian historians have sometimes seen that nation's revolutionary years as spanning nearly two decades, from the failed revolt of 1905 through 1921, when the Bolshevik government solidified its claim to power after three years of bloody civil war. If we draw these bookend dates closer to the actual revolutions that transformed nations and overthrew states, we might identify them as running, in Ireland's case, from the Easter Uprising of 1916 to the end of its civil war in 1923, with Russia's revolutionary years beginning with first the February, and then the October revolutions of 1917, and ending in 1921, at the close of its own civil conflict.[39]

The near convergence in the dates marking their nations' traumatic labor pains marks a radical split in Yeats's and Blok's poetic and personal paths. Yeats's astrologers had predicted well. He proposed to a young Englishwoman, Georgie Hyde-Lees, shortly after his refusal by Iseult Gonne, and the couple was married on October 20, 1917. Their daughter Ann Butler Yeats was born in 1919; she was followed by a son, Michael, in 1921. Yeats became a senator in the Irish Free State Government in 1922, and received the Nobel Prize for literature a year later. The Symbolist visionary had become an acknowledged legislator at last, though the "smiling public man" (219) apparently found official legislation less to his taste than its symbolic equivalent: "Do not be elected to the Senate of your country," he warned his friend Ezra Pound. His greatest poetic achievements still lay ahead of him—as did the dabbling with fascism that marks his most disturbing venture into prophetic politics.[40]

Yeats's successes coincide with Blok's decline. He wrote what were virtually his last poems, "The Twelve" and "The Scythians," in January, 1918, after eighteen months of poetic silence. He continued to write essays, and he served the government in various minor editorial and bureaucratic functions until his death from undiagnosed causes on August 2, 1921. His descent dovetailed neatly with the triumph of the Soviet state, and the convergence of the two events seemed no accident to both friends and foes of the new regime who perceived the poet's end, regardless of their affiliations, as marking the death of lyric poetry as such, along with the age and the class that had spawned it. They read his death, in other words, along Blokian lines, and I will return to Blok's posthumous influence on his own obituaries in a moment. For now, though, I want to address a different set of questions. How did champion mythmakers like Blok and Yeats confront and recreate the catastrophes they had long sought once these disasters crossed over from imagination in reality? And why did their lives and art diverge so radically at this crucial juncture in history?

"Yeats's 'The Second Coming' (1920) began with explicit references to the Russian Revolution and the First World War ('The falcon cannot hear the falconer / The Germans are [ ] now to Russia come')," James Longenbach notes. It was only in later variants that "the poem's apocalypse became mythical rather than historical." "Leda and the Swan" (1924) likewise began life as a meditation on "the Russian revolution and its aftermath," Kiberd comments, though Yeats insisted that all politics had vanished from the final version. Two of the greatest poems of the modern age thus took their initial inspiration from the event that marked the end of tsarist rule in Russia, and the lines Longenbach cites hint at the significance this cataclysm held for Yeats's symbolic vision.[41]

"The falcon cannot hear the falconer / The Germans are [ ] now to Russia come": what connects the famous opening line with the second phrase omitted from the final poem? The Germans had come to Russia twice in the preceding decade, once by way of the World War that brought down the monarchy, and the second time in the train car carrying Vladimir Lenin from Germany back to Russia in 1917. The German leaders hoped—rightly as it turned out—that the exported revolutionary would end Russian participation in the war by overthrowing Kerensky's Provisional Government. The Communist regime that replaced it became Yeats's emblem of the modern age gone horribly wrong, although not for the reasons we might suspect. "*Democracy*, to Yeats, was a bad word; it meant mob rule, as in Russia," Maddox comments. Yeats's mistrust of the masses extended even to his compatriots: "Let us have no faith in the people," he urges in a letter of 1911. But Soviet Russia best exemplified the "filthy modern tide" (345) that his poetry was intended to stem. Hence the aristocratic image of falcon and falconer, which evokes not just the medieval ideal Yeats venerates through a feudal pastime cultivated by the privileged few. It also summons up a world in which these few have, however tenuously, mastered the violent, animal instincts of their underlings and turned them to their own ends. When the falcons cease to heed their masters and abandon their place in history's grand scheme—"History is very simple—the rule of the many, then the rule of the few, day and night, night and day forever"—then "mere anarchy is loosed upon the world," as it had been in Soviet Russia (189).[42]

How is this madness to be staunched? How is history gone horribly wrong to be put right again? In his *Autobiographies*, Yeats celebrates "the symbolism of sex" that gives Blake's poetry its heightened meanings. Symbolic sex shapes Yeats's great poems as well; it provides the key to viewing his own life through the encompassing code he devised to bridge the gap between self, history, and nation. Yeats devotes the final chapter of *A Vision* to the quasi-historical significance of the mythic rape that is the subject of his controversial "Leda": "I imagine the annunciation that founded Greece as made to Leda," he explains. But we do not need the author's commentary to see the larger claims being made for Zeus's rape of the "staggering girl": "A shudder in the loins engenders there / The broken wall, the burning roof and tower" (218). Crisis and new creation—the fall of Troy and the rise of Greece—were born of the forced mating of winged divinity and hapless maiden. The comment from *A Vision* reminds us, though, that this is not the only such meeting to reshape history. Christ and Christianity were likewise born of an annunciation that took the form of a—rather gentler—encounter between an otherworldly winged creature and an innocent girl whose child, conceived through this meeting, will transform the world. "Surely some revelation is at hand," the poet-seer proclaims in "The Second Coming," and he ends the poem anticipating the next earthly avatar of cosmic transformation: "What rough beast, its hour come round at last / Slouches towards Bethlehem to be born?"(190).[43]

These lyrics bookend two other poems, also written in 1920 and 1924 respectively, which celebrate what appear to be more purely personal events. "A Prayer for my Daughter" begins literally where "The Second Coming" ends; it appears immediately after the more famous poem in *Michael Robartes and the Dancer* (1921;190). "Under this cradle-hood and coverlid / My child sleeps on," the speaker writes unremarkably enough. But the sleeping child is surrounded by a tempest-driven reality—the howling storm, the roof-leveling wind, the ocean's "murderous innocence"—that recalls the cataclysms of "The Second Coming." Symbolic and domestic realities intersect, just as they do in the more chilling "Prayer for my Son" (215–216), which appears a few poems before "Leda and the Swan" in *The Tower* (1928). "Bid a strong ghost stand at the head / That my Michael may sleep sound," the speaker begs (and just what deity does he address, we wonder).

> Bid the ghost have sword in fist
> Some there are, for I avow
> Such devilish things exist,
> Who have planned his murder, for they know
> Of some most haughty deed or thought
> That waits upon his future days,
> And would through hatred of the bays
> Bring that to nought.

What latter-day Achilles or Herod wishes to murder the hapless infant? And why should the poet's son be singled out for such brutal treatment? The prayer's prophetic language and guardian ghosts remind us that the first offspring of Yeats's marriage was neither daughter, nor son, but the personal mythology born of his wife Georgie's spirit writing, the otherworldly dictation that led in turn to the encompassing cosmologies of *A Vision*. The work was intended, Kiberd notes, "as a kind of Celtic constitution." It was first published in 1925, "a juncture when the new state, of which Yeats was by then a senator, was seeking to codify its own laws and customs." But it was also a cosmic autobiography of sorts, and the Yeatses interpreted their growing family through its prism. Could some prophet "prick upon the calendar the birth of a Napoleon or a Christ?" Yeats wonders in his introduction. The lonely feats he foresees in the "Prayer" likewise hint at the lofty company he anticipates for his male heir. By 1918, Maddox notes, the Yeatses' hoped-for son "had grown in their imagination to something much grander than an ordinary baby. It was to be a new messiah, redeemer, or initiate who, like Christ or Buddha, would introduce a new cycle of history."[44]

I will not enter here into the very different, clearly gender-based expectations the poet sets forth for daughter and son in his controversial lyrics. The poem's imagery reveals, though, both the spatial realization of Yeats's ideal state and the paradigmatic family on which it would be based. Let his daughter be a "flourishing hidden tree" whose secret verticality will resist the "assault and battery" of the "roof-levelling wind," Yeats intones in the first "Prayer." Natural heights become pinnacles of human accomplishment in the prayer for his son, whose future "haughty deed or thought" threaten the resentful masses who "hate the bays," the laurel wreaths meant to crown the triumphant few.[45]

"The theoretical self-image of the Anglo-Irish was aristocratic and gentlemanly," Kiberd comments. In practice, though, "they were a middle class masquerading as an aristocracy." "The middle class," Yeats himself wrote, is "an attitude of mind more than an accident of birth."[46] For Yeats as for his beloved Nietzsche, aristocrats are likewise a matter of attitude, not birth. Hence his purchase in 1916 of the tower that would serve for a time as his young family's home, and that lent its name both to the collection of 1928—its image graced the book's cover—and to the well-known poem. Descent and heights join forces in "The Tower" and "Meditations in Time of Civil War" (198–214), which celebrate the achievements of his Anglo-Irish ancestors, both literal and figurative, while laying out the terms of his inheritance for the generations of Yeatses, and properly Yeatsian Irishmen, yet to come:

It is time that I wrote my will,
I choose upstanding men . . .
                    I declare
They shall inherit my pride,
The pride of people that were
Bound neither to Cause nor to State,
Neither to slaves that were spat on,
Nor to the tyrants that spat . . .
(from "The Tower")

Having inherited a vigorous mind
From my old fathers I must nourish dreams
And leave a woman and a man behind
As vigorous of mind . . .
These stones remain their monument and mine
(from "Meditations in Time of Civil War")

In civilization as in nature, Yeats spurns the leveling forces that threaten to lay the mighty low, be they trees, towers, or the men who planted and built them. But violence that aspires upwards is another matter. Ireland's English conquerors, "rough men-at arms, cross-gartered to the knees" first ascended the winding stairs he calls home in "The Tower" (200). For Yeats, Howes notes, "Anglo-Irish civilization is based on barbarism"—but this is the barbarism of masters, not masses. "Its rich cultural identity originates in crime and violence," since "violence and greatness, blood and power go together." And this is key to his vision of human history generally: "I think that all noble things are the result of warfare; great nations and classes, of warfare in the visible world, great poetry and philosophy, of invisible warfare, the division of the mind within itself" ("J. M. Synge and the Ireland of His Time," 1910).[47]

Yeats's visionary history moves through cycles, be they gyres, great wheels, or historical cones. Blok was likewise in thrall to the Nietzschean notion of a history shaped by repetition, not progress. And violent upheavals are crucial to the health of the nation he celebrates as well. "Ceaseless battle—we only dream of peace / through dust and blood," he proclaims in "On the Field of Kulikovo" (1:285). His geometries of history were not nearly as ornate as those of Yeats or his own compatriots Andrei Belyi and Velimir Khlebnikov. Still in Blok's own great effort to meld personal genealogy with national, even cosmic history, his language inevitably calls to mind the elaborate charts and diagrams of *A Vision*. "I began constructing an epic poem called 'Retribution,'" he writes in the poem's preface. "I conceived its blueprint in the shape of concentric circles, which first became narrower and narrower, and then the smallest circle, having contracted to its innermost limits, begins once more to live its own life, to expand and extend what surrounds it and to act, in its turn, upon the peripheries" (1:478).[48]

The independent life he envisions for the final circle does not extend to his own family, whose history he sets alongside that of "the nineteenth century, iron age, cruel age" in the poem (1:484). The death of Blok's father in 1909 inspired his unfinished epic. In it the end of the family line coincides with the end of a society whose demise is long overdue: the nation's renewal depends upon it. Blok apparently hoped for some salvation conceived outside the family line proper. But the illegitimate future child he anticipates in his preface—"the seed is cast . . . into the womb of some quiet, womanly daughter of another nation" (1:480)—never appears in the poem itself. This other nation was in fact Poland; the poem's third chapter is set in Warsaw, where his father lived and taught. But the imagined offspring meant to represent a redemptive fusion of Russian and Polish Romantic messianism never finds its way into the poem as such.[49] And the unshackled bird of prey that presages disaster for Yeats is thus the poem's only hope of future liberation:

> Arise, go to the meadow in the morning:
> The hawk revolves in the pale sky,
> Tracing smooth circle after circle,
> Determining which nest
> Is least hidden among the bushes . . .
> Suddenly—birds twitter and rustle . . .
> He listens . . . one instant more—
> Descends on straightened wings,
> A terrified cry from neighboring nests,
> The sad squeal of the last chicks,
> Tender down tossed by the wind—
> He claws his poor victim,
> And once more, raising a vast wing
> Flies up to trace circle after circle,
> With a hungry, homeless eye
> He scrutinizes the lifeless meadow . . .
> No matter where you look—he's circling (1:499)

Blok's metaphorical nest of gentry comes to a grisly end, as it must. All who wish to survive history and its depredations should emulate its emissary, the hungry hawk, and not its sorry prey, who must learn to leave the nest and make do with homelessness.

"Come build in the empty house of the stare [starling]," Yeats bids the bees from his new tower home in "Meditations in Time of Civil War." The poem's subtitles reveal his commitment to house-building in past and future alike: "Ancestral Houses," "My House," "My Table," "My Descendants," and so on. The phrases suggest not only Yeats's drive to will his tradition into being. They also reveal his awareness of the "threat posed to the aristocracy by the violence of the civil war and the burnings of estates," Howes comments. Blok, the poet-gentleman, had inherited the tradition and family tree Yeats craved the old-fashioned way, by right of birth. And where Yeats the Anglo-Irish upstart must laboriously build his house in verse and stone, Blok seeks to annihilate his ancestral estate, at least poetically. "Retribution" might better have been called "The House That Collapsed," Chukovsky suggests. "Manor houses are rotting, moldering, crumbling into dust, with all their marble, cupids, gold and ivory, their high fences guarding centuries-old linden parks, their six-tiered, sculpted iconostases in the manor churches," Blok writes approvingly in 1906, just after the revolution that had seen so many estates vandalized and burnt by rioting peasants (2:33). His detailed inventory reveals nonetheless an intimate, loving knowledge of the way of life whose end he applauds. As Presto notes, Blok devoted the inheritance he received following his father's death to "house construction" (*domostroitel'stvo*), a thorough-going renovation of the family estate, Shakhmatovo, which he undertook in the same year that saw the beginning of "Retribution." Nonetheless he apparently practiced what he preached when his own estate was destroyed shortly after the October Revolution: "Do not fear the destruction of kremlins, palaces, pictures, books," he bids his readers in 1918 (1:225). After Shakhmatovo was pillaged, Chukovsky recalls, "it seems as if he hardly noticed the loss. When he related the story of its destruction, I remember how he waved his hand and said with a smile, 'Such was its predestined path.' In his soul his house had long ago been reduced to rubble."[50]

Come let us mock at the great," Yeats scoffs in "Nineteen Hundred and Nineteen":

> That had such burdens on the mind
> And toiled so hard and late
> To leave some monument behind,
> Nor thought of the levelling wind. (212)

His irony would have been lost on Blok, who celebrated the same forces that Yeats deplored as emblems of the modern age. The "Mother Russia" (*matushka Rossiia*: 2:49) he pursues is a pathless expanse that defies all efforts at civilization. It is an elemental force, "stikhiia," and its tokens are the wind, the storm, the blizzard (*v'iuga*) that overthrow all who would stand against them. Those who wish to court this amorphous goddess must abandon home and family alike to take up wandering.

This Russia seems to have triumphed in Blok's final poems, "The Twelve" and "The Scythians," which were written virtually simultaneously, within the same few weeks early in 1918. The road signs and markers of the old world have vanished in "The Twelve" (1:534), whose twelve revolutionary soldiers march through a universe that has been radically reshaped by an elemental force of nature:

> Black night.
> White snow.
> Wind, wind!
> A man can't stand upright.
> Wind, wind—
> Over all God's earth!

So run the poem's opening lines. The soldiers may celebrate the "world-wide fire" ignited by the revolution, but the poem itself is dominated by the "blizzard" that rages from beginning to end, and that might initially seem yet another incarnation of "Mother Russia" herself—but has in fact been utterly transformed. "We both love and hate the Russia so distant from us," Blok writes in 1908 (2:95). Ten years later only the hatred remains, or so the evidence of the late poems suggests.

I have mentioned the assembly of warriors Blok gathers before his Russian Venus in "The Divine Cannot Be Measured by the Mind." This masculine collective convenes once more in "The Twelve." This time around, though, they are common Bolshevik foot soldiers, not the heroes of ancient legend, and they come to bury Russia, not to praise her:

> Comrade, grasp your rifle, don't flinch,
> Shoot your bullet into Holy Rus' (*Sviatuiu Rus'*)
> That old-timer,
> Hut-dweller,
> With her fat ass!

But why should we take the soldiers' matricidal hatred for anything but an antipode to the myths of a redemptive motherland Blok had cultivated so carefully over the last two decades?

In "The Twelve," as critics noted early on, Blok combines his love of common forms like folk laments, gypsy dances, and "cruel songs" (*zhestokie romansy*) with revolutionary slang, soldier's marches, and street songs (*chastushki*) to create a poem in which the bardic gentleman's lyric musings have finally been drowned out by the maelstrom, the "music of the revolution." Was he embracing the revolution? Slandering it? Was the poem "anathema or hosanna"? Its multiple voices defied easy answers, and its interpretation proved controversial from the start: it was greeted by both applause and derision. Some revolutionaries rejoiced as the old world's most celebrated poet apparently joined their ranks; while other rebels attacked not just the boorishness of the poem's Bolsheviks, but their aimlessness as they wander uncomprehending through the snow from the poem's outset to its ambiguous ending. Many of Blok's former friends and Symbolist colleagues, on the other hand, refused to acknowledge the poet-turncoat on the streets.[51]

Chukovsky argues that the poem's Russia is of a piece with the nation whose primal passions Blok had embraced early on.[52] The poem itself tells a different story. Whatever it does or doesn't mean vis-à-vis the revolution, its storyline, such as it is, is clearly yet another transposition on a theme that had long preoccupied Blok: the love triangle. I will not enter into the biographical and literary variations on the theme that run through Blok's life-in-art here. But whether the affair involves Belyi, Blok, and Mendeleeva-Blok themselves, Colombine, Pierrot, and Harlequin in "The Puppet Show," or the Poet, the Light Blue Man, and the Stranger in the play by that name, unhappy triangles proliferate in Blok's art and life alike. "The Twelve" is no exception—but its love triangle takes a less exalted shape. The poem's central action concerns not revolutionary conquest, but lowbrow, garden-variety romance, with all its retrograde possessiveness and strife. Vanka, a renegade comrade-in-arms, has stolen Katka, a common prostitute, away from a spurned and jealous fellow soldier, Petrukha. Petrukha must choose his allegiances: will he join the revolutionary brigade in their assault on their wayward comrade and his beloved? Or will he stay true to the girl he laments in the poem's fourth section: "Oh you Katka, my Katka, / Fat-cheeked Katka." The poem's answer is unambiguous. "Halt, halt," the unnamed leader shouts:

> Andriukha, look sharp!
> Petrukha, take the rear!
> Rat-a-tat-tat-tat-tat-tat-tat-tat-tat! . . .
> And where's Katka?—Dead, dead!
> Shot straight through the head!

This is the only military action the unit actually sees. Small wonder, then, that the poem sparked arguments in revolutionary circles: the murder of a common streetwalker and her renegade lover would hardly have ranked among the revolution's chief ideological or strategic priorities. Just the opposite. Such anarchic behavior would in reality incur only the wrath of the powers-that-be, Leon Trotsky protested. Had a Red Guard like Petka actually been caught, he explains in "Aleksandr Blok" (1924), "he would have been sentenced to be shot by the Revolutionary Tribunal. The Revolution which applies the frightful sword of Terrorism, guards it severely as a State right." "Were Terror used for personal ends," he concludes, "the Revolution would be threatened by inevitable destruction."[53]

In his poem, Blok does indeed turn revolutionary violence to deeply personal purposes, although he struggles to imbue them with suitably political meanings. The twelve soldiers themselves are first introduced in the poem's second part—it has twelve—as is the story of Vanka and Katka. The part concludes with a revolutionary exhortation—"Keep the revolutionary pace! / The relentless enemy never sleeps!"—and a statement of the collective's mission, which involves, unsurprisingly, the elimination of this ruthless foe. And who exactly is this enemy: the bourgeoisie? the forces of world capitalism? the tsarist White Guard? No, to all of the above. The section ends with the lines I quoted earlier: the soldiers' prime target is none other than "fat-assed" (*tolstozadaia*), backward Mother Russia herself.

The "fat-cheeked" (*tolstomorden'kaia*), fickle streetwalker is just another incarnation of the vilified, feminized Rus' who is the Bolsheviks' chief foe, and this is why her execution proves so crucial to the revolution's proletarian apostles. Indeed, the poem's opening section, which evokes the range of symbolic bourgeois enemies as efficiently as any revolutionary lampoon, is populated exclusively by women or "womanish" men. There is the "old woman like a chicken" who invokes God's mother ("Okh Matushka-Zastupnitsa!") against the "Bolsheviks who'll drive us to our grave!"; the "young lady in furs" who "slips, / and splat—goes sprawling!"; the "long-skirted" priest; and finally the "long-haired" writer-prophet who echoes the distraught old lady: "Traitors! / Russia has perished!" The imagery comes straight from the new state's broadsides, with their benighted, roly-poly *babushki*, effete bankers, and portly priests overwhelmed by the forward-looking, virile forces of the revolution. Postrevolutionary Soviet culture generally revered "traditionally masculine values at the expense of conventional femininity," which was taken to represent the Russian backwardness that the Bolsheviks were destined to overcome. This cult of masculinity took the form, moreover, of the kind of collective comradeship shared by Blok's revolutionary twelve, who choose, as Vanka's fate demonstrates, female companionship over masculine solidarity only at their peril.[54]

But Russia is not the only suspect female in Blok's version of global revolution. In "Hugh Selwyn Mauberly" (1920) Pound laments the myriads of young men lost in the First World War for the sake of "an old bitch gone at the teeth," the "botched civilization" of rotting Europe.[55] The Europe of "The Scythians" (1:453–454) has likewise outlived herself. This "old coquette" is still "comely," though, and the poet speaks for the new Mongol horde, the Soviet forces en masse, as he describes the love and hate with which they will subjugate their seductive foe:

> We love flesh—its taste, its color,
> And its sultry, mortal scent . . .
> Are we to blame if your bones crunch
> Between our heavy, tender paws?

Holy Russia will be shot straight out, but the Scythians plan to ravish the aging courtesan Europe before her long-overdue end. In either case, the Soviet male collective emerges victorious, and the poet of "The Scythians" becomes the self-appointed spokesman for this barbaric horde.

Both poems might seem to represent Blok's desire to sacrifice his Beautiful Lady—be she harlot or deity—at the altar of a new, hyper-masculine Russia that has no use for aging earth mothers or otherworldly ladies. But the very language Blok uses to describe his barbarian conquest sends us back to the earlier poetry in unexpected ways. "Come from the horrors of war / Into our peaceful embraces," the horde bids an understandably reluctant Europe (these peaceful caresses had pulverized bones just a few stanzas earlier). And if she refuses, the poet's collective warns, "you will be cursed / By your ailing, belated descendants" (*bol'noe pozdnee potomstvo*). The phrase evokes nothing so much as Blok himself and his Silver Age gentry brethren as described in "Retribution" and elsewhere. Indeed, his unlikely Mongol horde possesses a surprisingly sophisticated and au courant European education:

> We love all—the heat of cold numbers,
>> And the gift of divine visions,
> We comprehend all—sharp Gallic thought,
>> And the gloomy German genius . . .
>
> We remember all—the hell of Parisian streets
>> And the coolnesses of Venice,
> The distant aroma of lemon groves,
>> The smoky vastness of Cologne.

Sultry flesh, Parisian hell, and distant lemon trees: this "barbarian lyre" is tuned to a peculiarly Baudelairean key. The masculine collective versus degenerate, feminine Europe: this fight is rigged in unexpected ways. The enemy appears to have infiltrated the barbarian forces from within; they have even received the dubious gift of divine visions (*dar bozhestvennykh videnii*) that had first sent the young poet off in search of his Beautiful Lady. For all its bloodthirsty brawling, this horde bears a suspicious resemblance to the past and class that Blok sought to escape.

Yeats loathed "the irrational, atavistic barbarism of the crowd" that Blok extols here and throughout his writing[56]—but the would-be Scythian cannot help conceiving this crowd in his own image. Even the barbarians' conquest of Europe becomes a more aggressive, Bolshevik variation on the heroic quest for a Beautiful Lady of uncertain reputation. Blok could not keep his divine visions from intruding into his hymns to a new revolutionary reality, and this failing lay at the heart of the storm surrounding his would-be epic.

Thus far I have focused on the soldiers'—and the poet's?—assault on Holy Rus' and her various feminized incarnations in "The Twelve." The most notorious of these beings appears, though, only in the poem's problematic conclusion. "Onward, onward, onward, / Working-class people" (*Vpered, vpered, vpered, / Rabochii narod*), the soldiers chant as they tramp through the snowstorm. But they themselves have no idea "what's ahead" (*chto vpered*). How could they? Even Blok claimed to be shocked by his final lines, which came to him of their own accord and refused to go away:

> Ahead (*vperedi*)—with a bloody flag,
>> Invisible beyond the storm
>> Unharmed by bullets
> With a tender tread above the storm,
> With a pearly haze of snow,
>> In a white wreath of roses—
>> Ahead (*vperedi*)—is Jesus Christ.

What on earth was Christ doing not just leading the forces of revolution, but usurping the privileged position (*vperedi*) to be occupied only by the most advanced social class (*peredovoi klass*), the proletariat, and their self-appointed guardians in the Communist Party? Friends and enemies of the revolution alike were outraged and baffled. But Blok could provide no explanation. He had always had a vexed relationship with that "feminine phantom" Jesus Christ, and was dismayed to find him taking pride of place in his revolutionary epic. "I don't like the end of 'The Twelve' either," he confessed at a public discussion in 1919: "I wanted it to turn out differently. When I got to the ending, I was surprised myself: Why Christ? But the closer

I looked, the more clearly I saw Christ. And so I made a mental note: 'Yes, unfortunately, Christ.'"[57]

Christ alone would be bad enough: but this luminous figure in pearls and roses is a peculiarly effeminate Redeemer. "Maidenhood, tenderness, femininity shine through [Christ's] masculine features," the Silver Age philosopher Vasilii Rozanov had proclaimed in 1911, hence "we worship the Maid in the Man." "The soul of the new man is wavering between the male and the female principles," Blok notes in an unpublished essay.[58] If we read "The Twelve" as Blok's attempt to end this wavering once and for all, to banish the feminine from both the revolution and his own poetic vision, the poem proves an unqualified failure. Holy Rus' has unexpectedly been resurrected in the person of the risen Christ, who cannot be harmed by the bullets intended for the motherland and her surrogates. The poet himself, who had hitherto managed to submerge his own voice and vision beneath the revolution's raging music, suddenly resurfaces alongside his unwanted guest. The poem's language suddenly turns unmistakably, lyrically Blokian—no slogans or street songs here.

Moreover, the poet-prophet alone is apparently privy to this unnerving vision: the pearly, tender Christ is hidden by the storm from those he leads. No one else can see him: is he really even there? Where have we heard this complaint before? "But You are a vision / I seek salvation": the doubts Blok expresses in an early lyric haunt him throughout his writings on his other-worldly, ambiguous beloved (1:30). I have mentioned that Christ usurps the position rightfully held by the Party and the proletariat. His situation looks familiar in other ways as well. He is not just ahead of (*vperedi*), but above (*nad*, as in *nadv'iuzhnoi*, "above the storm") his followers; he floats above the chaos that engulfs them. Above and beyond: this is how the Beautiful Lady typically appears to her anxious suitor. The Twelve may have thought they were hot in pursuit of a glorious revolutionary future. But they end by unwittingly joining in their own creator's quintessentially lyric quest for the eternal feminine in her latest, most baffling incarnation.

Life and Death Après La Lettre: The Posthumous Fate of Alexander Blok

In [Blok's] notebook for January 29, 1918, we read the very signifi-cant lines: "That Christ is going on before them is beyond doubt . . . It is He who is with them and there is still no other; should there not be Another—?" . . . Probably, Blok would have opened his eyes wide in

astonishment and fear had anyone suggested to him that this "Other"
was already living; that he was the great teacher and leader of the
proletariat, at once a real man and the true embodiment of the great-
est ideas which had ever developed on this earth and which made the
sayings of Christianity look naive and old-fashioned; that he was that
very Vl. Ilych Lenin whom, perhaps, he had occasionally encountered
at meetings or on the street.
                                    —*Anatoly Lunacharsky, "Alexander Blok" (1932)*

The longest way round is the shortest way home—or so it proved for
Blok, to judge by the enigmatic ending of his would-be epic. Yeats's vision-
ary history was transformed by the marriage that inspired *A Vision* and
the children who took their symbolic meaning from its pages. His cosmic
historiography now found its key not in thwarted courtships, but in "the
relations of men and women and the birth of children." I will not enter here
into Yeats's later poetic and political evolution. (Like so many other great
Russian poets, Blok could claim only an early and a middle period at best.)
At this critical juncture, though, Yeats found a way to convert his courtship
into marriage, to beget progeny who existed on physical and metaphysical
planes alike, and to tie his new family into the life of his nation, both sym-
bolic and actual, as he became not just a mystical, but a literal legislator by
serving in his new nation's government.

When Yeats died in 1939, after a long, lauded, and controversial career,
even the outbreak of World War II could not defeat his burial plans, which
were once again both specific and symbolically charged. "Many times man
lives and dies / Between his two eternities / That of race and that of soul /
And ancient Ireland knew it all," Yeats proclaims in his self-designated vale-
dictory poem, "Under Ben Bulben" (1939; 333–336). But Yeats, not Ireland,
knows all when it comes to this particular death:

> Under bare Ben Bulben's head
> In Drumcliff churchyard Yeats is laid . . .
> No marble, no conventional phrase,
> On limestone quarried near the spot
> By his command these words are cut:
>
>> Cast a cold eye
>> On life, on death.
>> Horseman, pass by!

History apparently had other plans: death overtook Yeats in France.
Since the war prevented the body's return to Ireland, he was buried at the

church of St. Pancras at Rocquebrune. Even here, though, he was not caught entirely off guard. As per his last-minute directives, the coffin was carried—upwards, of course—along a long, winding road to the top of a hill. But Yeats's final dictates were not to be thwarted even by a bona fide worldwide catastrophe. The poem's specifications were fulfilled at last when his body was dug up and reburied near Ben Bulben with all possible pomp and splendor in September, 1948. "Death and life were not / till man made up the whole." Be that as it may, Yeats managed his own exit from the world's stage with admirable aplomb.[59]

Unlike Yeats, Blok operates under the sign of courtship from start to finish. Even his wooing of the revolution ends by reverting to form; the outlines of his perpetually thwarted courtship of the Beautiful Lady appear, willy-nilly, in even his most apparently bloodthirsty hymns to the revolutionary brotherhood. He could reinvent neither self nor vision in his quest to serve the revolution he had awaited—or so it seemed—and his physical death was perceived as a postscriptum to a life-in-art that had already ended long since. Blok himself encouraged just such an interpretation. Kornei Chukovsky recalls attending a reading with the poet a few months before his death: "Onstage some two-bit orator, of whom there were so many in Moscow, merrily expounded to the crowd that Blok was already dead as a poet: 'I ask you, comrades, where is the dynamism in these lines? They're carrion, written by a dead man.' Blok leaned over to me and said: 'He's right. . . . He's telling the truth. I am dead.'"[60]

The spirits planned Yeats's wedding date well: October, 1917 could hardly be bettered for international resonance and lasting symbolic impact. Blok's death, in 1921, would seem to have been equally well timed—though it is only in hindsight, of course, that Blok's end seems preordained and not simply one more of the countless, unmarked fatalities produced by seven years of war, famine, disease, and calamity of every kind. His death coincided not only with the Bolsheviks' final victory in the Civil War. It also launched the series of poetic casualties that Jakobson would later commemorate in "The Generation that Squandered Its Poets" (1931). This series would culminate nine years later in the suicide of the state's most famous poetic celebrant, Vladimir Mayakovsky, just as Stalin assumed the reins of power. The deaths of the Silver Age's two greatest life-creators thus bracketed Russia's first postrevolutionary decade.

Blok's death invited—and continues to invite—conflicting interpretations. Was its cause a suitably symbolic syphilis, à la Ibsen's "Ghosts"? Or did he fall prey to the appropriately neurasthenic asthma that would claim his near-contemporary Marcel Proust just one year later? In either case, its timing was flawless, at least as far as revolutionary narratives—and poetic mythologies—are concerned. The death of the great Symbolist coincides not just with the victory of the Reds over their White opponents, but also with the triumph of prose over its own class enemy, lyric poetry, that I mention in my introduction. The demise of genre and artist together underlies the literary postmortems that emerged in the wake of Blok's death.

What Mandelstam called Blok's "posthumous life" and "posthumous fate" preoccupied literary scholars and revolutionary leaders alike. Blok overcame "'the lyrical' in himself" and perished, Boris Eikhenbaum laments in an essay called—what else?—"Blok's Fate" (1921), and "the destiny of an entire generation," he continues, was articulated in the poet's passing. Leon Trotsky's eulogy was, predictably, more caustic. "'The Twelve' is not a poem of the Revolution," he proclaims in "Alexander Blok" (1923). It is an end, not a beginning, "the swan song of the individualistic art" that was obliterated with the revolution, and its creator is a thorough-going product of the "old Russia, of its landlords and intelligentsia" for all his revolutionary sympathies. Blok's "lyric poetry," Trotsky predicts, "will not outlive its time or its author."[61]

Writing nearly a decade later, Anatoly Lunacharsky takes issue with his erstwhile comrade-at-arms. "Blok's works, and, therefore, his whole personality, are of considerable significance for us," he insists. But Lunacharsky's interest is taxidermical, not literary. "Here we have a perfect specimen," he marvels, "a product of the last, decadent stages of the culture of the nobility." Blok's "love affair with the revolution" was thus doomed from the start. This "scion of several noble families" "was conscious of the curse which hung over his class" and so sought to embrace a revolutionary future. But the "last poet of the gentry" could not endure the revolution's resolutely unlyrical aftermath. He could not bear an "'unmusical' revolution," a revolution that "before his eyes had become prose" and so committed a form of generic suicide: "Thus the poet, in his own way, cried, 'Morituri te salutant.'"[62]

It is hard to say what is most striking about these last two commentaries. Is it that two renowned revolutionaries felt compelled, nearly ten years apart, to write lengthy, learned disquisitions on the life and death of a Symbolist poet? That they saw the need to interweave his story with the story of the revolution that they themselves had helped to forge? That the revolution was itself shaped by members of the intelligentsia so obviously well versed in the culture they denigrate in the person of Alexander Blok? Or is it finally the degree to which they rely on Blok's own interpretation of his life and art in assessing his relationship to the revolution from their very different vantage points in 1924 and 1932? "Music of the revolution"; the "last child of a long line"; the "last scion of a dying class consumed by a powerful spiral of shocks that would embrace the whole world": the list of near-quotations from Blok's own poetry and prose that punctuate their essays could be continued almost indefinitely. The ways in which Blok's own vision of his symbolic significance infiltrated the minds of even the revolution's luminaries must be accounted a kind of posthumous success.[63]

In one of his final public appearances, Blok recalled Pushkin's death eighty-six years earlier: "Pushkin was not killed by Danthes' bullet. He died from a lack of air. His culture died with him" (2:354). So far as we know, Danthes' bullet played a much larger part in the great poet's death than did prevailing atmospheric conditions. But not for Blok. The confusion of literal and literary deaths was of course his stock-in-trade, and it is not surprising to find Eikhenbaum following his lead. "And then came the abrupt end of this tragedy," he mourns: "The stage death to which the whole course of the play has been directed turns out to be a real death . . . and we are shaken as spectators are when, in the fifth act of the tragedy and before their very eyes, the actor bleeds real blood. The footlights are turned off; Hamlet-Blok is truly dead."[64]

Eikhenbaum muddles life and art very much in the style of Blok himself. But what are we to make of Lunacharsky's equally messy conflation of literal and metaphorical endings? "At the moment of the *physical* death of his class," Lunacharsky insists, "[Blok] exhibited the maximum revolutionary impulse of which the consciousness of the nobility was capable" (my italics). What is wrong with this picture? For Blok, Pushkin dies not of bullet wounds, but of suffocation. Eikhenbaum's tragic hero perishes, as he must, in the fifth act's bloody close, while Blok's entire class perishes with him in Lunacharsky's ideologically foregone conclusion, as the poet's physical death merges with the symbolic end of the landed gentry following the revolution's triumph. The death of the poet; the demise of an outmoded genre; the defeat of a doomed aristocracy: literal, literary, and ideological deaths converge neatly in a life story that Blok had taught admirers and enemies alike to read. Indeed, Lunacharsky cites "Retribution" at length in explaining his subject's fraught life and its timely ending. "[Blok] should be regarded as a scion of the line of the nobility's ideologists," he lectures, "and his place is—to extend the metaphor—at the end of that line."[65]

"Romantic Russia's dead and gone," as Yeats might have put it. Or at least so it seemed to Blok's contemporaries. But lyricism proved far harder to kill than Lunacharsky was willing to admit in his belated obituary. Blok's antipode, in Lunacharsky's reckoning, was Mayakovsky, and Mayakovsky was, he assures us, "revolted" by "lyricism," by the "musical chirping" and "saccharine melodies" of his Symbolist precursors.[66] Blok's death dovetailed neatly not only with the symbolic life story he had labored to create throughout his work. It turned out to be a near-perfect fit with the larger narrative of genres, generations, classes, and nations that the new Soviet regime was then in the process of creating. The all too lyrical suicide of the revolution's self-proclaimed bard and herald at the decade's close would prove far harder for the revolution's mythmakers to digest.

2

Whitman, Mayakovsky, and the Body Politic

I am the poet of slaves, and the masters of slaves.
I am the poet of the body.
And I am.

—Walt Whitman, untitled

Whitman the Futurist

You of the mighty Slavic tribes and empires! you Russ in Russia!
—Walt Whitman, "Salut au Monde!" (1856)

In 1913, the French Futurist Guillaume Apollinaire marked his entrance on the literary scene by figuratively killing off an overwhelming poetic parent. In the fantastical funeral Apollinaire invents for Walt Whitman, he celebrates his great precursor's flesh even as he lays it to rest: "Everyone that Whitman had known was there . . . the stagedrivers of Broadway, negroes, his old mistresses and his comerados [*sic*]. . . . Pederasts came in great numbers. . . . It is believed that several of Whitman's children were there, with their mothers, white or black. . . . At sundown, a huge cortege formed with a ragtime band in the lead. Whitman's coffin followed, carried by six drunken pallbearers."

Due to the size of Whitman's corpse, Apollinaire continues, the tipsy pallbearers were forced to crawl on their knees in order to thrust his enormous coffin into its merely human-sized tomb. "You cannot carry around on your back the corpse of your father," Apollinaire insists elsewhere. But his dubious anecdote demonstrates how difficult it was for modern poets to dispose of Walt Whitman. He inspired the avant-garde writers of Europe and the Americas even as they struggled to surpass an outsized poetic parent who is, by his own account, "kosmic," "lusty, phallic, with the potent original loins."[1]

"I am a habitan of Vienna, St. Petersburg, Berlin," Whitman announces in "Salut au Monde" (1881). "I belong in Moscow, Cracow, Warsaw" (293). Posterity justified his grandiose claims in ways that he could not have anticipated. Whitman made no secret of his own legislative ambitions: "A few first-class poets, philosophs, and authors . . . must stamp . . . [the] real democratic construction of this American continent," he insists in "Democratic Vistas" (934). But his poetic politics were taken far more seriously by Eastern European followers accustomed to heeding bardic wisdom than by his American contemporaries. Indeed, Whitman was indirectly responsible, so Czesław Miłosz claims, for changing the shape of modern history by way of one such disciple, the Montenegrin Gavrilo Princip. Princip, he explains, took the American poet's hostility to Europe's crowned heads too literally and shot Archduke Ferdinand under his hero's influence, thus making Whitman indirectly "responsible for the outbreak of World War I."[2]

Other Eastern European disciples, including Miłosz himself, were more restrained, though hardly less fervent in their admiration. I don't intend to trace the history of Whitman's reception in Russia here. (I will return to his Polish acolytes in Chapter 8.) By the time Vladimir Mayakovsky came to him, though, he had already found two champions on Russian soil, the Symbolist poet Konstantin Balmont and the critic and translator Kornei Chukovsky, who returned at intervals throughout his life to the task of finding a compelling Russian voice for Whitman's verse. All modern poetry, Balmont insists, moves between the poles marked out by Whitman and Poe. Chukovsky is less sweeping in his claims for Whitman's influence. But in *My Whitman* (*Moi Uitman*, 1966) he notes that for the poets of Russia's Silver Age, Whitman became "the very air they breathed."[3]

Mayakovsky was one such poet, as Chukovsky's account of their first meeting reveals. The Futurist had already read Chukovsky's early translations of Whitman, which he did not hesitate to criticize, though he knew no English: he spoke, Chukovsky notes, "as though he had written the poems himself." The two spent the evening reading Chukovsky's most recent translations; and Mayakovsky's comments on Whitman's life and writing point to precisely those places where the future bard of the revolution overlaps most closely with the celebrant of American democracy. Mayakovsky "singled out those lines which came closest at the time to his own poetics":

> Under Niagara, the cataract falling like a veil over my countenance . . .
> ["The waterfall Niagara is a veil for my face" as Chukovsky has it]
> The scent of these arm-pits is aroma finer than prayer . . .
> [I] am not contained between my hat and my boots . . .
> I do not require the stars to descend,
> They are good just as they are . . .
> Dazzling and tremendous how quick the sunrise would kill me,
> If I could not now and always send sunrise out of myself . . . (61, 51, 32, 52)

All but one of these quotations derives from the "Song of Myself" (1855, 1881), and it is no surprise that the Russian Futurist should find common ground with his American precursor in Whitman's great hymn to himself. Both poets were specialists in the art of self-celebration, and both constructed massive bodies in verse to house the monumental egos that are the source and subject of their work. Both intended these bodies, moreover, to exemplify, even incorporate the politics and people of a flourishing revolutionary state. The two writers found themselves confronted, though, by postrevolutionary societies in which self, poetry, and society held radically different meanings. Whitman may have suffered from the more or less benign neglect that unacknowledged legislators have come to expect in most of the English-speaking world. But Eastern European poets pay upon occasion a steep price for their place in the public domain. Mayakovsky's fate may be read as an object lesson in the dangers of acknowledged—or attempted—legislation in a state where Romantic self-glorification had given way to utopian visions of an encompassing collectivity achieved by resolute party leaders and not their poetic minions.

Let me return here, though, to the resemblances between the Russian poet and his American forebear. "I am not contained between my hat and my boots," Whitman boasts, and his claim points to another similarity between the American poet and his Russian rival. Whitman carefully crafted his transformation from Walter Whitman, erstwhile schoolteacher, typesetter, house-builder and journalist, to Walt Whitman, flesh and spirit of the nation. Chief among the props he used in this metamorphosis was the hat adorning his head in the first of a series of strategically posed photographs that shaped his image in the minds of readers for generations to come. In this photograph, Whitman poses as a "working-class rough," "dressed as a day laborer in workingman's trousers, a shirt unbuttoned to reveal his undershirt, [his] hat cocked jauntily on his head": an engraved version opens the earliest edition of *Leaves of Grass*.[4]

Whitman blurred from the start the line that divides life from art, the poet from his writing. He was an accomplished practitioner *avant la lettre* of the life-creation I discuss in Chapter 1, and found a hospitable reception in Russia's Silver Age where extravagant self-fashioning was all the rage. It is no accident that Chukovsky chose Whitman's ostentatiously proletarian photograph to open the earliest editions of his translations. Mayakovsky, whose infamous yellow blouse made appearances in his public performances and poetry alike, clearly spotted a fellow master of *épatage* in the poet whose laborer's clothes marked his own revolt against the genteel "profession of authorship" as practiced in mid-nineteenth century America.[5]

Chukovsky recalls Mayakovsky declaiming a celebrated line from "Song of Myself": "Walt Whitman, a kosmos, of Manhattan the son" (210). He speculates that such lines inspired Mayakovsky to insert his own name and biographical particulars into early works like "Vladimir Mayakovsky: A Tragedy" (1913) and "A Cloud in Trousers" (1914–15). Certainly the questions Mayakovsky put to Chukovsky suggest that he recognized a rival life-creator in his American forebear: "How did Whitman read his poetry on stage? How often did the public hiss him? Did he wear outrageous get-ups? How exactly did they trash him in the papers? Did he knock Shakespeare and Byron?" Chukovsky remarks that Mayakovsky appeared to be "measuring [Whitman's] biography against his own." More than this—he is clearly checking the credentials of a formidable fellow Futurist.[6]

Chukovsky recognized early on the affinities that linked Whitman to Futurism. In "Ego-Futurists and Cubo-Futurists" (1914), he calls Whitman "the first Futurist poet." Elsewhere he notes that the Futurists "acknowledge only Whitman among the world's poets." Mayakovsky himself conceded only that Whitman "wasn't a bad writer." But his grudging admission clearly stems from the same impulse that leads Apollinaire to bury and praise his poetic progenitor in the same breath. Mayakovsky's one explicit reference to Whitman in his verse sheds light on the source of this rivalry.[7]

In "150,000,000" (1919–20), Mayakovsky's first effort at a revolutionary epic, he cuts his—and his fledgling nation's—American competition down to size. He peoples his grotesque Chicago, the capital of his caricatured capitalism, with "all kinds of Lincolns, Whitmans, and Edisons." Whitman himself, stuffed into a "snug dinner-jacket" and "rocking like a rocking chair to an unheard-of rhythm," apparently serves in Woodrow Wilson's corrupt and well-fed retinue.[8] Stripped of his worker's disguise, Whitman stands unmasked in "150,000,000": he is not the people's poet, but the pet of their bourgeois masters. Through Mayakovsky's dismissive simile ("rocking like a rocking chair"), Whitman's iconoclastic poetic rhythms, intended to regenerate the American body politic, become instead an old man's senile fancies, to be replaced presumably by his descendant's more percussive beat. Finally Whitman, the titanic force, the prophet "contain[ing] multitudes" (87), is himself reduced to hordes of mass-produced "Whitmans" (*Uitmeny*), a commodity along the lines presumably of Frigidaires or Model-T Fords. "Who but I should be the poet of comrades?" Whitman asks in "Starting from Paumanok" (1860, 1881; 179). Mayakovsky's tacit retort is clear: "I myself, Mayakovsky."

Why should Mayakovsky feel compelled to settle scores with his American competitor in precisely this poem at precisely this time? One answer lies in the company that the "Whitmans" of "150,000,000" keep. Mayakovsky implicitly refutes all American claims to populist heroics, be they in politics (Lincoln), technology (Edison), or poetry (Whitman). The revolution and its offspring are destined to surpass their bourgeois brethren on all fronts, the poem suggests. But Whitman comes in for particular abuse here, abuse that his fellow populists-manqués are spared. Another poem of the period reveals that Mayakovsky alone should be counted as the true poet-genius in any future reckoning: "*I* want to stand / in the ranks of the Edisons, / In Lenin's rank, / In the ranks of the Einsteins" (my italics; 1:294). Only the Soviet leader and the revolutionary poet are dignified by grammatically singular forms. Collectivity is left to lesser luminaries—the Edisons, Einsteins, and of course, the Whitmans of this world. Mayakovsky was apparently willing to share the spotlight with his illustrious peer in the political sphere—though Lenin chose not to take him up on his offer. But the new state clearly had no place, as Mayakovsky saw it, for two "barbaric yawps" both operating at "the top of their voice." In "150,000,000," he leaves no doubt as to who will triumph in this shouting match of Titans.

Postrevolutionary Russians saw things differently. Whitman may have gone largely unnoticed at home during his lifetime—but his success just after the Russian Revolution exceeded even his prewar fame. And it came right as Mayakovsky was laboring to establish himself as bard-in-chief for the new state. In the introduction to the 1923 edition of his translations, Chukovsky stresses Whitman's affinities with postrevolutionary Russian culture. Cosmism, biocosmism, proletarian poetry, collective verse, political and sexual liberation, the celebration of technology, the cult of masculine camaraderie: all were first rehearsed in Whitman's writings, Chukovsky suggests. Many of his compatriots apparently agreed. Poets of the Proletarian Culture movement (Proletkult) and young revolutionaries alike were drawn to their American precursor, as Whitman Societies formed in towns across Soviet Russia. In a diary entry of 1922, Chukovsky recalls his encounter with one group of fervent young "Whitmanians" (*uitmeniantsy*): "They want to kiss and work and die like Whitman," he marvels.[9]

This was the reception that the homegrown prophet craved and failed to gain. Small wonder that Mayakovsky should feel compelled to fill Whitman's mythical hat and boots as he worked to commandeer his place as the premier "poet of the coming democracy."[10] In "150,000,000," Mayakovsky announces his programmatic collectivity in typically oxymoronic fashion. "150,000,000 speak with *my* lips. . . . No one is the author of *my* poem," he trumpets in the would-be epic's opening (my italics; 3:91). "I print[ed] it without my name," he recalls in his memoirs, and thereby extended an open invitation to his hoped-for mass audience. "I want[ed] everyone to add to it, improve it. But nobody did," he notes ruefully. Could it be that Soviet society was unwilling to contribute collectively by means of "*his* lips" to "*his* poem"? Perhaps they did not want to speak, or kiss, or work like Mayakovsky. Or maybe this had never really been Mayakovsky's goal. "Somehow they all knew my name though," he concludes in summing up the poem's reception (1:43). For all his ostentatious anonymity—"150,000,000 is the name of this poem's master," he proclaims (3:91)—lyrical self-advertisement, not socialist self-effacement, was Mayakovsky's stock-in-trade. And it proved to be increasingly incompatible with a state that bore little resemblance to what he called—what else?—"my revolution" (1:42).

Apocalyptic Bodies

With
my own hand
I touch
the bodiless word
"politics."

> —*Vladimir Mayakovsky, "Kazan" (1928)*

Most critics see Whitman's greatest influence at work on the prerevolutionary Mayakovsky, whose outsized self takes center stage, and not on the postrevolutionary bard who tailors his talents to the needs of the newly formed people's state. They emphasize Whitman the "poet of the self," in other words, over Whitman the "bard of democracy." Chukovsky, for one, locates the apex of Whitman's influence in Mayakovsky's epic poem "Man"

("Chelovek," 1916–17).[11] The poem itself leaves little doubt as to who the Man in question is. It reads like a Whitmanesque self-apotheosis gone ber-serk, with suitably perverse stations of the avant-garde cross marking the poet's progress: "The Birth of Mayakovsky," "The Life of Mayakovsky," "Mayakovsky's Passions," "The Ascent of Mayakovsky," "Mayakovsky in Heaven," "The Return of Mayakovsky," and finally, "Mayakovsky for the Ages." The segment Chukovsky mentions points, though, to the place where self and politics intersect for Whitman and Mayakovsky alike. He cites a passage in which Mayakovsky invites an awestruck public to admire the spectacle of his mammoth form:

> How should I
> not sing myself,
> if my whole self
> is an undivided wonder,
> if my every movement is
> an enormous,
> inexplicable miracle. (3:67)

Mayakovsky is not simply a poet of the self. Like Whitman, he houses his monumental ego in a suitably oversized body, and this body is the tortured hero of all his early work. Only in "150,000,000," though, does Mayak-ovsky first attempt to turn his form to the purposes that Whitman's poetic self had been crafted to serve early on. In "150,000,000," he emulates Whit-man's feat in creating a poetic body designed to incorporate a youthful, expansive, postrevolutionary state. Like his precursor, he works to locate the juncture where the poet's self fuses with the body politic.

This was the task that Whitman's self was meant to perform from the start. "One's self I sing," he exclaims in his first "Inscription," "a simple separate person, / Yet utter the word Democratic, the word En-Masse." How is this seeming paradox to be achieved? The lyric's next line gives a hint: "Of physiology from top to toe I sing" (165). "All comes by the body," he announces in "By Blue Ontario's Shores" (1881), with what is surely an intentional pun (470): all his writings might be taken as a gloss upon this statement. Both the preface to the first edition of *Leaves of Grass* (1855) and his programmatic letter to Ralph Waldo Emerson, written a year later, demonstrate that for Whitman democracy and poetry are alike rooted in the physical self. The unfettered body, with its boundless energy and sexual vitality, is the equivalent of the natural laws of liberty and equality upon which American democracy was founded. And both self and state are ide-ally unconstrained by the moral, aesthetic, and political strictures of old

Europe. The poet's activity becomes exemplary: he is flesh of the nation's flesh and bone of its bone. America, democracy, the body, and the bard: Whitman's writing maps out the symbiotic relations between what he sees as coterminous entities. The poet's own body is a poem ("And I will make the poems of my body," 179) and America is both the body politic ("for the union of the parts of the body is not more necessary to their life than the union of These States is to their life," 1330) and "the greatest," "the amplest poem" (5, 471). The poetic revolution Whitman effects in *Leaves of Grass* will, he suggests, continue and amplify the political revolution begun some eighty years before his first poems appeared.

In his letter to Emerson, Whitman energetically propounds his new poetic creed. The task of the truly American writer is to be "electric, fresh, lusty, to express the full-sized body, male and female—to give the modern meaning of things, to grow up beautiful, lasting, commensurate with America" (1328). The true bard, he insists in the 1855 preface to *Leaves of Grass*, "is to be commensurate with a people . . . he incarnates [the nation's] geography and natural life and rivers and lakes" (7). His flesh encompasses "the endless gestation of new states . . . the perfect equality of the female with the male . . . the large amativeness—the fluid movement of the population" (8). The poems themselves, in their various redactions, generate multiple variations on these themes.[12] The poet mates with the land that bore him, "attracting it body and soul to himself, hanging on its neck with incomparable love, / Plunging his seminal muscle into its merits and demerits" (472). He peoples its expanses with his offspring: "I pour the stuff to start sons and daughters fit for these states" (259). And he takes its fertile form for his own: "My ever-united lands—my body / . . . made out of a thousand diverse contributions one identity" (323).

Whitman thus takes a traditionally lyric impulse—the desire for one man or woman—and works to convert it to epic purposes. In *Leaves of Grass* he translates "the auto-erotic into the programmatically mystical, the hetero-erotic into the programmatically procreational, and the homo-erotic into the programmatically fraternal and democratic," James Miller explains. Other critics have been less charitable. All Whitman's "privacy leak[s] out in a sort of dribble, oozing into the universe," D. H. Lawrence complains in his *Studies in Classic American Literature*. (Soviet critics charged Mayakovsky with similar forms of cosmic sloppiness.) "There had always been a curious correspondence between Whitman's body and the body politic of America," Betsy Erkilla asserts—though few of his nineteenth-century compatriots could be persuaded to perceive it. Whitman managed nonetheless to craft a myth in which his evolving poetic body and

America's shifting political fortunes came to seem uniquely congruent to later generations.[13]

Mayakovsky attempts to tailor his poet's body to Soviet requirements throughout the twenties, from the overgrown Ivan-Russia of "150,000,000" to the grotesque poet-cum-factory that concludes "Homeward!" ("Domoi!" 1925) and the revolutionary latrine-cleaner who discards ideological cast-offs in "At the Top of My Lungs" ("Vo ves' golos," 1930). But his efforts were less than successful. Whitman did not have to contend with a state increasingly intent upon regulating poetry and bodies alike. He was free to generate his poetic myths, however scandalous, unhampered by the political pressures brought to bear upon Russia's revolutionary poets. More than this—the very lack of an audience freed him to perceive the ideal fusion of self and nation as pure potential, a dream to be achieved not at the present moment, but in a still-ripening future. Hence the endlessly growing "leaves of grass" that will one day form the very ground beneath our feet. Mayak-ovsky faced a world in which the much-ballyhooed future had, so the revolution's makers claimed, already arrived. And its shape, as articulated by these leaders, was not a good fit for the mammoth form of a compulsively self-aggrandizing Futurist.

Both friends and enemies agreed that Mayakovsky's limitations as a political poet grew from the distinctive nature of his lyric gift. "Even when he attempts 'a bloody Iliad of the Revolution,' or 'an odyssey of the famine years,'" Roman Jakobson comments, "what appears is not an epic but a heroic lyric on a grand scale."[14] A heroic lyric articulated, of course, by a heroic lyrist of equally impressive proportions. For all its vast size, the erotically charged body of Mayakovsky's poetry resists the fusion of lyric and epic modes that marks Whitman's most effective civic verse. Mayakovsky may have railed against the lyrical clichés that riddle his precursors' poems (with Blok among the chief sinners). His own work, though, does not resist lyricism: it stretches egotistical sublimity to its outermost limits. Lyrical truisms are renewed in his work through what we might call, following Shklovsky, not *obnazhenie priema*, but *voploshchenie priema*, not the baring of the device, but its incarnation.

Mayakovsky never articulated a clear-cut vision of the body's role in culture; he left behind no programmatic statement of the kind that punctuates Whitman's work from the start. He lacks not only his precursor's—at times exhausting—optimism. He is also constitutionally uncivic. "When Mayakovsky embarked upon his career," Lunacharsky remarks, "he was still beyond the sphere of influence of [that] gigantic social body, the revolutionary proletariat."[15] Lunacharsky is characteristically hamhanded here—as with Blok, he combines his gifted subject's own imagery with standard-issue Soviet rhetoric to hammer home his obvious points. There's something to his comment nonetheless. Mayakovsky explicitly identifies his body with the nation only after the revolution's success made this more or less imperative. He attempts to imbue his outsized sufferings with social import early on. But the "rallying cries" he attached post factum to "A Cloud in Trousers" ("Oblako v shtanakh," 1914–15)—"Down with *your* love," "Down with *your* art," "Down with *your* social order," "Down with *your* religion"— read like afterthoughts. They are undeveloped appendages grafted onto the "vast, sinewy bulk" (*zhilistaia gromadina*) that "moans and writhes" in the throes of unrequited love throughout the poem (3:550, 8).

Mayakovsky's poetic body may have been the outgrowth of his "emotional elephantiasis," as Victor Erlich puts it; or the expression of an insatiable, "mayakomorphist" desire to recreate the world in his own image, as Leon Trotsky scoffs. It resisted, in either case, his efforts to make it over in the image of a revolution that ostensibly represented the will of an entire class, and a party that claimed to speak for the people en masse. The party, in turn, was ill at ease with the gifts of a flamboyant self-celebrant struggling to tune the state's collective marches to the key of his own "backbone flute." "The Futurist poets," Trotsky claims, "have not mastered the elements of the Communist point of view and world attitude sufficiently to find an organic expression for them in words; [these elements] have not entered, so to speak, into their blood." The Futurists are alien organisms in the new Soviet corpus, as he sees it. For all their revolutionary grandstanding, they remain the offspring of "rebellious persecuted Bohemia," products of the same bourgeois, fin de siècle artistic milieu that gave birth to their Symbolist rivals.[16]

Trotsky is clearly grinding his own ideological axes. But he was not alone. Chukovsky had charged the Futurists with similar sins a decade earlier. Only Whitman, he insists, is a bona fide Futurist; unlike his decadent descendants he is a genuinely political poet. His ear is attuned to that "titanic word: democracy"; his work proclaims the radical social changes of the coming era and not just bohemian pipe dreams. Whitman's Futurism, Chukovsky explains, "arose not in a parlor hung with yellow silk, but amidst the hubbub of the democratic masses."[17] Chukovsky's claims may seem puzzling in view of the revolutionary activities that repeatedly landed the young Mayakovsky in tsarist prisons. And dead prophets hailing from distant lands are doubtless easier to embrace than strident iconoclasts proclaiming their rhymed manifestoes on neighboring street corners. Certainly the Soviet authorities would find Mayakovsky himself far more congenial after his death than before.

It is not my goal in any case to establish which poet was more truly Futurist or more authentically democratic. Yet if we take "political" to mean, as Webster suggests, "consisting of citizens," then Chukovsky's assertion that Whitman was political in a way Mayakovsky was not makes poetic sense vis-à-vis the distinctive mythologies each poet forges in his work. "This is the city . . . and I am one of the citizens," Whitman exclaims in "Song of Myself" (76), and his poetic body itself serves as an ideal polis. It incorporates multitudes and accommodates differences as it bridges the gap between the individual and the collective, the poet and the crowd.

Mayakovsky's body, on the other hand, is not even big enough for him—"I feel / that 'I' / is too small for me" (3:11)—let alone for the masses he hopes to incorporate in the revolution's aftermath. The giant's form he laments in "To His Beloved Self the Author Dedicates These Lines" ("Sebe, liubimomu, posviashchaet eti stroki avtor," 1916)—"What Goliaths conceived me," he wails (1:122)—condemns him to a self-absorbed isolation that is the antithesis of Whitman's idealized self en masse. Mayakovsky attempts to convert this inflated body, "so huge / and so useless" (1:122), to political purposes in "Fifth International" (1922). But like some monstrous balloon in the Macy's parade, he floats helplessly above a transformed planet he has grown too large to inhabit: "The earth is invisible. You can't see your own shoulders. Only heaven. Only clouds. And my massive head in the clouds."[18] The size of Whitman's poetic body permits him to become "himself the age transfigured," at least in his mythologies (23). Mayakovsky cannot manage this feat even in his poetic imaginings. His vast body is a defect, a deformity: "Anatomy went insane / On me," he complains in "I Love" ("Liubliu," 1922; 1:137). The expansiveness that makes Whitman a mate for his nation and age, in his poetic vision at any rate, serves only to thrust Mayakovsky beyond the bounds of the Soviet body politic.

For all their differences, Whitman's and Mayakovsky's outsized poetic bodies share a common heritage. They are alike both in their bardic aspirations and in their quintessentially Romantic orientation. They share the Romantic dream of a "rebirth in which a renewed mankind will inhabit a renovated earth where he will find himself thoroughly at home," a rebirth brought about by "the visionary poet as both herald and inaugurator of a new and supremely better world." The model for all such Romantic visionaries is, of course, Christ himself, whose body unites "all categories in identity: Christ is both the one God and the one Man, the Lamb of God, the tree of life, or vine of which we are the branches, the stone which the builders rejected, and the rebuilt temple which is identical with his risen body." Both explicitly and implicitly, Whitman and Mayakovsky model their outsized selves on the god-man whose apocalyptic body is the vessel through which a truly cosmic revolution is achieved.[19] But would-be poet-saviors take many shapes, and Whitman's poet-Christ differs from Mayakovsky's in telling ways. His poet is the Redeemer whose body "filleth all in all" (Ephesians 1:23). The "kosmic" poet, Whitman proclaims, is he "who includes diversity and is Nature": "Who, constructing the house of himself or herself, / not for a day but for all time, sees races, eras, dates, generations, / The past, the future, dwelling there, like space, inseparable together. ("Kosmos"; 516–17). "Not in him, but off from him things are grotesque, eccentric, fail of their full returns," Whitman reminds us in "By Blue Ontario's Shore" (475).

Grotesque and eccentric: the terms are made to order for Mayakovsky's poet-Christ, who sees not Whitman's relentlessly healthy universe, but only the damaged and the incomplete. He is Christ on the cross, Christ in revolt ("Father why have you forsaken me?"), condemned by God and man alike to agonies so outsized that they blacken the cosmos and crowd all merely human griefs from view. "I am where pain is—everywhere," he proclaims in "A Cloud in Trousers": "I nailed myself to the cross / In every drop of a torrent of tears" (3:16). In "War and the World" ("Voina i mir," 1915–16), he rebukes the "rotting souls" of the dead for their small-scale sufferings:

> You've got it good!
> But how I am
> supposed to bring love to the living
> crossing battle lines,
> through the cannons' thunder?
> If I stumble,
> the last particle of love
> will sink forever in the smoking abyss. (3:36)

Blok got his revolutionary redeemer all wrong, Mayakovsky charges in "About That" (1923). That "gentle" "little man (*chelovechek*)" "calm and kind" with his head swathed in a "wreath of moonbeams" "is no Jesus," he insists. But his own politically correct Christ as exemplary "Young Communist (*komsomolets*)" appears and vanishes in the space of a few lines, only to be replaced shortly thereafter by the solitary Savior Agonistes who is Mayakovsky's poetic trademark (3:157–158).

"The bodies of men and women engirth me, and I engirth them," Whitman exults in "I Sing the Body Electric" (1855, 1881; 118). When Mayakovsky looks around him, though, he sees not Whitman's community of kindred bodies, but a sea of menacing human flesh: "the meat-massed, bull-snouted horde" (3:39). These are not fellow forms to be consecrated through the poet's flesh, but enemies bent on his annihilation: "Crucify him, crucify him" (3:16) Mayakovsky's poet-Christ responds with a singularly gruesome salvation. "If you don't up and slit people's veins," he explains in "War and the World," "the infected earth / itself will die" (3:42). The form of communion he proposes is no less unsettling: "I myself, / flaying the skin from the living, / gnaw the world's meat" (3:55).[20]

"Who degrades or defiles the living human body is cursed," Whitman pronounces in "I Sing the Body Electric." "Who degrades or defiles the body of the dead is not more cursed" (124). One incident Chukovsky recalls in his memoirs points to the rift that divides Mayakovsky's poetic body from his precursor's. Chukovsky had just recited his recent translation of "This Compost" (1881) to Mayakovsky. Much of the poem must have been to Mayakovsky's taste—though he admitted only that it was "amusing" (*zaniatno*). "Where have you disposed of their carcasses [i. e. the carcasses of the 'sour dead']?" Whitman asks the earth. "Where have you drawn off all the foul liquid and meat?" But Mayakovsky attacked Chukovsky for his supposed mistranslation of another line: "I will not touch my flesh to the earth as to other flesh to renew me" (495). He mocked Chukovsky's "mushiness" (*patoka*) in rendering Whitman's "flesh" as the Russian equivalent, *plot'*. Mayakovsky did not know English. He insisted, though, that Whitman must have meant "meat" (*miaso*), and Chukovsky not only acceded, but claims later, oddly enough, to have found "meat," not "flesh" in the English original.[21]

Chukovsky and Mayakovsky thus agree to a Bloomian misprision, whereby a strong poet of the present willfully misconstrues the work of a powerful precursor.[22] They "mayakomorphize" Whitman's body, transforming his "flesh" into "meat"—and the misreading speaks to the rift that divides the Russian poet from his predecessor. Whitman is of course the optimist incarnate, the poet-redeemer sent to put the world to rights. His poem celebrates "the resurrection of the wheat," as it extols the earth's capacity to restore dead matter to new life through the "prodigal, annual, sumptuous crops" that spring from "endless successions of diseas'd corpses." It praises the "divinity" of an earth that turns mere "meat" into transfigured "flesh." The words themselves appear in proximity in the poem's opening segment, as Whitman contrasts his living "flesh" with the "foul meat" of "distemper'd corpses" that rot beneath the ground (495–497). Whitman tacitly tells of his own Christ-like restoration to life through the miraculous bounty of the earth.

Mayakovsky's mistranslation undoes this miracle, appropriately enough, for such wonders do not exist in his poetic cosmos. If Whitman's universe is apocalyptic, in Northrop Frye's sense—"man attempts to surround nature and put it inside his (social) body, [in] the sacramental meal"—then Maya-kovsky's exemplifies Frye's vision of the demonic cosmos, "the world of the nightmare and the scapegoat, of bondage and pain and confusion," "the world that desire totally rejects"—or that totally rejects desire.[23] Mayak-ovsky's poetry details the agonies of "human meat" (*chelovech'e miaso*; 1:70). The scent of his own "burnt meat" (*zharennoe*) permeates "A Cloud in Trousers" (3:12); a "red snow / of juicy chunks of human meat" marks the outbreak of hostilities in "War Is Declared" (1:70); and sexual intercourse is a hideous "wallowing of meats in down and quilting" in "War and the World" (3:40). Mayakovsky's human meat can never be redeemed, for God and the devil are alike made of meat in his relentlessly fleshy cosmos (3:98, 3:28). In this world resurrection means only to succumb once more to the tortures of the flesh: "Buried bones rise from the burial mounds, / And meat grows over them" (3:58).

According to Chukovsky, Mayakovsky revised Whitman's line to read: "I will not press my meat to the earth so that her meat might renew me." The misreading is apt, since the world itself is made of meat in Mayakovsky's vision. Mating with this world leads not to spiritual redemption, but to stomach-turning reproduction:

> The whole world will sprawl like a woman,
> all heaving meat, ready to give in;
> things will come to life—
> their thingy lips
> will lisp:
> "la-di-da, la-di-da, la-di-da!" (3:18)

I spoke in my first chapter of the programmatic resistance to procreation that marks that poetics of Russia's Silver Age. Mayakovsky outdoes his Symbol-ist rivals and then some. In the demonic realm, Frye notes, "the Eucharist symbolism of the apocalyptic world" finds its parodic counterpart in "the imagery of cannibalism." In Mayakovsky's bloodthirsty cosmos, one either eats or is eaten, while the poet-savior reigns as its premier "cannibal." "I myself, / flaying the skin from the living, / gnaw the world's meat," he boasts in "War and the World" (3:55).[24]

In Whitman's vision, spirit and flesh are indivisible: "I am the poet of the body, / And I am the poet of the soul" (46). Flesh threatens to consume the spirit in Mayakovsky's poetic cosmos. Some demon of incarnation seems to pursue him as one lofty abstraction after another succumbs to the horrors of the flesh. Thoughts lie "dreaming on a sodden brain, / like an obese lackey on a greasy couch," or "crawl from the skull, sick and clotted, / like clumps of blood" (3:7, 28); a metaphorical heart aflame with passion reeks of "burnt meat" (3:12), while "the little corpses of dead words rot" (3:14). Shklovsky may have seen "the resurrection of the word" at work in the Futurists' verbal experiments.[25] Time and again, though, Mayakovsky seems to preside at its—gruesome—funeral.

In Mayakovsky's pre- and postrevolutionary writing alike, the good and the bad, or rather the better and the worse, are divided not by abstractions like ideology or virtue, but by how much meat they have on their bones. "I've / hated fat people / since childhood," Mayakovsky announces in "I Love" (3:136), and his visceral reaction takes the place of political orthodoxy even in the explicitly propagandistic "150,000,000." The revolutionary Mayakovsky is a hunger artist. His ill-fed collective hero, Ivan-Russia, literally incorporates hordes of ravenous "human and animal carcasses" whose political fervor is fueled by starvation alone (3:96–97). The enemy in this Bolshevik comic book is an implausibly obese Woodrow Wilson "swimming in fat": "Wilson chows down, / his fat expands, / his bellies grow, / one story on top of another" (3:93, 110).

Both Lenin and Trotsky objected violently to Mayakovsky's perverse parable. Lunacharsky, Lenin fumed, "should be horsewhipped" for abetting such outrageous publications.[26] And no wonder. One would be hard put to find the "positive hero" in this bizarre battle of a rebellious Russian "piglet" squashed by the bloated American "elephant" Woodrow Wilson (3:93). These extremes—the grotesquely diminished "carcass" versus the grossly overfed human "stomach in a Panama hat" (1:88)—are the only bodies that keep Mayakovsky company within the world of his poetry. There is "nothing on earth in between" (3:116). Even his giant's form affords him more anguish than joy. "I've been given a body / What do I do with it?" Mayakovsky might ask with the young Mandelstam. Unlike Mandelstam, though, he finds no answers. In this nightmarishly corporeal cosmos, the body is both inescapable and repellent.[27]

"The average man of a land at last only is important," Whitman insists in "Democratic Vistas" (72), and Whitman's ideal hero is precisely the "divine average" (182) that his imagined democracy demands. "The man with one ear," the man with one arm," "the man with one eye and one leg," "the man without a head": these are the disciples of the reluctant messiah "Vladimir Mayakovsky" in the "tragedy" by that name (3:341–359). Whitman's corporate self holds room for outcasts; he embraces "the blind, the deaf and dumb, idiots, hunchbacks" (266, 294). But these bodies must be made whole through the poet's ministrations, for the true goal of this "most robust poet" (1328) is "to help in the forming of a great aggregate

Nation . . . through the forming of myriads of fully develop'd and enclosing individuals" (1328, 668). The future will hold no cripples, for the poet's body wills it so.

Whitman's ideal vigor is far removed from the maimed forms that limp across the pages of Mayakovsky's verse. It is difficult to imagine two critics further apart on the political spectrum than Trotsky and Yuri Karabchievsky. Both agree, though, that pervasive fragmentation plagues the poet's work. "In the entire creative personality of Mayakovsky," Trotsky claims, "there is no necessary correlation between component parts; there is no equilibrium." Karabchievsky seconds his complaint: "The fragmentary, fractured nature of all his work means that . . . the excerpt is always better than the poem, the line is always stronger than the stanza."[28] Both critics have in mind the construction of Mayakovky's verse. And the poems' famous, fractured "step-ladder" construction does indeed embody his fragmented vision in the same way that Whitman's expansive, quasi-biblical lines are meant to project an ideal wholeness. But their comments hold for his poet's body as well. Mayakovsky's poetic self is both oversized and incomplete. "I've been crippled by love's ailment," Mayakovsky moans in "About That" (3:177). His misshapen form flaunts its scars in poem after poem: he's "as lonely as the last eye / Of a man going blind" (1:59); he is made of "lips alone" (3:7); his hypertrophied heart bursts from his chest (3:137–138); and his bloodied soul is torn to shreds time and again (1:57; 3:178; 3:53).

What is true of Mayakovsky's body is true of the world at large. The poet cannot escape the stunted specters who first make their appearance in "Vladimir Mayakovsky." He may dream of a glorious Soviet future without cripples (2:34); but the postrevolutionary present is peopled by "wholesale consumers of crutches and prosthetics" (2:400). Whitman was no stranger to the shattered bodies that populate Mayakovsky's poems. He served as a nurse during the Civil War and the chief impetus to his taking on such work was a visit to his brother, then recuperating in an army camp. "One of the first things that met my eyes," Whitman recalls, "was a heap of feet, arms, legs, & c. under a tree in front of a hospital."[29] Whitman tended to such fractured bodies in life and poetry alike. His verse may extol whole, healthy forms; yet all bodies, well or ailing, are part of the larger body politic in Whitman's vision, and each member must be healed if the whole is to survive. "From the stump of the arm, the amputated hand," Whitman writes in "The Wound-Dresser" (1865, 1881), "I undo the clotted lint, remove the slough, wash off the matter and blood" (444–445)." "Agonies," he exclaims in "Song of Myself," "are one of my changes of garments; / I do not ask the wounded person how he feels . . . / I myself become the wounded person" (65). He is both the injured and their savior as he ministers to the crippled body of the nation—or so his writings would have it. And his version of wholeness must have seemed both politically and poetically imperative to a poet aiming to save a fractured nation through his various ministrations.

All injury tends towards wholeness for Whitman's miraculous physician, who heals wounds as easily as he changes his clothes. But wholeness was illusory to Mayakovsky, whose poetic imagination tended relentlessly towards dissolution. Certainly the reality that surrounded him did little to dispel such a notion. World war, revolution, civil war, disease, and famine: Russia was spared little in this century's first decades, and these sufferings, not surprisingly, find their way into Mayakovsky's poetry. In *Mayakovsky's Resurrection* (*Voskresenie Mayakovskogo,* 1985), Yuri Karabchievsky charges the poet with crossing the line from metaphor into reality through poetic incitements to violence that too often mirrored Bolshevik practice. "Our feet know / which corpses / to walk on," Mayakovsky warns in one controversial lyric (1:182).[30] Frequently, though, one feels something like the opposite: the horrors of war seem to exist chiefly to provide grisly objective correlatives for Mayakovsky's tortured imagination.

The broken limbs Whitman mends in "The Wound Dresser" are both literal and symbolic; they belong to real victims and to Whitman's larger poetic vision at once. In "War and the World," Mayakovsky relishes the "monstrous hyperboles" (3:44) that World War I has furnished for his art: "Human meat had been minced for miles around Kovno," he exults (3:49–51). In the poem he describes the kind of spectacle that horrified Whitman: "In a rotting wagon four legs for forty men" (3:51). But his reaction belongs exclusively in the realm of Mayakovskian hyperbole: through the powers of the Futurist poet-Christ, "chopped off legs / will seek out / their masters, / severed heads will call out their own names" (3:58). Mayakovsky did no military service. Nonetheless he sees himself as the war's greatest casualty: "Each of my stanzas is a chest pierced through by every lance, / a face contorted by every gas" (3:52). "War and the world" is Mayakovsky's constant theme: the world lays siege to the body, and the body revolts against both its master and the cosmos. His talents find their best outlet in times of war and revolution, of worldwide conflagration. For all Mayakovsky's hymns to the coming utopia, he is more at ease with a state in shambles than with a thriving community at peace. Or so, at any rate, we might speculate. His times provided him with no such refuge— though Soviet attempts at postrevolutionary stabilization would put him to the test.

Cosmic Consummation

*The direct trial of him who would be the greatest poet is today. . . .
[I]f he does not attract his own land body and soul to himself and
hang on its neck with incomparable love and plunge his semitic mus-
cle into its merits and demerits.*

— *Walt Whitman, "Preface,"* Leaves of Grass *(1855)*

*From the heaven of poetry
I throw myself
into communism,
because
without it there is no love
for me.*

— *Vladimir Mayakovsky, "Homeward!'*

Whitman's celebration of sexuality was not intended merely to release
the American people from the straitjacket of outdated European mores. It
marked his own efforts to unleash the "the measureless wealth of latent
power and capacity" of a still-expanding nation (944). His verse, he insists,
is a "song of procreation," and his voice is "strong with reference to con-
summations": "Sexual organs and acts! do you concentrate in me!" (248,
609, 183). An exhausting agenda, to say the least. Still as a poet, at any rate,
he practices what he preaches. "My lovers suffocate me!" he complains in
"Song of Myself," "crowding my lips, and thick in the pores of my skin"
(80). His voracious poetic lovemaking is not undertaken for its own sake.
Its goal is the creation of a mightier nation: "This day I am jetting the stuff
of far more arrogant republics" (73). To this end he courts his country ("For
you these from me, O Democracy, to serve you ma femme!" [272]), his reader
("Camerado, this is no book. . . . It is I you hold and who holds you" [611]),
the earth ("Far-swooping elbowed earth! Rich apple-blossomed earth! /
Smile, for your lover comes!" [47]), and God himself ("As God comes a lov-
ing bedfellow and sleeps at my side all night" [29]). Only through constant
couplings can he bring about the new race and nation, "beautiful, gigantic,
sweet-blooded" (610), that his verse is intended to inaugurate. This symbolic
procreation will create, ideally, a people that surpasses its precursors both
physically and politically. Similarly grandiose notions would be voiced, in a
rather different context, by early leaders of the Soviet state.

Mayakovsky is no less obsessed with procreation, though it takes a rather
different shape in his verse. "Through life I drag / millions of enormous pure

loves / and millions upon millions of tiny, sordid lovelets," he complains in "A Cloud in Trousers" (3:23). Indeed all of his poetry reads like an extended quest to find the one object, be it public (the state) or private (a woman "as large as me" [2:373]), that can answer his large-scale needs. But "A Cloud in Trousers" also suggests why Mayakovsky's "gigantic love" (*liubovishcha*; 1:122) is doomed to remain unrequited. In his poetic cosmos, procreation breeds not liberation, but endless repetition, "millions upon millions of tiny, sordid lovelets" (*liubiata*—the coinage suggests progeny or spawn). "Copulation," Mayakovsky warns, is a "bloody game," the "wallowing of meats in down and quilting, / As people crawl on top of each other to sweat, / shaking cities with their creaking beds" (3:40, 45). His courtship of the world is the antithesis of Whitman's. The globe itself is willing—"The whole world will sprawl like a woman, / all heaving meat, ready to give in"—but the poet resists, for he knows what will follow. For Whitman such coupling leads to the creation of "a hundred millions of superb persons" who will people a vital new nation (609). For Mayakovsky, though, it breeds only hordes of subhuman "things" destined in their turn to become obscenely genteel papas "sleeping sweetly, eyeless, earless, /. . . . While [their] children play croquet, / On [their] bellies" (3:18, 1:88). Procreation perpetuates the relentlessly fleshy, bourgeois status quo that Mayakovsky is determined to destroy. It will trap him in a "familial perpetuum mobile" (2:151).[31]

Mayakovsky apparently finds an ideal mate in the revolutionary nation whose red body sprawls beneath him in "Fifth International." Like Blok before him, though, he resists the culmination of his symbolic courtship. He keeps his distance from his beloved, with his "giant's head" planted firmly in the clouds. Only in the twenty-first century, when worldwide revolution is achieved and Soviet Russia presumably no longer requires his services, does he resume his human form ("Mayakovsky! Be a person again!") and return to earth.[32] He leaves a strategic gap in the middle of "Fifth International," and the ellipsis is telling. It allows him to circumvent the kind of imaginative consummation with his native land that Whitman articulates in his verse. And it permits him to escape the merely human time in which revolutionary nations adjust their utopian expectations to a less than idyllic reality.

"Let's reconstruct the human race," Mayakovsky exclaims in "I Protest" ("Protestuiu," 1:360). One of the defects to be erased is the mundane copulation he associates with capitalist decadence. "In Chicago . . . [they] hugged the effeminate stump of meat . . . kissed all over, stripped naked, rollicking," he insists in what is perhaps yet another dig at his American poetic rival ("150,000,000"; 3:115). But the revolution did not succeed in remaking the species overnight, and the attractions of home and family persisted into the radical twenties. The Soviet Mayakovsky thus found himself forced to continue railing against the inexplicable attractions of "family happiness," with its "broads," "love," "children," and "dear little old daily life" (*staren'kii, staren'kii bytik*): "How many ideals have died . . . beneath the blanket!" he laments (2:51–54, 149).[33]

It is not entirely clear how Mayakovsky expects the denizens of Russia's brave new world to reproduce.[34] But Soviet Russia should not proceed by time-honored routes that breed only continuity where there should be radical change. "Can't you see the enemy's menace / behind love's pleasures?" he warns his straying comrades (3:25). The enemy he has in mind is not just the worldwide bourgeoisie, but time itself. "I'm against time, that thieving murderer," he proclaims in "I Protest" (2:360). Elsewhere time has a distinctly female face. It is woman, after all, who threatens to ensnare him in time's vicious circle: "Hurry up and die, old woman . . . Here we come, a gang of your young grandsons" (1:358). But Mayakovsky's ideal nation is also no country for old men: "My country is an adolescent . . . May we grow a hundred years without old age" (3:332). And his ideal revolution ends time itself as it attains "Eden" with a single stroke (2:289): "A thousand years of 'Formerly' collapse today," he proclaims in "Revolution" (1917; 1:131).

In "A Cloud in Trousers" Mayakovsky sketches a portrait of the revolution's ideal bard, who bears of course the poet's own name:

> I don't have a single gray hair in my soul,
> And no senile tenderness!
> The might of my voice has expanded the world,
> and I come forth—a beautiful
> twenty-two-year-old. (3:1)

Critics have pointed to Whitman's influence on Mayakovsky's beautiful boy.[35] His likely source in "Song of Myself" is telling, though. Unlike Mayakovsky, Whitman was a latecomer both to poetry and to the revolution he celebrates; and this belatedness informs his sense of his own and his nation's selfhood. Like Mayakovsky, Whitman is careful to identify his age. But the self he celebrates is no longer young—though it is, he stresses, admirably fit. "I, now thirty-seven years old in perfect health begin / Hoping to cease not till death," he announces in "Song of Myself" (188). Elsewhere he painstakingly places himself in relation to a revolution that has likewise reached maturity: "Full of life now, compact, visible, / I, forty years old the eighty-third year of the States . . ." (287).

Mayakovsky, the bard of youth, has no use for age. "Let's kill the old people, / and turn their skulls into ashtrays" he modestly proposes in

"150,000,000" (3:99)—a suggestion to which Trotsky responded in mock horror, "Ash-trays made of skulls are inconvenient and unhygienic." In "Democratic Vistas," Whitman insists on the "ceaseless need of revolutions, prophets, thunderstorms, deaths, births, new projections and invigorations of ideas and men" in poetry and politics alike (991). His pronouncement might seem to anticipate Futurist calls to "place the world on a new axis." But Whitman is himself middle-aged as he undertakes his great project, and unlike Mayakovsky, he is not the coeval of the revolution he celebrates. By the time he turned to poetry this revolution was already history; he thus could not conceive, like Mayakovsky, of a "revolution that places a period after the past" (2:39). He must forge a different myth, and a different kind of mythic time, and the equivalence he finds between himself and a nation flourishing in its prime is key to his poetic mythology.[36]

"America is not finished, perhaps never will be," Whitman proclaims in his letter to Emerson (1333). In his verse he monitors both the Union's "endless unfolding" in time and the growth of his own self as "projected through history" (49, 177). "Span of youth! Ever-pushed elasticity! Manhood balanced and florid and full! . . . Old age superbly rising! Ineffable grace of dying days!" he exclaims in "Song of Myself" (80–81). His task is to respond to the evolving shape of the nation that is at once his parent, his child, his lover, and his very self. "The proof of a poet," he declares in the first *Leaves of Grass* (1855), "is that his country absorbs him as affectionately as he has absorbed it" (26). By this reckoning, Whitman was a failure. His love affair with his nation went largely unrequited in his lifetime. In spite of his populist aspirations, "the great mass of American people remained, and would remain, all but oblivious to his work." And this in turn became yet another feather in the revolutionary cap that Soviet Russia placed upon his head: the "bourgeois" American public's neglect of their great bard was read as indirect testimony to the innately "socialist" leanings that placed him beyond the pale of his nation's politics. The modern poet wins by losing, though, so Jean-Paul Sartre suggests, and Whitman's vision was designed to accommodate apparent disappointment. "Whether I come to my own today or in ten thousand or ten million years, / I can cheerfully take it now, or with equal cheerfulness I can wait," he announces in "Song of Myself" (46). "Poets to come!" he proclaims elsewhere, "You, a new brood . . . you must justify me" (175). Here certainly he found some vindication.[37]

"I know the amplitude of time," Whitman boasts in "Song of Myself" (46). Mayakovsky could make no such claim. It is one thing, after all, to court rejection by the benighted bourgeoisie and another to be spurned by the proletarian masses and their masters. Mayakovsky's vision left him with little room to maneuver when the Bolshevik revolution—inevitably—failed to fulfill his Futurist fantasies. His poetic body, titanic and eternally "twenty-two," was not designed to withstand the vicissitudes of time: his confession, in a late poem, that "I'm no longer twenty, / I'm thirty and then some," reads like an admission of defeat (2:369). His poet's body was at its best during war and revolution, where its outsized agonies found their match in the bloody anguish of the age. It was a poor fit for a state attempting to regain its economic and political equilibrium through compromise (Lenin's New Economic Policy) and coercion (Stalin's Five Year Plans).

The state did not hesitate to remind Mayakovsky of his defects. Larger-than-life lyricism does not a revolutionary poet make, Trotsky warns in *Literature and Revolution,* as he mocks both the poet's monstrous body and the generic confusions it creates: "Mayakovsky has one foot on Mont Blanc and the other on Elbrus . . . [he] speaks of the most intimate thing, such as love, as if he were speaking about the migration of nations." A world in which Mayakovsky is the measure of all things produces both physical and generic aberrations. The avant-garde colossus who straddles continents sings of love and politics in the same breath—and small wonder, since the same unrequited passion propels both kinds of song. The revolution, like so many other beloveds, had failed to return Mayakovsky's affection, and the new state had little use for epic laments sung by bourgeois bohemians with revolutionary pretensions.[38]

Trotsky's own prescriptions for physiological correctness reveal that Mayakovsky was hardly alone in his overblown imaginings. The state in its postrevolutionary "constructive" phase, Trotsky explains, requires that we outgrow "man's extreme anatomical and physiological disharmony" as we master the "processes of [our] own organism, such as breathing, the circulation of the blood, digestion, reproduction"; we will then achieve a new level of "social and biological" being and be better prepared to serve the collective's need for "social construction."[39] Trotsky would soon find himself discarded by the revolution he had helped to shape. His vision here, though, is of a piece with postrevolutionary dreams of a new species of Soviet "machine-men" who would dispense with the "lyrical disorder" of their less enlightened brethren. These new men require a new brand of lyrics, Trotsky explains, a poetry that promotes "the psychological unity of the social man." Mayakovsky's lyrical and anatomical disharmonies were hardly what he had in mind.[40]

Mayakovsky himself seemed to sense that his brand of physiological fantasy did not meet the state's specifications as early as "Fifth International" (1922): the larger the poet grows, the further he moves from the nation. On one level the poem celebrates Russia's revolutionary successes; on another, it admits that the poet is a poor fit for the state he ostensibly serves. Following "Fifth International," Mayakovsky's poetic body is no longer the protagonist of his political poems—though its enemies, the bloated forms of the old tsarist and new socialist bourgeoisie, continue to proliferate. Two bodies cannot occupy the same space at the same time, the physicists warn. And by 1924, the task of embodying the state had clearly passed to the political, and not the poetic, avant-garde. The place at center stage was taken by another monumental form, that of the nation's martyred leader, Vladimir Lenin. In his epics, odes, and elegies Mayakovsky praises Lenin with what were already canonical clichés: "Lenin is still more living than the living," "the most humane of men" (3:186, 194). But Lenin also takes on attributes of Mayakovsky's poet-Christ. He is "larger than the largest" (1:367); the nation rises on the blood of his suffering body (1:276, 364; 3:237, 246); and he speaks with the "voice of thunder" (1:276). The once-proud poet is humbled by the master's posthumous presence: "I am happy. / The flowing water of a resounding march / carries off my weightless body. . . . I rejoice to be a fragment of [his] strength" (3:251).[41]

Lenin's body may live forever, but Mayakovsky's will not, or so an image from his final, unfinished epic suggests. "At the Top of My Lungs" ostensibly celebrates the poet's legacy to his "comrades in posterity":

> Rummaging
> in today's
> petrified shit,
> studying the twilight of our days,
> you
> may
> ask about me, too. (3:333)

Mayakovsky's "ponderous, crude, palpable" verse "will break the bulky mass of years," he announces. But the terms in which he envisions this poetry—"an ancient, ominous weapon" pokes out from "petrified shit"—evoke the graveyard or the junkyard more readily than the dialogue "of the living with the living" that he promises his descendants (3:333–335). Whitman's poetic body was designed to last a lifetime and beyond. In his farewell poem "So Long!" (1860, 1881) he bequeaths his readers the living form incarnated in *Leaves of Grass:* "Camerado, this is no book. . . . / I spring from the pages into your arms—decease calls me forth" (611). The inheritance Mayakovsky leaves his descendants is more ominous. "With the passing years," he mourns in "At the Top of My Lungs," "I come to resemble / excavated, long-tailed monsters" (3:336). Mayakovsky's monstrous body has become a dinosaur, an antediluvian skeleton able perhaps to amuse the occasional passerby or edify some future researcher. But it cannot embody the drives of a nation pressing forward into the future through the first Five Year Plan.

In this passage, moreover, Mayakovsky does not speak of how he will appear to comrades in some distant future. He has already become an outsized relic of days gone by, not the Soviet standard bearer he had claimed to be. Like Blok before him, he had outlived himself, or so he feared. Rather than Whitman's life in death ("decease calls me forth"), Mayakovsky finds himself, at the age of thirty-three, condemned to a kind of death in life. His giant's body perishes not just at the hands of a state that has no use for its anarchistic energies. Like the dinosaur he evokes, it expires from built-in limitations. "All the middle ground has been destroyed," Mayakovsky exults in "150,000,000" (3:116). For Mayakovsky's poetic body, there is no happy medium, no golden mean: it occupies center stage or it vanishes from the scene. It is more living than the living or the deadest of the dead. Forced to choose between the Soviet state of the future and his avant-garde "song of myself," Mayakovsky opts not just to step on the throat of his song, but to throttle the mammoth body it celebrated.

The Immortal Mayakovsky

But the immortal Mayakovsky lives on.
—*Anatoly Lunacharsky, "Vladimir Mayakovsky, Innovator" (1931)*

Resurrect me!
—*Vladimir Mayakovsky, "About That" (1923)*

Or so it seemed. But poets who end their lives in spectacular, spectacularly well-timed fashion may in fact be guaranteeing their future immortality. This proved to be the case for Mayakovsky. He may have outlived his welcome in Soviet Russia, but he left behind a beautiful corpse, according to at least one eyewitness report. "His face," Boris Pasternak records, "had returned to the time when he called himself a beautiful twenty-two-year-old. Death had caught a facial expression which rarely falls into its clutches. It was the expression with which you begin a life, not end it." The deathbed scene might have been scripted by Mayakovsky himself.[42]

He also left behind a dilemma for a state that found itself faced with the suicide of its best-known artist at a crucial moment in its own self-transformation. The motivations for Mayakovsky's self-inflicted death have been endlessly debated: were they political, personal, or some unwieldy amalgam of the two? I do not intend to weigh in here with further speculations. For the state, though, there could only be one answer. Political dissatisfaction was not an option, hence the poet's reasons must have been by default entirely private. "The preliminary investigation indicates that his act was prompted by motives of a purely personal nature," the official newspaper *Pravda* concluded the morning after the suicide. This seeming solution in fact created further ideological problems, complications that state officials found exceptionally difficult to explain. "It is very strange," Jakobson remarks, "that on this occasion such terms as 'accidental,' 'personal' and so forth are used precisely by those who have always preached a strict social determinism."[43]

"Accidental," "personal": where have we heard these terms before? They make up two-thirds of the triumvirate that form Mandelstam's prescient, parenthetical description of a postrevolutionary lyric that is also, ominously, "catastrophic."[44] Mandelstam's generic definition was a perfect fit for the official postmortem. Mayakovsky had been killed, the state concluded, by his own lyricism. He had fallen prey to the kind of retrograde writing long since relegated to Trotsky's famous dustbin. The revolution's bard was dead, shot through the head by a lyrical class enemy who had infiltrated the ranks of the faithful. This was not suicide, in other words, but generic assassination. If this summary sounds farfetched—and it does—then let us turn to one of Mayakovsky's official eulogists, Anatoly Lunacharsky, for a version of the poet's death worthy of the master himself at his most grotesque.

Like other party leaders, Lunacharsky railed against Mayakovsky's "lyrical whining" during the poet's lifetime. The Mayakovsky he conjures up posthumously is a different matter. This poet was from the start "revolted by all lyricism," Lunacharsky insists in "Vladimir Mayakovsky, Innovator" (1931), and this, in turn, "undoubtedly was the influence of his dormant Marxist feelings," he assures us. It took only the Bolshevik revolution to bring this nascent Marxist to the fore, since at heart the poet was on the right track from the start. "Mayakovsky was a materialist"; "Mayakovsky was a hard worker"; "Mayakovsky [was] poetry's labourer," "producing poems which are a 'product of production.'" As a "big man"—Lunacharsky follows the poet's lead in stressing his "Herculean frame"—Mayakovsky knew he had found his match in the no less "Herculean, vast scope" of the proletarian revolution and its leader. "He came upon these tremendous phenomena on his life's road" and "he saw . . . that this was what he had been yearning for, a direct realisation of the gigantic process of reconstruction!"[45]

So why did this happy giant have to die? This is where Lunacharsky's tendentious tale takes its bizarre Gogolian twist. Mayakovsky, it turns out, had an evil twin, a "soft petty bourgeois" armed with "sentimental lyric[s]." "You dare not speak in the name of Mayakovsky!" the poet warned this insidious double time and again while grabbing him "by the neck most forcefully, passionately and triumphantly" and "bend[ing] it in two." The double somehow survived these repeated neck-wringings, but was apparently so incensed when Mayakovsky finally "stepped on his throat" that "the double killed him for this." Curiouser and curiouser, as Alice says.[46]

The fate of this murderous double remains unclear in Lunacharsky's little fable: he suggests that he may have taken flight with Trotsky who is also mysteriously implicated in Mayakovsky's demise. But announcements of the good Mayakovsky's death proved premature in any case. "The 'metal' [i.e. 'Stalinist'?] Mayakovsky," "the revolutionary Mayakovsky" "lives on," courtesy of "the creative revolutionary vanguard of humanity" which "proclaims itself to be . . . not an ally of Mayakovsky's double, but an ally of the Mayakovsky in whom his socio-political personality became crystallized [*sic*]."[47]

But the double likewise failed to die. He survived in legend and writing alike, and the poet's perpetual fragmentation and self-contradiction proved to be his most vital gift to future poets and readers. He bequeathed several selves to posterity: the lovelorn lyrist, the avant-garde iconoclast, the revolutionary standard bearer. These mismatched Mayakovskys continued to quarrel posthumously, and their mutual incompatibility would stir controversy decades later in another fledgling state, the postwar Polish People's Republic. But that is another story.

3

The Death of the Book à la russe:
The Acmeists under Stalin

Only that historian will have the gift of fanning the spark of hope in the past who is firmly convinced that even the dead will not be safe from the enemy if he wins.
> —Walter Benjamin, "Theses on the
> Philosophy of History" (1940)

Did they publish André Chenier? Did they publish Sappho? Did they publish Jesus Christ?
> —Osip Mandelstam, quoted in Anna Akhmatova,
> "Mandelstam" (1954)

In *Of Grammatology* (1967), Jacques Derrida apocalyptically proclaims what he calls "the death of the book," the death, that is, of the self-contained, organically unified, self-explanatory text. The postmodern age, he continues, has replaced the now defunct book with the notions of "writing" (*écriture*) and of a "text" that undermines or explodes any metaphorical bindings that might attempt to confine it within the safely "logocentric" limits of a single, self-sufficient volume. "The destruction of the book, as it is now underway in all domains" is a "necessary violence," Derrida claims. The rhetorical violence with which he marks the unnatural death of the book finds its counterparts in the famous proclamations of Michel Foucault and Roland Barthes, whose respective essays "What Is an Author?" (1969) and "The Death of the Author" (1968) commemorate the passing of the autonomous, individual creators of the objects known in less enlightened ages as "books." "[The work] now attains the right to kill, to become the murderer of its author," Foucault announces. His phrase—indeed, all the phrases I've cited—are bound to give the Slavist pause, not least because such metaphors have had, in recent Russian history, an uncomfortable habit of realizing themselves as they pass from theory into practice.[1]

"There are some countries where men kiss women's hands, and others where they only say 'I kiss your hand.' There are countries where Marxist theory is answered by Leninist practice, and where the madness of the brave, the martyr's stake, and the poet's Golgotha are not just figurative expressions." Roman Jakobson's observation dates from 1931; it is peculiarly apt, though, in the postmodern philosophical context in which Barthes, Foucault, and Derrida operate. All three theorists developed their concepts in an environment in which men "only say 'I kiss your hand,'" that is to say, in which the literal implications of "the death of the author" remain unactivated. They deal explicitly with the development of "literature," the "author" and the "book" in Western, "bourgeois capitalist" civilization. The notion of the author, and the concept of the autonomous human subject that underlies it, are "the epitome and culmination of capitalist ideology," Barthes explains, and "the image of literature" in bourgeois culture is, as a consequence, "tyrannically centered on the author, his person, his life, his tastes, his passions."[2]

What happens, though, when an actual tyrant centers his attention on the author's person, life, and passions? The student of Stalinist-era writing is uneasily aware of the cultural specificity of Barthes', Derrida's and Foucault's dead authors and books. All the world's a text, these theorists proclaim; and within this textual kingdom, Derrida claims, "the 'literal' meaning of writing [is] metaphoricity itself." All three theorists are provocateurs or, as Allan Megill puts it, responsive or "reactive" thinkers who seek "to attack received ideas, to demolish previous platitudes." They are practitioners of what their great precursor Friedrich Nietzsche calls "the magic of the extreme." Their dead authors and books trace their lineage back to the God whose death Nietzsche proclaims in *The Gay Science* (1887). Like Nietzsche, they require a bland backdrop, middle-of-the-road, middle-class, complacent, commonsensical, for their extreme pronouncements to have the desired effect. Like Nietzsche, they demand an audience "made up of us folks here—living in the 'ordinary' world, earning money, raising families, catching buses, experiencing pleasure/leisure of various sorts, and undergoing the vagaries of nature."[3]

Like Nietzsche, or Blok or Mayakovsky, for that matter, these theorists need a bourgeoisie to shock. Unlike the poets, though, they are not the product of a government increasingly preoccupied with eliminating not just its middle-class enemies, but the writers whose work betrayed, willy-nilly, their suspect origins and thus could not be shaped to state purposes. They require a context in which texts are not responsible for the actual deaths of their creators, in which books may metaphorically bomb in the marketplace or die, in filmed form, at the box office, but are not literally destroyed by anxious writers in their quest for self-preservation or by a state determined to maintain absolute control over its master script of past and present alike. "The twentieth century has given us a most simple touchstone for reality: physical pain," Czesław Miłosz comments; one might extend his thought and say that the true test of any theory of authorship must be a dead body.[4] The dead authors and books of Barthes, Foucault, and Derrida can retain their purely metaphorical status only in a society that has long since lost the habit of literally destroying writers and texts for their verbal crimes against the state. If the literal meaning, in other words, of phrases like "the death of the author" or "the end of the book" is the first meaning that comes to mind, as it does for the Slavist, it undermines the very core of these theorists' arguments. It undoes our capacity to conceive of language as mere metaphoricity or of the world as pure interpretation. Indeed, in such contexts, we begin to perceive language not metaphorically, but magically: we need only try the discomfiting experiment of pronouncing "fatwa" and "Salman Rushdie" in the same sentence to experience the urge to knock wood or spit over our shoulders.

The "author" was born, Foucault remarks, "only when [he] became subject to punishment and to the extent that his discourse is considered transgressive . . . an action situated in a bipolar field of sacred and profane, lawful and unlawful, religious and blasphemous." This also describes exactly the kind of situation in which the real-life author (not the "author" in quotation marks) may be called upon to die for his or her transgressive verbal actions, and this is the sort of culture in which Osip Mandelstam and Anna Akhmatova found themselves living and writing during the period of so-called "high Stalinism," that is, from the early 1930s until the outbreak of World War II and the Nazi assault on the Soviet Union. "Do calm him down! It's only in bourgeois countries that they shoot people for poems," Mandelstam's prison guard implored his wife shortly before the poet was sent into exile. Mandelstam himself, however, took a perverse pride precisely in the murderous ways that the Soviet state chose to express its regard for his chosen calling. "If they're killing people for poetry," Nadezhda Mandelstam recalls her husband saying during their years of exile in the 1930s, "that means they honor and esteem it, they fear it . . . that means poetry is power." Such power has its limits, needless to say; the kind of valorization that leads poets to nonmetaphorical scaffolds and prison cells lends itself all too readily to the posthumous mythmaking that views both life and work as mere preludes to the martyr's unhappy fate. Whether poetry should ideally be a matter of life and death is a vexed question, to say the least. The fact remains that in certain circumstances, the poetic word has consequences that far outreach the limits of postmodern *écriture*. What I want to address now are the distinctive forms of poetic power that Mandelstam and Akhmatova derive from writing in a society that paid poets the dubious compliment of taking their persons and their texts with the utmost seriousness.[5]

In her memoirs, Nadezhda Mandelstam speaks of writing in the "pre-Gutenberg era" of Russian literature, and her phrase suggests the nature of the "death of the book" as it took shape in Stalinist Russia. By the early 1930s, both Akhmatova and Mandelstam had undergone what Akhmatova calls a "civic" or "civil" "death" (*grazhdanskaia smert'*—a more literal translation might read "death as a citizen"). They became official non-persons, practitioners of a suspect genre and adherents of an outmoded, "pastist" poetic philosophy, Acmeism: "It does not make new poets of you to write about the philosophy of life of the Seventeenth Century into the language of the Acmeists," Trotsky had warned early on. The purported defenders of bourgeois subjectivity ceased to be subjects in any publicly recognized sense. Both writers were virtually barred from print. As literature and the arts were transformed into handmaidens of the state, only those writers willing to contribute to what Mandelstam calls "the book of Stalin" (*stalinskaia kniga*), the epic text of Soviet letters and life then being scripted by the master artist, Stalin himself, had access to the paper, printers and presses that would guarantee their works a public, "civic" life.[6]

Their poetry continued to live, however, a furtive, underground existence as it was written on scraps of paper and hidden, or circulated in manuscript among friends, or read aloud and hastily memorized. Such a situation would scarcely seem conducive to the cultivation of the poetic power Mandelstam celebrates in his remarks to his wife. Yet it is just at the time that the final nails were being driven into Mandelstam's and Akhmatova's civic coffins, the time of the First Congress of Soviet Writers (1934) and the official birth of Socialist Realism (1932), that Mandelstam pronounces his own social command (*sotsial'nyi zakaz*) for himself and his fellow Acmeist. "Now we must write civic verse" (*Teper' stikhi dolzhny byt' grazhdanskimi*), Akhmatova recalls him announcing in 1933; and the ironies of his proclamation are manifold. In the first place, he and Akhmatova had been barred from public life precisely for their failure to write civic poetry, or at least the kind of civic poetry the regime required. They were considered lyric poets par excellence, famed or defamed as the composers of "chamber poetry." As such, they were unwelcome in a state that demanded, with increasing insistence, only triumphal marches and collective hymns to accompany the nation's uninterrupted progress towards a glorious future. The dweller in the personal and accidental realm of lyric poetry could claim no civil rights in a state dedicated to the eradication of all that is private, personal, and unplanned. According to the new work plan for poetry, poets could speak for and to the people only by renouncing their lyric selves as they "dissolve in the official hymn," in Akhmatova's phrase.[7]

Under Stalin, Eikhenbaum remarks, the "lyric 'I'" became almost taboo. How could practitioners of a forbidden genre, noncitizens barred from public discourse, hope to speak for and to the larger audience that a truly "civic poet" requires? For Akhmatova and Mandelstam do indeed produce their most ambitious, audaciously "civic" poetry precisely at the height of Stalin's terror—I have in mind Mandelstam's sequence of "Verses on the Unknown Soldier" ("Stikhi o neizvestnom soldate," 1937) and Akhmatova's famed *Requiem* (*Rekviem*, 1935–40). Mandelstam provides a tacit answer to this question by way of the example of civic writing he gave Akhmatova. He followed his social command—"Now we must write civic verse"—with a recitation that was in effect his declaration of a sui generis form of civil, or civic, war (*grazhdanskaia voina*), that is, of war waged against the state on behalf of its citizenry. The poem he recited to Akhmatova was the famous "Stalin Epigram" (1933), a lyric published only posthumously that proved to be, nonetheless, his death warrant.[8]

> We live without feeling the land beneath us,
> Our speeches can't be heard ten steps away.
>
> But whenever there's enough for half a chat—
> Talk turns to the Kremlin mountaineer.
>
> His fat fingers are plump as worms,
> And his words are as sure as iron weights.
>
> His mighty cockroach moustache laughs,
> And his vast boot-tops gleam.
>
> A mob of thin-necked chieftains surrounds him,
> He toys with the favors of half-humans.
>
> One whistles, another mews, a third whimpers,
> He alone bangs and pokes.

He forges one decree after another, like horseshoes—
One gets it in the groin, another in the head, the brow, the eye.

Every execution is a treat
And the broad breast of the Ossetian.

On hearing the "Stalin Epigram," Boris Pasternak reportedly exclaimed: "This is not a literary fact, but an act of suicide." Mandelstam's interrogator likewise saw his unauthorized lines as exceeding the reach of literature proper: they were a "provocation," a "terrorist act," he charged. And Mandelstam apparently ceded the point: the poem was, he confessed, "a widely applicable weapon of counter-revolutionary struggle." All three agreed that these were not words, but deeds.[9]

They were actually a little of both. They exist on the boundaries between language as metaphor and language as action, and thus incidentally illustrate the difficulties of speaking, as Barthes and Derrida do, of language as exclusively metaphorical. The poem itself concerns the possibilities and dangers of different kinds of speech. Mandelstam contrasts the inaudible "half-conversations" of those who oppose or fear Stalin and the dehumanized mewing and whining of those who support him with the language of the Great Leader himself, who demonstrates the real-life consequences of his speech on the bodies of his subjects as he energetically forges new decrees: "One gets it in the groin, another in the head, the brow, the eye" (*Komu v pakh, komu v lob, komu v brov', komu v glaz*). The energy and efficiency of Mandelstam's diction and syntax in these phrases enact the power of the language he describes.

Mandelstam counters this form of language as action with his own verbal deed, the epigram, and he authorizes the collective "we" he requires for his civic verse precisely by way of his linguistic feat. The poet-prophet is exempt from the linguistic limitations he perceives in the citizenry at large. "*Our* speeches can't be heard ten steps away," he thunders. The phrase itself demonstrates, though, that he himself is prepared to proclaim *vo ves' golos*, at the top of his voice, what he insists the Russian people think but dare not say aloud, as the subsequent line reveals: "But whenever there's enough for half a chat— / Talk turns to the Kremlin mountaineer." Unlike the leader who reserves the powers of speech for himself alone—"He alone bangs and pokes" with his words like "iron weights"—Mandelstam derives his verbal authority and force from the multitudes whose innermost thoughts and fears he claims to articulate.

I have been speaking of the "Stalin Epigram" as a form of action, a deed, and I do not mean the terms metaphorically. "Burn with your word (*glagolom*) the hearts of men," God bids the poet in Pushkin's "Prophet" (*Prorok*, 1826). In his notebooks of 1931–32, Mandelstam recognizes the real-life implications of certain kinds of speech: "Only in government decrees, in military orders, in judicial verdicts, in notarial acts and in such documents as the last Will and Testament does the verb [or "word"—the modern Russian for "verb" coincides with the Old Russian term for "word," *glagol*] live a full life."[10] By treating his "Stalin Epigram" as a de facto will and testament, Mandelstam could complete the prophet's mission and compete with those verdicts and decrees whose "full lives" threatened to deprive him and other Russians of their own more vulnerable existences. Poetic legislation thus trumps the murderous official variety.

Mandelstam was prepared to take the real-life consequences of his verbal act—"I'm ready for death," Akhmatova recalls him saying—and the poem precipitated his first arrest in 1934, which was followed by three years of internal exile, a second arrest in 1937, and finally his death early in 1938 in a gulag transit camp. Indeed, according to auditors who witnessed his clandestine recitations of the "Stalin Epigram," Mandelstam appeared to be staging performance-provocations intended to reach the ears of his epigram's subject. He recited the poem to selected groups of friends and acquaintances, some of whom were almost guaranteed to pass it on to the authorities. The poem in fact existed only in performance—Mandelstam himself transcribed it for the first time only at his police interrogation in 1934—and it was as oral performance that it precipitated his arrest.[11]

This is no accident. "Those rhymes must have made an impression," Mandelstam remarked in the wake of Stalin's call to Pasternak.[12] They did indeed. In the epigram, Mandelstam describes the ominous power of Stalin's spoken words. Through his performance of the epigram, Mandelstam demonstrates the equal force of the poet's speech. The poet's voice, condemned to "civic death" in the private domain, may seem inaudible—but it travels much further than "ten steps away." It bypasses the whole elaborate state apparatus designed for the control and repression of the written word to reach the ears of the leader himself, who is compelled to countermand it through the verbal action that took the shape of the orders that led to Mandelstam's arrest and exile. The "Stalin Epigram," as poem and provocation, thus paradoxically becomes Mandelstam's most direct testimony to the power and efficacy of the spoken poetic word.

In Derridian philosophy, Western civilization revolves around an illusory opposition between "fallen," artificial, written language and untainted, "natural" speech. We find a similar dichotomy at work in Mandelstam's late poetics—and yet, once again, the context in which Mandelstam lived and worked gives this opposition a very different coloration than it assumes in Derridian thought. "Writing and speech are incommensurate," Mandelstam insists in "Conversation about Dante" (1933), and in "Fourth Prose" (1930) he leaves little doubt about where his own preferences lie. "I have no manuscripts, no notebooks, no archives," he proclaims. "I have no handwriting, for I never write. I alone in Russia work with my voice, while all around me consummate swine are writing." There is an element of truth in Mandelstam's characteristic hyperbole; he did in fact compose aloud and on his feet, and he and his wife transcribed the lyrics only after they had been completely formed in the poet's mind and speech.[13]

For the Mandelstam of "Fourth Prose" and the revealingly titled "Conversation," though, the idea of a corrupt and fallen written language is based not on Western cultural mythologies but on Soviet reality. When all agencies of printing, reproduction, and distribution lie in the hands of the government, any author "who first obtains permission and then writes" becomes involved in an act of collaboration with the state whose blessing he has received. He composes his work on what Mandelstam calls "watermarked police stationery" and his "authorized" writings thus take their place in a continuum that begins with state-sponsored poetry and ends with the state's most ominous decrees: "Crude animal fear hammers on the typewriters, crude animal fear proofreads the Chinese gibberish on sheets of toilet paper, scribbles denunciations, strikes those who are down, demands the death penalty for prisoners."[14]

In such a society, only unauthorized speech or, specifically, oral poetry, readily transmissible through the voice alone, can speak a language free of complicity in state atrocities; only the poet who works "from the voice" can hope to challenge its monopoly on written language. "They have sullied the most pure Word, / They have trampled the sacred Word (*glagol*)," Akhmatova writes in a lyric of the period, and Western logocentric mythologies are not what is at stake here, as Akhmatova's own poetry makes clear. In the prose text that opens *Requiem*, Akhmatova derives the authority to compose her tribute to the purges' victims not from any official source but from an unauthorized, oral communiqué from an anonymous fellow sufferer:

> In the terrible years of the Ezhov terror, I spent seventeen months in the prison lines of Leningrad. Once somebody "identified" me. Then a blue-lipped woman standing behind me, who had of course, never heard my name, came to from the torpor characteristic of us all and asked me in a whisper (everyone spoke in whispers there), "But can you describe this?"
> And I said, "I can."
> Then something like a smile slipped across what had once been her face.

As in the "Stalin Epigram," the poet justifies her civic, collective "we" by virtue of her ability to articulate aloud what other suffering Russians only whisper.[15]

Akhmatova resembles Mandelstam in her emphasis, here and elsewhere, on the face and mouth that articulate what Mandelstam calls "sounds forbidden for Russian lips." Both poets had drawn from the start on what Shklovsky terms "the articulatory dance of the speech organs" in creating their verse. Both Akhmatova and Mandelstam, Eikhenbaum comments in 1923, derive their poetic force from "the mimetic movement of the lips, the intensification of purely linguistic, articulatory energy." They turn this energy to new purposes in their later work. "A human, hot, contorted mouth / Is outraged and says 'No,'" Mandelstam writes in a poetic fragment from the thirties. Akhmatova and Mandelstam insistently call attention to the mouths, lips, and tongues that firmly root speech in the body that may be called upon to account for its verbal crimes against the state. Mandelstam makes these lips the basis for a defiant "underground" poetics in the opening lines of one late poem. "Yes, I lie in the earth moving my lips, / But every schoolchild will learn what I say," he announces defiantly from the grave to which he has been confined following his "civic funeral."[16]

Oral poetry is not the only genre that Mandelstam and Akhmatova practice in their efforts to avoid signing their names to the massive, collective text being spun out by the state apparatus with the assistance of the obedient tribe of hired scribes whom Mandelstam denounces in "Fourth Prose." Mandelstam and Akhmatova were effectively barred from print throughout the 1930s. They could have no hope of seeing their own names and poems printed in anything remotely resembling a conventional book, and the written form that their poems took were handwritten copies scrawled on scraps of paper or laboriously transcribed by hand into unprepossessing school copybooks. I'm thinking now of Mandelstam's "Moscow" and "Voronezh Notebooks" as well as the "burnt notebooks" Akhmatova commemorates in the *Poem without a Hero* (1940–66). "It is more honorable to be learned by heart, to be secretly, furtively recopied, to be not a book, but a copybook in one's own lifetime," Maksimilian Voloshin had written shortly after the revolution. His words proved prophetic.[17]

Mandelstam follows Voloshin's lead as he makes a virtue of necessity by turning humble, unpublished scraps of paper into a crucial genre of the underground poet. In the "Conversation about Dante," Mandelstam inverts the apparent order of things as he condemns "official paper" to oblivion and assigns true permanence only to the rough drafts (*chernoviki*) that cannot be captured on official paper and made to serve official purposes. "Rough drafts," he insists, "are never destroyed. . . . The safety of the rough draft is the statute assuring preservation of the power behind the literary work." It is a theory made to order for poets denied access to official paper of any sort, and Akhmatova provides testimony to its efficacy and force in the first dedication to her *Poem without a Hero*. "Since I didn't have enough paper, / I'm writing on your rough draft," Akhmatova explains, and the rough draft she has in mind can only be a page taken from one of Mandelstam's perpetually unfinished notebooks. She thus bears witness to the power of the unprinted word and to the indestructibility of the rough draft that has already outlived its less fortunate, more perishable creator.[18]

Akhmatova creates a telling variant on this poetics of the incorruptible rough draft in her late work. "Manuscripts don't burn," Mikhail Bulgakov proclaims in a famous phrase.[19] In Akhmatova's poetics of the unofficial text, manuscripts do burn, and poems do perish—and this is precisely what guarantees their integrity and, finally, their immortality. In her Stalin-era writings, Akhmatova cultivates the genre of the "burnt notebook" and its subsidiary, the "poems written for the ashtray": the phrases' meanings are both literal and metaphorical.[20] She was in fact forced to burn her private archives more than once, in the hopes of keeping illicit writings out of official hands. Some of the burned texts vanished for good—but others survived, either in her own memory or in the memories and copybooks of friends.

This literal destruction and resurrection of the poetic text prompts the metaphor that enables Akhmatova, the banned lyric poet, to take on Stalin himself as she forges her own collective, civic voice to speak for the masses who have been either figuratively or literally obliterated by Stalinist collective rhetoric. The lyric poem can fall victim to Stalinist oppression just as the lyric poet can, and their voices are suppressed for the same reason: they speak for the private, individual realm that the regime was bent upon destroying. In this distinctive redaction of the Romantic myth, poem and poet alike become arch-victims, the most fitting representatives of the millions of victims, whether living or dead, whose individual selves the state had worked to efface in the name of the collective.

For both Akhmatova and Mandelstam, their civic authority is under-written by their very perishability and the perishability of their works. It is precisely because the poets and their poems are subject to literal, physical death that they are authorized to speak for the dead and dying victims of a nation under siege by its own rulers. In their greatest "civic" poems, Mandelstam and Akhmatova turn Stalinist rhetoric on its head, as the artificial collective imposed from above meets its match in the genuinely communal voice that rises from below, through the throat of the poet prematurely consigned to civic burial. In the "Verses on the Unknown Soldier," Mandelstam employs the militaristic rhetoric of the Five Year Plans, with their class warfare, enemies of the people, saboteurs, provocateurs, and wreckers, to recruit his own idiosyncratic infantry of misfits and ne'er-do-wells. And, as Susan Amert demonstrates in her study of the late work, Akhmatova in her *Requiem* counters the state's inflated rhetoric of the "motherland" with her own "song of the motherland" woven from the wails of the wives and mothers left behind by Stalin's victims. "I renounce neither the living nor the dead," Mandelstam announced shortly before his own death. And in their civic poetry Mandelstam and Akhmatova speak for both the living and the dead by virtue of their faith in the lasting power of dead authors and dead books.[21]

4

Akhmatova and the Forms of Responsibility: *The* Poem without a Hero

If only Russia had been founded
by Anna Akhmatova . . .
                            —Adam Zagajewski, "If Only Russia"

Haunted Houses

Remorse—is Memory—awake—
Her Parties all astir—
A Presence of Departed Acts—
At window—and at Door—
            —Emily Dickinson, "Remorse—is Memory—awake" (1863)

"Il faut que j'arrange ma maison (I must put my house in order)," said
the dying Pushkin.
            —Anna Akhmatova, "A Word about Pushkin" (1952)

I found when I had finished my lecture that it was a very good house,
only the architect had unfortunately omitted the stairs.
                            —Ralph Waldo Emerson, quoted in
                            Barbara Packer, Emerson's Fall (1982)

In 1884, a middle-aged widow began work on a house in California's
Santa Clara Valley, near San Francisco; the construction ended only with her
death several decades later, in 1922. The builder's name was Sarah Winchester.
Her deceased husband, William Winchester, had inherited a vast fortune from
his father, who had manufactured the first successful repeating rifle, a weapon
whose lethal efficiency had influenced the outcome of the Civil War. The cou-
ple's only child had died in infancy, and William himself fell victim to tuber-
culosis in 1881, leaving Sarah the sole heir to the family's ill-gotten—as she
thought—wealth. The grieving widow came to believe that her husband's and
child's deaths were the work of the many unhappy spirits whose lives had
been cut short by the rifles that bore the family name. "You must start a new
life," a medium told her, "and build a home for yourself and for the spirits
who have fallen from this terrible weapon too. You can never stop building. If
you continue building, you will live. Stop and you will die."[1]

Mrs. Winchester took the medium at her word. "She had her pick of
local workers and craftsmen," a local historian records, and for nearly forty
years, "they built and rebuilt, altered and changed and constructed and
demolished one section of the house after the other." There were no blue-
prints: Mrs. Winchester presumably chose not to provide angry ghosts with
a readymade road map to the intentionally baffling building. She sketched
out tentative plans instead on scraps of paper and tablecloths. The house
eventually grew to include some 160 rooms—doubts still exist as to the
precise number—of which approximately forty were bedrooms. She slept in
a different room every night in order to evade the vengeful phantoms that
might otherwise trouble her sleep; an elaborate system of bells alerted ser-
vants to her whereabouts. Mrs. Winchester and her builders devised other
ways to outwit the restless spirits that plagued the unhappy house. "There
were countless staircases which led nowhere; a blind chimney that stopped
short of the ceiling; closets that opened to blank walls; trap doors; double-
back hallways; skylights that were located one above another; doors that
opened to steep drops to the lawn below; and dozens of other oddities,"
according to the local chronicler.[2]

What does Mrs. Winchester's perpetually unfinished Mystery House (its
tour book title) have to do with Anna Akhmatova's incomplete magnum
opus, *Poem Without a Hero*? An unfinished epic born of Stalinist Russia
would seem initially to share little with an architectural oddity that now
serves chiefly to draw tourists to an unprepossessing corner of the Bay Area.
Both, though, are the work of women who could not shake the sense that
they were haunted by the sins of the past, their own and others': "How can
it turn out / That I'm to blame for all," the speaker laments in the *Poem*

(2:125). Their only hope for some form of salvation, however problematic or provisional, was to labor away at their life's work by way of atonement—or evasion. Akhmatova began writing the *Poem* in 1940, "the year in which worlds collapsed" (1:229), and the year in which she completed her master-piece *Requiem* (1935–40). Unlike Sarah Winchester, she apparently planned to finish her project: 'The Poem's text is final. No future additions or omis-sions are foreseen," she wrote hopefully at the end of several variants (2:367). Still each ostensibly completed version ended, like its precursors, by requir-ing endless amendments, appendages, and renovations. "[I] was continually adding to and revising something that was to all appearances finished," Akhmatova confesses in one of her numerous prose commentaries on the *Poem*. She kept rewriting it until her death in 1966, and arguments continue to this day as to which of the poem's many manuscripts came closest to its author's final wishes.[3]

My guess would be that this confusion, like the intentionally bewildering structure of the Mystery House, is precisely the legacy its creator intended to leave for future generations of baffled admirers. The *Poem* became a ready-made companion piece to *Requiem,* a "fellow traveler" (*poputchitsa*) that "walked beside it," Akhmatova remarked in 1961. The pair seems singularly ill matched in several respects. Indeed, their creator herself commented on the incongruity of placing the "funereal" *Requiem* alongside her "motley" *Poem,* at once "clowning and prophetic": *Requiem,* she remarked, would have been better served by a sisterly "Silence" at its side.[4]

Akhmatova speaks here of tone, and she is right: *Requiem*'s wrenching sobriety is scarcely a fit for the *danse macabre* of the *Poem*'s first part or the satiric wit of the second. Other disparities are just as glaring. Like so many modern verse epics, both *Requiem* and the *Poem* create their own forms rather than adhering to time-honored templates. These forms could not be more different, though. *Requiem* is both encompassing and compact; a nation's torments are miraculously contained within the space of eight or ten pages. The *Poem,* on the other hand, incorporates three wildly disparate sections, with varied lengths, structures, tones, and topics—not to men-tion addenda ranging from stage directions to quasi-scholarly footnotes and bits of ostensibly private correspondence. It also comes encumbered by an unwieldy entourage of proliferating variants and commentaries: "Again the Poem doubles," Akhmatova observes in 1961, "something going alongside—another text . . . since the Poem is so capacious, not to say bottomless."[5]

When Alexander Solzhenitsyn first heard *Requiem* read in the early six-ties, he criticized what he saw as its inappropriate lyric self-absorption, and thus inadvertently echoed the Soviet critics who repeatedly attacked both

Akhmatova and her chosen genre for their bourgeois self-preoccupation. "But really, the nation suffered tens of millions, and here are poems about one single case, about one single mother and son," he chided the poet: "I told her that it is the duty of a Russian poet to write about the suffering of Russia, to rise above personal grief and tell about the suffering of the nation." He could not have been further from the mark. As Susan Amert notes, the sequence of ten lyrics that presents the speaker's Stalin-era Via Dolorosa is framed by the magnificent opening and closing texts that imbue the lyric "I"'s singular suffering with collective resonance:

> The hour of remembrance comes again.
> I see, I hear, I sense you:
>
> She who scarcely reached the window,
> And she who no longer treads native ground,
>
> And she, who tossed her pretty head
> And said: "Coming here is just like coming home."
>
> I wish I could call you all by name,
> But the list's been taken, there's nowhere to look.
>
> For them I wove this wide shroud
> Of their own poor words, which I overheard.
>
> I remember them always and everywhere,
> I won't forget them in new grief,
>
> And if others shut my tortured mouth,
> Through which a nation of a hundred million shrieks,
>
> Then let them recall me in turn
> On the eve of my memorial day . . . (1:369)

Lyric and epic merge in *Requiem,* as Akhmatova counters the Soviet's "state hymn" (2:125) of enforced collectivity with her own collective voice made up of the shattered selves and unheard words of the nation's tormented mothers and wives, including, of course, Akhmatova herself, who is both poet-prophet and fellow sufferer.[6]

The poet who ends *Requiem* defiantly proclaims her mandate to speak for the "hundred million" victims whose sufferings she commemorates. But Akhmatova's situation, as poet and person, was far more complex than *Requiem*'s magnificent conclusion might suggest. The imagined mon-ument—the poet as stone-clad Niobe—that concludes *Requiem* is Akhma-tova's retort to the bombastic mass grave that Mayakovsky celebrates in "At the Top of My Lungs" (1930): "Let our common monument be / the socialism built in battle," he crows. As Amert observes, the "nation of a hundred million" for whom Akhmatova claims to speak in *Requiem* is likewise a challenge to Mayakovsky's self-proclaimed collective authority, this time in an earlier work, "150,000,000" (1920): "150,000,000 speak through my lips," he insists in the poem's opening. Neither the ordinary reader nor the Soviet state saw fit to endorse his grandiose assertions in his lifetime. But were Akhmatova's pronouncements any better founded? She never saw *Requiem* published in its entirety in her native land—it first officially appeared in Russia only in 1988—though the periodic cultural thaws initiated by Khrushchev repeatedly raised her hopes. Instead a small circle of confidants committed the poem to memory, and Akhmatova would occasionally recite it to carefully selected individuals or groups. She feared even to write the full poem down, as her ritual of poem-burning attests. Even after Stalin's death Lydia Chukovskaya was reluctant to call the work by name in her clandestine *Akhmatova Journals*. The poem that claimed to speak for an entire nation could scarcely make itself heard even among the chosen few to whom it had been entrusted.[7]

"We cannot sympathize with a woman who does not know when to die," the Soviet critic Viktor Pertsov wrote of Akhmatova in 1925. In her bitterly ironic "On the Occasion of the Fiftieth Anniversary of My Literary Career," Akhmatova quotes from memory the review cum obituary that had marked the beginning of her protracted "civic death," with its intermittent, short-lived resurrections, some forty years earlier.[8] In the decades following Pertsov's pronouncement, Soviet readers, if they read her at all, saw her chiefly through the prism of a state censorship that presented her at best as a relic of a long-vanished past: "I'm so quiet, so simple, *Plantain, White Flock,*" Akhmatova writes mockingly in the *Poem* (2:125). She had remained frozen in time, the beloved—or reviled—"poetess" of the early collections, *Evening* (1912), *White Flock* (1917), *Plantain* (1921), and especially *Rosary* (1914).

Akhmatova laments her enforced solitude time and again in Chukovskaya's *Akhmatova Journals*. But such isolation can prove an—ambiguous—blessing to a poet reared on the Romantic myth of the poet-martyr, the poet-outcast: "No, without the hangman and the scaffold / The poet can't exist on earth," she writes only half-ironically in one version of her poem "Dante"(1936; 1:236). Chukovskaya recalls Akhmatova reciting a defiant poetic credo directed against those who would consign her to a premature "civic" burial:

> They'll forget me? Here's what startled them!
> I've been forgotten a hundred times,
> A hundred times I've lain in the grave,

Where I may be today.
And the Muse grew mute and blind,
Moldered in the earth like a seed,
So that afterwards, like the Phoenix from the ashes,
She might rise in the sky-blue ether.

"Did they publish Sappho? Did they publish Jesus Christ?" (2:187). Akhmatova quotes Mandelstam's phrases in her memoirs on her friend—but he was not alone in his vision of the unpublished poet as oppressed redeemer. Akhmatova seems to refer obliquely to Mandelstam's fate when she notes that "eleven people knew *Requiem* by heart, and not one of them betrayed me"; of the eleven to whom Mandelstam recited his infamous "Stalin Epigram," one proved to be a Judas, as the poet himself apparently anticipated.[9]

"Because he cannot escape the task of raising his voice against cruelty and injustice, the poet is *par excellence* the victim in a repressive society, a property which [*Requiem*'s] 'I' shares with others of her trade," Kees Verheul remarks; and, as Nancy Anderson observes, "for Akhmatova in the late 30's Russia was a nation of victims." Anderson also notes, though, that the Soviet Union's population at the time was about 170,000,000. What has become of the 70,000,000 not counted among in *Requiem*'s 100,000,000 sufferers? Certainly prosodic necessity plays a part in her choice here. Still, it is difficult to imagine her voluntarily ceding 50,000,000 Russians to Mayakovsky, whose "150,000,000" gave a rough approximation for the entire country's population at the time the poem was written. The question, though, is not her grasp of Stalin-era demographics; it is rather the nature of the collective voice and vision she conceives in her involuntary isolation.[10]

"Innocent Rus' [the noun is grammatically feminine in Russian] writhed / Beneath bloody boots, / And the tires of the Black Marias," Akhmatova writes in *Requiem* (2:363). Clearly the nation's oppressors, the wearers of bloodied boots and drivers of Black Marias, are not to be numbered among its true constituents. Does this division lie then, as the phrase I've just quoted suggests, along the lines of gender? Are the suffering women Akhmatova commemorates the true embodiment of an authentic, non-Soviet Rus'? In an essay on *Requiem* as a women's epic, Stephany Gould notes that the female population of Soviet Russia in the late thirties came close to the figure Akhmatova gives in her poem. But even here the poet's "we" proves problematic. Chukovskaya recalls reading *Sofia Petrovna*, her then-unpublished novella about the purges, aloud to Akhmatova in 1940. Like *Requiem*, the novella concerns women's sufferings under Stalin—but Chukovskaya's vision differs markedly from Akhmatova's in one regard. Like Akhmatova's speaker, and Akhmatova herself, Chukovskaya's

eponymous heroine loses her son to Stalin's purges. Unlike her poetic coun-
terpart, though, Sofia Petrovna refuses to recognize the wives and mothers
she meets in the prison lines as fellow victims: "She was sorry for them, of
course . . . but still an honest person had to remember that all these women
were the wives and mothers of poisoners, spies and murderers." She follows
the Party line that ruthlessly divides the faithful from the saboteurs and
traitors surrounding them even as that policy undoes both her son and her
own sanity. The "we" upon which Sofia Petrovna relies allies her with the
perpetrators, not their prey.[11]

Requiem's attempt to voice the experience of an authentic "we" as a chal-
lenge to the State's enforced collectivity must have seemed a heroic, but
doomed endeavor when the poem was first read and recited. In the event,
time proved Akhmatova right. The poem is internationally acknowledged as
both a masterwork of modern writing and one of the past century's greatest
testaments to an age of mass terrors. The lines in which the speaker yearns
to call each vanished companion by name are now "inscribed around the
memorial stone that commemorates the victims of repression in her adopted
city of St. Petersburg," Catherine Merridale comments. In violating the
State's interdiction forbidding mourning—the "traditional languages of
mourning" tempted forward-looking Soviet citizens to "face backward into
time, remember, brood on the realities of loss," the Bolsheviks warned early
on—Akhmatova managed to become, at least posthumously, her nation's
"muse of weeping."[12]

But Akhmatova's role as chief mourner for a stricken people is more com-
plex than *Requiem's* defiant epilogue suggests. "I called down death on
those I loved," she mourns in a poem written in 1921: "My word / Foretold
these graves"(2:209). Her lines proved all too prophetic. Her suspect poetry
and her personal fame would lead in coming decades to the repeated arrests
and protracted imprisonments of her son, Lev Gumilev. His unfortunate
last name, a lasting reminder of the poet-father executed for alleged coun-
terrevolutionary activities in the state's early years, did not help matters. Her
third husband, Nikolai Punin, was imprisoned in 1935 at least partly for the
crime of being married to Akhmatova.[13] The very poem in which Akhma-
tova struggled to articulate the nation's sufferings under Stalin might easily
have led, had it been discovered, to further sufferings for the son whose fate
she laments, as she well knew. Moreover, as *Sofia Petrovna* reminds us,
totalitarian systems are expert in implicating their victims in their crimes;
all who survive do so by the grace of the very state that has tormented their
families and friends. Akhmatova's lament in the *Poem's* second section—
"How can it turn out / That I'm to blame for all"—finds its counterpart in

a parallel phrase from Part One: "So how could it have turned out / That I'm the only one still living"(1:106). Her Silver Age cohort of poets and artists, the dramatis personae of the *Poem*'s first part, had largely vanished by 1940, from one more or less ominous cause or another. Survivors' guilt is a powerful force, especially when coupled with the inescapable complicity in an immoral system that was the regime's stock-in-trade.

"Isolate, but preserve": Stalin's dictate on Mandelstam's fate was followed far more faithfully in Akhmatova's case. Unlike Mandelstam and countless others, she survived the terror of the thirties, although at a great price. She escaped the devastating Nazi siege of Leningrad by way of a state-sponsored airlift to Tashkent organized in 1941 to ensure the safety of important cultural figures: "In the flying fish's belly / I was saved from the evil pursuit," she recalls in the *Poem* (2:131–32). The fifties saw her son in and out of camps, while she endured her persecutions not in prison, but in various tiny rooms in Moscow and Leningrad, with a small group of friends to assist her. "Ask my women contemporaries (*sovremmenitsy*)," Akhmatova writes in a passage omitted from later versions of the *Poem:*

> Convicts, exiles, captives,
> And we'll tell you,
> How we lived in frenzied fear,
> How we reared our children for the scaffold,
> The torture-chamber and the prison.
>
> Pressing our blue lips shut,
> Maddened Hecubas
> And Cassandras from Chukloma,
> We'll thunder in a soundless chorus
> (We, crowned with shame):
> "We dwell on the far side of hell."

Amert speculates that the stanzas were dropped from later variants "for censorship reasons." Certainly it is difficult to imagine this passage being any more palatable to the authorities than the earlier *Requiem*. And yet Akhmatova did apparently hope against hope that *Requiem* might appear in Soviet print one day, but she never tried to make the finished poem more acceptable to the regime through strategic omissions or alterations. Just the opposite. She carefully monitored the memories of the select few who had learned the work in its entirety to check for mistakes and deviations.[14]

I suspect that Akhmatova had other reasons for excluding the offending stanzas. The chorus of outraged wives and mothers, past and present, she evokes here is clearly of a piece with the Stalin-era women whose ranks are joined first by the grief-stricken widows of Peter the Great's *streltsy*, his military elite, and finally by the mother of Christ herself in *Requiem*. Akhmatova's speaker enters this particular chorus by way of the back door, though. "Ask my contemporaries," she commands the unnamed "you" (*ty*) to whom she speaks: it is her contemporaries, not she, who swell the ranks of Stalin's female "convicts, exiles, captives" (*katorzhanok, stopiatnits, plennits*). She joins in their "we" (*i tebe rasskazhem my*) only once they have been transformed from prisoners themselves into the mothers of Stalin's victims and martyrs; "we reared children for the scaffold," she reminds her unnamed auditor. "The *Poem* takes its voices both from beyond the 'barbed wire,' and beyond the 'Iron Curtain,'" Roman Timenchik notes. But the voices that reach her from beyond camp walls in the poem's "Epilogue," its third and final segment, are not her own:

> From beyond barbed wire,
> In the dense taiga's very heart—
> I don't know the year—
> Now a handful of camp dust,
> Now a tale from a chronicle of terror,
> My double goes for interrogation. (2:130)

This double endures the first-hand agony that Akhmatova herself had eluded by chance or fate. "Always through her own 'non-death (*nepogibel'*),'" she heard "sounds *from there*, from the mirror world of the taiga (*taezhnogo zazerkal'ia*)," Chukovskaya comments. "She discerned the sounds and outlines of the other, inevitable destiny she had miraculously escaped." Akhmatova had not been forced to follow the "funeral route" to the east "along which they led my son," as she writes in the *Poem*'s epilogue (2:132). She had likewise been spared the bombardment that had left her beloved "city in ruins" "seven thousand kilometers away" from her safe haven in Tashkent (2:129). What comes under siege in the *Poem* is instead precisely the choral "we" of the omitted stanzas and of *Requiem*, the "we" that triumphally asserts the speaker's right and obligation to speak for all the suffering women of her tormented nation.[15]

"150,000,000 is the name of this poem's master," Mayakovsky crows in the opening of his would-be revolutionary epic. As the poet Anatoly Nayman observes, *Requiem* is not simply a repudiation of official Soviet writing. It is also a continuation of the genre that Mayakovsky hoped to initiate: "Strictly speaking, *Requiem* is the ideal embodiment of *Soviet poetry* that all the theorists describe. . . . This is poetry which speaks on behalf of the people and for the people. Its language is almost that of the newspaper;

it is accessible to the people." "The hero of this poetry is the people," he remarks. But "who is the hero of the poem without one?" as Lev Loseff asks. The secondary literature attempting to identify the poem's prototypes and locate its enigmatic hero is vast, and I will not attempt to summarize it here. What interests me is the conspicuous absence of a coherent hero in the *Poem*. The speaker-heroine of *Requiem* may contain multitudes. but the *Poem*'s attenuated speaker might well complain with Mandelstam that "there is not enough of me left for me."[16]

One of the *Poem*'s key features, Kees Verheul observes, is "the peculiar lack of stability in the personal identity of the I."[17] Instead of multiple subjects subsumed into the speaker's defiant voice, we get a self split into proliferating alter egos and doubles, as the poet's voice alternates with or is transmitted by the series of personified nouns that ventriloquize the poem as it progresses. Its narrative, such as it is, is advanced or interrupted at various points by "words out of darkness" (*slova iz mraka*, lines 161–179); an unidentified voice (221–350); an unnamed woman or her shadow (*ten'*), (206–221); the wind, which "recalls or prophesies" 351–398; Silence (*Tishina*) which recites lines 399–439; the poet's conscience (*sovest'*, 440–451); a theme (*tema*) rapping at the window (454–455); and the curiously disembodied "author's voice" (*golos avtora*) which concludes the poem and which is presented in much the same way as sui generis earlier narrators such as "the wind" or "Silence."[18] This is not to mention all the other human voices and quoted texts that have their say in other passages, or the human doubles who may or may not speak for the poet herself.

I have not yet identified the most important of these poetic surrogates, though: this is the *Poem* itself, or better, herself. *Poema*, the Russian word for "epic" or "narrative poem" as opposed to lyric, is grammatically feminine, and Akhmatova is quick to exploit the possibilities that this bit of grammatical serendipity affords. Within the *Poem* proper, it is easy enough to distinguish the *Poem* as text from the *poema* as character. Near the end of the *Poem*'s second section, "Obverse" (*Reshka*), the *poema* herself awakens to wrest temporary control of the text from its ostensible creator:

> But the hundred-year-old enchantress
> Awoke suddenly and wanted
> To make merry. I'm beside the point . . .
>
> . . . . . I had no idea how
> To rid myself of this lunatic:
> I threatened her with the Star Court
> And chased her back to her native garret—(2:127)

The poet apparently does not pack the *poema*-Pandora back into her box quickly enough, though. The interloper manages to commandeer the final two stanzas of "Obverse," in which she contradicts the poet's account of the genre's literary origins: "My only genealogy / Is sunshine and legend, / July itself brought me forth"(2:127).

The *poema*'s cameo performance as narrator is relatively short within the *Poem* itself. But the line between the two blurs beyond the boundaries of the poetic text proper. A personified version of the *Poem* features prominently in two of the prose texts appended to later variants. "It came to visit me for the first time at the House on the Fontanka on the night of December 27, 1940 . . . I hadn't summoned it," Akhmatova explains in "In Place of a Preface," while in the "Letter to N.," she complains that "the *Poem* has tracked me down time and again, like attacks of an incurable disease" (2:99). Many poets have, of course, been subject to unexpected visitations of the muse; there is nothing so unusual in this. But this particular muse cum doppelgänger seems to have demonstrated remarkable persistence. One of the *Poem*'s most salient features, Akhmatova writes in her notes, is "how it has persecuted me"(3:157). She details the nature of this torment in other prose fragments: "Sometimes the Poem aspired to become a ballet, and then nothing could hold it back"; "More than anything, it tormented me in Leningrad in 1959, turning again into a tragic ballet." And she is not the *Poem*'s only prey: "People simply come in off the streets and complain that the *Poem* has tormented them," Akhmatova moans. At times the *Poem* bears a disconcerting resemblance to Gogol's renegade "Nose." What should be a mere appendage of its owner asserts its independence and upstages its would-be master: "It really was behaving very badly, so much so that I fully intended to deny that it was mine, like the owner of a dog that has bitten someone in the street who assumes an air of ignorance and strolls off without quickening his pace." "Rumor has it," she complains elsewhere, "that it is trying to overpower other works of mine that are in no way related to it, and, in this manner, to distort both my literary development (such as it is) and my biography."[19]

Akhmatova receives her "social command" (*sotsialnyi zakaz*) in *Requiem* from the anonymous "woman with the blue lips" who asks "Can you describe this?" to which the poet replies unhesitatingly, "I can." The finished poem represents the fulfillment of that promise: self, society (as opposed to state), and poetic form function in perfect accord. The Akhmatova of the *Poem,* on the other hand, takes her marching orders from "the old shaman woman" that is the work itself. Akhmatova is answerable neither for the poem ("it might be better if it were anonymous," she comments), nor to its audience. In the prefatory "Letter to N.," she relishes the outrage of those "women" who greet the apparently incomprehensible work with "sincere indignation"(2:98). She is, moreover, fully responsible neither for herself as speaker nor as biographical entity: the poem threatens to usurp her very life story, she insists.[20]

In *Requiem,* as Amert demonstrates, Akhmatova takes Soviet forms and turns them against the very state they are meant to celebrate, in part by filling these forms with profoundly un-Soviet content.[21] The *Poem*'s structural complexity and its programmatic inaccessibility mark it, on the other hand, as *formally* anti-Soviet.

> He shouldn't be very unhappy
> Or, more important, secretive. Oh, no!—
> The poet should be flung wide open,
> And obvious to his contemporaries. ("The Reader," 1959; 1:253)

Akhmatova's sardonic prescription for Soviet poetry is reversed in the *Poem*'s many variants: one of its incarnations within the text is after all the "Confusion-Psyche" (*Putanitsa-Psycheia,* 2:101) who appears in the "Second Dedication."[22] "The Soul selects her own Society— / Then—shuts the Door": the Soviet poet lacks the luxury of lyric isolation, of ignoring the "Majority" and neglecting "Emperors," that Dickinson claims in her famous poem. "My editor was unhappy," the poet remarks in the *Poem*'s second part, "he growled, 'There are three themes at once'":

> Having read the final phrase,
>   You don't know who's in love with whom.
>
> Who met whom when and why,
>   Who is dead and who's alive,
>   And who's the author, who's the hero—
> And why today we need such
>   Debates on the poet . . . (2:123)

Akhmatova might seem simply to be rehearsing what had long since become standard attacks on Modernist obscurity (she was reading Eliot and Joyce while the *Poem* was being written). But inaccessibility had ominous implications in a state that demanded that poets' doors be left "wide open" at all times.[23]

"The *Poem* shouldn't have a living room" (*V 'Poeme' ne dolzhno byt' gostinoi*), Akhmatova remarks to Chukovskaya by way of explaining one excision. This was also her way of limiting the public space in an intentionally hermetic construct. She herself, she comments elsewhere, is forced to "enter my own *Poem* by way of the back stairs." The funhouse structure of the *Poem*—"this box has a triple bottom," Akhmatova warns (2:126)—defeats easy access even for initiates. *Requiem* was intended as a common monument, accessible, in principle, to an entire nation of victims—but the Akhmatova of the *Poem* takes delight in thwarting even the cultural elite that is presumably its intended audience. She returned more than once to the multiple interpretations it generated with feigned shock and dismay: "When I hear that the *Poem* is a 'tragedy of conscience' (Viktor Shklovsky in Tashkent), an explanation of why the Revolution took place (I. Shtok in Moscow), a 'Requiem for all of Europe' (a voice from the mirror [i.e., Isaiah Berlin]), a tragedy of atonement, and God knows what else, I become uneasy. . . ." But both the poet-author and the poet within the *Poem*, its would-be speaker, can claim no superior interpretation; they likewise lose their way time and again in the very work they both inhabit and create.[24]

"Break down the four-square walls of standing time," Ezra Pound bids his fellow Modernists in an early lyric. Akhmatova puts his prescription into practice in the spectral house that is the *Poem*'s chief setting. It is a space meant to confound all who enter. The stage directions that open Parts One and Two place the action in the House on the Fontanka (*Fontannyi dom*), part of the former Sheremetiev complex in Petersburg where Akhmatova lived, by her reckoning, "for thirty-five years" (the actual tally was apparently much shorter). Her little room expands to include places from across time and space: the Sheremetiev Palace ballroom, a theater, the Wandering Dog Cabaret, her editor's office, and her friend Olga Glebova-Sudeikina's bedroom. These rooms behave, in turn, like the uncanny chambers of a Gothic penny dreadful: ceilings expand and contract, walls part, specters and demons appear in mysterious mirrors. Even segments of her own *Poem* are apparently delivered by the haunted house's phantasmal hands and voices. A furtive "conscience" drops charred manuscripts upon her windowsill and disappears (2:120), while the wind wailing in the chimney recites her rhymes (2:122). When she is forced to abandon the House on the Fontanka, and evacuate her beloved Leningrad, the poet herself becomes a ghost in Part Three, haunting the city under Nazi siege: "My shadow falls on your walls / My reflection appears in your canals / My footsteps sound in the Hermitage's halls" (2:131).[25]

"I live as if in someone else's house, a house I dreamed, / Where I perhaps have died," Akhmatova writes in a poem of 1957 (2:293). Homelessness is a recurrent theme in the late work; at times indeed it seems as if she called down death not just on the people she loved, but on the places she cherished as well. "The main feature of my biography," she tells Chukovskaya, "is

that all the houses I've lived in have been erased from the face of the earth."
From her exile in Central Asia, she imagines her home as the *Poem* itself:

> I can see my poem (*poema*)
> From the road's bend—it's cool there,
> As in a home, where the darkness is sweet
> And the windows are open from the heat,
> Where there's not a single hero,
> >   But the poppies spill across the roof like blood. (1:269)

Even in welcoming Tashkent, the Gothic mansion that is Akhmatova's home
in verse is haunted by the specter of some obscure, unpunished crime. The
reminiscences of the *Poem*'s first part "are centered around an unspecified
motif of CRIME [*sic*]," Verheul observes. The final part, too, is shaped by
guilt as a double marches to the doom that the poet herself has escaped.
"Sins and poets don't mix," the speaker insists in Part One (2:108). But she
herself is dogged by a sense of impending retribution for some unnamed
transgression. "Whose turn is it to grow fearful, / To start, recoil, yield /
Atone for an ancient sin," she asks; "No one will judge me," she reassures
herself a few lines later (2:106). The respite is short-lived, though: "I punish
myself and not you," she tells a fellow culprit elsewhere (2:112).[26]

"Won't you tell me . . . the answer to my life," the speaker begs at the
end of one section (2:118). Akhmatova herself refuses, though, to give any
of her readers the final word on her unfinalizable opus. She is bemused
by the confusion she strews among critics and admirers as she collates the
multiple interpretations which become, in turn, part of the ever-expanding
Poem's extended family of notes, quotes, and commentaries, both others'
and her own. Its endless construction becomes a way of deferring indefi-
nitely the questions of personal and poetic responsibility that it both raises
and deflects.

The Life of the Poem

*I asked if she would ever annotate the Poem without a Hero . . . She
answered that when those who knew the world about which she spoke
were overtaken by senility or death, the poem would die too; it would
be buried with her and her century.*
>   —*Isaiah Berlin,* Personal Impressions *(1980)*

There is no death—we all know that.
>   —*Akhmatova,* Poem without A Hero

Akhmatova intended the *Poem* to be "a synthesis of the most important themes and images of her entire oeuvre," A. I. Pavlovsky observes. Anatoly Nayman concurs: "In every sense, this work lies at the center of her *oeuvre,* her fate, and her biography." Akhmatova had hoped at one point to write an autobiography that would combine "the narrative of my life and the fate of my generation." The *Poem,* which threatens to take over both her literary development and her biography, has apparently supplanted the prose work intended to fuse her own life story with that of her contemporaries. It becomes, in other words, the kind of master poem that Lawrence Lipking calls, following Stevens, a "harmonium," a work in which the aging poet seeks both to summarize her or his life in art and to align it with the greater story of the age that shaped and was shaped by that life. The term "harmonium" may originate with Lipking and his *Life of the Poet* (1981). The impulse it designates, though, is an ancient one, as Lipking demonstrates; he traces its origins back to Virgil, whose "master creation" is the "sense of an inevitable destiny: his life as a poet." Lipking finds his prime exemplar of the modern "harmonium" in Eliot's *Four Quartets* (1935–42), whose dates coincide very nearly with those of Akhmatova's *Requiem.* The work it influenced, though, was *Requiem*'s eccentric companion piece, which takes one of its many epigraphs in altered form from Eliot's late masterwork.[27]

Akhmatova received a copy of the *Quartets* in 1947 from Boris Pasternak, who found the American poet's obscurity too far removed from his own stripped-down later style to be of much interest. But Akhmatova took to Eliot's poem instantly. "Ruins and waste lands are my specialty," she writes in a letter of 1943. Small wonder that she should be drawn to the work of a poet who had made his reputation and become the voice of his generation with his own *Waste Land* in 1922. Akhmatova may not have known Eliot's early masterpiece (I suspect that she did, although I have no direct evidence). But she would have found traces of the earlier poem's desolate landscape scattered throughout the later work. The *Quartets* revisit the waste lands of European culture in the aftermath of one war from the midst of yet another conflagration—-"The parched eviscerate soil / Gapes at the vanity of toil, / Laughs without mirth. / This is the death of earth ("Little Gidding," 1942)—as the poet struggles to synthesize his own beginnings and ends with those of his troubled century.[28]

"My future is in my past" (2:122): the epigraph to the *Poem*'s second part has no direct counterpart in the *Quartets,* although Akhmatova attributes it to Eliot in early versions of the text (2:387). It echoes several of the *Quartets*' best-known phrases, though, as V. N. Toporov notes: "Time present and time past / Are both perhaps present in time future"; "In my beginning is my end," and so on. Toporov scrupulously traces the many echoes and reminiscences of Eliot's work in the *Poem*. For all that, though, the differences between the works are finally more salient and more significant than their similarities. The middle-aged Eliot was urgently concerned, Lipking notes, with meeting his own criterion for poetic success, which involved the creation of the poetic masterpiece that would reveal "a significant unity in his whole work." "An aging poet in this state of mind has no time for incidents or interruptions; he needs to arrive at his destination," Lipking comments. The destination at which Eliot arrives by the *Quartets'* conclusion seems determined at least in part by this very need to end conclusively and meaningfully, and to bring us along with him. "What we call the beginning is often the end / And to make an end is to make a beginning. / The end is where we start from," he reminds us, perhaps too insistently as the poem draws to a close. "We shall not cease from exploration," he proclaims in another well-known passage, "And the end of all our exploring / Will be to arrive where we started / And know the place for the first time." The tentativeness with which he begins the *Quartets*—"Time present and time past / Are both *perhaps* present in time future" (my italics)—is replaced in its ending by a programmatic assurance that includes both the poet and his audience: "we call," "we shall," "we will," he intones.[29]

"I was born in the same year as Charlie Chaplin, Tolstoy's *Kreutzer Sonata,* the Eiffel Tower, and it seems, T. S. Eliot," Akhmatova writes in her "Pages from a Diary"(1957). The date is off by a year in Eliot's case—but to these virtual contemporaries the century whose birth they witnessed must have seemed very different indeed. Such distinctions would not have been lost on Akhmatova as she first encountered the *Quartets*. The voices of her *Poem* come at times from beyond the Iron Curtain, Timenchik reminds us. The Eliot of the *Quartets* represents one such voice; the curtain had descended in 1946, just a year before Akhmatova came upon his little book. This was also the year of the infamous Zhdanov Resolution that marked the end of the relative cultural leniency of the war years. The resolution singled out Akhmatova and the prose writer Mikhail Zoshchenko as relics of a reprehensible bourgeois past that had no place in the newly triumphant Soviet socialist state. "The counterrevolutionary poetess" was excluded from the Writers' Union shortly afterwards; and any hope of publishing her work in state-controlled presses—and there were no others—vanished with her Union membership.[30]

The extended poem in which Eliot brings his life in art to its necessary conclusion not only managed to appear in print. Its claims to be a fitting end to a lifetime of writing were ratified by the Swedish Academy when Eliot received the Nobel Prize in 1948. For Akhmatova, the state, not the artist, claimed the right to place the period at the close of her life's work, and this period had been placed in a prerevolutionary Russia long since consigned to history's dustbin. Her borrowed epigraph takes on new meaning in this context. Even those admirers who remembered her work knew her chiefly, with a few exceptions, as the lady love poet of Russia's vanished Silver Age, as Akhmatova complains repeatedly to Chukovskaya. Her artistic present and future had been officially confined to a history that meant only one thing in Soviet terms: "the accursed tsarist past." Perhaps the programmatic inconclusiveness of her *Poem*—so unlike Eliot's desire to reach "the end of all his exploring" in the *Quartets*—represents in part her right *not* to end in spite of repeated efforts to strike her name "off the lists of the living."[31]

The Eliot of the *Quartets,* like all aging poets, is "haunted by the ghost of his past," Lipking remarks. For much of her Soviet-era existence, Akhmatova was herself viewed as the ghost of both her own and her nation's history. Following the Zhdanov Resolution, the most ruthless of her many "civic deaths," she led what she calls an "almost posthumous existence." This was not the first of her protracted "posthumous" periods: until the publication of her wartime poetry, the Soviet poet and editor Aleksandr Tvardovsky had "thought she was long dead, along with Blok, Briusov, and Gumilev," he notes in his diaries. "Every attempt at a continuous narration in memoirs is a falsification," Akhmatova comments in her "Pages from a Diary." Her observation may seem a mere Modernist truism, dating as it does from the late fifties. But Modernist clichés take on new meaning in what Akhmatova called the Soviet "Royal Court of Wonderland."[32]

Both her life and her work were filled with gaps not of her own making: "imposed lacunae and censor's omissions" punctuated the biography and poetry alike, Chukovskaya remarks. "Will they guess what's been left out?" Akhmatova asks Chukovskaya while preparing one of the several abortive *Selected Poems* that she hoped would one day find their way into print. Her question held for the life-in-art as well, which was distorted on both sides of the Iron Curtain, as she complains to Chukovskaya. The chief Western sources of information were no less distorted, she argues, than their Soviet counterparts. "They act as if I wrote nothing for twenty years. . . . And how could they possibly know, since I couldn't appear in print," she fumes.[33]

The *Poem,* Akhmatova moans in her notebooks, aims to distort her life and work alike. It engages, in other words, in the same sort of sabotage that has been inflicted upon Akhmatova by the Soviet state—or so her mock-serious lament suggests. Her comment provides yet another way of approaching the *Poem*'s various forms of difficulty: it is a peculiarly inharmonious harmonium. The state strives to strip Akhmatova of responsibility for both life and art, and the *Poem* mimics its inhospitable master. Akhmatova suggests the state's invasive power in several ways. The omitted lines and stanzas that punctuate Part Two remind us with their ghostly ellipses of the censor's role in shaping Soviet art, and of the venerable tradition of Russian censorship: the device is borrowed, of course, from Pushkin's *Onegin*. She refers in the same section to another long-standing Russian tradition, the trick of smuggling contraband content into literature by way of Aesopian language: her poem has "a triple bottom," she warns, and is written in "mirror script" (2:126). But the author herself is finally "beside the point," she confesses a few lines later (2:127). The threats to her autonomy derive from two sources: the *Poem* itself, that "century-old enchantress" who repeatedly usurps her role as author (2:127); and a regime that opposes in principle the very notion of the poet's "I." "Will I dissolve in the state hymn," she worries (2:125). The threats come from different sources and are treated with different degrees of seriousness—but their end result in each case is the diminution of an autonomous speaking subject. The poem's would-be hero is in either instance consigned to a less than heroic role.

Akhmatova dramatizes her plight as *poeta non grata* in the *Poem* in other ways. Endings and origins coincide by the conclusion of Eliot's *Quartets*. The life that is the *Poem*'s ostensible subject, on the other hand, stubbornly refuses to add up. This is not simply a matter of the intentional gaps and inconsistencies that riddle the work, nor of the multiple doubles drawn from different times and places who make it difficult at times to ascertain who is leading what life when and where. In Soviet Russia's "pre-Gutenberg era," a work that never officially appeared in print continued to lead a mysterious half-life in the multiple variants that made their clandestine way through the literary underground, regardless of authorial intent: unofficial texts have no copyrights. Akhmatova turns this situation to her advantage with the *Poem*. "The Poem's text is final," she claimed on more than one occasion. But by circulating multiple, conflicting manuscripts, she undermined—intentionally, I suspect—the capacity of any reader, contemporary or future, to determine which is the fixed, authoritative version of the text, and which is merely a wayward draft gone astray. For all her disavowals of responsibility for the headstrong *Poem*, Akhmatova makes sure that the final word always lies with an author who, willy-nilly, must hide behind the scenes, waiting to abridge, expand, or annotate each time the work seems in danger of reaching its conclusion.[34]

For Mikhail Bakhtin, Caryl Emerson comments, "death is the ultimate aesthetic act, a gesture that turns the whole of my life over to the other person, who is then free to begin an aesthetic shaping of my personality."[35] Through her unwillingness or inability to finish her magnum opus, Akhmatova resists such finalization, at least for her life in verse. She thus limits the freedom of readers hoping to find the key to the life in the work. I use the present tense here advisedly; the controversies around the *Poem*'s variants demonstrate that Akhmatova succeeded in keeping the upper hand even from beyond the grave. Seen this way, the question of poetry and responsibility seems to have come full circle, with Akhmatova asserting her power even as she dramatizes and laments her impotence, poetic and personal, in the *Poem* and the texts surrounding it. Indeed, the *Poem*'s first part particularly raises and complicates questions of the poet's responsibility for the very state of affairs that has led to her oppression.

The Theater of the World

Soviet political theater acquired a mythic dimension in the mid- to late 1930's, when Stalin cast himself as father of the nation. Earlier in the decade the nation had been the fatherland, but now it became the homeland or motherland in implicit union with the great father.
　　　—Jeffrey Brooks, Thank You Comrade Stalin! *(2000)*

Thus far I've interpreted Akhmatova's quasi-Eliotian epigraph as a response to a state that repeatedly attempted to relegate the poet and her work to a long-dead past. But this is only one possible interpretation of her gnomic phrase. Another variant—"As in the past the future ripens / So the past molders in the future" (2:107)—appears early on in the *Poem*'s first part, entitled "Nineteen Thirteen: A Petersburg Tale." And the "diabolical harlequinade" (2:122) that dominates the *Poem*'s most extended segment suggests ways in which the Soviet future may indeed have germinated in Akhmatova's, and Russia's, not so distant history. When Akhmatova read an early version of the *Poem*'s opening to Marina Tsvetaeva, Tsvetaeva responded "rather acidly," Akhmatova recalls, that "it takes nerve to write about all those harlequins, columbines, and pierrots in 1941." Harlequins, Columbines, and Pierrots: it doesn't require much effort to recognize the stock figures that were Blok's signature in "The Puppet Show" (1906) and elsewhere. Blok's poetic personae and their paramours are recurring characters in the "Petersburgian diaboliad" (2:108) that dominates Part One: the "Heroine," Akhmatova's friend, the actress Olga Glebova-Sudeikina, plays the roles both of Blok's "Columbine" and the "Donna Anna" from his "Steps of the Commendatore" (2:112); while Blok himself appears, inter alia, alongside his own Commendatore at one point in the *Poem,* and as the besotted cavalier who sends a rose to his unknown lady in "The Restaurant" at another (2:114). His chief role, though, is the demonic "man-epoch" (*chelovek-epokha*: 2:412), who sets the tone both for this Petersburg Walpurgisnacht, and for the age it embodies.[36]

Shortly before her death Akhmatova referred to the *Poem* as a "polemic with Blok." Why should Blok be Akhmatova's embodiment of an age gone terribly wrong? "All the women [in the Stray Dog Cabaret] turned into Columbines, young men who could love Columbines—into Harlequins, and enthusiasts and dreamers—into poor and sad Pierrots," one of Akhmatova's contemporaries comments. Blok was arguably his age's most accomplished practitioner of the "life-creation" I discuss in Chapter 1, and he inspired his admirers both by his own example and through the work that expanded not just their repertoire of roles, but also the rules on how to play them. What Akhmatova gives us in Part One is life-creation gone berserk. It is virtually impossible to draw a clear-cut line between the real-life figures taken from her prerevolutionary past and their theatrical counterparts, drawn largely from a fin de siècle stockpile of favorites: Faust, Dorian Gray, Don Juan, Casanova, Salome, the Demon, miscellaneous fauns and bacchantes, and so on.[37]

"Is this a mask, a skull, or a face," Akhmatova's puzzled speaker asks in Part One (2:106). The skull here is no accident: Silver Age "life-creation" had a nasty habit of turning into something far more sinister, Vladislav Khodasevich suggests in his tellingly titled *Necropolis* (1939). The "cranberry juice" shed by Blok's hapless Pierrot in "The Puppet Show" "sometimes turned out to be real blood" when Symbolist dramas were played out in reality, Khodasevich warns. And "Renata's End" (1928), his cautionary tale of life-creation gone awry, gives a variant of the story underlying the *Poem*'s first part. In the essay, Khodasevich describes the stormy life and death by suicide of a young would-be writer, Nina Petrovskaya, who makes the mistake of falling in love first with Blok's erstwhile companion-in-arms Andrei Belyi, another champion "life-creator," who soon abandons her "all too human love" in his quest for a transcendent "Woman Clothed with the Sun"; and then with the self-consciously demonic Valerii Briusov, who promptly makes artistic capital of their affair by writing it into his novel *The Fiery Angel.*[38]

Nina Petrovskaya killed herself only in 1928, after years of failed efforts to transform her life into art, to convert "her personality into an epic poem (*poema*)," Khodasevich tells us.[39] Akhmatova's thwarted "dragoon Pierrot" (2:115), the young poet Vsevolod Kniazev, did not outlive the Silver

Age culture that shaped and finally destroyed him; he committed suicide in 1913 upon discovering the infidelity of his chosen "Columbine," Glebova-Sudeikina. In other ways, though, their stories are strikingly similar. As commentators have noted, Kniazev's ghost haunts Part One, from the "First Dedication" bearing his initials, to the fourth chapter's epigraph, taken from one of his lyrics (2:101, 110, 119). Why should the death of a "silly boy" "who couldn't bear his first injuries" (2:120) prove the fulcrum around which the *Poem*'s enigmatic opening act revolves? Well, in the first place, he is the single figure foolish enough to attend the sinister masquerade clad only in his hapless human face: "You came here without a mask," the speaker reproaches him (2:111). Like the unfortunate Nina, his love also proves all too human, and the blood he sheds is genuine: "Why does a trickle of blood / Inflame your petal cheeks?" the speaker asks (2:111).

And like Nina Petrovskaya, he has the ill fortune to fall in love with some of the era's premier "life-creators": first, the poet Mikhail Kuzmin and, more to the point for my purposes, Glebova-Sudeikina, in whom Akhmatova saw the age personified. "Olga Sudeikina was a woman of her time down to her toes, hence closest of all to Columbine," she comments in one prose fragment. The actress becomes Blok's female foil in the *Poem,* a walking theater, a "human role" (*chelovek-rol'*), as one memoirist called her, who continues to play her various parts regardless of the toll they take on those around her (2:380). Khodasevich uses Nina Petrovskaya's troubled life to critique the "life-creating method" that he was the first to identify. He takes Blok to task for placing her death "in quotation marks"—"Nina Ivanovna Petrovskaya is 'dying,'" Blok writes in his notebooks—and rejects the Silver Age "cult of personality" that replaces "genuine, personal, concrete emotion" with its ersatz Symbolist substitute for the sake of cosmic drama. I have mentioned the language of guilt and retribution that runs through the *Poem*'s first part—and I am far from the first reader to see the work as what Shklovsky calls "a Poem of Conscience." Can Akhmatova's Silver Age morality play be read then, like Khodasevich's essay, as an attack on the lethal "life-creation" it so skillfully recreates?[40]

Certainly the entire *Poem*—indeed all of Akhmatova's late writing—works to undermine the Silver Age clichés she exposes in Part One. "There is no death—we all know that / It doesn't bear repeating" (2:109), the speaker remarks sardonically. In the *Poem* itself, though, the dragoon's—very real—suicide is only a prelude to the spectacular "range of deaths"(2:120) that would soon become available to artists and ordinary mortals alike. The poet "bears no guilt for anything. . . . / Poets and sins don't mix" she comments elsewhere (2:108). But the entire work bears witness to the force of at least one poet's sense of responsibility. It is the speaker's "old conscience," after all, who serves as her obdurate muse by unearthing the "burnt tale" of love and betrayal that becomes the unruly *Poem* (2:120).

The speaker is to blame for everything, she laments (2:125). But why is this speaker—who is clearly meant to represent Akhmatova as both poet and biographical entity—responsible for the amoral Silver Age antics of her contemporaries? In the same prose fragment where Akhmatova identifies Glebova-Sudeikina as the age's female incarnation, she also absolves herself of any obligations for her dubious heroine's behavior: "this shadow has assumed a separate existence and no one—not even the author—is responsible for her." Here as elsewhere, though, the *Poem* operates at cross-purposes with the author's own commentary. Glebova-Sudeikina was in fact one of Akhmatova's closest friends for many years; and the speaker herself confesses that this "Columbine of the 1910's" is "one of my doubles" (2:114). We needn't go far afield to seek out the real-world affinities between the two women that led to this particular doubling. Akhmatova's theatrical bent is evident in her many portraits, self-created or otherwise, and her contemporaries noted her flair for self-dramatization early on. "She holds herself like a queen in exile," the critic Lydia Ginzburg remarked following the revolution. The *Poem* hints at her theatrical gifts; the "black beads" and "lace shawl" the speaker wears while entering the world of her past evoke the characteristic costume of Akhmatova's early photographs and poetic self-portraits (2:106). And the pose she assumes before speaking—she turns "half-way" (*vpoloborota*: 2:105)—echoes Mandelstam's famous miniature of Akhmatova as tragic queen, "Half-way turned, oh sorrow" ("V poloborota, o pechal'," 1914).[41]

Time and again, moreover, Akhmatova implicates herself in her friend's most serious transgression: the suicide "is at your threshhold! / Across it . . . / May God forgive you," she writes in the *Poem* (2:120). Whose lines are these? Does the speaker address her erring heroine? Or does the poet's own conscience—who delivers the incinerated manuscript a few lines later—reproach her for half-forgotten sins? Akhmatova hints more than once in her conversations with Chukovskaya that she too had caused the suicide of a young man in the heyday of Symbolist life-creation and was thus complicit in the sins of her Silver Age contemporaries.[42] Be that as it may, within the *Poem* itself Akhmatova manages once again both to suggest and evade the question of her own answerability by way of her ambiguous doublings and shifting speakers.

All this still begs Tsvetaeva's tacit question: why on earth should Akhmatova resurrect her long-dead Harlequins and Columbines in 1941? Why dredge up some obscure Pierrot's suicide while worlds collide and crumble? In "Renata's End," Khodasevich attacks the Symbolist theatricalization of life that denigrates, even destroys "real feelings" along with the real human beings who possess them. Akhmatova's goal is finally, I think, quite different. Scholars have noted the puzzling overlap between her evocation of Kniazev's "senseless" suicide (2:120) and Mandelstam's death in the gulag in 1938. The *Poem*'s first dedication bears Kniazev's initials—"To the memory of Vs. K" (2:101)—but it is followed by the date on which Mandelstam was presumed to have died, December 27. Why would Akhmatova evoke in the same breath a "silly boy"'s romantic suicide, and the death of a friend martyred under Stalin? "I'm ready for death": Akhmatova recalls Mandelstam's phrase both in her memoirs and in the *Poem*'s first part (2:109), where it serves as a grim reminder of the real fate awaiting those poets who survived the Symbolists' satanic revelries unscathed. Both poets choose death—but one assumes the noble role of poet-martyr, while the other ends his life from thwarted love and wounded pride. By linking such disparate poet-victims, Akhmatova does more than merely accuse her Silver Age masqueraders of fiddling while Rome burned. Does she hint that their frivolous toying with life and death, a game that led more than once to real bloodshed, prepared the way for the large-scale life-and death-creation of the Great Impresario himself, Joseph Stalin? Does her forgotten poet-suicide prefigure in some way the massive bloodletting of the decades yet to come?[43]

Perhaps. But the year of Kniazev's death provides a more convincing link between 1913 and 1941. From her vantage point in the early 1940's, at the onset of yet another worldwide cataclysm, the poet sees what her misguided revelers cannot: "Along the legendary embankment / Not the calendar, but the real / Twentieth Century drew closer"(2:118). "He didn't know which threshold / He stood on, and which road / Would open before him," she writes of her love-struck poet. The words hold for all the "phrasemongers and false prophets" who populate the *Poem*'s first part (2:120, 107). Caught up in their petty, self-provoked tragicomedies, they miss the advent of the true cosmic drama then upon them, the drama that was still unfolding as she wrote and rewrote a lifework intended to be both retrospective and prophetic. This was the drama of the true Twentieth Century, a cosmic battle being waged by the one true State against the Poet and the Nation, and the fate of the human race hung in the balance. This was the drama that Mandelstam had anticipated when he spoke his appropriately prophetic line in 1934. This was the battle Akhmatova begins in *Requiem* and continues in the *Poem Without a Hero*.

The gaze of the Romantic poet-prophet, Ian Balfour writes, "penetrates beyond the props of everyday history to the theater of the world under the aspect of eternity."[44] Unlike Khodasevich, Akhmatova does not advocate a retreat from theatricality in favor of more mundane human emotions and experience. Just the opposite. "My lips no longer / kiss, but prophesy," she had written in 1915 (1:146). As a young poet, she may have fallen prey to Silver Age errors, but the price she had paid—and continued to pay—for past sins had also enabled her to take up her prophet's staff at last. She herself consents to play "the role of the fatal chorus" this time around; she will be her own collective in this cosmic drama (2:114). But she will also serve as the prophet who foretells and even directs the drama's action, as well as taking a leading role in the theater of modern history that the *Poem* enacts and predicts.

"She looked and moved like a tragic queen" and spoke "like a princess in exile," Isaiah Berlin remarked of his encounters with Akhmatova in Leningrad just after the war. Did he realize that he was repeating almost verbatim phrases first uttered decades earlier? Berlin recognized the poet's uncanny "genius for self-dramatisation." She was no less skilled at staging those around her—in art at least, if not always in life. Berlin not only inadvertently became one of the *Poem*'s most symbolically charged characters, the "Guest from the Future" whose shadow falls on the first part's macabre revelries (2:107). He proved to be one of its most astute interpreters as well, and Akhmatova integrates his remarks on the *Poem* into its ever-growing prose appendices. The meetings between Berlin and Akhmatova have been well described by Berlin and others, and I will not retell the story here. I want to focus instead on the part he played in the world-historical drama that Akhmatova saw at work in her life and strove to embody in the *Poem*.[45]

Berlin's spectral presence in the poem provides yet another gloss on Akhmatova's borrowed epigraph. The "Guest from the Future" "cannot penetrate" the ghost-filled ballroom that is one of the *Poem*'s chief sets. He is reflected, nonetheless, in "all its mirrors," and Akhmatova sets the stanza describing this mysterious guest smack in the middle of the haunted "white hall" filled with shadows from her past (2:107). The future—in the form of the stanza describing its human incarnation—is thus poetically embedded in the midst of the personal and cultural past that dominates the *Poem*'s opening segments. In Akhmatova's eyes, Berlin must have lent himself remarkably well to just such a juxtaposition. This young stranger from England, who was only the second foreigner she had met since 1917, knew not just her language and her culture, but even several friends who had formed part of the prerevolutionary milieu in which Part One of the *Poem* is set. Akhmatova's intuition, "almost second sight," had warned her to expect nothing less, she informed him.[46]

But the "Guest from the Future" was no mere reminder of past glories and shames. Akhmatova "saw herself and me as world-historical figures chosen by destiny to begin a cosmic conflict," Berlin comments. Indeed, circumstances seem to have conspired to imbue Berlin's visit with supernatural significance. His very name invited cosmic interpretation, combining as it did Old Testament prophecy with the city whose fate might be, as it soon seemed, to trigger the outbreak of World War III. Their first visit was interrupted, moreover, by no less a personage than Winston Churchill's son Randolph, who had foolishly gone looking for his friend. Of the Big Three, the former wartime allies, only Roosevelt was missing—since Stalin was, of course, always present in spirit, if not in fact. "Who is the third who walks always beside you," Eliot asks in *The Waste Land*. Akhmatova and her *Poem* are likewise shadowed by a mysterious "Other" whose spectral footsteps echo alongside their own. Uncanny doublings are, of course, the stuff the *Poem* is made of—but suspect Russian poets always recognized the possibility that their words might find an eager, if less than cordial, auditor in very high places. One identity for the *Poem*'s enigmatic companion and auditor might well have been, if not Stalin himself, then one of his many proxies. Indeed, shortly after Berlin's visits, a microphone was conspicuously installed in the poet's ceiling.[47]

In the modern poet's "heart of hearts," Auden observes, "the audience he desires and expects are those who govern the country." Such expectations were sometimes fulfilled in Stalin's Russia, where a poet's defiant words could reach a distant leader's ears, as Mandelstam had proven. And that ruler in turn might consult with yet another poet in the process of determining the blasphemer's fate, as in the famous phone call Stalin made to Pasternak about Mandelstam: "He's a master, isn't he?" he asked the flabbergasted poet. Stalin had taken an active interest in Akhmatova's fate for many years. "Where is Akhmatova? Why isn't she writing?" he reportedly asked at a meeting of literary prize winners in 1939—though he knew full well the answers to both questions. Akhmatova took pride in Stalin's "unflagging interest in her," according to one informant's report. And he was intrigued by her meetings with Berlin: "So our nun now receives visits from foreign spies," he allegedly remarked. Akhmatova saw Berlin's visits as partly to blame for her public fall from grace by way of the Zhdanov Resolution. In her "mysterious fate," he proved to be "the precursor of all my misfortunes," she writes in a later poem (1:293).[48]

The troubles he had caused were not limited to her life alone, the *Poem*'s "Third Dedication" suggests: "He will not become my dear husband / But we will earn the right / To trouble the Twentieth Century" (2:102). Their illicit conversations had far-reaching consequences, she insisted when she met Berlin once more twenty years later in Oxford: "we—that is, she and I—inadvertently, by the mere fact of our meeting, had started the cold war and thereby changed the history of mankind," he recalled.[49] Akhmatova was in earnest. Her vision of the poet's responsibility towards history has shifted radically since *Requiem*: she no longer simply preserves a forbidden past for posterity, as she had in the earlier poem. Through her words and actions, she actively, if at times unwittingly, changes the course of history in the making. Isaiah Berlin, the lifelong foe of historical master plans and fixed fates, whether singular or collective, inadvertently becomes Akhmatova's star-crossed accomplice in this predestined endeavor. "Beneath which starry signs / Were you and I born to woe?" she asks in a poem commemorating their encounters (1:284). This is the sweeping vision of poetic responsibility that finally shapes the *Poem*—or more precisely, that refuses to let it take a final shape.

For the *Poem*'s ending, true to form, has no final form. The different stanzas that conclude two of the fullest versions suggest, though, the nature of the prophetic vision that possessed Akhmatova in the last decades of her life. In one edition, the *Poem* concludes as follows:

> Seized by mortal dread
>> Of that which has become dust,
>>> And knowing the time for vengeance,
> With dry eyes downcast,
>> Wringing her hands, Russia
>>> Walked before me to the east. (2:132)

A more recent edition includes a final stanza found in a number of manuscripts:

>>> And en route to meet her own self,
>>> Unyielding into dread battle,
>>> As if from the mirror into reality,—
>>> Like a hurricane, from the Urals, from Altai,
>>> True to her duty, young
>>> Russia went to save Moscow.[50]

In both variants, Russia herself (Rossiia) becomes the last and most potent of Akhmatova's doubles: the nation springs from the mirror world of the *Poem* into reality itself, as the second text would have it. But this is no longer the meek, tortured Rus' who writhes beneath her tormentors' feet in *Requiem*. The violent potential implicit in the first ending ("knowing the time for vengeance") is realized in the second, where "young Russia" (*molodaia Rossiia*) plunges steadfast into battle (civil war?) in order to save the nation's revered ancient capital (another feminine noun, Moskva), presumably from the masculine state that had found its most ferocious embodiment in the Great Father, Joseph Stalin. Blok follows a long tradition of poet-prophets by courting the enigmatic Rus' that both surrounds and eludes him. Akhmatova puts a new spin on this Romantic tradition. As a woman poet, and a woman poet explicitly identified with old-world Russia by friends and enemies alike, Akhmatova can go her male colleagues and precursors one better. She and embattled Russia are female comrades-at-arms—the spurned, long-suffering woman takes revenge—or even mirror images. Shoulder to shoulder, they are ready to take on even the great dictator, the usurper father Joseph Stalin himself. She is thus the best and most fitting prophetic mouthpiece for her troubled nation and its destiny.

In either version, the *Poem* ends open-endedly—Russia's fate remains unknown—but this is the openness of a prophetic vision, not a Bakhtinian novel. The prophet walks a fine line, Balfour remarks. If his or her pronouncement is too specific, too narrowly construed, it dies with its creator or with the crisis that first called it forth. This is the scenario Akhmatova anticipates when she tells Berlin that the *Poem* "would be buried with her and her century." If the prophecy is too general, though, it loses its appeal to those contemporaries to whom it is at least partly directed, and whose situation it purports to address. Akhmatova claimed to despise "vaticination," "the poet's eye peering into a dimly discernible future," Berlin recalls. (This was during the same visit in which she informed him of their shared world-historical mission.) Her own *Poem* belies her claims, not least by its resistance to conclusion. Both final stanzas end in future-tending motion; the repeated verb form "shla" ([she] "went" or "was going") signals goal-driven action in progress, though attainment of the goal remains in doubt. By ending the *Poem* in multiple ways, moreover, Akhmatova projects the activity of interpretation into the future; neither its final version, nor its final meaning can ever be fully resolved. "Your Horoscope Is Long Since Cast," one of the *Poem*'s unearthly voices tells the speaker (2:116). But the poet alone is privy to this otherworldly prediction. The rest of us are left guessing at meanings that may still be unfolding as we read.[51]

The modern poet longs to gain the ear of the world's legislators, Auden warns. Akhmatova was not alone in her conviction that the poet played a key part in shaping the postwar world's fate. In 1962, nearly two decades after her encounters with Berlin, she met another illustrious foreign guest in Leningrad, Robert Frost. The purpose of his trip, which was sponsored by the American government, was to foster cultural bonds between the two superpowers. But Frost's plans were more ambitious. He encountered a number of eminent writers, and was duly impressed by Akhmatova's solemnity and sorrow. She was less taken by the ostentatiously folksy Frost, whose talk mixed poetry with lumbering and profits. "It was not fitting," she commented, "for a poet to reason in this manner." She recognized their shared eminence; "we're both candidates for the Nobel Prize," she told Chukovskaya. But the "muse of weeping" had more in common with the self-styled poet-farmer than she guessed.[52]

Frost overtly resisted all varieties of "postwar apocalypticism," James Longenbach remarks. "It is immodest of a man to think of himself as going down before the worst forces ever mobilized by God," Frost explains in his "Letter to 'The Amherst Student'"(1935). For all his studiedly homespun ways, though, he was "deeply committed to his poetic-prophetic-political role," his Russian-language interpreter, the Slavist F. D. Reeve, commented. "Frost prophesied the union of 'poetry and power' during the Kennedy presidency," Tom Paulin remarks, "because he shared Yeats's dangerous ambition of recovering the poet's ancient right to full membership of the state council." The backwoods prophet dreamed of meeting not only poets and artists, but, more importantly, the Soviet Union's commander-in-chief himself, Nikita Khrushchev. His dream was realized after some doing, and he and the Soviet leader talked for several hours. "We were charmed with each other," Frost recalled. "The poet's role in government," he told Khrushchev, was to bestow "character"—but his goals were not limited to character-building alone. He apparently hoped to resolve the conflict that Akhmatova, by her reckoning, had inadvertently begun through her meetings with Isaiah Berlin. During his talk with the Soviet premier, Frost suggested that East and West Berlin be reunited, thus ending the Cold War. Not surprisingly, Khrushchev proved less than amenable to his guest's suggestions. The American poet's forays into acknowledged legislation proved ineffectual, though Frost himself may not have realized it. "We're playing a great world game and with some style," he exclaimed delightedly after his visit. The game that Khrushchev was playing, though, was clearly public relations, and not the prophetic politics to which his would-be collaborator aspired.[53]

"We sat opposite one another in cozy armchairs," Akhmatova told Chukovskaya after her meeting with Frost. "I thought, 'every time that he was accepted somewhere, I was cast out. When he was rewarded, I was disgraced.'" But the life of the "disgraced poet" (1:236) has peculiar compensations, at least in its Stalinist incarnation. The very seriousness with which the dictator, whose visions of history are no less messianic than the poet's, takes his literary opponents would seem to encourage cosmic imaginings. Certainly that was the impression Berlin took from his meetings with Akhmatova and Pasternak alike. Pasternak, he recalls, returned repeatedly to the "cosmic turning points in the world's history, which he wished to discuss with Stalin." He saw World War II, like the revolution, as a "necessary prelude to some inevitable, unheard-of victory of the spirit," to which his still-unpublished *Doctor Zhivago* was destined to contribute. Pasternak "wished his work to travel over the entire world, to 'lay waste with fire' (he quoted from Pushkin's famous poem *The Prophet*) 'the hearts of men,'" Berlin remembers.[54]

In her conversation with Berlin, Akhmatova excoriated Chekhov for "the absence in his world of heroism and martyrdom, of depth and darkness and sublimity." But a world made up only of executioners and martyrs, evil overlords and heroic victims, may prove perilous to poets in their writing and lives alike. "Do not want to die for us, / do not want to live for us, / Live with us," the Polish poet Ryszard Krynicki bids his fellow writers at the height of the Solidarity movement of 1980–81. Easier said than done. How does the poet live with traditions demanding prophetic revelation or glorious self-immolation for the sake of the oppressed nation, if not for human salvation as such? "I loved them. / But I loved them haughtily," Cassandra confesses in Wisława Szymborska's "Soliloquy for Cassandra":

> From heights beyond life.
> From the future. Where it's always empty
> And nothing is easier than seeing death.
> I'm sorry that my voice was hard.
> Look down on yourselves from the stars, I cried,
> Look down on yourselves from the stars. . . .

Is the prophet's haughtiness, or the martyr's ardor, the best way to challenge a regime with its own claims to cosmic prophecy, and its own litany of martyrs to the sacred cause? This was the quandary facing Poland's poets as they set about rebuilding their nation and their traditions following the Second World War under the unsought auspices of the same messianic state that had shaped Akhmatova's poetry and fate.[55]

Avant-garde Again, or the Posthumous Polish Adventures of Vladimir Mayakovsky

Lenin
is still
> *more alive than the living.*
> > —*Vladimir Mayakovsky, "Vladimir Ilyich Lenin" (1924)*

He lives! He simply can't stop living!
> —*Wiktor Woroszylski, "Once More on Immortality" (1949)*

On Various Mayakovskys

That wasn't a man, that wasn't a poet; that was an empire, the coming world empire.
> —*Aleksander Wat,* My Century *(Mój wiek, 1977)*

In 1948, the young Wisława Szymborska found herself at the center of a controversy on the proper nature of progressive poetry in the fledgling People's Poland. Like many young intellectuals and writers, she was at the time a true believer in the ideology espoused by the nation's new rulers. Her poetics had not kept pace with her politics, though, or so some aggrieved readers complained in the columns of *Dziennik literacki* (*Literary Gazette*).

A group of puzzled students had, at their teacher's suggestion, written to Szymborska asking her to decipher her poem "Saturday in School," which had recently appeared in the paper. Their instructor, one S. Lewiński, explained in his own letter that his pupils were well-versed in avant-garde poetics, having covered "the futurists, expressionists, picadorians, skamandrites, quadrigists, meteorists, cadrists, czartakians, helionites, and proletarianists." They were baffled, though, by Szymborska's elusive imagery and oblique metaphors, which would likewise be incomprehensible, Lewiński warned, to the ordinary "worker and peasant." He urged her to abandon her avant-garde allegiances and follow the lead of a poet whose "stylistic simplicity" never fails to "astonish and delight us." Vladimir Mayakovsky, Lewiński continued, "is an inspired poet of the masses": "This is a prophet (*wieszcz*) whose poems 'Lenin,' 'Good,' or 'Left March' won't strain for a moment the brains of a shepherd from Kazakhstan or a lumberjack from Komi. They'll understand the poems instantly, absorb them, experience them, enriching in the process both their intellect and their class consciousness." "Do our revolutionary Polish poets write this way today?" he concludes. His question is clearly meant to be answered in the negative.[1]

Szymborska apparently took Lewiński's challenge to heart. She provided her disgruntled readers with a prose gloss to the enigmatic lyric clarifying its ideological content: "The full burden of labor rested on the shoulders of the proletariat, bent by oppression, but the fruits of that labor served to satisfy the property-owning classes and not the needs of entire nations . . ." And she also excluded all dubious avant-garde experiments from her debut volume *Why We Live* (*Dlatego żyjemy*, 1954), whose poems are by and large as self-explanatory as their titles: "What a Soviet Soldier Said to Polish Children in the Days of Liberation," "Our Worker Speaks Out on the Imperialists," "An Old Working Woman Reminisces over the Cradle of the People's Constitution," and so on.[2]

Lewiński's rhetorical query begs a more pressing question, though: did Mayakovsky himself ever really write this way? Not according to Soviet critics during his own lifetime, including, as we have seen, such luminaries of the revolution as Trotsky, Lunarcharsky, and Lenin himself: "Nekrasov I acknowledge, but Mayakovsky—excuse me, I can't understand him," he confessed. Jacek Łukasiewicz remarks that Lewiński was at least partly right about Mayakovsky's comprehensibility among the Komi woodcutters: the lumber camps of the Komi Autonomous Republic were largely staffed by forced laborers drawn from the intelligentsia "who had frequently completed Europe's best universities" and were thus intellectually equipped to tackle Mayakovsky's linguistic experiments. "I ought to be the poet of the people," Mayakovsky insisted shortly before his suicide in 1930. But he was plagued throughout his brief career as the self-proclaimed bard of the revolution by charges of obscurity, irrelevance, and narcissistic self-absorption, as I've discussed elsewhere. "The workers and peasants can't understand you" ran the standard charge.[3]

Only after his death were his "petty-bourgeois" origins, "anarchist-individualist tendencies" and "bourgeois Bohemian" aesthetics finally forgiven him, when Joseph Stalin himself rectified years of neglect by proclaiming in 1935 that "Mayakovsky was and remains the best and most talented poet of our Soviet epoch." His statement, needless to say, was not based upon a critical reevaluation of the great poet's works. "This shift in official Soviet attitude was predicated by the pressing needs of cultural politics of the moment," as Lazar Fleishman remarks. "On the one hand, it pretended to be a further manifestation of the anti-RAPP stance of Soviet leadership." (RAPP was the acronym of the short-lived Russian Association of Proletarian Writers.) On the other, "Mayakovsky was advanced to rebuke Bukharin (and his followers) who at the Congress of 1934 put forward Pasternak as a genuine expression of Soviet ideals in lyrical poetry." "Indifference to his memory and his works," Stalin concluded, "is a crime." Under Stalin, Boris Pasternak remarks, "Mayakovsky began to be forcibly imposed, like potatoes under Catherine the Great." His comment might seem initially to explain both the unrecognizably Socialist Realist Mayakovsky of Lewiński's letter and the seriousness with which Szymborska and others apparently took this sanitized, radically simplified bard of the revolution. Poland became, after all, a satellite of the Soviet state when Stalin's reign was at its height, and words like "indifference" and "crime" were not to be taken lightly.[4]

But Mayakovsky did not require Stalin's intervention to make his presence felt in Polish poetry. He had been an active force on the Polish literary scene since shortly after the First World War, and he actually visited Poland twice, first in May, 1927, at the invitation of the Polish Pen Club, and then for a week or so in 1929, not long before his suicide. But Mayakovsky's "legend had preceded him," another Futurist, Anatol Stern, remembers. "He had been among us long before he finally appeared." "Mayakovsky's influence came early, by the very beginning of the twenties," Aleksander Wat comments. "It reached Poland in 1918. I was reading Mayakovsky in 1919, 1920." Wat was both a founding member of Polish Futurism, a younger sibling of the Russian and Italian movements, and a leading leftist intellectual, although he apparently never actually joined the Communist Party. For Wat, as for so many other avant-garde writers then and later, Mayakovsky represented the ideal fusion of "the avant-garde position, formal innovation" and "communist, revolutionary writing": "Mayakovsky is the model, the archetype, the prototype for the mixing of those two elements," he concludes.[5]

Mayakovsky himself applauded Wat as a "born futurist," and Wat seems to claim the Soviet writer as the exclusive property of Polish poetry's more radical elements: "What Bryusov, Balmont, and Blok were for the Skamandrites, especially [Julian] Tuwim, Mayakovsky was for the futurists. He came as a revelation." But the Skamandrites, Modernist poets who espoused a more traditional poetics, also fell beneath Mayakovsky's spell. "The poetic shock I experienced reading Mayakovsky for the first time," Tuwim recalls, "can be compared only to the unforgettable shock you feel at the voice and vision of a sky riven by lightning bolts. Riot, uproar, thunder, flame—everything new, without precedent, miraculous, astounding, revolutionary." Tuwim went on to translate what Edward Balcerzan calls the "bible of Eastern European Futurism," Mayakovsky's "Cloud in Trousers," while his fellow Skamandrite Antoni Słonimski tackled the exuberantly revolutionary "Left March," among other works.[6]

Translating Mayakovsky apparently became a cottage industry among Polish poets in the twenties. Translators flocked to Mayakovsky from across the political and artistic spectrum. They included not only politically liberal poetic traditionalists like Tuwim and Słonimski, but also, more predictably, avant-garde leftists such as Stern, Bruno Jasieński, and Włodzimierz Słobodnik, alongside the more aesthetically conservative, avowedly communist poets Władysław Broniewski and Witold Wandurski. His first, official visit to Poland caused a "genuine storm," Stern recalls. Poets and journalists alike were struck by his "cosmic voice" and "massive form"—"Are they all that big back there?" one spectator wondered—while "swarms of [government] spies tracked his every move," Wandurski remembers. Mayakovsky's fans and translators packed the Wats' apartment for a private reading at which "the living, speaking locomotive" proceeded to "roar and reel" his way through "Left March": "the windowpanes shook and the doors of a cubist cupboard burst open of their own accord," one witness reported.[7]

Mayakovsky's suicide produced the same kind of aftershocks among his Polish admirers that Svetlana Boym describes amid their French counterparts in *Death in Quotation Marks* (1991). Soviet officialdom wrote off the suicide as a strictly personal affair: his death "has nothing in common with the public . . . activity of the poet," the official report announced. The state's representatives could scarcely do otherwise. For them to admit that their most visible poetic representative might have had reasons to be dissatisfied with the shape that Soviet life, literary or otherwise, was taking under the leadership of Comrade Stalin would be tantamount to committing political—and not just political—suicide themselves. Mayakovsky's failure as a poet, his insurmountable lyricism, becomes his private failure as well; and his regrettably individualistic death is safely cordoned off from the triumphal march of Soviet history.[8]

But neither the poet nor the ideology he claimed to represent could be faulted by the Polish poets who had taken Mayakovsky as their model of the avant-garde artist who successfully places his gifts in the service of the revolutionary regime. A whole issue of the radical journal *Miesięcznik literacki* (*Literary Monthly*) was devoted to anxious discussions, and evasions, of the suicide. The openly pro-Soviet, avowed communist Władysław Broniewski found one solution to this dilemma by interpreting the ambiguous event as a "death sustained in battle" in a poem entitled "April 14," the date of Mayakovsky's suicide:

> But the song won't fall silent
> raised on high from the catacombs to the forum:
> it will fly higher
> than the crematorium's black smoke.
>
> Let the word, like radium,
> scorch the tissues of our hearts.
> All praise to the fallen!
> We march onwards.[9]

Mayakovsky's word will scorch hearts, or at least some hearts, more effectively than that of Pushkin's prophet ("Burn with your word the hearts of men") ever could: radium's afterlife far exceeds that of even the most divinely inspired would-be bard. Indeed, Broniewski takes his poetic radium straight from the master's verse: "Poetry is the same as mining radium," Mayakovsky boasts in "A Conversation with the Tax Inspector about Poetry" (1926). The hero may have fallen, but the struggle will live on, Broniewski promises.[10]

And it did. "The battle for Mayakovsky" ("Batalia o Majakowskiego") became the rallying cry for a group of young postwar Polish poets eager, as their master had been, to lend their voices to the new state's collective hymn of praise. But whom were they battling? And which Mayakovsky were they fighting for? Was it the Bohemian bard whom Trotsky mocks in *Literature and Revolution*? Or was it his antipode, the well-behaved spokesman of the proletariat whom Lewiński uses to rebuke Szymborska and other misguided Polish practitioners of avant-garde poetics *après la lettre*? What happens when "mayakovshchina," the "mayakovskovitis" for which Soviet critics had castigated the poet and his followers during his lifetime, becomes the "majakowszczyzna" embraced by a new generation of young Polish communist writers? "I viewed the world revolution through the prism of Mayakovsky," the poet Wiktor Woroszylski confesses in his memoir *A Return to My Country* (*Powrót do kraju*, 1979). What revolution and which Mayakovsky did he see?[11]

Majakowszczyzna, or the Death and Polish Resurrection of Vladimir Mayakovsky

"Your poem is really 'I and Lenin,' while I want Lenin without your 'I.'"
"What you really want is poetry without my 'I . . .'"
> —*A conversation with Vladimir Mayakovsky, from the memoirs of Ilya Selvinsky (quoted in Wiktor Woroszylski,* The Life of Mayakovsky, *1965)*

The individual!
> *Who needs him?!*
The single voice
> *is weaker than a squeak.*
> > —*Vladimir Mayakovsky, "Vladimir Ilyich Lenin" (1924)*

It's bad for a person
> *to be alone,*
Woe to one alone! One alone's no soldier!
> —*Vladimir Mayakovsky, "Vladimir Ilyich Lenin"*

In his quasi-epic "About That" (1923) Mayakovsky anticipates his posthumous fate once "the slaughter is done": "The poet's tatters," he predicts, will "shine over the Kremlin / like a red flag in the wind." This ragged body-cum-banner was triumphantly hoisted in 1950 by a pugnacious group of openly pro-communist poets whom critics sardonically christened the "pimply ones" (*pryszczaci*) in honor of the still-adolescent complexion of their spokesman, a "pimply Bolshevik from Łódź" by the name of Wiktor Woroszylski (1927–96). In his manifesto "The Battle for Mayakovsky," Woroszylski declared war on the poetic classicists who edited the influential journal *Kuźnica* (*Ironworks*), Ryszard Matuszewski, Seweryn Pollack, and Adam Ważyk. Their prorevolutionary sentiments were at odds, he argued, with an artistic traditionalism that had not kept pace with the political realities and requirements of the new Polish

People's Republic. "What haven't the opponents of 'majakowszczyzna' defended?" Woroszylski charged: "They've defended fine craftsmanship and cultural tradition against the blockheads and barbarians. They've defended perfect classical form against the brutes who shatter stanzas. They've defended a poetic language subtly woven of Ledas, Endymions, and Persephones from the incursions of nonpoetic elements such as PPSer [*pepesz*, slang for a member of the Polish Socialist Party], socialist competition (*współzawodnictwo*), Pstrowski [a celebrated shock worker whose face would one day grace the 100-złoty note], ZWM [the Fighting Youth Union]." "Our revolt," he later explained, "took shape in language and form, in rhythmic and phonetic rasping, in prosaicized phrases, imprecise rhymes, and brutal, colloquial diction."[12]

So far so good. Modern poetry has a long and distinguished history of aggressively "unpoetic" writing. From Wordsworth to Whitman, from Baudelaire and Rimbaud to avant-gardists of every stripe: poets throughout the last two centuries have periodically imported intentionally banal, "unlyrical" elements of language and life into their verse as a way to shake up a readership grown accustomed to fancier poetic fare. And Futurists, Dadaists, and Surrealists were alike in their embrace of Soviet Russia's budding dictatorship. Mayakovsky, Khlebnikov, Wat, Jasieński, Breton, Aragon: all saw their linguistic experiments as speeding the birth of the brave new world emerging from the ashes of the old life that their poetry had helped to incinerate. Both the program and the patron adopted by Poland's "pimply ones" would seem to place them squarely in what was by 1950 a recognizably modern tradition of avant-garde rebellion. Woroszylski managed "to include everything" in the manifesto that Alicja Lisiecka calls "the most typical pamphlet of postwar Polish literature": "political fanaticism, the wrath and 'maladjustment' of rising stars in a constellation of heavenly bodies with readily recognizable surnames, indiscriminate personal attacks, a fascination with the writings of their Soviet colleagues, the rebellion of 'Romantics' against 'classics,' the present against the past, the young against the old."[13]

"Every Romanticism picks the classics it must combat," Woroszylski himself later confessed. "Battle, fronts, attacks, retreats, victory": these were the categories, he remarks elsewhere, through which he and his angry young friends perceived their mission in poetry and society alike. What better model could they find than the poet who had commanded his cadres of like-minded artists to man "the barricades of hearts and souls" in his "Order to the Army of the Arts" (1918): "To the streets, Futurists, / drummers and poets!"[14] But the movement to which Woroszylski and his contemporaries recruited their polonized Mayakovsky was an avant-garde with a difference. This avant-garde had a history; it was burdened by a legacy of failed fusions between experimental poetics and left-wing politics. The radical experimentation that marked Russian poetry of the twenties had been squelched by no less than Joseph Stalin himself—though Mayakovsky himself had done his best to help by rejecting his radical colleagues at LEF (the Left Front of Art) for the budding Socialist Realists of RAPP shortly before his suicide.

Early Polish fans of Mayakovsky's politics and poetics like Wat, Broniewski, Wandurski, and Jasieński, moreover, later found themselves in various Soviet prisons and camps, from which not all of them emerged alive. Even when they themselves survived, any dubious avant-garde tendencies they might have harbored did not.[15] Woroszylski and his fellow Mayakovskovites—Krzysztof Gruszczyński, Tadeusz Urgacz, and Andrzej Mandalian—had to battle not only their classicizing contemporaries, but also the avant-garde precursors who had, so they thought, fatally misinterpreted the shape that a truly socialist Mayakovsky should take. The proletarian prophet celebrated by the sermonizing schoolteacher S. Lewiński joins forces with the Mayakovsky embraced by the pimply young Turks of postwar Polish poetry. The martyred patron saint of rebellious writers from Broniewski and Breton to Frank O'Hara, Nicolas Guillen, and Julia Kristeva unexpectedly becomes the scourge of the very poetics he had helped to invent.

More than this—the battle for Mayakovsky was also a battle with Mayakovsky and even a battle against Mayakovsky, or so Woroszylski's early poetry suggests. Trotsky had announced the lyric's end shortly after the revolution—and Mayakovsky's irrepressible lyricism becomes Exhibit A in Trotsky's case against the self-proclaimed standard bearer in *Literature and Revolution*: "When he wants to elevate man," Trotsky charges, "he makes him be Mayakovsky." Anatoly Lunacharsky likewise called for an end to Mayakovsky's incessant "lyrical whining" in another postrevolutionary attack. Mayakovsky was unable to overcome what he himself called his "melancholic, sentimental lyricism," and his contemporaries saw even would-be revolutionary epics such as "Vladimir Ilych Lenin" and "Good!" (1927) as "steeped in individualism," suffused in a "personal, lyrical" intonation. He tried time and again to "step on the throat of my own song," as he writes with a mixture of rue and pride in his final, fragmentary epic "At the Top of My Lungs" (1930). But he never managed to suppress this song to his own—or anybody else's—satisfaction. It remained to his self-proclaimed disciples in Soviet Russia and its satellites to finish the job that Mayakovsky himself had left half-done.[16]

The new man demanded a new kind of lyricism, Trotsky and others had announced early on. And this new lyric poetry was to be resolutely anti-lyrical, born not of subjective perceptions, but through the "objectivity of historical necessity." Trotsky allowed for small-scale lyrics as a stopgap measure until a truly Soviet poetry emerged to take their place: a kind of NEP for poetry. Postwar Polish poets and critics were less tolerant. "Poetics arises from ideology and fulfills an ideological function," Adam Ważyk announced in an early essay—and only those who fail to recognize this function will fall into the capitalist trap of "speaking theoretically about a 'personal' lyric." Only "capitalist society," he warns, fosters the false division between "the socio-political sphere" and the "private, individual sphere" that makes the ostensibly "personal" lyric possible. "Marxism has successfully liquidated the contradiction between man's private and social natures," another postwar critic crowed: "The Socialist Realist poet will write a personal poem about Nowa Huta [the new steel works outside Krakow] and a political poem about love." The purely personal lyric seemed destined to go the way of the dodo—although ideology, not biology, would drive the last nail in its coffin.[17]

The young Woroszylski may have opposed Ważyk's neoclassical poetics, a poetics he saw as singularly ill-suited to appropriately Socialist Realist content. He would have had no argument, though, with Ważyk's mixing of ideology and genre. In his redefinition of lyricism, Ważyk carefully explains the necessity for quotation marks around the dubious adjective "personal" that so often and misleadingly accompanies the word "poetry": "I place the term in quotes since I see great peril arising from the very definition." Woroszylski is no less scrupulous in his debut volume *There Is No Death!* (*Śmierci nie ma!* 1949). In "About Love—A Chaotic Tale" ("O miłości—gawęda chaotyczna"), he sardonically deflates the erotic "histories that capitalism calls 'private'" and that feed its ostensibly intimate verse: "that's not love, it's bourgeois hysteria," he explains.[18]

Another poem from the same collection places tacit quotation marks around the personal lyric poem indirectly, by way of its aggressively anti-lyrical—and anticapitalist—frame. The poem takes as its starting point a brief newspaper citation concerning recent events in the United States: "The court pronounced a death sentence on Rosa Lee and her children." The story, as Woroszylski re-creates it in the poem's opening and closing sections, concerns the brutal beating of a black woman in the American South by her employer, one Mr. Startford. She and her two adolescent sons resist, which leads ultimately to Startford's death and their subsequent execution for his premeditated murder. Woroszylski draws a suitably Socialist Realist conclusion from this horrific tale. In America, he reminds us, "there are only two colors: black and white. / But the judges didn't know the third color / . . . which was called—The Red First of May!":

> the workers vow that Sammie Lee,
> the workers vow that Wallace Lee,
> the workers vow that Rosa Lee
> will live on in the red banner.
> So the story doesn't end: it begins.
> Rosa Lee lives on![19]

"Is there any question today that the strongest emotions—the strongest precisely in a poetic, artistic sense—come to us from the newspapers, with their straightforward, naked narrative of the deep changes taking place among the Polish workers?" Woroszylski exclaims in a programmatic piece entitled "The War for Literature in People's Poland"(1951). "Rosa Lee" combines his vaunted newspaper aesthetics with the impassioned critique of American social injustices that was de rigueur among Soviet Socialist Realists and their epigones. Mayakovsky himself had pointed the way early on as he reminded Soviet readers of the "unemployed workers" who "flung themselves headfirst into the Hudson [*sic*]" from the span he both celebrates and condemns in "Brooklyn Bridge" (1925). Woroszylski's poem proves most interesting, though, in its middle section as he clumsily works to combine social and aesthetic criticism by way of a personal poetic association. The Rosa Lee who is his poem's subject reminds him of a poem commemorating a different victim with a similar name:

> I remember I once read a poem,
> a good poem, Edgar Allen Poe wrote it,
> and it wasn't your ordinary poem,
> but a lament for a dead woman, a tribute,
> and her name still sticks in my memory,
> the name of a white woman: Annabel Lee.

Woroszylski proceeds to quote whole chunks of Poe's poem in Polish translation. But he also takes pains to add key details omitted by his gifted, if misguided precursor:

> And afterwards—(he didn't write this, but I know)—
> the poet's lonely evenings dragged on
> and the roar of alcohol filled his head, glowing like the great city's windows,
> and the poems also died slowly,
> like pastel, frail, flossy-haired women
> at dawn in hotel rooms.[20]

Poe's poetic fantasy is, like the poet himself, a product of the poisonous pseudo-privacy born of urban, capitalist existence, Woroszylski reminds us. Poe's lonely hell is as artificial as Baudelaire's infamous paradise; both his lyrics and their refined female victims are the stillborn children not of some imaginary kingdom by the sea, but of modern capitalist alienation in the making. Moreover, both the lyric poet and his favored genre stand indicted of neglecting the evils of the society they ignore in creating their insular fantasies—or so Woroszylski suggests by way of the awkward, parodic revision with which he begins the poem's third and final section:

> This story took place not so long ago
> in a land where the freedom's not free—
> there lived a woman whose name the courts know
> as the Negress Rosa Lee.
> (Było to bardzo, a bardzo niedawno / w republice, gdzie wolność się cli—
> / żyła tam kobieta i nazwało ją prawo / Murzynką Rosą Lee).

What does this all have to do with Mayakovsky? A few clues emerge from the strongest stanza in what is by and large an all too typical exercise in Socialist Realist political and poetic correctness. The poem comes to life fully only in the passage where Woroszylski imagines the melancholy afterlife of "Annabel Lee"'s unhappy author: "He didn't write this, but I know," the Polish poet confesses parenthetically. His perspicacity derives partly, of course, from the "infallible Marxist master key" that offered him and like-minded contemporaries a failsafe way to interpret human history from its barbaric beginnings all the way through to its foregone communist conclusion.[21] Other passages hint, though, at deeper affinities between the self-avowed communist poet and his seeming American antipode. Woroszylski's speaker concedes that Poe's poem is "good," apparently good enough "to stick in his memory" long after his initial reading. After citing various excerpts, moreover, he gives a rather surprising account of "Annabel Lee"'s reception among his revolutionary colleagues:

> I read this poem to my comrades—they said it's not like that,
> but Annabel Lee's death moves me even though it might not be real,
> since it happens that way, just love and suddenly your whole life,
> it happens that way, just hair and lips and eyes.
> So you're really wrong not to believe—
> that's the whole point, other things hurt even worse, hit even harder.

The speaker's comrades respond appropriately to the poem's dubious bourgeois content. His own reaction is less predictable. The revolutionary flag bearer unexpectedly becomes an apologist for Romantic passion: where have we seen this paradox before?

"From the heaven of poetry / I throw myself / into communism / because / without it there is no love / for me," Mayakovsky exclaims in "Homeward" (1925)—but communism and love made for uneasy bedfellows at best for the would-be bard of the coming utopia. It is, I think, no accident that Woroszylski christens another early poem "About Love—A Chaotic Tale." The title's first part sends us back to one of Mayakovsky's most notorious efforts to fuse his quest for "love the savior" (*spasitel'-liubov'*) with the emergence of the new Soviet state, his quasi-epic "About That." The first section of Mayakovsky's poem refers directly to Oscar Wilde and the scandalous "love that dare not speak its name": it is called "The Ballad of Reading Gaol" ("Ballada redingskoi tiur'my"). But the unspoken word of Mayakovsky's title—"That" is his coy substitute for "love"—is more banal. It refers simply to the garden-variety bourgeois passion which had long been the stock-in-trade of poets, and which this particular poet has found himself unwilling or unable to overcome:

> In this theme,
>> both personal
>>> and petty
> sung time and time again
> I've spun like some poetic squirrel,
> and I mean to go spinning again.[22]

The second part of Woroszylski's title—"A Chaotic Tale"—might easily be his tacit critique of the unstable mixture of philistine passions and progressive politics that makes up Mayakovsky's epic lament for lost love. He and his contemporaries preferred what had become Mayakovsky's canonical texts, the poems that were required reading for generations of Soviet schoolchildren, "Good!", "Vladimir Ilych Lenin," and "At the Top of My Lungs." Woroszylski recalls reciting Artur Sandauer's translation of "Good!" from memory along with his fellow Mayakovskovites, and Balcerzan describes the postwar enthusiasm provoked by the programmatic throat-stomping that concludes "At the Top of My Lungs." Woroszylski's "About Love" ends with an exhortation to just such collective self-throttling. The true poet, he insists, must defeat his lyric impulses and learn to "howl like a revolutionary agitator," "bawl" "in a bass of bellowing poems."[23]

The older Woroszylski was ruthless toward both himself and his generation of "dreary sectarians, thick-skulled schematists," "rigid, doctrinaire epigones of Mayakovsky, lacking both imagination and talent." He did not renounce his early allegiances, though. Instead he sought time and again to revise his youthful misreadings of his Russian master's life and art by returning to an ever more complex portrait of poet and writing alike. In 1952, Woroszylski left Poland for Moscow, that Mecca of budding revolutionaries, where he completed his doctoral dissertation on Mayakovsky's lyric poetry in 1956. This stay also marked the beginning of the long process of disillusionment that culminated in his ejection from the Party in 1966 over his support for the revisionist Marxist philosopher Leszek Kołakowski. The research, both official and unauthorized, that he conducted on this and subsequent trips led to the publication of his acclaimed biography, *The Life of Mayakovsky* (*Życie Majakowskiego*, 1965), which appeared in English translation in 1972. The book in turn became a play entitled *The Death of Mayakovsky* (*Śmierć Majakowskiego*), which was produced in Warsaw in 1967. Neither the biography nor the play made it past the censors in Mayakovsky's homeland, though; and I will return to Woroszylski's provocative life of the poet later in my discussion.[24]

The play's title alone is enough to alert us to one key source of controversy in biography and drama alike. *There is No Death!* Woroszylski's debut volume proclaims, and in this he follows the lead of the Mayakovsky who enthusiastically endorsed the Soviet dream of "abolishing death." "Official Marxism-Leninism," Irene Masing-Delic remarks, saw "genuine immortality in 'the preservation of the results of human activity'"—she takes her quotation from the Soviet *Atheist Dictionary* of 1983—and it categorically rejected "any form of personal immortality in either transcendental or earthly regions." Socialist immortality may, however, be achieved by way of revolutionary martyrdom, and this is the fate that Mayakovsky envisions in "At the Top of My Lungs": "I don't give a damn for monumental bronze / I don't give a damn for marble slime / . . . Let socialism, built in battle, be our common monument." Like the Lenin of his famous paean, Mayakovsky will live on in the glorious heaven on earth that his work has helped to forge. This is how orthodox Soviet thought came to interpret, or elide, Mayakovsky's own less than glorious suicide. A film biography I saw as a student at Leningrad State University in the late seventies ended not with the poet's death, which went unmentioned, but with what was presumably his miraculous assumption into the Soviet pantheon as a camera panned heavenwards while the narrator intoned Mayakovsky's famous lines from his early poem "Listen" ("Poslushaite"): "If the stars are switched on—- / it must mean somebody needs that? / it must mean somebody wants them there?" The poem itself predates the revolution by several years. In its late Soviet incarnation, though, Mayakovsky's unspecified "somebody" could easily be taken for that strategically unnamed socialist luminary who had first placed Mayakovsky's star in the revolutionary firmament where it now twinkled so brightly.[25]

This is also the kind of immortality that Woroszylski foresees for his Rosa Lee. Her defiance costs both her own and her children's lives, but she survives nonetheless in the minds and deeds of the workers she inspires. Woroszylski endorses the programmatic optimism of the newborn People's Poland throughout the collection, which reads, as its euphoric title suggests, like a communist valediction forbidding mourning amidst the unfolding glories of the revolutionary "first day of creation" one poem extols. The volume's final poem, "Once More on Immortality" ("Jeszcze o nieśmiertelności") sums up its insistence on the new communist creed that supersedes Christianity's feeble previous efforts at transcendence:

> So, if he wanted to find
> immortality in our times
> the Israelite worker Christ
> wouldn't die on the cross,
> he'd be a Communist Party member.
> a volunteer, with a grenade belt,
> who'd perish beneath the imperialists' first tank . . . [26]

"Once more on immortality": perhaps the Polish poet as would-be Soviet prophet—"Literate young [workers] collectively / read the Manifesto like a sermon"—protests too much. I have said that Woroszylski's battle for Mayakovsky might also be read as a battle with Mayakovsky, and the quote I've just given is a case in point. Mayakovsky was, of course, no stranger to the figure of the crucified Christ who dies at the hands of an ignoble present so that the glorious future might be born. But the martyred Mayakovskian poet-Christ would hardly have allowed himself to be laid, for all his protestations, in the tomb of the unknown soldier that is the likely destiny of Woroszylski's proletarian savior. Anonymity was never Mayakovsky's strong suit. Moreover, crucifixion, not armed battle, was his preferred mode of martyrdom from his earliest poems on: "Crucify him, crucify him," hostile audiences cry in "The Cloud in Trousers." These crucifixions sometimes take the shape of a singularly challenging form of suicide: "I have nailed myself to the cross," he announces in the same poem. And his metaphorical crucifixions, whether imposed or self-inflicted, are not provoked by revolutionary motivations alone. The "nails of words" that pin him to the paper at the end of "The Backbone Flute" are driven by thwarted love, not revolutionary fervor.[27]

Love, martyrdom, and suicide: these quintessentially lyrical, supremely un-Soviet, themes unify the whole of Mayakovsky's life and writing, as

Roman Jakobson observes. "CAUTION, POLITICAL POETS, / trumpeters of the imagination, stevedores of feelings," Woroszylski warns in one early poem, "I summon you to cooperative labor in the name of the miner Pstrowski": "Who will provide more, provide better, more and better / poetic coal to warm / their comrades from the cities, villages and abroad?" Selfless poetic shock workers, not spectacular poet-Christs, are what the socialist state requires from its would-be laborers of the imagination. The Mayakovsky who thought and wrote otherwise must be carefully excised from the hearts and minds of his latter-day Polish acolytes—even if it means that they themselves must tacitly fight the master under whose banner they claim to march.[28]

Love, Death, and the Socialist State

Then the first poet rose to his feet and recited a poem about a girl who broke off with her beloved, a young man working at the lathe next to her own, because he was lazy and failed to fulfill his production quotas. The young man did not want to lose his girl, and so he proceeded to work with such enormous zeal that the red star of a socialist hero of labor was soon pinned to his machine.

—Milan Kundera, Life is Elsewhere *(1973)*

The middle-aged lady . . . said: "Why do you want to meddle with love, comrades? Love will be the same till the end of time, thank goodness."

The organizer replied: "Oh, no, comrade, you are mistaken!" . . .

"Then where's the difference?" asked the lady.

"Here: that in the past, love—even the greatest love—was always a kind of escape from social life which was distasteful. But the love of today's man is closely connected with our social duties, our work, our struggle for unity. And that's where its new beauty lies."

—Kundera, Life is Elsewhere

Death. In those days of compulsory joy it too belonged among the forbidden topics.

—Kundera, Life is Elsewhere

In an essay written near the end of his life, Woroszylski reminisces about his participation in a Polish conference dedicated to Mayakovsky in 1993. The conference prompted him, he recalls, to "think about 'my

Mayakovsky,' who changed so much for me as the years passed": "At first he thrilled me with his ruthless negation of the existing world and bombastic faith in an ideal new world. Then I became fascinated by his enigmatic fate, marked for tragedy from the start up through its final, fatal end. I tried to decipher it by compiling documents, inadvertent disclosures, and contradictory accounts in my book *The Life of Mayakovsky*. Still later, after a long break, I returned to my abandoned readings and noted with astonishment the iconoclastic imagery of crosses, crucifixions, Golgothas—alongside his passionate hope for the birth of a different existence, which might be termed the longed-for "civilization of love."[29]

Love, death, and crucifixion: by this account, Woroszylski recognized these key themes in Mayakovsky's poetry only after the decades that had produced a manifesto, a short-lived movement, a dissertation, and a lengthy, meticulously researched biography (the Polish edition runs to some eight hundred pages). It strains belief—not least because Woroszylski, unlike some of his contemporaries, was not confined to the Mayakovsky available in Polish translation, who was subject, like his less illustrious literary colleagues, to the censor's prohibitions and whims. His satirical plays, to give just one example, could be published only after Stalin's death; a 1956 production of Mayakovsky's *Bathhouse* in fact marked the beginnings of the Polish Thaw (*Odwilż*), which, like its Soviet counterpart, initiated the posthumous relaxation of Stalinist cultural restrictions.[30] Woroszylski apparently picked up a good working knowledge of Russian during a childhood spent in Poland's easternmost provinces. He later went on, as I've mentioned, to receive a doctorate in Russian literature at Moscow State University, and produced biographies not just of Mayakovsky, but of Esenin, Saltykov-Shchedrin, and other Russian writers. He became, in short, a recognized expert on Russian literature generally and Mayakovsky in particular.

How could Woroszylski have missed what seems so obvious to far less knowledgeable readers of Mayakovsky today? My guess is that he didn't— though he may have been loathe to admit it—and that his battle for and with Mayakovsky took place along lines first mapped out by the master himself. A passage in the preface to Woroszylski's *Selected Poems* of 1982 suggests as much. "What do I now know about my former self and my youthful poems?" Woroszylski asks, and his answer invites us to read between the lines of both his Mayakovsky and the poetry inspired by him. "They were Romantic," Woroszylski confesses: "I searched for the meaning of life in the simplified world that made up the terrain of my poetic experiences—and I found it most often in a beautiful death. I was probably reacting in part to the many deaths, deaths lacking all heroic justification, that I had witnessed during the war. . . . But I see as well the instinctive rejection of ordinary life in which, all ideology to the contrary, the shivers of Romantic emotion rarely seized me."[31] We should expect nothing less from the ardent reader of Poe who briefly tips his hand in "Rosa Lee."

Elsewhere Woroszylski confesses that "in twentieth-century poetry I acknowledged only the Russians, with Mayakovsky and Esenin at the fore." One would be hard-pressed to come up with two modern specialists more adept in the art of beautiful dying than these spectacular suicides who left lyrics alongside or in lieu of final letters: Esenin famously wrote his last poem in his own blood. Indeed, Woroszylski's biography of Mayakovsky concludes with Pasternak's description of the poet's miraculously rejuvenated corpse. "His face," Pasternak recalls, "restored the time when he called himself the beautiful twenty-two-year-old, because death had captured a facial expression which rarely falls into its clutches. It was the expression with which you begin life, not end it." The biography's closing lines call to mind Woroszylski's confession that the urge to write the life stemmed from his need to decipher its enigmatic ending.[32]

But we need not leap ahead to the mid-sixties to find Woroszylski's preoccupation with Mayakovsky's suicide and with death, beautiful or otherwise, at work in his writing. *Why We Live* runs the title of Szymborska's debut volume: Woroszylski's first book might easily be called *Why We Don't Die*. It opens with a poem entitled "On the Reverse Side of Wincenty Pstrowski's Obituary" ("Na odwrocie nekrologu Wincentego Pstrowskiego"), which commemorates the death and resurrection of postwar Poland's most lauded shock worker, a coal miner who exceeded his quota many times over before his—apparently short-lived—death. "Can you wake a corpse? You can!" the speaker exults. He proceeds to outline the means by which the dead are resurrected in the newborn People's Poland. Death itself, for starters, is politically incorrect. She (the noun is feminine in Polish) is a "black marketeer, mired in the swamp," but since all right-(or rather left-)minded Poles have recognized "THAT THERE IS NO DEATH," "she flees through Dakota," a state presumably chosen so that Woroszylski could create his very Mayakovskian rhyme of "w błocie / na Dakocie" ("in the swamp / through Dakota") while signifying the prescribed larger ideological oppositions. Moreover, he concludes,

All our miners resurrect
Pstrowski daily
with dynamite and pickaxes.
Pstrowski rolls along, rough, black, heavy—
on carts, freightcars, steamers.

And on Saturdays after work,
maidens, Silesian and otherwise, burst into song
about Pstrowski.

The volume concludes, moreover, with "Once More on Immortality," which ends with the following lines:

let's put paid
to this immortality business
with the most immortal point of all
which is called
c o m m u n i s m .[33]

Between these relentlessly optimistic bookends, we find, though, not only the predictable paeans to workers' achievements—the poems Woroszylski hopes will serve as "pocket Dneprostroys," model factories in miniature, for present and future Polish proletarians—and hymns to fallen comrades both at home and abroad, whether in war-torn Spain, Soviet Russia, or the American South. The theme of collective resurrection through labor gives way to a different consideration of death elsewhere, though. I have already mentioned Woroszylski's "About Love—A Chaotic Tale." It is preceded by another poem with the conspicuously un-Soviet title of "An Intimate Letter" ("List intymny"). Chaotic love and private correspondence—the titles themselves suggest the suspiciously lyrical terrain that Woroszylski treads here. The first takes the form of a missive from the poet to a despairing comrade who apparently cannot reconcile himself with the shape his longed-for revolution has taken. "It can be tough: your neck bent / by others' business, others' battles. / It's tough: to be grown over by a home, / a third skin, a world of trivialities," the speaker writes sympathetically, even as he counsels his downcast colleague to "keep your eyes glued / to the pocket-sized poster of your party membership card." The "intimate letter" thus ends by discouraging intimacy in favor of solidarity with the "imperishable" working class taken en masse.[34]

The next poem is less sympathetic as it recounts the cautionary "chaotic" tale of a "certain student from Łódź / who committed suicide . . . / from love!" In his "comic land of curtains and family portraits," where "Papa trades hard currency, while mama / puts up jam and gossips," their "son, a student . . . —threw himself out the window from love!" Love, suicide and "little old daily life" (*staren'kii, staren'kii bytik*): this ill-fated triumvirate looks strikingly familiar to any reader of Mayakovsky. "Love's boat has smashed up on daily life (*byt*)," the Soviet bard laments in the poem he incorporated into his own final "intimate letter." In an equally well-known earlier piece he had fulminated against precisely such lyrical pseudo-disasters. "Why up the number of suicides?" he chides Esenin in the poetic reprimand he wrote following the peasant-poet's death. "You'd be better off increasing ink production!" Woroszylski rebukes his dead student by way of an even better-known literary self-immolation: "Of course, woman is fickle, hence young Werther's sorrows, / but if I met him, I'd say—So what's your problem, / friend, there's no demand for Werthers nowadays!"[35]

The stricken Werther, a lovesick student, a despondent revolutionary mired in the quotidian: it doesn't take any great leap of imagination to see Mayakovsky's ghost lurking behind the poems' various heroes and antiheroes. "About Love" is, among other things, a slap in Mayakovsky's own incurably Romantic face. Love takes a new and different shape in People's Poland, Woroszylski reminds us repeatedly. "Today / even on the newspaper's third page / you can learn about great love," he insists in "About Love": "So this party secretary in Opole, Comrade Mrochen, / don't ask him about love, take a good look at his labors, / and you'll hew your own epic called 'I love.'" The sneer at Mayakovsky's own "I Love" ("Liubliu"), a typically outsized lyric-cum-epic of 1922, is unmistakable. "An Intimate Letter" and "A Chaotic Tale" form Woroszylski's tacit rebuke to the unhappily bourgeois lyric tendencies that his precursor was unwilling or unable to outgrow.[36]

"Those who forget the past are doomed to repeat it," Santayana famously remarked. Those who revise the past are likewise destined to reenact it, or so Woroszylski's example suggests. His lightly concealed combat with Mayakovsky marks not only an effort to outdo his overwhelming precursor both ideologically and aesthetically. By tacitly challenging Mayakovsky's own versions of love and death, he apparently works to suppress equally suspect tendencies in himself. "It's always like that with me," Woroszylski confides en passant in "About Love": "I start out lyrically, / Eyes beyond compare, the sun, / Then I pick up speed and howl like a revolutionary agitator." His Mayakovskian bellowing is called upon time and again to stifle his equally Mayakovskian passion for the retrograde poetic warblings that lead to untimely lyric deaths.[37]

"He can't stop living," Woroszylski proclaims of a singleminded socialist who falls in battle but lives on in grateful proletarian hearts in "Once More on Immortality." Mayakovsky's posthumous resilience in postwar Poland was apparently due less to stalwart revolutionary virtue than to the ongoing conflict between self, song, and (socialist) society that animates his life and work. The poet himself may have died, inappropriately enough, at his own hand, but the struggles that led to his premature end did not perish with him. The fight for, with, and against Mayakovsky lives on, both within the work of individual poets and in the programmatically collective communities they inhabit—or so Woroszylski's own later life and work suggest. The fate of another aggressively pro-Soviet artist, Woroszylski's friend and comrade-in-arms Tadeusz Borowski (1922–51) demonstrates the persistence of the "Mayakovsky problem" in postwar Poland. A precociously gifted poet, Borowski received what Jan Kott calls a true twentieth-century "European education." His leftist parents were persecuted under Stalin in the thirties, while he himself was active in the Polish underground resistance under Nazi domination in World War II, and spent the last part of the war first in Auschwitz, and later in Dachau. His wartime experience not only produced the thinly disguised autobiographical tales on life in Auschwitz that remain his lasting contribution to modern European fiction. It also led him, like so many other young Polish intellectuals, to embrace the communist ideology that promised a glorious future to replace the corrupt bourgeois democratic past whose failures, so the argument went, had led to the rise of the fascist nations and a cataclysmic war. He joined the Party shortly after the war and devoted his considerable talents to propagandizing for the new state.[38]

Like Woroszylski, Borowski was an ardent admirer of the Soviet Union's official bard. "The true writer of the working class is not Eulenspiegel [a code name here for the poet Konstanty Gałczyński], but Mayakovsky," he announced in 1950, the same year that saw the appearance of Woroszylski's manifesto and short-lived movement. Borowski's suicide a year later produced the same kind of shockwaves sent out by Mayakovsky's death twenty-one years earlier. Borowski himself spoke obsessively in his final days of the "Mayakovsky case," Miłosz recalls, and his compatriots were quick to perceive the parallel. "Borowski's suicide," Wat remarks, "was similar to Mayakovsky's. Borowski would come to see me when Stalinism was at its height to talk about his own schizophrenia, his profound disenchantment, his excessive zeal as a communist, his fanaticism as a means of destroying himself." His acute political disillusionment was compounded, moreover, by the kind of disastrous love affair that Mayakovsky laments in his final lyric. The true revolutionary, Woroszylski writes in his poem "Nowotko" (1952), "loves, suffers, and burns for a million." Closer to home, though, yet another gifted communist had just died for the same volatile, politically incorrect mix of ideological and personal reasons that had prompted his precursor's suicide two decades earlier.[39]

Woroszylski's paeans to various glorious deaths on officially approved battlefronts earned him a place of honor in a 1955 anthology of Socialist Realist verse entitled *The Poetry of People's Poland* (*Poezja Polski Ludowej*): "A communist's death / is never lonely. / I loved deeds and people, / the deeds and people will remain, / . . . so it's not hard to die." But his poem on Borowski's death—"he could have lived on and on, / so why this funeral?"—was itself buried without its telltale dedication in the middle of his collection *Fatherland (Ojczyzna, 1953)*, where it is bracketed by the hymns to socialist collectivism, entitled "We" and "About Us," that open and close the volume. "The planet shakes / from the march of our million feet," Woroszylski exults: "Daily labor knows each of us / like childhood friends." In "After a friend's death," though, he mourns the loss of his strategically unnamed companion, which was, he observes, even crueler than the "deaths of childhood friends." The impulse behind that most lyrical of genres, the elegy, quietly undermines his programmatically collective bombast. But the poem's true subject was disclosed only after communism's fall, when it appeared, dedication intact, as the opening lyric in Woroszylski's *From Travels, Sleep, and Dying: Poems 1951–1990 (1992)*.[40]

In the collection's afterword, Woroszylski calls this poem the first of his early works to raise the questions that would preoccupy him in his mature writing. He returned years later to Borowski's troublesome suicide in his novel *Literature*, published only in the émigré press.[41] The urge to decipher Mayakovsky's equally baffling death marks the impulse behind his monumental biography, as Woroszylski comments. Love, death, and the collective; Romanticism, lyricism, and the Soviet State: why should these particular combinations of conflicts and contradictions continue to absorb Woroszylski long past his youthful infatuation with Marxist utopias in the making?

Let us return in this context to his description, in 1993, of the biography's beginnings. "I became fascinated," Woroszylski recalls, by Mayakovsky's "enigmatic fate, marked for tragedy from the start up through its final, fatal end." He tried, he continues, "to decipher it by compiling documents, inadvertent disclosures, and contradictory accounts in my book *The Life of Mayakovsky*." Both the impulse behind the book and the method that informs it are revealing. The mature Woroszylski identifies Romanticism as the heart of the ardently pro-Soviet "majakowszczyzna" that shaped his early postwar years. But a deeply Romantic notion of the poet informs his later, more skeptical work as well. "Now I understand that the primary category of poetry is fate," Woroszylski remarks in the preface to a volume of selected poems that appeared in 1982, a year he spent interned in a government camp for dissidents after the imposition of martial law in December, 1981.[42] It is the same notion that underlies the biography written some fifteen years earlier.

If Woroszylski's goal is to trace Mayakovsky's life through to its tragic, preordained conclusion, why does he choose his unorthodox method of compiling documents, disclosures, and contradictory accounts? Why does he include not only the poet's own writings and remarks, but the voices of family members, friends, enemies, rivals, politicians, and journalists, among others? Why does he not confine himself to Mayakovsky's own eminently Romantic view of his martyr's path through the minefields of first, imperial Russia, and then the Soviet state? In his earlier life of the nineteenth-century Russian novelist Saltykov-Shchedrin, Woroszylski "experiment[ed] with the possibility of identifying completely with my hero and speaking in the first person 'as Saltykov.'" This "nineteenth-century utopian who wanted to change the world," "an engaged writer whose maximalism lay at the heart of both his personal suffering and his extraordinary opus," clearly shares common roots with the Mayakovsky who haunts Woroszylski's imagination. Why then does he decide to present Mayakovsky, as he writes, "from the outside, avoiding all conjectures, hypotheses, and personal emotions"?[43]

The Woroszylski of the mid-sixties is not only a disillusioned Marxist. He is also a Romantic who has learned to recognize and resist his own revolutionary Romanticism, or so the evidence of the biography suggests. "I contain multitudes," Whitman boasts. "150,000, 000 speak with my lips," Mayakovsky insists. Mayakovsky's disciple and translator Władysław Broniewski later became the involuntary practitioner of yet another variety of group authorship in a 1949 volume of Mayakovsky translations, when his then-suspect name was replaced by the politically impeccable nom de plume "collective translation." Long past his early infatuation with Marxist utopianism, Woroszylski shared his favorite's yearning to find a group, a "we," capable of accommodating or absorbing his complex poet's "I." This endlessly thwarted quest for an adequate collective is a chief theme of the biography. Likewise, throughout his turbulent life, with its difficult passage from devout Marxist to staunch dissident, Woroszylski himself "thought and spoke in the plural about 'we,'" one friend recalls. But this "we"—in its later stages, at any rate—was anything but simplistic. The word "our," Woroszylski himself remarked in the early eighties, "signifies different communities, sometimes tiny, sometimes vast. At times, it may mean history as such, with all its pathos and poverty."[44]

His notion of history had changed since the early years when it meant annihilation of a despised "world order" and all merely "ahistorical life" for the sake of the "glorious march of history towards universal happiness" in which he and his like-minded comrades would inevitably take the lead. "My little histories descend from History," Woroszylski observed in a late volume tellingly entitled *Histories* (1987). Małgorzata Łukasiewicz comments that the phrase encapsulates the "parabola of Wiktor's adventures with history":

"great, rapacious History . . . disintegrates into a multitude of small, individual histories." She contrasts these little histories with Woroszylski's monumental earlier biographies of Mayakovsky, Saltykov-Shchedrin, Pushkin, and Esenin.[45]

In fact, though, the Mayakovsky biography is evidence that Woroszylski's notions of history and self had already undergone a sea change since he first launched his "battle for Mayakovsky." The book is proof positive that such a battle can never be won. It tells an inconclusive tale pieced together from a variety of stories, large and small, recounting the adventures of various Mayakovskys drawn toward and dissenting from a diapason of "we's." For the young Woroszylski, self was to be subsumed entirely in the grand forward march of Marxist history, and he impatiently hammered his Mayakovsky into the prescribed collective shape that Mayakovsky himself had been unable to assume. By 1966, he had recognized that a single "I"—particularly one as rich and troubled as Mayakovsky's—comprises many selves and many histories. The book is assembled chronologically from documents of all kinds—memoirs, autobiographical writings, love letters, political invectives, artistic polemics, poems, newspaper articles, state documents, and so on—with a minimum of authorial commentary. Just as no one relationship, no one kind of "we"—be it familial, ideological, emotional, literary, subversive, or conformist—can exhaust the complexity of the self that forms and is formed by others, so no one genre—lyric, epic, manifesto, letter, reminiscence, jeremiad, proclamation, denunciation, and so on—can exhaust the personality that shapes and is shaped by the shifting histories that surround it. I suspect that such notions, no less than the sometimes unofficial sources Woroszylski turned to in retrieving his little histories, led to the book being barred from Russia even after its successful publication in Poland.[46]

The biography itself may have been banned in Mayakovsky's homeland. But it was politically inexpedient to repress completely the works of the poet who inspired it. "Paradoxically," Andrei Sinyavsky recalls, "many Soviet young people arrived at dissidence via Mayakovsky, via the revolution's officially recognized poet": "In the early sixties in Moscow, young people began gathering by Mayakovsky's statue to read poems and argue about everything under the sun. For some, the statue on Mayakovsky Square became a baptism of fire, even the execution place of unofficial Russian poetry. Others waited there for the plainclothes agents they knew were coming. Thus Mayakovsky was transformed from standard bearer of the revolution and the Soviet state into . . . a symbol of opposition." His comment underscores, yet again, Mayakovsky's irresistible appeal to the rebellious young, even if in this case they are rebelling against precisely the leftist ideology that led to his enshrinement in the first place, and that has traditionally formed part of Mayakovsky's appeal to generations of Western avant-garde admirers.[47]

Woroszylski's case is more complex. In Chapter 2, I spoke of Mayakovsky's programmatic resistance to maturity, his refusal to step beyond the limits set by avant-garde time frames demanding immediate, apocalyptic transformation. Woroszylski's half-century of reading Mayakovsky demonstrates that Mayakovsky can, despite his own best efforts, be read maturely. The very complexities and contradictions Mayakovsky struggled to erase from his life and writing can be used, as Woroszylski proves, to develop a vision of lyric, personality, and history that runs counter to the very credo the Russian poet had embraced in his early attempt to escape from his many Mayakovskys embroiled in their multiple, inconclusive histories.

6

Bringing Up the Rear: The Histories of Wisława Szymborska

The historian calmly leafs through Gilgamesh, that most ancient epic of humankind, and immediately latches on to what he needs, i.e. "one of the earliest testaments to the formation of the state leadership's social base." The poet isn't equipped to relish the epic for such reasons. Gilgamesh might just as well not exist for him if it holds only such information. But it does exist, because its titular hero mourns the death of his friend. One single human being laments the woeful fate of another single human being. For the poet this fact is of such momentous weight that it can't be overlooked in even the most succinct historical synthesis.
      —Wisława Szymborska, *from* Nonrequired Reading *(1996)*

The reality of wool and that of the finished suit; that's how one might see the relationship of history as we know it in deeds, in action, in textbooks, and history as unused potential. . . . We shouldn't think that things could never turn out otherwise in the history of politics, art, music, literature. We must keep in mind the vast supplies of wool from which our suits are made. Rough bales of that wool, secured against time's ravages, are packed in scrupulously guarded warehouses. My guess is that their stockrooms don't just hold wool for

coming centuries. They also store the unused wool of distant times, the wool of events that never came to pass, nations that were never realized, cities that remained unbuilt, the wool of people who were never born, of those who died too soon, of those whose lives didn't turn out, the wool of unwritten epics and symphonies, of unpainted pictures, of thoughts that never came to mind, the wool of a world in which fate worked differently.
                                —*Adam Zagajewski,* Another Beauty *(1998)*

Little history picks up where Great History leaves off.
                                —*Tadeusz Nyczek,* 22 × Szymborska *(1997)*

On a recent train trip from Krakow to Warsaw, I began chatting with the other occupant of my compartment, a retired engineering professor who collected stamps. He asked where I was from and how I happened to know Polish. I told him I was a Slavist who'd been drawn to the language by way of Poland's great postwar poets, some of whom I happened to translate. The usual response I get when Poles, be they cab drivers or Ph.D.'s, find out that I'm a non-Pole who's learned Polish well enough to translate their poetry is enthusiasm, to say the least: Poland's a wonderful place to be a translator with an obviously non-Slavic last name. But this engineer's response was telling in a different way. When I mentioned my admiration for Szymborska, Miłosz, and Herbert, he said that of the three he could only read Herbert, since only Herbert had never been affiliated with the Communist Party.

Technically speaking, he was right—though his remark demands qualification in ways I won't attempt to address here. After the war, Miłosz served in the Polish diplomatic corps for several years before seeking political asylum in France in 1951; I'll return to this episode in my final chapter. And Szymborska, like Woroszylski and so many other young artists, embraced the party as what seemed to be the only possible salvation from a Europe whose "bourgeois nationalism" had apparently been discredited not just by the rise of fascism, but also by the failure of Western democracies to recognize and combat its threat early on. For Poles particularly, the Western commitment to liberty and justice had a suspiciously hollow ring. The Allies not only failed to honor their pledges to protect Poland from foreign aggression at the war's outset. At Tehran and Yalta, they had, through Churchill and Roosevelt, quietly signed away its future sovereignty as well.

Szymborska joined the Party at the age of nineteen in the early fifties—at the same time that the stubbornly unaffiliated Herbert was busy writing his unpublishable poems "for the desk drawer," in the Polish phrase. She returned her party card only in 1966, in a show of support for the philosopher Leszek Kołakowski, who'd been expelled from the party earlier that year. In an interview of 1991, Szymborska speaks of the unexpected benefits she drew from her years as a true believer. "If it weren't for the sadness, the sense of guilt," she comments, "I might not even regret the experience of those years. Without it, I wouldn't know what belief in the one true cause really is. And how easy it is not to know what you don't want to know. And what mental gymnastics you're capable of when you're confronted with other worldviews." "Reality," she remarks elsewhere,

> sometimes seems so chaotic, so terrifyingly incomprehensible that you long to uncover its permanent order, to distinguish once and for all between what's important and what's trivial, what's outdated and what's new, what's useful and what's obstructive. It's a dangerous temptation, since so often a theory, an ideology that promises to classify and explain everything instead sets up a barrier between the world and [our notion of] progress.

My retired engineer was clearly far from Marxist. But his schematic take on his poetic compatriots illustrates precisely the tendency to tidy up messy realities, past and present, that Szymborska sees at work in her own early embrace of Marxist doctrine. "Once a communist, always a communist"— the life story is as unequivocal and clear-cut as the deceptively straightforward curriculum vitae she proposes in "Writing a Resumé": "Memberships in what but without why."[1]

He is not alone in his reductive retrospection. In their sui generis biography of the poet, Anna Bikont and Joanna Szczęszna recall meeting Szymborska's former high school teacher, one Sister Mianowska, who refused to discuss "that lady who won the Nobel Prize." She couldn't forgive Szymborska's early hymns to Lenin and socialism, or her elegy—"heartfelt," Szymborska comments—on the death of Joseph Stalin.[2] Her Nobel Prize was not received with universal jubilation. Several months after the award had been announced, an irate hotel receptionist in Warsaw felt compelled to explain to me how I'd been taken in. Szymborska had engineered the whole thing, she insisted, from the early espousal of communism when that served her purposes to the split with the Party that would guarantee her favor in the West and eventually bring her to the attention of the Swedish Academy. Szymborska apparently possessed Cassandra's gift without its unhappy consequences. She knew that decades of scraping by on piecemeal editorial work were a safer bet than any lottery. They were bound to lead to Stockholm, wealth, and glory in the end.

It is just this kind of narrative that Szymborska comes to suspect in her mature writing. Time and again she warns against both clear-cut histories derived from hindsight and foregone futures constructed with the help of one ideology or another. More than this: she mistrusts narrative as such, the human proclivity, as she views it, for using more or less Procrustean storylines to tidy a recalcitrant reality. This might seem initially to bring her into line with what Frederic Jameson calls the postmodern "incredulity toward metanarratives." But Szymborska is an awkward postmodernist, not least because of the genre she uses to undermine all manner of master plots. The New Historicists share, of course, the postmodern suspicion of the Western "grand narratives" that they seek to replace with less biased accounts of history and culture. But they are no less suspicious towards the notoriously "antinarrativistic" lyric that seeks an unwarranted exemption from human making and being. I've dealt with these anti-lyric biases at some length in my introduction. It may be worth mentioning, though, that the very term "New Historicism" implicates its practitioners indirectly in the kind of progress-based Western metanarrative they disclaim. The adjective that precedes this most recent brand of historicism cries out, after all, for its inevitable Madison Avenue companion, "improved."[3]

Such inadvertent investment in large-scale storytelling is part of the human project as such, Szymborska's poetry suggests. Indeed, Marxism's success in the American academy might be dictated partly by deep-seated narratological needs, or so we might speculate on reading her work. She herself steers clear of the kind of generalizations that I am guilty of here: "I prefer myself liking people / to myself loving humanity," she explains in one typically self-effacing lyric (214). Still, the species as viewed through the shifting lens of her poems seems driven by a persistent narrative impulse, which operates on every level to which its senses, knowledge, and imagination have access. The post-Marxist Woroszylski dissents from the Great History he had earlier embraced by creating in his poetry and prose an interlocking network of "little histories." He shares his project with a range of postwar Polish poets who might be called the "little historians" and whose ranks would include Miłosz, Herbert, Różewicz, and Białoszewski, among other luminaries. One could easily assemble an anthology of postwar Polish lyrics dedicated to recuperating alternate histories, vanquished histories, and vanished histories of all sorts from these and other writers' work. Certainly Poland's experience of seeing its own history rewritten time and again by one conquering nation or another has sensitized its writers to the ways in which individuals and peoples alike may be revised or deleted entirely by official chroniclers past and present.

But beleaguered nations also breed mythologies best embodied by long-suffering or martyred bards, mythologies to which even the most skeptical poets may succumb: "Perhaps I was born so that the 'Eternal Slaves' might speak through my lips," Miłosz muses in *The Captive Mind.* You would search Szymborska's mature writing in vain for a similar pronouncement. The work of the poet is "hopelessly unphotogenic," she explains in her Nobel lecture (xiii). The poet's life is equally unprepossessing as she presents it, or declines to present it, in the poems. She gives us no "Retribution," no *Quartets,* no *Poema* either with or without a hero. She makes no effort to place an equals sign between her own life and that of her age or nation. Szymborska is arguably the greatest of Poland's "little historians" precisely because of her immunity to barddom and the seductive counternarrative it provides for poets raised in the traditions of unhappy, captive nations.

There are "poets with biographies" and "poets without biographies," Boris Tomashevsky notes. There are the poets, that is, whose works and lives are inextricably entwined in their readers', and their own, minds: Byron, Pushkin, Mickiewicz, Whitman, Rimbaud, Blok, Mayakovsky, Akhmatova, Miłosz . . . the list could be continued indefinitely. And then there are the writers who strive to keep their private lives behind scrupulously shut doors. The mature Szymborska is a poet without a biography par excellence, largely due to her own resistance to clear-cut narratives both in writing and in life. The younger poet, though, had her biography handed to her ready-made: the Soviet-style Socialist Realism imported to postwar Poland provided foolproof templates for citizens and states alike. In Socialist Realist writing, "individual human fates, like the fates of lyric 'I's," Jacek Łukasiewicz remarks, serve only "as models for problems set by the Party as it directs both the nation's industrialization and the development of socialist consciousness among its inhabitants." Szymborska's early poetry is replete with such exemplary "I's." "I want to die a communist," one noble Soviet soldier predictably proclaims in the title poem of her first published volume, *Why We Live* (1954). Another early poem finds ways to fill the interval between birth and death with suitably communist content: "It's not enough that my heart's on the left side. / I want to think, to act, to speak. . . . It's not enough to reject your class. It's harder / to live usefully among the people." But even this is not enough, another lyric suggests: "Dying, I want to befriend / a young communist medical student."[4]

Life and death by the book: this is the formulaic existence that Szymborska dissects in a later poem on the hagiographic afterlives of heroes. "Yes. she loved him very much. Yes, he was born that way. / Yes, she was standing by the prison wall that morning. / Yes, she heard the shots" ("Pietà," 88).

The poem was based, her biographers note, on Szymborska's 1954 visit to "the mother of Nikola Wapcorow, a Bulgarian poet and communist shot by the Nazis in 1942."[5] Her pilgrimage thus coincided with the publication of *Why We Live;* she clearly must have registered the limits of the formulas she was helping to promulgate, to judge by the way she revises them a decade later. Here what is unspoken speaks loudest. The mother's rote answers serve inversely to underscore the particulars of intimate experience concealed behind the official party line.

Szymborska's poem could easily be taken as political commentary, a critique of censorship perhaps, or of Socialist Realism's attempt to eliminate the line that divides public from private existence: "Marxism has liquidated the contradiction between the private and social natures of human beings," one postwar critic exults.[6] But such readings would be misleading. "We are children of our age, / it's a political age. / . . . all affairs—yours, ours, theirs—are political affairs," Szymborska writes in "Children of Our Age," from *People on the Bridge* (1986).[7] "Apolitical poems are also political," the poem continues, in a line that sounds uncomfortably familiar to any habitué of English departments today. And indeed, the poem's purported master key for unlocking all the world's messy mysteries—variants of the adjective "political" (*polityczny*) appear twelve times in the space of twenty-odd lines and conclude each of its first six stanzas—stands revealed as purely academic by the poem's end. This politics consists exclusively of the ritual repetition of its own name. It has no bearing on the larger reality it purports to explain: "Meanwhile, people perished, / animals died, / houses burned, / and the fields ran wild / just as in times immemorial / and less political" (200–201).

After her early experience as a true believer, "Szymborska never again drafted her poetry into any kind of battle," Nyczek remarks. "After the difficult crisis of the fifties," Szymborska herself explains, "I understood that politics was not my element." In Communist Poland, she saw her task not as opposing the regime per se, but as "appealing to those cells in the reader's brain which hadn't yet submitted to the invasion of the Polish People's Republic." "Politics is a vampire that wants to suck all the juices out of us," she comments elsewhere. A prose piece from the early eighties implicitly addresses her own leap from the political avant-garde to the poetic rearguard. "The poet can't keep up," she laments, "he lags behind. In his defense I can only say that someone's got to straggle in the rear. If only to pick up what's been trampled and lost in the triumphal procession of objective laws." The poet abandons the advance guard of Great History's triumphal progress, in other words, to take her place in its wake where she tends to the world's hidden histories; she becomes the poetic patron saint of "lost and overlooked things," the literary caretaker of a cosmic lost-and-found.[8]

The implications are clear for Soviet Marxist historiography, with its conveniently prefabricated master plots for individuals and nations alike. And Socialist Realism followed suit: it "denigrated lyric poetry" in favor of forms governed by a "storyline" (*fabula*). But Szymborska uses her poem to poke holes in more than one kind of story. The mother's ritualized retelling of her noble child's life and death in "Pietà" is familiar from countless variants in the nightly news and Sunday papers: its very title suggests a template applied to suffering mothers and martyred sons throughout the ages. In one talk, Szymborska recalls a film in which Charlie Chaplin, unable to close his overflowing suitcase, simply snips off all the bits and pieces that don't fit: "That's how reality fares when we try to squeeze it into the suitcase of ideology." The ideologies she has in mind are not confined to Eastern Europe's recent totalitarian past. They are the inevitable explanatory tales we construct in our ceaseless, doomed efforts to whittle our unwieldy human experience down to more manageable proportions. Lyric poems thus become crucial because of their antinarrativistic tendencies; they pick up the bits that the storyline proper leaves out.[9]

If "Pietà" concerns, at least in part, the Soviet system and its formulas for secularized sainthood, then another poem, written some two decades later, provides an equally unsettling look at another kind of hagiography. "In Broad Daylight" provides a young Polish poet-martyr, Krzysztof Kamil Baczyński (1921–44), with the "ordinary" biography and mundane daily existence denied him by his heroic early death from a German bullet:

> Sometimes someone would
> yell from the doorway: "Mr. Baczyński, phone call for you"—
> and there'd be nothing strange about that
> being him, about him standing up, straightening his sweater,
> and slowly moving toward the door.
>
> At this sight no one would
> stop talking, no one would
> freeze in mid-gesture, mid-breath
> because this commonplace event would
> be treated—such a pity—
> as a commonplace event. (192–193)

"A man who dies at the age of thirty-five," Walter Benjamin famously remarked, "is at every point of his life a man who dies at the age of thirty-five"—or

at least so he "will appear to remembrance." What chance does an extraor-
dinarily gifted young poet who dies in the Polish Home Army heroically
resisting his nation's invaders have of being remembered as anything other
than an extraordinarily gifted young poet who dies in the Polish Home
Army heroically resisting his nation's invaders? Baczyński's fate looks dis-
comfitingly made to order for a national tradition that, in Julia Hartwig's
words, gives up its best "for the dragon of force and violence to devour / The
young boys the beautiful girls / the best minds the most auspicious talents."
But his fate was not foreordained, Szymborska reminds us: "About his ear,
just grazed by the bullet / when he ducked at the last minute, he would / say:
'I was damned lucky.'" And it does not exhaust the human potential for
banality as well as greatness that a different outcome—"a jamb, a turn, a
quarter inch, an instant" (111)—might have unlocked.[10]

   "In Broad Daylight" was published in Szymborska's collection *The Peo-
ple on the Bridge,* which appeared in 1986, at the height of martial law. It
came out, that is to say, in a Poland besieged by its own rulers whose poetry,
"under the shock of December 1981 [when martial law was declared], had
wrapped itself in a pall, clutched the nation's flag in one hand, a rock in the
other, and headed for the barricades."[11] The time was ripe for a corrective,
however gently applied, to the Polish cult of the poet-bard. The anecdotes
with which I began this chapter point to the high status of poetry in Polish
society even today: one would be hard-pressed to produce American engi-
neering professors or hotel clerks with strong opinions on Robert Pinsky or
Rita Dove either way. But they also point to the perilously close association
between poetry and politics in Polish society: woe to the poet who fails to
fulfill his or her obligations as the nation's unofficial legislator in the face
of foreign oppression. In "In Broad Daylight," Szymborska tacitly reminds
us that state ideologies are not the only form of tunnel vision to hamper
recognition of ordinary experience and particular, irrepeatable lives. The
oppositional ideologies cultivated to counter the state's official story can be
just as ritualized and confining as the doctrines they were devised to resist.
Both heroic biographies, whether poet's or communist's, end necessarily in
martyrs' deaths.

   But what about the miracle of ordinariness? What about the resistance
hero who survives fascist and totalitarian terrors only to be faced with the
commonplace indignities of old age? Such are the unphotogenic trials that
an aging Baczyński would confront: "Goateed, balding, / gray-haired, in
glasses, / with coarsened, weary features, / with a wart on his cheek and
a furrowed forehead, / as if clay had covered up the angelic marble." "The
price, after all, for not having died already / goes up not in leaps but step

by step," she reminds us (192). Szymborska rejects the heroic biographies proffered by victorious state and captive nation alike in favor of the miracles of daily existence in which she "really see[s] nothing ordinary."[12] Or so the story I've told thus far suggests.

Such oppositions are far too easy, though, as Szymborska's tacit dismantling of competing Polish and Soviet martyrologies implies. If everyday existence is so ideally ideology-free, then how do we account for the unquenchable thirst for master narratives that has apparently shaped human history from its beginnings? This is the message suggested by another poem dating, like "Pietà," from the sixties. In "A Palaeolithic Fertility Fetish," Szymborska turns to a vanished matriarchal culture far removed from the "paternal state socialism"[13] of the postwar Polish People's Republic. Yet the prehistoric fetish to whom Szymborska gives voice in this lyric—in a characteristically virtuosic act of poetic ventriloquism—speaks to the same drive for a stripped-down, simplified version of human history that shapes more recent doctrines and myths. Or rather, it embodies such drives in their purest form:

> The Great Mother has no feet.
> What would the Great Mother do with feet.
> Where is she going to go.
> Why would she go into the world's details.
> She has gone just as far as she wants
> and keeps watch in the workshops under her taut skin . . .

From the Great Mother—messy reality held in check by the cult of unencumbered fecundity—to the Great Father and Teacher, Joseph Stalin and beyond: the human need for Great Histories survives the manifold forces that topple these histories time and again. Rather than seeking to escape from these master narratives into our private lives, then, we would be better advised to track down their sources in the commonplace stories that we tell ourselves and one another every day. This, at any rate, is one message underlying a series of lyrics that deal not with heroes and martyrs, but with the tales told by those who miraculously manage to escape the potential calamities awaiting us at every turn—those lucky enough, in other words, to lead an ordinary life.

"Anyone who has lived through wars and revolutions knows that in a human anthill on fire the number of extraordinary meetings, unbelievable coincidences, multiplies tremendously in comparison with periods of peace and everyday routine. One survives because one was five minutes late at a given address where everybody got arrested, or because one did not catch a train that was soon to be blown to pieces." Miłosz's comments on *Doctor*

Zhivago might almost serve as a prose gloss to Szymborska's well-known poem "Could Have."

> It could have happened.
> It had to happen.
> It happened earlier. Later.
> Nearer. Farther off.
> It happened, but not to you.
>
> You were saved because you were the first.
> You were saved because you were the last.
> Alone. With others.
> On the right. The left.
> Because it was raining. Because of the shade.
> Because the day was sunny.
>
> You were in luck—there was a forest.
> You were in luck—there were no trees.
> You were in luck—a rake, a hook, a beam, a brake,
> a jamb, a turn, a quarter inch, an instant.
> You were in luck—just then a straw went floating by.
>
> As a result, because, although, despite.
> What would have happened if a hand, a foot,
> within an inch, a hairsbreadth from
> an unfortunate coincidence.
>
> So you're here? Still dizzy from another dodge, close shave,
> reprieve?
> One hole in the net and you slipped through?
> I couldn't be more shocked or speechless.
> Listen,
> how your heart pounds inside me. (111)

"Was that an accident, fate, or providence?" Miłosz asks.[14] Szymborska's response is to rephrase the question. She gives not the story of a single survivor, but a template for creating the narratives survivors use to explain their apparently miraculous escapes—and recent American history lends grim testimony to its accuracy. The artist Jenny Holzer chose to commemorate September eleventh by projecting this poem, in English translation, onto a Manhattan skyscraper and photographing it for the *New Yorker* magazine. And indeed, anyone with friends or friends of friends living in New York at the time heard shocked versions, in the first phone calls, of Szymborska's poem: the train was late, the car didn't start, the meeting was postponed. "My apologies to chance for calling it necessity," Szymborska writes elsewhere (142). How do we weave the stories that create apparent necessity out of terrifying chance ("you were in luck")?

This is the question that lies behind "Could Have." Szymborska shifts the emphasis of the survivor's tale from the syntagmatic to the paradigmatic, as Roman Jakobson would say. She shifts attention from the "axis of combination" to the "axis of selection" by breaking down the syntagmatic elements of the survivor's tale, the sequence of events that leads by apparent necessity to the miraculous reprieve.[15] "I was in luck, it happened farther off, I was saved because it was raining in the forest, if they'd been a quarter inch closer, if I'd been an instant later, I would never have squeaked through": such would be one version of events pieced together from Szymborska's poem. It would be contradicted, though, by the other, equally plausible accounts assembled from other options. "Earlier," "later," "nearer," "farther off," "but not to you"—so runs a partial inventory of the possibilities presented in the first stanza alone. The ostensibly singular survival stories that furnish this plethora of possibilities end paradoxically by affirming a shared need for a distinctive narrative structure to convert terrifying happenstance into ineluctable fate. To put it more humanly—the poem creates community from seeming isolation. Our lives may be different, but our stories are finally the same: "Listen, / how your heart pounds inside me."

I used the word "happenstance" a moment ago—and this is no accident. This is the term that Stanisław Barańczak and I used to translate the Polish "przypadek" that begins a later lyric, "Seance," which opens as follows:

> Happenstance reveals its tricks.
> It produces, by sleight of hand, a glass of brandy
> and sits Henry down beside it.
> I enter the bistro and stop dead in my tracks.
> Henry—he's none other than
> Agnes's husband's brother,
> and Agnes is related
> to Aunt Sophie's brother-in-law.
> It turns out
> we've got the same great-grandfather. (242–243)

"It has to mean something," the poem's speaker insists—and it does. The ways we weave the connective tissues that link our fates and keep our ordinary lives from feeling random may be dubious: "We want to shout: / Small world! / You could almost hug it! / And for a moment we are filled with joy, / radiant and deceptive." What we do share, though, are the strategies by which we forge these illusory connections. As it turns out, we've got something in common after all.

We want neat beginnings and tidy endings with tightly plotted chapters in between, Szymborska suggests as she works to unravel these carefully patched-together life stories. It is no accident (once again) that the poem I've just cited comes from a collection called *The End and the Beginning* (1993). "Every beginning is only a sequel, after all, / and the book of events / is always open half through" (245): so reads the inconclusive conclusion to "Love at First Sight," which sympathetically dismantles the persistent romantic fable of its title. The poem itself gently pries open the lovers' airtight narrative to happenstance's more uncertain charms:

> They'd be amazed to hear
> that Chance has been toying with them
> now for years.
>
> Not quite ready yet
> to become their Destiny,
> it pushed them close, drove them apart,
> it barred their path,
> stifling a laugh,
> and then leaped aside. (244–245)

If and when the lovers' tale reaches the desired denouement, it will only be followed by yet another episode in the never-ending story, Szymborska warns in "A Tale Begun":

> The world is never ready
> for the birth of a child.
>
> Our ships are not yet back from Winnland.
> We still have to get over the S. Gothard pass.
> We've got to outwit the watchmen on the desert of Thos,
> fight our way through the sewers to Warsaw's center,
> gain access to King Harald the Butterpat,
> and wait until the downfall of Minister Fouché.
> Only in Acapulco can we begin anew. (210–211)

But we never do begin anew. Only "the detail / is unyielding," Szymborska insists elsewhere (87). Here, though, the details are endlessly mutable: "We haven't got the trucks, we haven't got the Minghs' support. . . . No news so far about the Tartars' captives." What remains intact is the framework used for a tale begun time and time again.

Our tales about beginnings meet their match in the conclusions we reach about our endings, or so other lyrics suggest. In her exquisite "Elegiac Calculation," Szymborska questions the human need for closure of a different kind, as she carefully dismantles the formulas and conventions we use to ease ourselves by an impassable divide:

> How many, after a shorter or longer life
> (if they still see a difference),
> good, because it's beginning,
> bad, because it's over
> (if they don't prefer the reverse),
> have found themselves on the far shore
> (if they found themselves at all
> and if another shore exists)— . . . (236)

Another poem suggests the larger implications of the tidied-up afterlives we try to give the dead:

> We read the letters of the dead like helpless gods,
> but gods, nonetheless, since we know the dates that follow . . .
> The dead sit before us comically, as if on buttered bread,
> or frantically pursue the hats blown from their heads.
> Their bad taste, Napoleon, steam, electricity,
> their fatal remedies for curable diseases,
> their foolish apocalypse according to St. John,
> their counterfeit heaven on earth according to Jean-Jacques . . .
> We watch the pawns on their chessboards in silence,
> even though we see them three squares later.
> Everything the dead predicted has turned out completely different.
> Or a little bit different—which is to say, completely different . . . (118)

"Hindsight's twenty-twenty," the saying goes. But Szymborska does not merely expose our tendency to treat past histories as a series of "foregone conclusions," in Michael André Bernstein's phrase. Her concern is finally with what Frank Kermode calls the "anthropomorphic paradigms of apocalypse" we use "to give ourselves meaning."[16] She not only hints at the teleological impulses that have shaped Western history from its Judeo-Christian origins—"the foolish apocalypse of St. John" is of course itself a teleologically minded rereading of the Hebrew Bible, the text that provided Western culture with its most enduring paradigm of end-directed history—to more modern incarnations, from Rousseau's "counterfeit heaven on earth" to Napoleon and the Romantic cult of the Great Man, to technology and the worship of progress ("steam, electricity").

We are of course the latter-day inheritors of all these variations on a teleological theme, the poem's final lines remind us: "The most fervent of them [the dead] gaze confidingly into our eyes: / their calculations tell them that they'll find perfection there" (118). "Our twentieth century was going to improve on the others," Szymborska comments ruefully in "The Century's Decline." We were to be, in other words, the proof in the pudding, the pièce de résistance of all our benighted precursors' grand designs. Needless to say, we've let our ancestors down in a large way: "Too many things have happened / that weren't supposed to happen, / and what was supposed to come about has not" (198–199). And if we have failed to redeem their various myths of progress—"good and strong / are still two different men" (198–199)—then whence do we derive the authority with which we, their enlightened offspring, so blithely dismiss their misguided prophecies? Aren't we falling back on the same notions we mock?

In the late sixties or early seventies, when "The Letters of the Dead" was likely written (it appeared in 1972 in the collection *Should Have*), one phrase in particular must have resonated with Szymborska's compatriots. Rousseau was not the only great modern thinker whose prophesied "heaven on earth" had proven false. The promised land of the Polish People's Republic was also a sham: the materialist kingdom of Marx, in its Soviet imperialist redaction, had spectacularly failed to materialize on Polish soil or elsewhere. Even erstwhile true believers had become diehard skeptics. In *The Captive Mind*, Miłosz argues that Marxism's enduring appeal lies largely in its capacity to combine our most pervasive, propulsive teleological traditions into one compelling, quasi-scientific master plot: the Enlightenment cult of progress meets Romantic historiosophy by way of Isaiah. "He reads one after the other / Isaiah and *Das Kapital* / then in the fervor of discussion / confuses his quotations," as Zbigniew Herbert writes of his alter ego in "Mr. Cogito and a Poet of a Certain Age."[17]

Szymborska suggests something similar as the arch-apocalyptist John joins forces with the proto-Romantic Jean-Jacques and two key nineteenth-century technological advances, steam and electricity. The young Szymborska had conflated such traditions unironically in an early hymn to Lenin: "The grave in which this Adam / of a new human race lies / will be crowned by flowers / from planets still unknown," she exults. The history which began with Adam will find its culmination not in Christ or the Second Coming, but in the interplanetary apotheosis of the Soviet state's founding father. Lenin himself was not immune to such interplanetary fantasies, as an interview with H. G. Wells reveals. "If we succeed in making contact with other planets," he told the writer, "all our philosophical, social, and moral ideas will have to be revised, and in this event these potentialities will become limitless." All our theories will need to be adjusted upwards, in other words; our notion of progress will be inflated to cosmic proportions.[18]

What does the mature Szymborska make of such quasi-scientific fictions? Instead of extending Western teleological tendencies onwards and upwards ad infinitum, she turns them against the very notions of progress that underpin Soviet Marxism. Darwin's "survival of the fittest" became, in Soviet hands, the justification for an inevitable class struggle with a preordained outcome: only the proletarian righteous would survive, while lesser species (aristocrats and, of course, the despised bourgeois) would be forced to step aside or, ideally, vanish from the face of the earth completely, much like their doomed analogues in the animal kingdom, the dinosaurs. In the ungainly, but remarkably seductive amalgam that was Soviet communism, the anthropocentricism in which the Judeo-Christian tradition is rooted—"let them have dominion over the fish of the sea, and over the fowl of the air, and over the cattle, and over all the earth" (Genesis 1:26)—joins hands with the Darwinian evolution and proletarian revolution that are catalyzed in turn by the nineteenth century's boundless faith in technology taken to cosmic extremes.

In her early poetry, Szymborska subscribed wholeheartedly to this vision: "Humans, earth's inhabitants / are the highest form of matter," she announces in *Why We Live*.[19] What if, the later poet asks, we deprive such human-made teleologies of their anthropomorphic conclusions? What if evolutionary changes and technological advances have not stopped with us (and why should they)? We look down on the so-called lesser species with whom we share the planet: "A dead beetle lies on the path through the field. . . . The horror of this sight is moderate" (151). How might we look in turn when "seen from above" (151)? One of the many "miniseries" that run throughout Szymborska's work concerns this question, as she hands pride of place in the great chain of being to various hypothesized observers from outer space. Human progress looks pitiful indeed when viewed from this perspective:

> He has only just learned to tell dreams from waking;
> only just realized that he is he;
> only just whittled with his hand né fin
> a flint, a rocket ship . . . ("No End of Fun," 106)

Perhaps our grand historical schemes scarcely register on their intergalactic monitors:

> Maybe thus far we aren't of much interest?
> The control monitors aren't usually plugged in?
> Only for wars, preferably large ones,
> for the odd ascent above our clump of Earth,

for major migrations from point A to B?
Or "maybe just the opposite":
They've got a taste for trivia up there?
Look! on the big screen a little girl
is sewing a button on her sleeve.
The radar shrieks,
the staff comes at a run. ("Maybe All This," 248–249)

"God is in the details," it's been said. Perhaps our extraterrestrial observers take delight in the tiny, human particulars that get overlooked in the "triumphal procession" of the ideally teleological histories we construct for ourselves time and again? Perhaps advancement doesn't necessarily mean endless expansion of the big picture? Perhaps progress doesn't actually progress the way it should? Perhaps there's something to be said for fine-tuning?

If this is true, it may be time to review the way we imagine our collective past as well, to see what's been lost or abandoned en route to our predestined future. "If I'm perceived as a person who lives by modest observations, details, I won't protest since that's the way it is," Szymborska has remarked. The poet Julian Przyboś, she continues, "concluded [from my poems] that I'm myopic. That is, I can only really see small things from close up. I don't see large panoramas so precisely."[20] Szymborska's poetic myopia proves a useful corrective to panoramic pasts as well as radiant futures. In "Census," she points to the inescapable sins of omission that plague even the great narratives on which the Western tradition is based:

On the hill where Troy once stood,
they've dug up seven cities.
Seven cities. Six too many
for a single epic.
What's to be done with them? What?
Hexameters burst,
nonfictional bricks appear between the cracks,
ruined walls rise mutely as in silent films . . .

"History rounds off skeletons to zero," she notes elsewhere. "A thousand and one is still only a thousand" ("Starvation Camp near Jaslo," 42). In "Census" she laments the unnamed masses who never make it close enough to history's pages even to be rounded off: "reckless squatters jostle for a place in history / . . . Hector's extras, no less brave than he, / thousands and thousands of singular faces" (81–82).

"There are no empty spots . . . in the dense fabric of history," Szymborska writes in a prose piece on Montaigne. "Or rather, there are—there's just no way to prove their existence." The poet, though, can make us aware that each narrative we spin out of the past, however accurate, excludes by necessity countless other plot lines, whether potential or actual, major or minor. More importantly, as a disillusioned graduate of the Joseph Stalin school of teleological progress, she can warn us to be on our guard against what Bernstein calls "apocalyptic history" in his study of *Foregone Conclusions*. His book deals specifically with the misrepresentations of the Holocaust that results from transforming possible outcomes into inescapable endings: "No one came to Frau Hitler in Braunau and said, 'Unto you the Führer is born.'" [21] The comment might stand as an epigraph to one of Szymborska's best-known poems, "Hitler's First Photograph":

> And who's this little fellow in his itty-bitty robe?
> That's tiny baby Adolf, the Hitlers' little boy!
> Will he grow up to be an L.L.D.?
> Or a tenor in Vienna's Opera House?
> Whose teensy hand is this, whose little ear and eye and nose?
> Whose tummy full of milk, we just don't know:
> printer's, doctor's, merchant's, priest's?
> Where will those tootsy-wootsies finally wander?
> To a garden, to a school, to an office, to a bride?
> Maybe to the Bürgermeister's daughter? . . . (196–197)

It is a shockingly inappropriate opening for the twentieth century's most infamous biography: could Hitler have ever been an infant? By surrounding him, moreover, with the kitschy props and silly chatter that are the standard accoutrements of every happy, well-fed baby—"A little pacifier, diaper, rattle, bib, / our bouncing boy, thank God and knock on wood, is well"—Szymborska pushes us towards the impossible. The name Adolph Hitler becomes equivalent not to Satan or the Antichrist, but to the kid next door, the neighbors' noisy newborn who keeps you up at night.

Apocalyptic history lets us off the hook. The Antichrist's brand of evil is Evil with a capital E; it is qualitatively different from our own petty flaws and peccadillos. Moreover, the future of the Antichrist is foreordained; it can't be contained by merely mortal efforts, and it has nothing to do with our mundane daily routines. Szymborska's poem suggests otherwise. "Where will those tootsy-wootsies finally wander?" the speaker asks, and the question would have been genuinely open back in 1889, unimaginable as that is in hindsight: in Braunau, "a small, but worthy town . . . no one hears howling dogs, or fate's footsteps."[22]

Beware of the ways we tell tales, Szymborska warns. In "Census," she pulls threads from the epic tale that sets Western literature in motion. She tackles an even more celebrated beginning in "Lot's Wife," written in the mid-seventies. Her revisionary history turns back to the beginning to end all beginnings, to Genesis and the roots of the Judeo-Christian teleological tradition. It recalls the famous cautionary tale, elliptical in the extreme, that describes the punishment of the righteous Lot's unnamed wife, who violates Jehovah's prohibition while fleeing her sinful hometown of Sodom. "But his wife looked back from behind him, and she became a pillar of salt" (Genesis 19:26): this is the biblical account in its entirety. Szymborska turns from the unremembered masses to a single unnamed victim whose fate has become synonymous with the kind of "feminine" disobedience that prompted all our earthly travails.

> *Lot's Wife*
> They say I looked back out of curiosity.
> But I could have had other reasons.
> I looked back mourning my silver bowl.
> Carelessly, while tying my sandal strap.
> So I wouldn't have to keep staring at the righteous nape
> of my husband Lot's neck.
> From the sudden conviction that if I dropped dead
> he wouldn't so much as hesitate.
> From the disobedience of the meek.
> Checking for pursuers.
> Struck by the silence, hoping God had changed his mind.
> Our two daughters were already vanishing over the hilltop.
> I felt age within me. Distance.
> The futility of wandering. Torpor.
> I looked back setting my bundle down.
> I looked back not knowing where to set my foot.
> Serpents appeared on my path,
> spiders, field mice, baby vultures.
> They were neither good nor evil now—every living thing
> was simply creeping or hopping along in the mass panic.
> I looked back in desolation.
> In shame because we had stolen away.
> Wanting to cry out, to go home.
> Or only when a sudden gust of wind
> unbound my hair and lifted up my robe.
> It seemed to me that they were watching from the walls of Sodom
> and bursting into thunderous laughter again and again.
> I looked back in anger.
> To savor their terrible fate.
> I looked back for all the reasons given above.

I looked back involuntarily.
It was only a rock that turned underfoot, growling at me.
It was a sudden crack that stopped me in my tracks.
A hamster on its hind paws tottered on the edge.
It was then we both glanced back.
No, no. I ran on,
I crept, I flew upward
until darkness fell from the heavens
and with it scorching gravel and dead birds.
I couldn't breathe and spun around and around.
Anyone who saw me must have thought I was dancing.
It cannot be excluded that my eyes were open.
It's possible I fell facing the city. (149–150)

Szymborska replaces the single sentence of Genesis with forty-four lines containing no fewer than twenty-five possible explanations for the behavior that the Bible describes so perfunctorily. The poem thus joins the company of Szymborska's many poem-lists in which a harried speaker struggles to keep up with a reality that resists all efforts to contain it in lyric form. This particular list, though, is even more unruly than usual. This is due not just to the speaker's own confusion—she herself doesn't know precisely why she did it—but to our confusion about the speaker. Who is turning back here? The answer seems clear enough—Lot's wife herself. And to what does she return? The picture begins to blur the minute we ask the question. The poem responds not to the biblical text itself, but to subsequent versions of events: "*They say (Podobno)* I looked back out of curiosity" (my emphasis). This wife responds not to Genesis itself but to later, apocryphal attempts to supplement the official story by aligning it with Pandora's box or Eve's temptation. She looks back, in other words, neither to Sodom itself, nor to Genesis, but to ways in which the biblical account has been amplified and distorted over time. Szymborska's speaker is what Dostoevsky would call a "fantastic" narrator, whose ability to tell the story we are hearing is contradicted by the very story he or she tells. (William Holden's dead screenwriter in *Sunset Boulevard* is a prime example.) A pillar of salt has been posthumously endowed not just with consciousness and speech, but with the awareness both of her own history and of the subsequent histories of that history.

The least we might expect from such a long-sighted speaker would be an effort to set the record straight. But the poem's second line already warns us not to anticipate precisely what the first line seems to promise: a direct eyewitness account. The speaker doesn't say she "had other reasons" (*miałam inne powody*) for turning back apart from curiosity; she says she "*could* have had other reasons" (*mogłam mieć inne powody*). The speaker herself, in other words, isn't quite sure why she did it. What follows is not so much a definitive version as a catalogue of possibilities, a list of every reason that might conceivably have led to her fatal faux pas. She gives us not history, in other words, but hypotheses. Moreover, her various conjectures refuse to hang together: they range from the sublime ("hoping God had changed his mind") to the ridiculous ("a hamster on its hind legs tottered on the edge"), from petty spite ("to savor their terrible fate") to pragmatic self-preservation ("checking for pursuers"). They span the spectrum of human emotion and encompass the range of life on earth, from insect to reptile to mammal and even beyond, up to the God who may or may not be the cause of her anguished flight.

The only possibility she omits is one that might form the basis of a single coherent narrative: this string of speculations cannot be reassembled into a satisfyingly straightforward chronicle of events. The implications of this are manifold. In "May 16, 1973," Szymborska reminds us how little we retain of even what we might reasonably claim to know best, our own first-hand experience: "I was filled with feelings and sensations. / Now all that's like a line of dots in parentheses" (246–247). In "Lot's Wife," as elsewhere, Szymborska suggests that human motivations are contradictory, confused, and varied; that we ourselves never fully remember the whole story of our lives (if indeed we know it to begin with); and that we give an unequivocal account of our own histories only by reducing or even falsifying the personal past we purportedly represent.

Such confusion, moreover, is endemic to the kind of mass flight from the shattered city that Lot's wife recalls, as Szymborska knew all too well from her experience in wartime Poland, and as newspapers and broadcasts continue to remind us daily. "Some people flee some other people. / In some country under a sun / and some clouds. / They abandon something close to all they've got," she writes in a lyric written some two decades after "Lot's Wife" ("Some People," 262). The frantic flight of Szymborska's speaker is both irretrievably particular and all too common; neither the first-person singular, nor the third-person plural can do it justice. Her story, moreover, cannot be safely confined to the past tense, exiled to the epic beginnings of a tradition of which we are the improved, latter-day inheritors. Human pasts are—so these poems suggest—both endlessly repetitive and irrecoverably personal. As such, they defeat all efforts to provide them with a comfortably fixed and final narrative form.

Throughout her writing, Szymborska resists the notion of "existential historicism," that is, a faith in our imaginative capacity to enter fully into a distant mind formed by a vanished past:[23] if we ourselves can't be trusted to provide a reliable record of our own histories, how on earth can we adequately represent the lives of others? As she unpostmodernistically insists, though, "reality demands" that we must try (232). She uses other viewpoints time and again in her writing, be they those of tarsiers, terrorists, or extraterrestrials. But she employs them to expand the resources of what one of her cosmic visitors calls human "speech's personal best," "the conditional" (106): that is, our ability to say "what if," to imagine, however imperfectly, a world or worldview other than our own. The use of the first-person in "Lot's Wife" is especially puzzling, though. The temporal perspective fits the modern Polish poet far better than the hapless wife of ancient chronicles. Indeed, the poem's first two lines read more smoothly when revised to eliminate this discrepancy: "They say *she* looked back out of curiosity / But *she* might have had other reasons." The whole poem could easily be altered to read as a series of speculations posed by a contemporary writer imagining a past she cannot access, a past that may never have actually existed: "*She* looked back mourning her silver bowl. / Carelessly, while tying *her* sandal strap," and so on.

Such revisions would help make sense of the oddly modern turns of phrase that surface in the poem's conclusion: "I looked back *for all the reasons given above*"; "*It cannot be excluded* that my eyes were open"; "*It's possible* I fell facing the city." "For all the reasons given above": this is the answer to a questionnaire or a multiple choice exam, not an explanation for personal past behavior. Like the other phrases, it betrays the disconcertingly double-voiced speaker's roots in the modern age. The bureaucratic jargon is a typically twentieth-century way of framing, distorting, or even erasing individual biographies. This kind of language would be all too familiar to unwilling adepts of "newspeak" (*nowomowa*), the "hermetic poetics" of double- and triple-talk employed in the People's Republic[24]—though the bureaucratese that Szymborska evokes here is also familiar to anyone versed in any of the many non-Soviet dialects of red tape and paperwork spoken today. By inserting these distinctively modern phrases into the monologue of her ostensibly archaic speaker, Szymborska calls attention, in typically oblique fashion, to the distinctively modern vantage point—both hers and ours—from which we view this or any distant history.

She also calls to mind certain habits that have remained unchanged, so she claims, from ancient times to our own. In a brief prose piece, Szymborska recalls the posthumous fate that befell the single woman ever to reign in ancient Egypt: "Soon after Hatshepsut's death . . . they energetically set about erasing her name from the list of pharaohs. Every cartouche bearing her name, every likeness of her as pharaoh, every written reference to her was destroyed. We know this sort of thing very well from other sources. Through large stretches of our twentieth century undesirable political personages were likewise forced to vanish from public memory from one day to the next. Their names disappeared from newspapers and encyclopedias, and palm trees suddenly sprouted over their pictures in group photographs." "Trimming history to fit present needs," she concludes, "is an iron rule of all satraps." Szymborska knew such rescripted histories at first hand. The very subject of history, Sheila Fitzpatrick notes, was banned for a time from post-revolutionary Soviet school curricula "on the grounds that it was irrelevant to contemporary life." The Soviet state had not managed to obliterate history completely in the name of the radiant future by the time "Lot's Wife" was written some fifty-odd years later. It had, however, perfected the art of periodically airbrushing its own past, and those of its colonies, in pursuit of its shifting interests.[25]

History belongs to the victors: the phrase has a special resonance for Poles, whose nation has been bisected, trisected, and even excised from the map of Europe at various points over the last two centuries. Postwar Polish writers have become specialists, as I've suggested, in "episodes inscribed on the margins of Great History,"[26] and Szymborska's version of "Lot's Wife" clearly draws upon her experience of history used and abused by colonizing powers, totalitarian dictators, or some combination of the two. But this does not exhaust its frame of reference. The problem is not simply that the Lots of the world (and the wrathful deities who back them) are all too often entrusted with the task of recording our past. Humans invariably revise their own histories in the process of relating them, she suggests. And this proclivity is writ large when states undertake the retelling of entire races and nations both in life and on the page. This tendency is not confined to the victors—though they generally have better luck in making their versions stick. But victims, be they persons or nations, can likewise skew history to their own purposes, and Szymborska is wary of contributing either to the official version of events or to a counter-history designed to supplement or subvert the official story.

"Who will mourn for this woman? / Is she not the least of losses? / My heart alone will never forget / She who gave her life for a single glance." So ends Anna Akhmatova's version of "Lot's Wife" (1922–24), composed in the immediate aftermath of Russia's years of revolution and civil war. "Time, forward!" was the fledgling state's rallying cry—but Akhmatova defiantly turns back to commemorate a long-vanished woman who likewise refused to obey commands from on high as she, too, turned back to bear witness to a perished past. She thus performs what Szymborska sees as a key function of the lyric poet in an age of Great History: "One single human being laments the woeful fate of another single human being."[27]

Unlike Akhmatova, though, Szymborska does not seek to restore a forgotten past in her own "Lot's Wife": she calls attention to a missing history only to render it still more inconclusive. Early Soviet denunciations of the lyric were echoed decades later by postwar Polish poets struggling to renounce bourgeois "lyric lamentations," "individualism" and "formalism" in the name of a collective "poetry that would speak to the sensibilities of workers and peasants, that would enter the hearts of the [nation's] most progressive people." Instead of taking her place in the state-orchestrated collective hymn to the coming future, Akhmatova uses the first-person singular voice of the lyric poet to commemorate a single vanished past: an isolated heart recalls a solitary glance.[28]

Szymborska is no less suspicious of Great Histories, and no less insistent upon the need for lyric supplements to cast doubt upon canonical pasts and foregone futures. But Akhmatova's defiantly single-minded speaker knows precisely what she's retrieving and why. Szymborska is the child of a different age; for the reformed True Believer, uncertainty itself becomes a virtue. The lyric's self-consciously inadequate witness provides the best defense against would-be authoritative histories large and small. "Four billion people on this earth, / but my imagination is still the same," she laments in "A Large Number." "It's still bad with large numbers":

> My choices are rejections, since there is no other way,
> but what I reject is more numerous,
> denser, more demanding than before.
> A little poem, a sigh, at the cost of indescribable losses . . . (145)

Each choice is a loss. Every history we choose to tell—whether plural or singular, public or private, authorized or not—is told only at the cost of countless other stories that might have been, that were but went unseen, that were seen and then forgotten or erased. Both personal narratives and grand master plots are rooted in a deeply human need to make consequence of chaos.

I have used "we" repeatedly in this chapter, and in this I have followed Szymborska's lead. "We are," "we read," "we watch," "we call," "we still don't see," "we just don't know," "we may well be": her poetry is replete with verbs in the first person plural. But this is a plural with a difference, as my last examples suggest. Szymborska rejects the staunch collective based on Common Knowledge in favor of a more unstable community derived from shared uncertainty. "We lived in the plural," Adam Zagajewski laments in a poem of the mid-eighties; he has in mind not just the enforced collectivity of a sovietized society, but the oppositional collectives forged to combat their state-imposed counterpart. He and his fellow poets of Poland's "Generation of '68" would come to see the lyric's task as defending an "I" endangered by an ever-expanding variety of "large numbers," including at times that of their own dissident community.[29]

The "large number versus the single being" is the great theme of Szymborska's poetry, Zagajewski argues in his review of her collection *A Large Number* (1976). Her writing demonstrates that "poetry must take its direction from particularity, specificity, individualism," Stanisław Barańczak insists in his own discussion of the volume. But the relationship between the poet's "I" and the large number is more fraught than these remarks suggest. What does it mean to have an individual viewpoint? What does it mean to be a single self? What is the "I," lyric or otherwise? Szymborska's speakers range from tranquillizers to lemurs to Lot's wife and beyond, as yet another poet of '68, Julian Kornhauser, notes. Even when she speaks as something approximating herself, though, it is only to cast that self into doubt: "Why after all this one and not the rest? / Why this specific self, not in a nest, but a house? . . . Why on earth now . . . and why on earth?" (128).[30] The lyric viewpoint, in turn, becomes the basis of a new kind of collectivity. "We," such as we are, are brought together by our need for a shared story that turns out differently, we insist, each time we tell it:

> With smiles and kisses, we prefer
> to seek accord beneath our star,
> although we're different (we concur)
> just as two drops of water are.
>   ("Nothing Twice," 20)

Counterrevolution in Poetic Language: Poland's Generation of '68

> *It is possible to speak of revolutionary poetry or art, in the sense of poetry or art which awakens emotions favorable to revolution, that is, which contributes to the destruction of the existing institutions of power. However, when leaders call for revolutionary poetry or art they have nothing like that in mind; quite the opposite, they want poetry and art which help to stabilize their domination.*
>
> *—Leszek Kołakowski, "Revolution— A Beautiful Sickness" (1979)*

Streetfighting East and West

"The Generation of '68": the term will seem self-evident to any aging baby boomer. The student rebellions of 1968 shook college campuses and city streets, after all, from Berkeley to Berlin, from Paris to Prague and Warsaw. Only a few months and some eight hundred miles seem initially to separate the upheavals that convulsed Warsaw in March 1968 from the student strikes that shook Paris in May later the same year. Both rebellions were, as Daniel Cohn-Bendit remarks, "anti-authoritarian revolts" par excellence. In both capitals, students resisted a hated state and its tainted offshoots—the academy, the courts, the press—by taking to the streets in unprecedented numbers, provoking the despised establishment to strike back with police action and mass arrests. And in both cases this anti-authoritarianism took a self-consciously linguistic turn: language itself became a key battlefield in the struggle of generations. In Poland, students and writers alike sought to subvert the pervasive "newspeak" (*nowomowa*) imposed by a regime that demanded absolute control not just over the minds and bodies of its inhabitants, but over the very relationship between language and the reality it ostensibly described. Polish students called for the linguistic recuperation of the "unrepresented world," the everyday reality erased or distorted beyond recognition by the Polish dialect of a Sovietspeak that claimed monolithic, monologic rights to both representation and reality as such.[1]

The French revolts likewise focused on a "guerilla war of speech acts" that worked to disrupt the "verbal rituals" and "forms of linguistic exchange" on which the status quo relied. May of 1968 "opened up a Pandora's box of language," Yve-Alain Bois comments. We in the American academy still live with this Parisian Pandora's theoretical offspring today, as tenured professors and anxious job-seekers alike embrace the esoteric vocabulary and anti-authoritarian worldview of theorists whose visions were shaped in fundamental ways by the experience of May, 1968: Roland Barthes, Michel Foucault, Jacques Derrida, Julia Kristeva, Jacques Lacan, Pierre Bourdieu, and others.[2]

These theorists have taught us, among other things, to "interrogate"— with a vengeance—the seeming transparency of ordinary speech. The phrase "Generation of '68" is a case in point. Its seeming obviousness conceals as much as it reveals—but Western commentators have turned a blind eye to its richest contradictions. Dennis Hollier's thumbnail description of the student revolts provides a prime example of such blindness. "The years 1966–1970," he observes, "witnessed the emergence of an international student movement, whose chief centers were Berkeley, Berlin, Milan, Paris, and Tokyo, and whose mobilizing theme was the Vietnam war." His list of cities in revolt stops short at the Berlin Wall, and his reluctance to venture past Checkpoint Charlie is telling. "I supported the May 1968 movement," one of Poland's premier dissidents, Adam Michnik, comments in an interview with Cohn-Bendit, himself a participant in the French revolts, some twenty years after the fact. Such support was a one-way street. Paris's protesters were oblivious at best to the protests being held—and suppressed—just a day's train ride away to the east. And their intellectual inheritors have generally sustained this less than illustrious tradition.[3]

The chief international event catalyzing the Warsaw revolts, Michnik comments, was not Vietnam, but the "Prague Spring" of 1968 that blossomed under the leadership of Alexander Dubček, who held out the possibility of a "socialism with a human face" not forged by fiat from afar, but generated by the more local desires of individual nations and their inhabitants. "Polish students were chanting Dubček's name in the streets of Warsaw," one historian notes. "We cried out, 'Poland awaits her Dubček'!" Michnik recalls. The subsequent Soviet invasion of Czechoslovakia, in which Polish troops took part, marked, he adds, "the worst [day] in my life." For Parisian students and intellectuals, though, the short-lived Prague Spring, if acknowledged at all, met as often as not with "incomprehending, even hostile reactions." Its participants were, one leftist group charged, "willing victims of petit-bourgeois ideologies (humanism, liberty, justice, progress, secret universal suffrage)." Warsaw's riots went unmentioned.[4]

Prague and Vietnam: the catalysts of the student uprisings East and West point to a fundamental schism in the anti-authoritarian revolt that was, Cohn-Bendit notes, "our generation's common experience." This rift finally led Michnik to recognize the "profound difference" between himself and his Western counterparts, for all their shared anti-authoritarian sympathies. In the Eastern bloc, protests against American participation in Vietnam were mandated from above: they meant supporting the establishment, not resisting it. Members of a communist society were expected, even required, to protest en masse the invasion of a fledgling people's democracy by the forces of bourgeois capitalist aggression. The Soviet bloc status quo came close, in short, to the program espoused by the Parisian resistance, at least in this regard—though the official newspapers attacked the Parisian protesters no less viciously than their Polish counterparts, Michnik remembers. But Polish students could openly protest neither the invasion of Prague, nor their own country's—involuntary—participation in quelling the very dreams to which they themselves aspired.[5]

The People's State's crackdown against the March protests was swift and effective: Michnik met the news of the invasion of Czechoslovakia while awaiting trial for his participation in the '68 protests. He subsequently spent eighteen months in jail in what proved to be the first of many imprisonments for his dissident activities, and was thus unable to complete his undergraduate degree.[6] Like many of the Polish protesters, he had begun his dissident career as a Marxist revisionist hoping to reshape the state from within. The regime's response to the Warsaw protests, combined with the Soviet invasion of Czechoslovakia, helped to disabuse him and likeminded thinkers of the notion that Eastern bloc communism might prove amenable to such reforms.

Parisian students fighting for a utopian socialist future to replace a tarnished bourgeois present could hardly be expected to sympathize with their contemporaries resisting the incursions of a leftist utopia in power. French students and intellectuals may have rejected the Stalinism that precursors like Jean-Paul Sartre had defended so stalwartly. They inherited, though, his reluctance to criticize, or even recognize, the phenomenon of left-wing oppression generally—a reluctance shared by their American intellectual descendants. The Algerian war marked French intellectuals' turn away, Danielle Marx-Scouras remarks, "from Moscow to the Third World." They realized with a shock that Sartre's generation had neglected French complicity in Third World oppression even while espousing Marxist egalitarian ideals, that diehard leftists could, in other words, combine the theoretically uncombinable by "being simultaneously Stalinist and imperialist." The Soviet Union was thus "not necessarily at the vanguard of history." By "shifting from Russia to the Third World," however, France's "New Left" could bolster "Marxism while condemning both Stalinism and colonialism." Stalinism and imperialism, Stalinism and colonialism: the terms are used here as virtual antonyms. These intellectuals need only have turned to their own divided continent, though, to find the Soviet empire actively sustaining Stalin's legacy by violently enforcing his imperial claims on unwilling colonies closer to home.[7]

Revolutions and Poetic Language

If I had the time, I could show that Stalin was logocentrist.
            —Jacques Derrida, Moscou aller-retour *(2005)*

There is, it seems, a hidden link between theories of literature as écriture . . . *and the growth of the totalitarian state.*
            —Czesław Miłosz, Nobel Lecture *(1980)*

Prague, Michnik remarks, was only one formative experience for young Polish dissidents in the spring of 1968. He cites a key local catalyst as well. Polish students first took to the streets, he recalls, when the government shut down a production of the great Romantic Adam Mickiewicz's *Forefather's Eve* for its anti-Russian sentiments. Both the production itself and its abrupt conclusion marked, one student commented, "one of the culminating points in the life of my generation." Another student participant, the critic Tadeusz Nyczek, comments that Mickiewicz "became the hero of the 'March generation'; mass meetings were held around his statue in Warsaw and Cracow, and his name became the slogan for freedom of the word." One would, I suspect, search in vain for a comparable phenomenon among the other student insurrections of '68. It points to the surprising—to Western eyes, at any rate—centrality of Romantic poetry in Polish resistance movements, and not among students alone. A striking worker would later pin lines from Byron's "Giaour" in Mickiewicz's translation to a makeshift altar in the Lenin Shipyard in Gdańsk, the birthplace of the Solidarity Movement in 1980; resisting dockers and miners circulated excerpts from Mickiewicz and his fellow Romantic Juliusz Słowacki at meetings and demonstrations.[8]

I can't speak to the place of Romantic poetry in the French student uprisings and workers' strikes. I would guess, though, that Hugo's impact on revolutionary politics in recent French history was less noticeable than that of Mickiewicz in Poland. Poetry played a key role just the same in the theories generated by the upheavals of 1968; Kristeva's monumental *Revolution in Poetic Language* (*La révolution du langage poétique*, 1974) was not an isolated event. "Mao Zedong is the only man in politics and the only communist leader since Lenin to have frequently insisted on the necessity of working upon language and writing in order to transform ideology," Kristeva insists in an essay on Barthes.[9] The revolutionary leaders apparently worked hand in glove, for theoretical purposes at least, with the great modern innovators in poetic speech. Mao and Mallarmé, Lenin and Lautréamont: such unexpected pairings are standard fare in the writings of both Kristeva herself and her fellow participants in the avant-garde literary group Tel Quel, whose affiliates included at various points Lacan, Barthes, Foucault, Derrida, and other theoretical luminaries.

Epigraphs drawn from Mallarmé and Marx adorn Tel Quel's collective manifesto "Division of the Assembly." The document attempts to trace the aesthetic and political genealogy of the "cultural revolution" that emerged in the wake of May, 1968: "To specify the historical dimension of what is 'happening' now, we have to go back beyond effects situated in the 1920s and 1930s (Surrealism, Formalism, the development of structural linguistics) in order to more correctly situate a more radical break at the end of the last century (Lautréamont, Mallarmé, Marx, Freud)." "Ideas do not exist separately from language," Marx proclaims at the manifesto's outset. He might well have been puzzled, though, by its subsequent summons "*to articulate a politics* logically linked to a non-representational dynamic of writing: that is: an analysis of the misunderstandings provoked by this position; an explanation of their social and economic characteristics; a construction of the relations of this writing to historical materialism and to dialectical materialism" (italics in original). The guidelines for radical transformation are even more impenetrable elsewhere. At one point Tel Quel charges its revolutionary confreres with the incendiary task of "inscribing a theoretical 'jump' in relation to which Derrida's 'Differance' situates a position of reorganization."[10]

Tel Quel's call to fuse revolutionary politics and avant-garde aesthetics would be enough to send us back to the historical avant-garde even without the manifesto's parenthetical mentions of various precursor movements. Tel Quel's guiding spirit, Philippe Sollers, makes the point more cogently elsewhere: "One cannot make an economic and social revolution without making at the same time, and on a different level, a symbolic revolution." Similar notions inspired both French Surrealism and the Russian avant-garde in its theoretical (Formalist) and poetic (Futurist) incarnations alike. "History occurs the first time as tragedy and the second time as farce," Marx famously remarks in *The Eighteenth Brumaire* (1852). Tel Quel's members were determined not to repeat the mistakes of their Surrealist precursors, who had, Marcel Pleynet comments, begun as avowed revolutionaries only to end as a bourgeois "salon phenomenon." Tel Quel's theorists took their forerunners to task on several fronts, denouncing, among other things, the "Trotskyist 'deviation'" that had led the Surrealists to misunderstand both the true function of dialectical materialism and the proper "relations between intellectuals and the revolution." The members of Tel Quel, "monomaniacs of the idea of Revolution," were forced to look elsewhere for an ideal fusion of innovative linguistic theory, radical poetic practice, and revolutionary politics.[11]

They found it, under Kristeva's guidance, in the Russian revolution and its immediate aftermath, a period in which, as they saw it, avant-garde aesthetics and politics not merely coexisted, but collaborated in the creation of a truly revolutionary state. In "The Ethics of Linguistics"(1974), Kristeva celebrates "the aesthetic and always political battles of Russian society on the eve of the Revolution and during the first years of victory," as she laments the advent of "Stalinism and fascism" that put an end to a febrile decade of radical experimentation in art and life alike. By this point, Stalin was fair game. Even Sartre had finally denounced his former allegiances by the early sixties (although Nikita Khrushchev had beat him to the punch by several years). Still the myth of a revolutionary Russia shaped in equal parts by avant-garde artists and radical Marxists survived to inspire French theorists of revolutions, poetic and otherwise, a half-century later.[12]

"Poetry is a bayonet thrust into the belly of its time. . . . Words take to the streets, attack, practically force their way into houses." The phrases, taken from Krzysztof Karasek's "Through the Firing Holes of Mouths" (1971) would be at home in any Futurist or Surrealist manifesto. With one key difference: the early twentieth-century avant-garde struggled to disrupt the linguistic complacency of its favored enemy, the bourgeoisie, in hopes of furthering the communist revolution that would, so it hoped, transform its poetic practice into political reality. The "Generation of '68," on the other hand, turned its verbal weapons against the very "Utopia in power" that their avant-garde precursors and contemporaries had sought. The boundary between art and life, between word and deed was no less permeable for the Polish poets than it had been for previous avant-gardes: "reality emulates the linguistic poetry / that pursues it," Ryszard Krynicki claims in a poem from the early seventies. The poets of "Generation of '68"—or the Polish "New Wave," as the movement was also known—were "poets of contestation" who sought, no less than their Western counterparts, to operate "on the borderlines between life and art." But the nature of their political opponent and the peculiar status of the poet in Polish society led to new permutations on these quintessentially avant-garde preoccupations.[13]

"They aim water cannons / at our mouths, I'm becoming a Surrealist, / I'm defenseless, I desire, / the whole thing is a lie." These lines are taken from Wit Jaworski's "May 68 (Image)": read in translation, both the poem's title and the lines themselves would seem to point to France, not Poland.[14] Even a cursory glance at the manifestoes and poems of Poland's "Generation of 68" reveals touchstones shared by Tel Quel and their Polish contemporaries: Surrealism, Formalism, structuralism, Marxist dialectics, Bakhtinian carnival. Both movements were preoccupied, moreover, with problems of language and representation: linguistic poetry, in one variant or another, was central to the enterprise of the Poles as well as the Parisians.

But the Polish "ground zero of literature" (Zagajewski) looked radically different than the "writing ground zero" embraced in revolutionary Paris. Czesław Miłosz refers indirectly to the rift that divides Western European theory from Eastern European practice in his Nobel lecture of 1980; and his remarks suggest key ways in which the Polish cultural terrain differed from its Parisian counterpart in 1968. "There is, it seems, a hidden link between theories of literature as *écriture*, of speech feeding on itself, and the growth of the totalitarian state," he claims. "In any case, there is no reason why the state should not tolerate an activity that consists of creating 'experimental' poems and prose, if these are conceived as autonomous systems of reference, enclosed within their own boundaries. Only if we assume that a poet constantly strives to liberate himself from borrowed styles in search of reality is he dangerous." His remarks are nothing if not provocative. Contemporary literary critics would no doubt be quick to dismiss his linkage of French literary theory and totalitarian practice as mere reactionary rhetoric. And Miłosz's own experience had taught him many times over that totalitarian regimes are not hospitable to experimental modes of artistic expression in a world where art, like everything else, exists not for its own sake, but for the good of the state. Still his apparent hyperboles were verified in important ways by the experience, linguistic and otherwise, of Poland's poetic "Generation of '68."[15]

More surprisingly, though, Miłosz finds unexpected support for his yoking of *écriture* and totalitarian states among the writings of the Tel Quelians themselves. I have mentioned their fondness for coupling revolutionary leaders with esoteric poets in their texts. The pairing that begins Jean-Joseph Goux's "Marx and the Inscription of Labour" (1968) is particularly revealing. Goux begins with citations from Derrida's *De la grammatologie* (1967) and Marx's *Das Kapital*, and argues for Marx as a key precursor to Derridean antimetaphysical linguistics: "Marx's critical analysis, considered in its relation to writing, undermines the system of the sign. It denounces not only the assured distinction between linguistic and non-linguistic signs but above all the linguistic (and political) mystification of signifier, signified and referent." Marx and Derrida both do battle, that is, with accepted bourgeois standards of referentiality, with the seemingly transparent language whose function is not to reveal, but to obfuscate the world's hidden order in hopes of upholding the political and social status quo. Their followers in Tel Quel continued this linguistic battle to the same end. "Reality as such," Danielle Marx-Scouras comments, "does not exist for Tel Quel." As Foucault remarks, "It is the world of words that creates the world of things."[16]

Certainly the leaders of the former Eastern bloc hoped that language might, if not precisely create "the world of things," then at least conceal the sorry state in which Marx's utopian dreams found themselves some hundred years after the first volume of *Das Kapital* made its debut. French students and theorists discovered with a shock that the ostensible pluralism of French democratic society in fact masked hidden forces of power and repression, that "a university examination and a police interrogation" were akin in ways belied by the academy's pretense of scholarly objectivity and neutrality.[17] The students of Warsaw and Krakow had no illusions about the relations between power and language, or about the source from which the power controlling both their language and their reality emanated. Their strikes were prompted, after all, by a Soviet-backed government shutting down a Polish play for its anti-Russian sentiments. But the conclusions they drew from their experience were radically different from those of their Parisian contemporaries, to judge at least from the works of the poets who served as their spokespersons.

The theorists of Tel Quel questioned the very notion of referentiality in the wake of their discovery that words referred not to objects, but to complex political and ideological systems that shifted meanings in ways that had no bearing upon either some form of objective reality or the desires and capacities of individuals struggling to articulate their personal experience. Language is always finally metaphorical, and writing, or *écriture*, is ultimately self-referential, a series of texts engaging neither with the world as such, nor with individual writers, but with other texts in an endless, intersubjective *mise en abîme*. The task of the Tel Quelian—who is of course not a "writer" *in sensu stricto*—thus becomes to unmask this hidden relationship of texts in hopes of liberating us from the illusion of language as representation.

Poland's poets of '68 were all too familiar with the notion of an encompassing system of language that referred to no world beyond itself, and that shifted its meanings not in response to some extralinguistic reality beyond its borders, but in accordance with one tacit political agenda or another. "The hermetic poetics of socrealism" is, after all, the logical extension of what François Furet calls the "compulsory and fictitious language" of the totalitarian state, a language "insulated from reality and leading inexorably to unity."[18] For these poets—most notably, Ryszard Krynicki, Stanisław Barańczak, and Adam Zagajewski—the rejection of representation that Tel Quel celebrates in "Division of the Assembly" signified not avant-garde subversion, but the linguistic status quo, the state monopoly on speech and print that they sought to resist in their verse. The poets of '68 had seen their forerunners seduced by myths of avant-garde poetry and politics imported from the East in the aftermath of World War II. They could not share, however, their Polish precursors'—or French contemporaries'—enthusiasm for the early years of the Russian revolution. As true children of the Soviet system, the first generation born and educated in the Polish People's Republic, they were unwilling heirs to what proved to be the revolution's lasting linguistic legacy.

"We alone are the government of the Planet Earth," the Futurists had proclaimed in 1917. The Futurists' "we" apparently included their political as well as their artistic brethren; they generously planned to share world dominion with their more practical-minded colleagues. But as Mayakovsky's later career demonstrates, the love affair between the political and the poetic avant-garde in revolutionary Russia was one-sided from the start. The fledgling Soviet state initially tolerated the Futurists and other would-be poetic revolutionaries for lack of more trustworthy, and comprehensible, alternatives. Lenin articulated the role he imagined for art in his future regime early on, and it was anything but avant-garde. Art was to be "a cog and a screw" in the "great Social-Democratic mechanism," he announced in "Party Organization and Party Literature" (1905): it would be not subversive, but submissive, a tool in the hands of the socialist state. His prophecies proved far more accurate than those of his Futurist contemporaries.[19]

The young state's relationship to language was nothing if not utilitarian—but it did not lack for imagination. The new leaders proved no less adept than their avant-garde contemporaries at what the Futurists called "language creation." And the vast web of official abbreviations—NEP, VAPP, RAPP, MAPP, Agitprop, Proletkult, Gosizdat—that was the state's first step towards casting what Martin Malia calls its "logocratic spell" on the Soviet masses answered the new government's needs far more successfully than any "transsensical" Futurist incantations.[20] One early coinage in particular presaged the regime's gift for inventing a self-contained code that served chiefly to keep unsavory realities at arm's length. In 1917, it christened the first incarnation of what would later become the KGB as the Cheka, short for "Chrezvychainaia komissia," or "Extraordinary Commission": the incarceration and execution of suspect individuals and groups lay among the extraordinary functions concealed behind both its august title and circumspect acronym. Poland's postwar rulers thus inherited a linguistic system developed through decades of exhaustive experimentation conducted under a wide range of historical and political circumstances. The poets of '68 began to challenge the state-held monopoly on both language and representation at a time when the regime could no longer hope to conceal the gap between the reality of daily life in People's Poland and the elaborate codes devised to paper over discrepancies between the radiant socialist future and a less than glorious quotidian.

The Re-represented World

Calling things by name is literature's only chance. . . .
  —*Julian Kornhauser and Adam Zagajewski,*
    The Unrepresented World *(1974)*

WRITING IN ITS PRODUCTIVE FUNCTION IS NOT REPRESENTATION.
  —*Tel Quel, "Division of the Assembly" (October, 1968)*

If somebody claims to have created a "revolutionary chair," one may be sure that it is a chair on which it is impossible to sit.
  —*Leszek Kołakowski, "Revolution—*
    A Beautiful Sickness" *(1979)*

"The unrepresented world" (*świat nie przedstawiony*), "the unfal-
sified world" (*niefalszowany świat*), "the unduplicitous world" (*świat nie
zaklamany*): the similarities between the three phrases are obvious. All three
combine a conspicuously negated adjective with a single noun, "world."
And all refer to the undoing of some form of obfuscation, linguistic or oth-
erwise, designed to distort or conceal this much-maligned world. But the
disparities in their sources are as telling as the similarities in their form and
sense. The first two terms are rallying cries taken from the writings of key
figures who emerged on the literary scene in the late sixties, Julian Korn-
hauser, Zagajewski, and Barańczak. The last phrase derives, though, from a
recent history of the Polish People's Republic co-authored by one of Poland's
premier dissidents, Jacek Kuron.[21] I have referred thus far to Poland's mili-
tant students and its dissenting poets by the same name, "The Generation
of '68." This confluence is not simply a matter of convenience. Nor is it a
sop to the illusions of avant-garde poets who longed, like their European
precursors and contemporaries, to speak not for some like-minded coterie
or clique, but for a generation or a nation.

I have mentioned the role that Mickiewicz played in the uprisings of 1968.
He was not the only poet whose impact helped to shape subsequent events.
In an interview of 1993, Michnik speaks of the political and cultural "cli-
mate created by the poetry of Barańczak, Krynicki, and Zagajewski." The
generation's poets "worked out a new language for its conversation with
reality," he remarks elsewhere: "We ceased to be slaves of others' words."
It is no accident that modern Poland's most distinguished dissidents should
evoke their generation's poets in describing the political changes that began
in 1968 and culminated over a decade later in the birth of the Solidarity
movement. "The organization of a democratic opposition, of an independent
[underground] press and publishing houses, and of free trade unions": the
poets of '68 fostered all three developments both by example and through
active participation.[22]

Poems by Barańczak, Krynicki, Zagajewski, and others circulated not
only among students and dissidents, but also among the disgruntled citi-
zens whose numbers were legion in a grotesquely inefficient state backed
by a long-hated neighbor. Why should this particular avant-garde have suc-
ceeded where so many others had failed? How did the Polish sixty-eighters
manage to bridge the gap between theory and practice, between poetry and
public, in a way that eluded Futurism, Surrealism, and the countless other
isms that proliferated in the first part of the twentieth century? Certainly
the Polish tradition of unauthorized bards who speak to and for the nation
at large had primed both artists and audiences alike for just such writing.

And the poets of '68 were acutely aware of the social burden laid upon them by their Romantic precursors: "If you live in the world's center," Zagajewski writes in an early poem, "you must account for everything / The living and the dead are watching you." The entire generation emerged "under the sign of Romanticism," Nyczek remarks. And the programmatic essays of Barańczak, Kornhauser, and Zagajewski reveal a sustained effort both to revise their Romantic legacy and to reclaim it from their immediate precursors in Polish poetry.[23]

But this heritage alone would not be enough to guarantee this particular generation's success: the modern Polish tradition has had its share of esoteric avant-gardes whose vast aspirations were in inverse proportion to their contemporary popularity. We must look elsewhere for the causes of this unexpected phenomenon; and the contrast between Poland's sixty-eighters and their Parisian counterparts in Tel Quel proves instructive here. Both groups were, as I've noted, obsessed with questions of language—but they turned their linguistic inquiries in very different directions. This is where we begin to see the distinctiveness of Poland's sixty-eighters not just on the international scene, but among the historical avant-gardes whose heirs they were no less than their Parisian contemporaries.

"Today's authentic art goes hand in hand with revolutionary activity," André Breton had proclaimed. "Like the latter, it leads to the confusion and destruction of capitalist society." The early twentieth-century avant-garde consecrated itself to what Maurice Nadeau calls "a totalitarian activity of creation" designed to overthrow a world in thrall to the loathed middle class. Everyday speech would be replaced by a subversive poetic dialect designed to disrupt bourgeois reality, not reproduce it. In a manifesto of 1926, Bréton celebrates "that enormous enterprise of re-creating the universe to which Lautréamont and Lenin dedicated themselves entirely." Only Lenin and his successors on the political vanguard finally succeeded, though, in the avant-garde task of reshaping, if not the universe, then at least a large chunk of Europe and Asia. The avant-garde dream of re-creating the language that articulated this brave new world thus fell to them, and not their poetic confreres. The Soviet language, Andrei Sinyavsky remarks, serves not "as a means of communication among people," but as "a system of incantations supposed to remake the world," or failing that, at least provide "a substitute reality." One would be hard pressed to find a better thumbnail sketch of the avant-garde poetic project generally.[24]

The Polish poets were, like their avant-garde precursors and contemporaries, leftist in their sympathies, at least initially. Their opponents, however, were not the complacent bourgeois who had been the bane of vanguard artists from Baudelaire to Mayakovsky, from Rimbaud to Aragon, Jasieński, Wat, and beyond. The Soviet-backed state deprived Poland's "Generation of '68" of what would have been its traditional target, the middle class, and its traditional medium, the experimental language that Kristeva celebrates as "the very place where the social code is destroyed and renewed." For a poetic avant-garde, be it Futurist, Surrealist, or Tel Quelian, the enemy of poetic language is everyday language, with its assumptions of transparency, communicability, and ready exchange value, "like prices on merchandise," as Marx complained. The avant-garde poet insists upon an artistic code that takes risks beyond the reach of mere mortal practitioners of daily speech.[25]

Poland's poets of '68 approached things differently. The regime claimed to speak in theory for the masses whose lives and voices they distorted beyond recognition in practice. The very name of the Polish People's Republic (*Polska rzeczpospolita ludowa*), betrayed the state's stranglehold on its subjects' language; the Polish people had little to do with the shape of their postwar nation, which was not a republic by any stretch of the imagination. The poets of '68 accordingly set out not to disrupt the representative functions of language, but to restore them. They strove to use this reclaimed speech to represent precisely the quotidian experience—"conferences and children's camps," "party meetings and soccer matches, the Race for Peace and political jokes, hospitals and parade banners," "Houses of Culture and brawls at village weddings," "libraries and beer halls"—disdained by the communist state and avant-garde artists alike. In *The Mistrustful and the Arrogant* (1971), Barańczak sets forth his generation's poetic program by quoting Wittgenstein—"the limits of my language are the limits of my world"—only to dismiss him. "For the poet-'linguists,'" he insists, "language is instead a window on the world." The reactionary position rejected by Paris becomes the subversive stance of Poland's poets in revolt.[26]

What did this poetry look like in practice? To begin with, only one branch of the "Generation of '68" laid claim to the title "linguistic poetry" proper. Language was the generation's shared "field of operation"—but the two chief groups disagreed on the strategies that would open windows onto an unrepresented reality. The Krakow-based movement that christened itself, with typically avant-garde braggadocio, NOW (TERAZ), endorsed what they called "straight speaking" (*mówienie wprost*). If the state programmatically refused to call things by their true names, then these poets—with Julian Kornhauser and Adam Zagajewski at their helm—would compensate for its failures with a vengeance. But before discussing the "straight speakers," I want to turn to the "linguistic poets" proper, and to Ryszard Krynicki and Stanisław Barańczak particularly. Krynicki and Barańczak were the chief exponents of a Poznań-based linguistic poetics that worked to expose the contradictions of a state language that claimed to speak for Polish reality as such. Their task, as Barańczak saw it, was to unmask the "conflicts, heterogeneity, and ambiguity lurking beneath a surface of harmony, accord, and transparency." As Krynicki put it, "unequivocality is fatal."[27]

Barańczak speaks of an ongoing "duel with the newspaper" as the movement's modus operandi. A guerrilla war conducted not from building to building or room to room, but from phrase to phrase and word to word would be more like it. Krynicki's early poetry combats the univocal speech he fears by wreaking linguistic havoc with official formulas, or by registering the ways in which reality itself rejects or revises such phrases. To flip through the pages of Krynicki's early work is to encounter a kind of Socialist Surrealism derived from the linguistic and existential phenomena peculiar to life on what he calls the "Planet Fantasmagoria" of People's Poland. One brief early lyric begins with a typically untranslatable pun. "Act of Birth" (*akt urodzenia*) takes its name from the bureaucratic term for "birth certificate," that is, the document registering one's official right to exist. The privilege of such existence is dubious, though, as the poem itself reveals:

> *Act of Birth*
> born in transport
> I came upon the place of death
>
> the cult of the individual unit
> of measures
> and weights
>
> the military unit
>
> progressive paralysis
> paralyzing progress
>
> each day I listen to
> the latest news
>
> I live
> in the place of death

This act of birth unexpectedly delivers the poet into the place of death, or at least a place of dead language, the reified officialese he modifies in order to effect a true linguistic act of birth by the poem's conclusion. The poem may end in death; its final phrase seems to compress an entire lifetime into a premature obituary. But the poet himself is no longer governed by his birthplace, as the poem's final, active verb suggests: "I live" (*żyję*).[28]

"Act of Birth" begins, though, with ominously passive, impersonal forms: "urodzonemu w transporcie, / przypadło mi miejsce śmierci," literally, "the place of death befell / me, born in transport." The expression "in transport" (*w transporcie*) adds to the complications of an already troublesome delivery. With the outbreak of World War II, the phrase came to designate the mass deportations, either into Soviet exile or to Nazi or Stalinist camps, that displaced Polish citizens in the millions from 1939 to 1946. It speaks both to the poet's own origins—Krynicki was born in 1943 in a work camp in Austria, where his parents served as forced laborers under Hitler—and to the fate of what he calls elsewhere his "portable nation" (*ruchomy kraj*).[29] Like the poet, postwar Poland was itself born "in transport," as its boundaries were forcibly shifted some 150 miles westward in accordance with Stalin's demands at Tehran and Yalta, resulting in new mass migrations of uprooted populations.

The poem's second and third stanzas effect another form of linguistic transformation. Nikita Khrushchev's famous denunciation of Stalin's "cult of personality" (*kult jednostki* in Polish) is converted first into weights and measures, and then into military jargon by way of yet another untranslatable pun: the Polish "jednostka" can designate both a single human being and a unit in various senses. Krynicki's wordplay unpacks the contradictions contained within Khrushchev's famous phrase. The flaws of the Soviet state cannot be traced to the crimes of a single dictator, however monstrous. They lie in the reduction of the individual human ("jednostka") to a single, quantifiable unit in a quasi-objective system ("jednostki / miar i wag") imposed and sustained by one military unit or another ("jednostki wojskowej"). Such procedures had been part of the Marxist-Leninist project since its own bloody act of birth some fifty years earlier. They were alive and well in the People's Poland that gave birth in turn to Krynicki's poem.

The poem's fourth stanza begins with a fixed phrase imported not from politics, but pathology, "progressive paralysis" (*paraliż postępowy*). The stanza's two lines remind us, though, that "progress" and its various derivatives were key terms in a Soviet Marxist lexicon that worked to evoke through magical incantation the transformed reality it could not achieve in practice. By shifting the regime's beloved catchword into a different linguistic context, Krynicki tacitly reveals the underlying reality that the state-mandated talk of progress works to conceal. The relentless forward motion that the state extols marks instead its ideological dead end. In another poem of the period, reality itself, in the form of a failed neon light, pulls the plug on the state's ideologically charged forward motion by creating its own untranslatable pun. The slogan "The press speeds progress" ("prasa toruje postęp") becomes "the press poisons progress" ("prasa t_ruje postęp") by way of an unlit letter "o": "the press hastens progress" versus "the press ha_te_s progress" might be one imperfect translatorly solution.[30] The state's decline is induced, such puns suggest, by its refusal to confront the gap between theory and practice, its efforts to paper over a troublesome reality with self-perpetuating Soviet Marxist jargon. The state's version of "progress" is in fact "paralyzing"; it produces not forward motion, but stasis, that is, the place of death.

"There's no news in the Truth and no truth in the News": so runs the old joke about the two chief Soviet Russian newspapers, *Pravda* (The Truth) and *Izvestiia* (The News). Regardless of its ostensible content, the "latest news"—the news the poet listens to as "Act of Birth" draws to its conclusion—consists of endless updates on the unchanging state of affairs that Krynicki describes in another early poem, "The World Still Exists":

> nothing changes
> you wait each day for an apartment allocation
> you wake up the world still exists
> you get home from work the world still exists
> you read in the paper
> that the Chinese have discovered a bone
> which may revolutionize science
> and topple Darwin's theory
> you go to bed drift off
> before hearing all the latest news
> you sleep dream about nothing
> you wake your bones won't revolutionize science
> you go to work along Red Army Street
> the world still exists nothing's changed
> along the street's left side
> depending on which way you're headed
> along with the entire nation
> along the leftist side
> along the street's ultraleftist side
> along its levitating side
> along its far left wing
> you see a slogan the street's highest goal is man
> along the right etc. the slogan the street's highest
> you can't make out what's below
> raindrops airplanes snowflakes fall below
> nothing's changed
> cars slam the enigmatic letter

into the asphalt &
time flows in immobility like an electrical current

but your child coming home from preschool already knows
that the highest goal is

etc.

Hegelian bad infinity meets Soviet Marxist progress in People's Poland, as daily life, with its numbing repetitions and endless deprivations, gives the lie to the lofty rhetoric imposed on that reality from above: "the street's highest goal is man." Under the new dispensation, the street—the symbolic locus of subversive energies in political revolutions and modern poetry alike—has been plastered over by progressive slogans and bombastic place names that bear no relation to the ordinary life passing down its ideologically charged sidewalks. "Minor league reality" (*drugorzędna rzeczywistość*) is the best antidote to revolutionary bombast, though, in the program of the sixty-eighters. The poet, himself a citizen of this cut-rate quotidian, may not be able to change the world. But he can at least expose the grotesque gaps between radical rhetoric and pedestrian daily practice by staging absurdist linguistic collisions between the two as he trudges along the street's "leftist side, its ultraleftist side, its levitating side, its far left wing."[31]

"You had such a vision of the street / As the street hardly understands": Eliot's lines, taken from his early "Preludes," exemplify the tacit elitism that marks the relationship of political and poetic avant-gardes alike to the urban masses that are their ostensible subject. Like many of Krynicki's early lyrics, "The World Still Exists" gives us instead a vision of the street that the ruling elite can hardly understand. The poem is scarcely a straightforward description of urban reality in the People's Republic. Still its very title must have read like a provocation or battle cry when it first appeared in the early seventies. The world still exists in spite of the regime's best efforts to transform it, or failing that, to conceal it behind a smokescreen of Marxist-Leninist slogans the way that crumbling buildings were once covered in outsized murals of Marx and Lenin. "Poetry has ceased to be incomprehensible," Krynicki writes in an early version of the poem. Krynicki himself is not an easy poet—far from it. The forms of difficulty he employs in his early poetry, though, are designed not to defy language's representational capacities, but to expand them, to open up new possibilities for depicting a spurned reality.[32]

His fellow Poznanian Stanisław Barańczak employs different tactics in orchestrating his poetic skirmishes between the language of the state and the speech of daily life. In *The Mistrustful and the Arrogant*, Barańczak aligns Bakhtin's "carnival" with the forces of oppositional poetry directed against "whatever is stable, official, immobilized, reified." In one of his best-known lyrics, he uses recognizably Bakhtinian techniques to draw the body into battle as he punctuates an official's ideally self-referential speech with a sound track of less dignified bodily functions:

> *A Delineated Era*
> We live in a delineated era (*clearing throat*) and thus
> we must, isn't it the truth, take this fully.
> into account. We live in (*pitcher*
> *glugging*) a delineated, isn't it the truth,
> era, an era of unending struggles on behalf, in
> an era of increasing and intensifying and
> so on (*gulping water*), isn't it the truth. Conflicts.
> We live in a delineated e (*glass*
> *clinking*) ra and I'd like to underline this,
> isn't it true, that certain guidelines
> will be outlined along these lines, sentences
> will be lined out that don't adequately line up, in addition
> calculations out of line with, isn't it the truth, will be realigned
> (*expectorating*) of those who. Any questions? I don't see any.
> Since I don't see them, I see that I'll be called on to express,
> expressing in conclusion the conviction that
> we live in a delineated era, that's the
> truth, isn't that the truth,
> there is no other.

In "The World Still Exists," Krynicki brings the street's official redaction into uncomfortable contact with the street as lived experience. In "A Delineated Era," Barańczak disrupts a spew of fluent bureaucratese by including all the mundane acoustic accompaniments that we are meant to edit mentally from such pronouncements. In both cases, the official linguistic version of events is undermined by the verbal representation of a reality best passed over in discreet silence. [33]

Barańczak's speaker also provides a prime example of what we might call, following Miłosz, "totalitarian *écriture*." This speaker aims at absolute inclusiveness by way of a language so ideally self-generating and self-referential that expressions and phrases can be relied upon to finish themselves without undue exertions on his part: "an era of unending struggles on behalf, in / an era of increasing and intensifying and / so on." Indeed, there is no real speaker, no particularized human subject, to speak of in "A Delineated Era." The pronouncement could be delivered by any of a multitude of adepts grown fluent in the officially mandated dialect of statespeak, just as any body placed at a podium might produce the poem's disruptive soundtrack of generic gulps and glugs. The poem's self-propagating officialese proves nonetheless to be as playful an etymologist as any Western practitioner of *écriture*. Words take on a life of their own in the absence of an individualized speaker, and one root in particular sends out various shoots and branches as the poem progresses: "I'd like to *underline* this, / isn't it true, that certain *guidelines* / will be *outlined* along these *lines,* sentences / will be *lined out* that don't / adequately *line up,* in addition / calculations *out of line* with, isn't it true, will be *realigned* . . . of those who." In Polish the key forms all derive from a single root meaning "line," *kres;* I've tried to approximate this wordplay in my English version.

But are these phrases really entirely self-referential? A closer look reveals what Seamus Heaney calls "the government of the tongue" at work between the lines. The guidelines to be outlined along certain unspecified lines apparently serve to guarantee that "sentences / will be lined out that don't adequately line up." The poets of this generation were no strangers to the censor's operations. Much of their work was published either abroad or underground; what did appear through official conduits seldom survived the censor's pen intact.[34] Linguistic self-referentiality came at a cost in People's Poland. Language could not be left to its own devices. It had to be tended, guarded, monitored, while suspicious words and phrases were taken into custody or banished into linguistic oblivion.

More than this—the perpetrators of such gaffes and blunders were themselves in danger of being overruled, or so one strategic ellipsis suggests: "in addition / calculations out of line with, isn't it true, will be realigned . . . of those who." My English version cannot do justice to the artfully mangled syntax of the Polish original. In either case, though, "of those, who" (*tych, którzy*) is left dangling ominously at the phrase's fractured end. "The game of autonomous language itself came into being in precisely the place where man had just disappeared," Foucault claims.[35] Barańczak's little poem suggests that this game plays out differently in totalitarian states. "Those who" refuse to disappear of their own volition, "those who" tamper with the game's rules, may be forcibly removed from print and perhaps from other places as well. The manner in which they will be stricken from the record is left conspicuously unsaid.

Barańczak is as adroit as any deconstructionist in unpacking the paradoxes concealed in apparently commonplace turns of speech. The speaker's most conspicuous verbal tic contains exactly the kind of linguistic self-contradiction that delighted Derrida. In the space of the poem's twenty lines, he repeats five times the untranslatable "nieprawda," a seemingly empty phrase, a placeholder much like "you know," "isn't it," "you don't say," and so on. The word, however, holds two totally incompatible meanings. It is both declarative in a negative sense, meaning "untruth, lie, falsehood" (*nieprawda*), and interrogative in a positive sense, meaning "isn't that so?" "isn't that the truth"? It means, in other words, both *"isn't* it true?" and "it *isn't* true," and Barańczak exploits the word's double sense in the poem's final lines, which I have given as follows: "that's the / truth, isn't that the truth, / there is no other" ("taka / jest prawda, nieprawda, / i innej prawdy nie ma"). The truth is whatever the state says it is, and in the absence of any metaphysical truth, of *Prawda* with a capital P, falsehood (*nieprawda*) will do as well as anything else. Given the speaker's impeccable credentials—he is, after all, the mouthpiece of the state—the question is clearly rhetorical.

Barańczak takes on the ambiguities of daily speech in the People's State from a different angle in another lyric, "And Nobody Warned Me":

> And nobody warned me that liberty
> might also lie in this: I'm
> sitting in the station house with drafts of my own poems
> hidden (how ingenious!) in my long johns,
> while five detectives with higher educations
> and even higher salaries waste time
> analyzing trash they've taken from my pockets:
> tram tickets, a dry cleaning receipt, a dirty
> handkerchief and a baffling (I'll die laughing) list:
>> celery carrots
>> can of peas
>> tom. paste
>> potatoes;
>
> and nobody warned me that captivity
> might also lie in this: I'm
> sitting in the station house with drafts of my own poems
> hidden (how grotesque!) in my long johns,
> while five detectives with higher educations
> and even lower foreheads have the right
> to grope the entrails wrested from my life:
> tram tickets, a dry cleaning receipt, a dirty
> handkerchief and most of all that (I can't bear it) list:
>> celery carrots
>> can of peas
>> tom. paste
>> potatoes;

and nobody warned me that my entire globe
lies in the gap that parts opposing poles
which can't be kept apart.[36]

The key to Barańczak's lyric lies in two disparate interpretations of the
suspiciously innocuous detritus pulled from the hapless poet's pockets after
he's been hauled in for interrogation. The poem's heart is not the interroga-
tion itself, nor is it the hidden poems. It is a tiny written document that is
neither political nor poetic, but personal and pragmatic: a shopping list,
handed to him by his wife perhaps as he headed out to work that morning.
"The personal is the political," ran the slogan in the sixties—but the five
detectives with their higher educations need no training in reading politics
into the most unlikely places. Even the seemingly harmless confession that
William Carlos Williams tapes to his refrigerator in "This is Just to Say"—

I have eaten
the plums
that were in the icebox

and which
you were probably
saving
for breakfast . . .

—could easily be given a sinister spin by a suspicious state and its army of
well-trained subordinates, Barańczak's poem suggests.[37]

But the problem here is not how the state interprets the poet's grocery list.
The poem's chief ambiguities lie elsewhere. "Nobody warned me," the poet
mourns in the lyric's conclusion, "that my entire globe / lies in the gap that
parts opposing poles / which can't be kept apart." What are these opposing
poles that are both segregated and inseparable? The answer is not entirely
clear, but it surely involves the space between poetry and the state. The two
are apparently kept at a safe distance in the poem's first stanza by the poet's
stratagem of concealing his lyrics in his long johns, while well-paid apparat-
chiks waste their time analyzing trash. The joke is on these functionaries—
"I'll die laughing"—in the poem's opening lines. This situation is reversed
in the poem's second stanza. Or rather, the situation remains unchanged,
but the poet's interpretation of this situation shifts diametrically. What had
been the emblems of freedom, ingenuity, and farce are transformed into
their opposites, captivity, grotesquery, and violation: "I can't bear it."

Why? Well, on a purely human level, the response seems natural enough;
the ingenuity it takes to fool the state comes at a price. The poems them-
selves may be safe, but the private life that gave them birth has been placed

on public display. This answer is only partial at best, though. I have said that the little shopping list is not poetic—but that is not entirely true. It may be composed in the pragmatic shorthand of daily life rather than the abbreviated lines of free verse, but the shopping list not only looks like a lyric in miniature. It is the lyric heart of Barańczak's poem. In her memoirs Nadezhda Mandelstam recalls hiding her husband's manuscripts in pots and pans, places where the secret police would never think to search. Pots, pans, and poetry: the very incongruity of this recipe apparently served to keep the state at bay. But is this mix really so inconsistent? "If only you knew what sort of trash / Verse grows from, knowing no shame," Akhmatova declares in "I've got no use for odic hosts."[38] The detritus of daily life is precisely the kind of mulch that poetry requires, Barańczak's lines suggest.

One of Mandelstam's late lyrics begins with a snippet of intimate dialogue seemingly taken straight from daily life: "No, not a migraine, but hand me the menthol pencil." Williams's famous poem likewise grows from the private communication between intimates on a conspicuously homespun subject. A recent poem by Zagajewski parenthetically exposes the lyric genre concealed behind such seemingly banal documents and dialogues: "Carrots, onions, celery, prunes, almonds, bread crumbs, caster-sugar, four large / apples, green are best (your love letter)." One study of the "Generation of '68" focuses on the cat-and-mouse "game with the censorship" that informs its representatives' writing. In "And nobody warned me," the lyrics concealed in the poet's winter underwear are part of this game; the shopping list is not. What has been violated is the poet's right to a private life beyond the long reach of the state. And the essence of this existence lies in the scribbled fragment that embodies the lyric impulse in daily life.[39]

For Harold Bloom, Mark Edmundson remarks, "one of the main reasons poetry matters is that it teaches you how to talk to yourself." Such inner dialogues rank among the threats that the lyric poses in a totalitarian state. Barańczak's poem "Fill Out Legibly" suggests how Eastern Europe's purveyors of Orwellian newspeak might have read Dickinson's "letter to the World / That never wrote to Me." "Does he write letters to himself? (yes, no)," the unnamed framers of an ominous questionnaire demand—and it's all too clear what the correct response should be. "Poetry is not heard, but overheard," John Stuart Mill remarks in one well-known definition of the lyric's audience. Lyric eavesdropping takes on new meaning in cultures where the walls have not just ears, but microphones: in "Moscow's evil living space" "the walls are damn thin," Mandelstam complains, just in case state-monitored poets should take a notion to deviate from their assigned task of "teaching the hangmen to warble." In the lyric, T. S. Eliot insists, the poet speaks "to himself—or to nobody." Just such soliloquies come under scrutiny in Wisława Szymborska's "Writing a Resumé": "Write as if you'd never talked to yourself / and always kept yourself at arm's length," the solicitous speaker cautions.[40]

"And Nobody Warned Me" goes to the heart of a dilemma faced by Barańczak's poetic generation. The poem itself was written in 1980, more than a decade after that generation had first emerged on the political and poetic scene. It indicates how successfully that generation's poetry had engaged the attention of a state that routinely sought to confiscate it and punish its distributors and creators. It also demonstrates, though, the dangers of the game that consists of being a political poet, a bard who must both speak for his oppressed nation and outwit the state that keeps his poems from reaching the citizens whose concerns they are intended to address. Such obligations may endanger the private impulse that lies at the heart of lyric creation, and that is the poet's best defense against the impredations of a programmatically collective state. Poetry is best equipped to engage in "permanent rebellion, criticism, demystification" precisely because of its "individual point of view, its unrepeatable vision of the world," Barańczak insists in an early essay.[41] Revolt, unmasking, demystification: all are catchwords of avant-gardes past and present. But avant-garde art has historically been a collective phenomenon; it thrives on groups, factions, credos, causes. Hence the abundance of isms—Futurism, Surrealism, dadaism, simultaneism, expressionism, formism, imagism, vorticism, cubism, and so on—that proliferate in histories of modern art, both in Poland and abroad. How can the individual, irrepeatable viewpoint that Barańczak defends be reconciled with this avant-garde predilection for plurals?

Only with great difficulty—or so the writings of his poetic contemporaries, the Krakow-based "straight speakers" Adam Zagajewski and Julian Kornhauser, suggest. "I'd give a lot / for this poem to be a box / of matches, an unshaded lamp / on the desktop, a dry-cleaner's slip," Kornhauser insists. For the straight-shooting poets of "NOW," the poem should be as ordinary and "as necessary as bread and air," Nyczek comments: the illumination and purification it provides should be no more esoteric than what is yielded by matchbooks, light bulbs, and dry-cleaners. Kornhauser provides a less sanitized image elsewhere. In his programmatic "Poetry," the lyric becomes "that dirty hotel towel, / that passes from hand to hand and always / smells like the same gray soap." In "And nobody warned me," poetry consists of a little scrap of writing that is both banal and profoundly personal. In Kornhauser's "Poetry," the scribblings on a white page become instead the traces left by the countless anonymous hands among which the poem cum hand towel circulates. Poetry's public functions efface the very notion of privacy. "I am others" (*ja to inni*), Kornhauser asserts elsewhere, revising Rimbaud's famous pronouncement in favor of a more programmatically appropriate plural.[42]

Zagajewski and Kornhauser both claimed to speak not for themselves alone, but for an entire generation. Zagajewski's early poems frequently operate "In the First Person Plural," as the title of one early poem reads. The titles of his first two volumes likewise speak to his notion of a public poetry that is, like Kornhauser's hand towel, not for the squeamish. The first was called *Communiqué* (*Kommunikat*, 1972), that is, as Webster's has it, "any communication or piece of information spoken, written or printed, as an official utterance"; while the second was entitled *Butcher Shops* (*Sklepy mięsne*, 1975). Its title poem runs as follows:

> An African not a Black
> one doesn't hear these days about the Blacks
> killed in coal mines
> those are African workers with smashed
> skulls asleep beneath a heap of brains
> one doesn't hear these days about the butcher
> the former knight of blood
> butcher shops are museums for a new squeamishness
> bureaucrats not executioners
> one doesn't hear these days about the dogcatcher
> whom children hate
> In the twentieth century under the regimes of reason's new rule
> certain things no longer happen
> blood on the streets on the hoods of cars
> and on unhooded cars
> a man white with terror
> a European eye to eye with death
> One doesn't hear about death any more
> deceased not dead
> that is the proper word
> I say it and suddenly perceive
> that my mouth's been packed with cardboard
> of the kind once known as silence.[43]

Like the "linguistic poets," Zagajewski seeks to teach his readers to read "between the lines of newspapers and communiqués."[44] "Butcher Shops" apparently emerged from just such an experiment in revisionary reading. It is a response to some sanitized newspaper account of "African workers" killed in a mining accident or perhaps murdered in a strike, and the poet urges his own readers to retrieve both the victims' racial identity ("one doesn't hear these days about the Blacks") and brutal fate ("smashed skulls asleep beneath a heap of brains"). This leads him to address other forms of butchery that lie concealed beneath the modern age's veils of euphemisms, from the mundane squeamishness that keeps us from acknowledging the consequences of our own carnivorous appetites ("one doesn't hear these days about the butcher") up to the screen of strategically opaque official-ese that permits "bureaucrats not executioners" to commit their large-scale crimes with impunity.

The poem ends, though, not with language triumphantly restored, but with language lost once more: "I say ['deceased'] and suddenly perceive / that my mouth's been packed with cardboard / of the kind once known as silence." The speaker is denied even the dignity of lapsing into true silence. His mouth is stuffed instead with an ersatz alternative; he is gagged by his own euphemistic pseudo-speech. Why is this? The answer lies in the paradoxical circumlocutions that the poet must employ to achieve his approximation of straight talk in "Butcher Shops." I have mentioned this generation's ongoing tug of war with the censor, and Zagajewski himself comments in a recent interview that this game made fully realizing their dream of plain speech impossible. "Each house conceals a second / hidden house your every move / might be a different one everything you say / could be said differently": these lines from his early poem "New World" speak to the difficulties of speaking straight in People's Poland.[45]

Zagajewski and Kornhauser railed against the Aesopian language of their precursors in *The Unrepresented World*. But poets' theories often fail to match their practice. "In one's prose reflexions one may be legitimately occupied with ideals, whereas in the writing of verse one can only deal with actuality," Eliot remarks. The actuality faced by Zagajewski and his generation was one that made talking straight to a larger public possible, paradoxically, only by means of carefully chosen circumlocutions. The collection *Butcher Shops*, unlike its predecessor, passed through the censorship unscathed, and one reason must certainly be the brand of Aesopian speech Zagajewski himself employs in the title poem.[46]

The Unrepresented World called for the linguistic resurrection of the concrete realia that shaped daily life in the People's Republic. "Butcher Shops," however, apparently confines itself to attacking the modern age generally for its euphemistic refusal of reality: "In the twentieth century under the regimes of reason's new rule / certain things no longer happen," the poet charges. It's hard to argue with this level of generality—the regimes and their various *raisons d'état* remain strategically unnamed. Specific keywords would have alerted savvy readers to a more local interpretation. The poem's black victims have been converted into "workers" (*robotnicy*), a transformation well suited to a regime whose ideology placed class above race, with the working class taking pride of place in the Marxist caste structure. The "bureaucrats" who have supplanted "executioners" evoke the elaborate government systems that facilitated mass murder in the Soviet Union and Nazi Germany alike. And the phrase "the regimes of reason's new rule" uses its deceptive plural to mask what is surely a reference to the quasi-scientific basis of Marxist-Leninist thought, which was intended to replace the false theological underpinnings of earlier states.

But initiating readers into a new kind of reading between the lines was hardly the dream of the Young Turks who had challenged precursors and contemporaries alike in *The Unrepresented World*. Perhaps the gap between intention and reality is precisely what dumbfounds the speaker in the poem's closing lines. More than this—for a poem that claims to "look truth in the eye," as the title of one of Barańczak's poems runs, the actual text is conspicuously short on particulars.[47] The People's Poland of the early seventies—with its own typically understocked butcher shops, its own bureaucrats and dog catchers—is nowhere to be seen.

The difficulties of articulating a particularized, personal reality in a world that promotes generic vision and public being are precisely the point in Zagajewski's powerful early lyric "Philosophers" (1974):

> Stop deceiving us philosophers
> work is not a joy man is not the highest goal
> work is deadly sweat Lord when I get home
> I'd like to sleep but sleep's just a driving belt
> transporting me to the next day and the sun's a fake
> coin morning rips my eyelids sealed as before
> birth my hands are two *Gastarbeiter* and even my tears
> don't belong to me they participate in public life
> like speakers with chapped lips and a heart that's
> grown into the brain
> Work is not a joy but incurable pain
> like a disease of the open conscience like new housing projects
> through which the citizen wind passes
> in his high leather boots[48]

Zagajewski uses a single citizen's voice to articulate an attack on the unnamed, but readily guessable philosophers of work whose ideals are contradicted by his daily being: "work is not a joy man is not the highest goal." The slogans this speaker attacks run parallel, moreover, to the mottoes mangled in Krynicki's "The World Still Exists"—further proof, if we needed it, as to the particular world, and worldview, mirrored in both poems. And it contains precisely the kind of realia that "Butcher Shops" lacks; one wonders what the censors were thinking when they let this lyric slip through the cracks. The slogans, the *Gastarbeiter*, and especially the "citizen" in the penultimate line root the speaker's diction in a very specific cultural climate. The "new housing projects" (*osiedla*) immediately summon up the vast cement blocks (*bloki*) scattered across the urban landscapes of People's Poland. And the "public life" that consists of an endless series of "speakers with chapped lips" clearly derives from the "delineated era" ventriloquized in Barańczak's poem.

These particulars are used, paradoxically, to express the resistance of the world they evoke to true individuation. French philosophers of the sixties embraced the "philosophical anti-humanism" of Marx that had, they complained, too often been "contaminated" in practice by the residues of a "bourgeois ideology" that persisted in addressing "problems of law and the person," in Althusser's phrase. The task of the new French thinkers was, as Jean-François Lyotard explained, to make "philosophy inhuman." The People's Republic that emerges in Zagajewski's lyric has beaten them to the punch. The speaker defies the definitions of man thrust on him from above. But a state built upon the glorification of labor has stripped him of the capacity to identify a self that lies beyond its reach; and its public language sabotages his efforts to articulate private experience.[49]

"Man is not the user of language," Lyotard proclaims.[50] Certainly that is true for Zagajewski's tormented speaker, whose diction and imagery are dictated by the very state he attempts to escape. His sleep cannot provide dreams or even physical rest. It serves instead as an assembly line, a mechanized conduit transporting him to his next day's labors in the service of the state: sleep is required for work, and work is in turn the foundation upon which the state rests. The very hands that perform this labor are, moreover, not his own; they are resident aliens, described by a term imported from government economics, *Gastarbeiter*. The state's appropriation of private property extends even to his tears, which become a mere extension of official rhetoric: "they participate in public life / like speakers with chapped lips."

Even the ethical functions of the individual conscience have been invaded by the state's public space. The phrase "open conscience" (*otwarte sumienie*) might initially seem of a piece with Polish expressions such as "pure" or "peaceful conscience" (*czyste, spokojne sumienie*). This conscience is an "illness," though, and its openness is linked with the "new housing

projects," vast and badly built, in which enforced collective existence takes
precedence over the seeming privacy afforded by four walls, a floor, and a
ceiling of your own. "If you must scream, then do it quietly (the walls have
ears)," Barańczak warns in one of his "housing" poems. In another he sar-
donically celebrates the joys of project life in multiplicate:

> We each have our refuge in cement,
> Plus the prescribed single balcony . . .
>
> The clocks strike simultaneously
> We fight and make up identically,
> Our period of rest is, as they say, adequate;
>
> At the gray hour we view from our window
> the hundred-watt bulbs in the other windows . . . [51]

A conscience, like a living space, should be private, opaque; the ease with
which the "citizen wind" penetrates the projects he patrols in "Philoso-
phers" is suspicious, to say the least. "The Soul selects her own Society— /
Then—shuts the Door": easier said than done in such impersonal and per-
meable places.

Precisely the right to privacy is at stake in the most complex and engaging
poems of the "Generation of '68." Zagajewski's "Philosophers," Barańczak's
"And nobody warned me," Krynicki's "Act of Birth": all mark efforts to
reclaim through language the private self and space that are the traditional
domain of lyric poetry. The truly radical project of these poets is not finally
their collective, generational embrace of a programmatically public poetry
intended to challenge a programmatically collective state. It is the undercur-
rent of stubborn singularity that underlies many of their most important early
writings. "In forty years or so," Barańczak concludes in "The Real Thing":

> when we're all
> dead,
> it will turn out (to general surprise), that
> this generation did not live
> in a period of thriving diaries:
> although our solitude en masse
> would seemingly have spawned just such
> phenomena, diaries
> somehow went unborn, those secret
> embryos conceived in a mind fertilized by reality
> (or the reverse)
> were stifled before birth, in the cramped
> wombs of our collective flats. . . . [52]

Zagajewski (to whom this poem is dedicated), Krynicki, and Barańczak may initially have viewed their chief poetic task as giving public voice to collective dissatisfactions. All three achieved this goal with striking success—and at considerable personal risk. Finally, though, the most subversive weapon each poet possessed was a distinctive lyrical gift that persisted in its efforts to articulate private experience in a state recognizing only collective existence.

Lyrical Resistance

[There is] a more real, literal, visible program in this literature. More practical, more prosaic, but perhaps no less important than its great heroic project. I have in mind the defense of individual words. Individual phrases, formulations. All those petty, seemingly inessential elements of which literature is made . . . Writers, defend those little words. They are literature's substance, its foundation, its wealth, its liberty. Not every word can be replaced by another one.
                    —Tadeusz Nyczek, Speak but the Word *(1985)*

The adjective . . . is the indispensable guarantor of the individuality of people and things.
                    —Adam Zagajewski, Two Cities *(1991)*

Perhaps Derrida was right: a faith in language's capacity for representation does presuppose outmoded notions like the existence of truth, a belief in some sort of fundamental human nature, and faith in an individual imagination that may at moments access these transcendent values. The Marxist thought that marked the death of metaphysics for the French poststructuralists inadvertently kept metaphysics alive among their Polish contemporaries: metaphysics marks their revolt against programmatic materialism. Such might be the message one takes from the later careers of Zagajewski, Krynicki, and Barańczak. The trajectories of these careers are strikingly different in ways that I will not explore here. For all their biographical and artistic differences, though, all three poets have devoted much of their more recent writing to a quest for the transcendent sense that informs—so they hope—our daily being. And this shared quest cannot simply be dismissed as a rejection of the more radical poetic politics of their youth. "Metaphysics, and mysticism in particular, were considered alien to the rationalism" of this generation's thought, Nyczek notes. But the "metaphysical relations of the poet as an individual human being and the universe, the cosmos" inform even their most apparently "diagnostic," "documentary" early writing. "Mysticism for Beginners"—one might easily compile an anthology of poems, early and late, by Barańczak, Krynicki, and Zagajewski under the title of Zagajewski's well-known poem.[53]

The poets of '68 were as acutely aware of the socially constructed nature of what we take for reality at a given time and place as any of their French contemporaries. Just such an awareness had influenced their precursors, the poets of earlier generations—Miłosz, Szymborska, Woroszylski, Borowski, and others—whose wartime experiences led them to embrace, however briefly, Marxist thought in its postwar Soviet variant. This awareness survived their disillusionment with Marxist ideology: "All concepts men live by are a product of the historic formation in which men find themselves," Miłosz comments in *The Captive Mind*.[54] The reality we perceive has been created by the language through which we perceive it: this notion permeates the poetry of the Polish sixty-eighters. But the conclusions they drew from this concept were radically different from those that inform the writings of their Parisian counterparts. "Reality Demands": the title of Szymborska's poem might serve as a post factum summation of the generation's program. "Reality," "objective truth," "an unfalsified image of the world": their manifestoes are peppered with such unpopular terms. They coexist, I should add, with references to Gramsci, Wittgenstein, and Barthes: their vision of truth and the language that strives for it was anything but naive. Poetry's task, as they saw it, was to wrench language away from its prescribed social functions in hopes of revealing glimpses of a human reality that had survived the various ideologies and social constructs designed to distort or disguise it.

"like everyone i've lost faith / in poetry / and prefer concrete facts / to their mythologization," Lothar Herbst confesses in "Transcription VIII" (1971). His generation's antilyrical tendencies were counterbalanced from the start, though, by a sense that lyric singularity was their best defense against the collective mythologies foisted on them by a hostile state. I've already quoted Barańczak's quintessentially avant-garde prescription for the poetry of his generation: "Permanent rebellion, criticism, demystification." He proceeds, though, to ask an unsettling question: "Why poetry?" His answer seems calculated to enrage the collectivist sensibilities of his avant-garde precursors and contemporaries: "Because in the modern world it preserves an individual viewpoint, a particular, irrepeatable perspective on the world." By virtue of its singular viewpoint, moreover, the lyric poem becomes the unlikely guarantor of those bourgeois pipe dreams, individual human rights: "By defending the right of the individual to freedom in every sphere of life, it must also defend the right to independent judgment—a crucial right in an era of dogmas imposed from above and universalized through the tuba of mass transmission. Poetry is thus a natural counterweight to any dogma accepted en masse—and the natural opponent of all that strives to become an impersonal system and thus threatens individual freedom." The book from which these quotes are taken could not be published in Poland; it first appeared in the Paris-based publishing house "Kultura" in the late seventies. Barańczak's comments, though, would have been no more welcome in post-'68 Paris than they were in People's Poland. Among Parisian intellectuals, what Engels called "the old metaphysical bric-à-brac" of humanist values and personal rights had been thoroughly debunked by the poststructuralists and their followers: "The humanism of the last three or four centuries is secretly totalitarian," one Foucauldian proclaims.[55]

Still for the Polish sixty-eighters, this variety of totalitarianism apparently seemed preferable to the kind they had come to know at home. In a poem of the mid-eighties, Barańczak celebrates, only half-ironically, his panoply of distinctly unpoetic "petit-bourgeois virtues." Zagajewski makes an even more shameful confession in a lyric written a few years earlier:

> Probably I am an ordinary middle-class
> believer in individual rights, the word
> "freedom" is simple to me, it doesn't mean
> the freedom of any class in particular.

Zagajewski's poetic career makes especially clear the perils and paradoxes inherent in the artistic programs of the sixty-eighters—how can the lyric voice be harnessed to collective action?—as he explores the potentials of this singular gift in the face of collective pressures from both state and, more surprisingly, opposition alike.[56]

In "Lyric Poetry and Society," Theodor Adorno argues for the lyric as a socially critical genre because it insists on keeping its distance from its dreary neighbors in reality. "Released from the heaviness of things," the lyric "should evoke images of a life free from the impositions of the every-day world, of usefulness, of the dumb drive for self-preservation." And it effects its utopian "dream of a world in which things would be different" by way of this divorce from dailiness. Adorno's otherworldly lyric was the sort of poetry against which Poland's sixty-eighters had declared war. Such abstract, impractical poetry was, however, eminently acceptable to a regime determined to obliterate all traces of daily life from public language, poetic and otherwise. For all their differences, the "straight speakers" and the "poet-linguists" were dedicated to resurrecting the particulars of life as lived in the People's Republic through maximally specific language. And poetry was ideal for such purposes due to what Barańczak calls its "propensity for particularity."[57] The search for a private self and speech shapes the richest and most engaging of Barańczak's, Krynicki's, and Zagajewski's early poems. But how can this search coexist with the need to speak "in the first person plural"? Is one collective voice necessarily the best weapon against another? Isn't a system bent on the eradication of individual personality and vision better combated by a voice that embodies those qualities most in danger of liquidation? Doesn't the accidental, personal voice of lyric poetry acquire singular power under such circumstances?

These questions are present in the programs and poetry of both "linguists" and "straight speakers" from the start. But it was Zagajewski who chose to depart most radically from the collective obligations of both his generation's and his tradition's poet-bards in the mid-eighties. Zagajewski has exchanged his "collective subject" for a mere "lyric speaker," his erstwhile comrade-in-arms Julian Kornhauser charged in a review of Zagajewski's controversial third volume of essays, *Solidarity, Solitude* (*Solidarność i samotność*, 1986). The collection was published in Paris in 1986, and followed in the wake of two equally provocative volumes of poetry, *Letter: Ode to Plurality* (*List: Oda do wielości*, 1983), and *To Go to Lvov* (*Jechać do Lwowa*, 1985). "I have the urge to become a dissident from dissidents," Zagajewski writes in *Solidarity, Solitude*, as he declares his newfound allegiance to "unusual, singular, exceptional things, such as a giraffe's neck." Fighting words indeed, especially when uttered at yet another time of national crisis, the period of martial law declared after General Wojciech Jaruzelski's brutal suppression of the Solidarity movement at the end of 1981. Poland's writers were being called upon once more to take the people's part against the state, and poetry "headed for the barricades" yet again, as Nyczek comments.[58]

Zagajewski's reputation for irresponsible lyricism—among some Polish critics and readers at any rate—dates from this time. "Birds, trees, wind," Kornhauser laments in a review of *To Go To Lvov*, "now carry him beyond space and time. . . . He has brought himself to a halt in order to forget about conflicts." Kornhauser misreads Zagajewski in ways I will not attempt to address here. But he has also apparently forgotten key elements of their own earlier manifesto. "The aesthetic value of an apt description becomes in some imperceptible way an ethical value as well, " Zagajewski insists in *The Unrepresented World*: his remark is of a piece with the calls for specificity and concreteness that punctuate the volume. Such particularity extends, Zagajewski's later work suggests, to the poet's need to cultivate not just solidarity, but solitude, his singular self and viewpoint—not least in hopes of pointing others to their own irrepeatable individuality.[59]

In one early lyric Zagajewski describes an encounter with a group of students: "What should we do they asked me / nineteen of my lyric I's": the poet gives no reply. A later poem from *Letter: Ode to Plurality* suggests that the best response might be to rephrase the question entirely:

> I lived in the plural, we lived
> in the plural, among friends
> strange to us and friendly enemies,
> so rarely on my own, our own, so little
> loneliness in such a lonely
> land. Even poems said
> we, we poems, we lines, we
> metaphors, we points. The I
> slept like a child beneath the cloth
> of a distracted gaze

The task of the poet, Zagajewski's later work suggests, is to keep this "I" awake at any cost, both for his own sake and for the sake of society at large. The "ordinary middle-class believer in individual rights" explains:

> I remember
> the blazing appeal of that fire which parches
> the lips of the thirsty crowd and burns
> books and chars the skin of cities. I used to sing
> those songs and I know how great it is
> to run with others; later, by myself,
> with the taste of ashes in my mouth, I heard
> the lie's ironic voice and the choir screaming . . .

The crowd's voice not only threatens to efface the individual identities of those who comprise it. It runs the risk of becoming what it hates, the burner of cities and books. And the poet who runs with the crowd, whose songs help to set it aflame, is at least partly to blame. Engagement has its dangers, Zagajewski reminds us.[60]

Thus far I have been speaking of lyric singularity in the context of programmatic collectivism and the collective opposition it provoked. Zagajewski's more recent poetry invites us to take such considerations much further, though. I have in mind specifically the fate of his most famous lyric, which appeared on the final page of the first *New Yorker* issue to be published after September 11, 2001:

> *Try to Praise the Mutilated World*
> Try to praise the mutilated world.
> Remember June's long days,

and wild strawberries, drops of wine, the dew.
The nettles that methodically overgrow
the abandoned homesteads of exiles.
You must praise the mutilated world.
You watched the stylish yachts and ships;
one of them had a long trip ahead of it,
while salty oblivion awaited others.
You've seen the refugees heading nowhere,
you've heard the executioners sing joyfully.
You should praise the mutilated world.
Remember the moments when we were together
in a white room and the curtain fluttered.
Return in thought to the concert where music flared.
You gathered acorns in the park in autumn
and leaves eddied over the earth's scars.
Praise the mutilated world
and the gray feather a thrush lost,
and the gentle light that strays and vanishes
and returns.[61]

It is perhaps not so surprising that a Polish poem should have been chosen to commemorate this national tragedy. A sense of overwhelming loss and hard-earned wisdom made poems like Miłosz's "Song on the End of the World" or "Dedication," Szymborska's "The End and the Beginning," "Could Have," or "Hatred," or Herbert's "Marcus Aurelius" compelling choices for journalists, artists, educators, and individual readers looking for ways to come to grips with the disaster. All three poets are masters at converting the horrors of modern Polish history into meditations, at once personal and universal, on the nature of our shared human experience.

Zagajewski's poem seems at first a misfit in this company. The lyric "I" is virtually invisible in many of the poems I've just listed, and this is no accident. "The true home of the Polish poet," Miłosz insists, "is history," and he or she is thus preoccupied "less with the ego" than with history's dramas.[62] But Zagajewski's poem, though used to commemorate a historical cataclysm, might serve equally well as a textbook illustration of Eliot's and Mill's famous dictums. We eavesdrop upon a poet urging himself to create ("try to praise") as he recalls lyric moments ("remember June's long days") and awaits the muse's return, the resurgence of "the gentle light that strays and vanishes." The *New Yorker*'s former poetry editor, Alice Quinn, remarked that this poem, written long before the terrorist attacks in Manhattan and Washington, was pinned to bulletin boards and refrigerators throughout New York in its aftermath. As its translator, I received emails from across the country after it appeared. In the lyric, the poet speaks to himself or to nobody, Eliot claims. How could Zagajewski, in speaking to himself, end by speaking to so many? How could a seemingly private poem possibly fulfill a public function?

"Try to praise the mutilated world," the poet bids himself as the poem begins; and forms of this exhortation recur four times in the space of the poem's twenty-one lines. This is the poet's difficulty, then; he suffers not from solipsistic self-absorption, but from a nagging need, an ethical compulsion even, to praise a world that is, and has always been, defaced by history's cruelties. Lyricism (praise) confronts history (the mutilated world); and its fragile, qualified victory (the straying light's evanescent return) is achieved only through persistence, particularity (the gray feather), and a stubborn refusal to let either lyricism or history vanish entirely from view. I have mentioned the poem's traditional lyric topoi. Indeed, taken in isolation, the poem's June, its wild strawberries and wine, its music, thrush, and fluttering curtains all teeter on the brink of poetic cliché. But they are not isolated here. "Remember the moments when we were together / in a white room and the curtains fluttered," the poet writes. Even in his remembered moment of solitude with a wife or lover, his windows are open to the winds of the world beyond. This poet is, if anything, too aware of history's nightmares, and he struggles to keep the lyric self alive in the face of history's inexorable opposition. The lyric recollections with which he begins—"wild strawberries, drops of wine"—are quickly overtaken by the nettles that in turn "methodically overgrow / the abandoned homesteads of exiles." Here as throughout Zagajewski's writing, the natural world is steeped in human history, and though he makes no explicit mention of it, this history is clearly informed by modern Polish experience. Human habitations—be they modest homesteads or stylish yachts—are in constant danger, and the dangers they face come from other human beings as well as nature. "You've seen the refugees heading nowhere, / you've heard the executioners sing joyfully." This world is difficult to praise.

But praise it he must, and so must we. Why? "History rounds off skeletons to zero," Szymborska comments in "Starvation Camp Near Jaslo." "For 120 dead," Zbigniew Herbert observes, "you search on a map in vain":

> they do not speak to the imagination
> there are too many of them
> the numeral zero at the end
> changes them into an abstraction

Herbert's lament was inspired by an experience we all know far too well; it comes from a little poem called "Mr. Cogito Reads the Newspaper." We live in an age of "large numbers," as Szymborska writes elsewhere, and we are bombarded by them daily. Their dehumanizing abstraction hit home in the months following September 11.[63] The number of victims reported in the media may have dropped from five thousand or more down to somewhere around three thousand as the data grew more precise, but the multiple zeroes and the lives they erased seemed painfully inadequate, as the *New York Times* recognized through the moving profiles of individual victims it ran week after week in the wake of the disaster.

Zagajewski's poem addresses history's victims only obliquely, through its refugees and abandoned homesteads. The poet struggles instead to keep the lyric "I" awake in the face of history's overwhelming depredations. But this "I" is not confined to the poet alone, in spite of the poem's seemingly self-enclosed dialogue of self and soul. Neither is it the inflated "I" of the many would-be poet-prophets and poet-Christs who have sought since Romanticism to take upon themselves the torments of the world en masse. This poet invites us instead to join in his struggle to face the world's large-scale sufferings and—more difficult still—to praise its ephemeral joys. The self that writes exhorts the self that reads to stay awake, despite awareness almost past bearing, and to sustain itself in its labors through the private store of lyric recollections that each of us carries within. The poet's indirect invitation is the more persuasive since he himself recognizes the difficulty of the task he undertakes: "Try to praise," "you must praise," "you should praise," he urges. This poet is no teacher from on high; he struggles, as we do, to see both the scars and the beauties, and to keep the seeing self alive. His urging is the more compelling precisely because it is not heard, but overheard. We follow his example not because he demands it, but because his own struggle so fully engages our sympathies. In spurring himself, and us with him, to recollect and revive our own inner lives, he also reminds us obliquely of the rich inner worlds that are lost each time the homesteads are abandoned as the executioners sing. Each vanished self had his or her own Junes and acorns, his or her own hidden wounds.

Lyric privacy is not a matter for poets alone. "Once one divides the world into history and poetry, then one obliterates the difference between a history which favors man, which is habitable and human, and the kind which produces concentration camps," Zagajewski asserts in *Two Cities*.[64] This may seem initially like uncharacteristic poetic grandstanding on Zagajewski's part. What he seems to mean, though, is far closer to the sense that so many readers apparently derived from "Try to Praise." The lyric poet summons us to remain stubbornly singular ourselves, whatever the cost, and thus to see all history, whether past or passing, as composed of similarly irrepeatable beings, and not as mere data, the vast, unfathomable numbers that obliterate, willy-nilly, all traces of the individual existences that serve as their raw material. Lyric history, as Zagajewski envisions it, retains its humanity through its specificity and thus remains habitable and human in spite of the endless exiles and executioners.

This is why Zagajewski and his contemporaries finally part company so completely with the "antihumanist" philosophy of their French contemporaries. Miłosz hints at a secret bond, as I've noted, between *écriture*—that poststructuralist echo chamber of texts speaking to texts without human intervention—and the totalitarian state. It would be silly to push his analogy too far—but it would be equally misguided to ignore it. Each phenomenon is born of the fascination with grand theory that marks the century just past. Each leads to the erasure of individual beings in theory alone, in the first case, and in practice—quite spectacularly—in the second. The French poststructuralists proudly proclaimed the "death of the subject," while their Polish contemporaries were busily orchestrating its resurrection. In their rebellion against a state based on grand theory, Zagajewski, Krynicki, and Barańczak chose as their weapon an instrument dedicated, as they saw it, to the preservation of the specific experience of human beings in the singular. This, not their early collective manifestoes and battle cries, proved to be their lasting legacy to postwar poetry, both in Poland and beyond.

8

The Unacknowledged Legislator's Dream: Czesław Miłosz and Anglo-American Poetry

Archimedes thought he could move the world if he could
find the right place to position his lever. Billy Hunter
said Tarzan shook the world when he jumped down out of
a tree.

I sink my crowbar in a chink I know under the masonry
of state and statute, I swing on a creeper of secrets
into the Bastille.

My wronged people cheer from their cages. The guard-
dogs are unmuzzled, a soldier pivots a muzzle at
the butt of my ear, I am stood blindfolded with my hands
above my head until I seem to be swinging from a
strappado.

The commandant motions me to be seated.
"I am honoured to add a poet to our list." He is
amused and genuine. "You'll be safer here, anyhow."

In the cell, I wedge myself with outstretched arms
in the corner and heave, I jump on the concrete flags to
test them. Were those your eyes just now at the hatch?
—Seamus Heaney, "The Unacknowledged
Legislator's Dream" (1975)

The Unacknowledged Legislator's Dream

In *The Waste Land*, T. S. Eliot famously called April "the cruellest month." It has also been more recently christened—coincidentally, one hopes—as American National Poetry Month. What does this mean in practice? Not much, I'm afraid. Editors push forward the publication dates of whatever poetry volumes they happen to have on hand in hopes of a few extra sales. Bookstores and libraries reserve a display case for Billy Collins, Sylvia Plath, Robert Frost, or Maya Angelou. And one or two prominent poets make appearances on Public Broadcasting or National Public Radio to try and explain what they do and why it matters before returning to their usual spot offstage.

In one well-known poem, Yeats gently mocks his own standing as a national icon, a "sixty-year-old smiling public man" standing awkwardly on display "among school children."[1] Few anglophone poets in modern times have been privileged to share in his public embarrassment: Eliot certainly, Frost, perhaps Carl Sandburg, and more recently Seamus Heaney, whose translation of *Beowulf* became an unexpected bestseller a few years back. If poets writing in English rarely find readers outside the ranks of critics, professors, and fellow poets, what can the occasional foreigner who stumbles onto the scene possibly expect, burdened as he or she is with an impenetrable accent and unpronounceable last name? One recent American poet laureate, Joseph Brodsky, did his best to convince American readers to pick up at least their own classic authors from time to time. Emily Dickinson alongside the Gideon Bible in every Holiday Inn, Walt Whitman next to *People* magazine at the grocery checkout stand—so ran a few of his modest proposals. Brodsky himself enjoyed great esteem among American intellectuals and writers, but his impact was by and large restricted to their ranks—and even here his influence rarely extended, I suspect, to the actual practice of American poets writing today. In any case, his poetry never reached the larger public he craved.

"If you have not read the Slavic poets, / so much the better," Czesław Miłosz wrote over forty years ago in his poem "To Robinson Jeffers" (1963). He could not have begun a poem that way today—and for this he was himself largely to blame. For many years now, American poets and critics have been reading Miłosz, along with his compatriots (many of whom they first encountered in the anthology of postwar Polish poetry he edited in the mid-sixties), with an intensity and attentiveness seldom accorded to a living poet whose words reach them only in translation. Miłosz's impact reaches far beyond American poetry—English-speaking poets from various parts of the globe have acknowledged their debt to Miłosz and his fellow Poles in recent decades. For the purposes of this chapter, though, I'll be looking most closely at his influence on American writing, with a few incursions into English and Irish terrain. Robert Pinsky, Edward Hirsch, Rosanna Warren, Robert Hass, Charles Simic, Mary Karr, Carolyn Forché, Yusef Komunyakaa, Mark Strand, W. S. Merwin—so might run a partial, preliminary list of contemporary American poets who've felt the impact of Miłosz and his compatriots over the last few decades. And this is not to mention the other recent Nobel laureates, Seamus Heaney, Derek Walcott, and Brodsky himself, who've testified, in both prose and verse, to what Heaney calls the "altogether thrilling" experience of encountering Miłosz and other Polish poets in translation. Brodsky even learned Polish in order to read what he called "the most extraordinary poetry" of the twentieth century in the original.[2]

But Miłosz's impact extends beyond literary circles. If you had been browsing through the *Chicago Tribune* book review on October 5, 2003, you might have noticed a photograph of Miłosz at the top of page 3, just above the English version of a poem written some sixty years ago in Nazi-occupied Warsaw. Miłosz's "Song on the End of the World" was the third in a series of poems chosen annually by the Great Books Foundation and printed in the *Tribune* in a tradition begun shortly after September 11, 2001, when scores of people turned up at designated libraries and bookstores around the Chicago area to discuss Auden's "September 1, 1939" as a way of considering our more recent tragedy. (I should perhaps mention that the second poem in this series was also Polish, Wisława Szymborska's "Reality Demands.") Less locally speaking, a recent search on Amazon.com turned up close to a thousand references to Miłosz in American books in print. There were the expected mentions in anthologies and handbooks on unleashing your inner artist, as well as numerous scholarly references in works on poetry, politics, Eastern Europe, and so on. Miłosz also makes guest appearances, though, in books on yoga, childrearing, self-help, basketball, civil liberties, world mythology, Silicon Valley, Kissinger, modern Christianity, and ancient Zen. His name even figures in a guide to celebrities and their signs: he apparently shares a birthday with Mike Tyson. Tony Kushner quotes him in his plays; Bill Moyers cites him on Public Broadcasting; he turns up in Lewis Hyde's classic *The Gift* (1983), John Grisham's recent thriller *The Broker* (2005), and Frances Mayes's bestselling *Under the Tuscan Sun* (1997).

Miłosz sardonically travesties Horace in a poem from the early seventies: "Oh yes, not all of me shall die, there will remain / An item in the fourteenth volume of an encyclopedia / Next to a hundred Millers and Mickey Mouse" (320). The unexpected fame he achieved since receiving the Nobel Prize in

1980 propelled him into even stranger company some years back when an excerpt from his *Treatise on Poetry* ended up sandwiched between blurbs for an illustrated history of baseball and *Gourmet Paris 2001* in Borders Bookstore's monthly guide to new arrivals. He keeps more distinguished company in Jill Vongrubin's *College Countdown: The Parent's and Student's Survival Kit for the College Admissions Process*, in which a list of student must-reads includes "Miller, Arthur, Milton, John, Miłosz, Czesław, Molière, Montale, Eugenio, Moore, Marianne, Morrison, Toni."

Such a fate seemed unlikely, to say the least, when Miłosz chose exile—first in France and then the United States, where he taught Slavic literatures at Berkeley for thirty years—over continued cooperation with the Communist regime that came to power at the war's conclusion. He continued to write in Polish throughout his long exile, though this choice seemed to doom him to obscurity. His work could neither be published in his homeland, where it was officially banned, nor comprehended in his adopted country where his native tongue seemed as remote, he complains, as "one of the lesser-known African dialects" (3:146). He seemed in danger of becoming not even, as he laments elsewhere, "the greatest poet of the kingdom of Albania" (3:115), but a poet who was equally invisible, for different reasons, in both the land of his origins and his adoptive country.

How did it come to pass that Miłosz—along with several other unpronounceable poets whose names include 'z,' such as Zbigniew Herbert, Wisława Szymborska, or Adam Zagajewski—has moved so far beyond the circles to which poetry is ordinarily confined in the United States? I raised this question first in my introduction, but I'm afraid that I will not explore its ramifications and their significance—sociological? cultural? metaphysical?—in exhaustive detail here. Instead, I want to turn to the more limited, if no less illuminating, topic of Miłosz's reception in the States particularly and the various paradoxes of cross-cultural poetry and politics it reveals. Miłosz first became known among American poets not as a poet, but as a translator. In 1965, he edited the collection that put Polish poetry on the map for American writers, his *Postwar Polish Poetry*—which is still in print today. Time after time, I've heard poets speak of this book as a turning point in their own artistic development.

But the year that marked his next major venture into the Americanization of Polish poetry is more satisfyingly symbolic. Miłosz's edition of Zbigniew Herbert's *Selected Poems* (co-translated with Peter Dale Scott) first appeared in 1968. The causes and effects of the student revolts that erupted from Warsaw to Berkeley varied greatly, depending on which side of the Iron Curtain you happened to occupy, as I've noted in my discussion of

Poland's "New Wave." "The personal is the political," ran the slogan in the States—but the poetic was the political, as we've seen, for the students who swarmed Warsaw streets in 1968 when Mickiewicz's "Forefathers' Eve" was shut down by the Soviet-backed authorities. Shelley's "unacknowledged legislators" would have given their eyeteeth for such a reception. Small wonder, then, that his American descendants should be drawn at that moment to lyrics coming from a part of the world where poets were capable, even posthumously, of disturbing the peace, inflaming the young, and outraging the authorities. In the States, the 1960's witnessed, not surprisingly, the growing restlessness of American poets, chroniclers of the personal unjustly confined, or so they felt, to the margins of a society that had little use for the selves they lamented or extolled in their poems.[3]

The complaint is an old one. American poetry "cannot embody political vision," Sven Birkerts remarks in *The Electric Life* (1989). "Poetry is now largely a face-saving operation, with poets pulling their bitterness inside out and preening themselves on their own uselessness." Birkerts's reproach has a distinguished pedigree. Alexis de Tocqueville had observed some 150 years earlier that the American people were inclined to "look at the world with reference to themselves and not, as the Frenchmen, at themselves with reference to the world." And the results, as he saw it, were far from promising: "Nothing conceivable is so petty, so insipid, so crowded with paltry interests, in one word so anti-poetic, as American life." The would-be poet of the fledgling democracy had recourse to himself alone: "Among a democratic people poetry will not be fed with legendary lays or memorials of old traditions. . . . All these resources fail him; but Man remains, and the poet needs no more." One has only to reach for Whitman's *Leaves of Grass* to feel the force of Tocqueville's prophecy. American poetry arguably became, and in many ways remains, as Roy Harvey Pearce has claimed, "a poetry of the self," "a private poetry aspiring to be universal," an egocentric poetry insisting that "in its egocentricism lay its universality."[4]

Egocentric universalism: the phenomenon is hardly confined to the Americans, as any reader of Mayakovsky can attest. From Virgil to Dante, from Blake to Blok or Mayakovsky and beyond, Western writers have shared the experience that Lawrence Lipking sees as pivotal to the poetic vocation: "[T]he poet realizes that his own personal history, reflected in his poems, coincides with the universal spiritual history of mankind." The key difference lies perhaps not so much in the claims themselves as in how seriously they are taken by the poets' compatriots—or their audiences in translation. In any case, it was not simply the Americans who looked eastward in the late sixties in hopes of reconciling the schism between the private lyrist and the public life. "In Western Europe," the British poet A. Alvarez comments in his introduction to Herbert's *Selected Poems,* "we take for granted that there is a fundamental split between poetry and politics. The problem is not that the twain can never meet but that they can do so only at a great cost. The complexity, tension and precision of modern poetry simply doesn't go with the language of politics, with its vague rhetoric and dependence on clichés." "To all this," he concludes, "Zbigniew Herbert is an exception." So it may have seemed in the late sixties, when Herbert was first introduced to an Anglo-American audience. But Herbert as exemplary political poet would be joined over subsequent decades by other Eastern Europeans— with Miłosz at their helm—who might, so anglophone poets hoped, help them bridge the gap that Alvarez deplores.[5]

Until the Nobel Prize, Miłosz was known in Anglo-American literary circles chiefly for his translations of Herbert and other Polish poets, in spite of the publication of his own *Selected Poems* in 1973, followed by *Bells in Winter* in 1978. "No single writer of our time has with such profound effect brought another literature across the distances of language and history to the readers and writers of our own," the poet Jonathan Aaron remarked in 1981. "His contribution to our literary self-awareness has been and continues to be crucial." Aaron has in mind Miłosz's translations of Aleksander Wat, the volume of *Postwar Polish Poetry,* and especially Herbert's poems, which "stung," Aaron notes, English and American writers "into a new, unfamiliar awareness": "translated by Miłosz, the poems seemed even in English to be products of a sort of preternatural knowing," a knowledge for which Anglo-American poets apparently had no counterpart.[6] As awareness of Miłosz's own poetic opus has grown over the last few decades, he has come to seem the exemplar of the otherworldly knowledge that Aaron and his fellow poets found so compelling in Herbert. But all this begs the question—what is this uncanny consciousness to which Polish poets are ostensibly privy? And why should American poets be so drawn to it?

Herbert himself suggests an answer in "Prayer of Mr. Cogito—Traveler": "forgive me that I didn't fight like Lord Byron for the happiness of captive peoples / that I watched only risings of the moon and museums." The British Romantics, whose island empire spared them the horrors of revolt and invasion at home, were forced to seek their captive nations elsewhere: the revolutionary France of Wordsworth and Coleridge, the insurgent Greece for which Shelley wrote his lyrics and Byron gave his life. In his "Hebrew Melodies" (1815), Byron works to stir sympathy not just for the nationless Jews alone, but for all peoples "whose shrines are desolate, whose land a dream": the Greeks, the Irish, the Italians, and the natives of South America, as well as the hapless Poles. The Polish poet, though, is forced to play out this scenario in reverse. He must first flee his own captive nation if he is to savor the seemingly innocent pleasures of moonbeams and museums—although he must do penance for tasting the forbidden fruit of beauty for its own sake: "forgive me," Herbert's alter ego Mr. Cogito begs. Politics versus poetry, ethics versus aesthetics, uprisings versus moon risings and museums: the manifold ironies unleashed by Mr. Cogito's little plea take us straight to the heart of the paradoxical Polish conquest of Anglo-American poetic territory.[7]

In this sense, Miłosz's remarkable career in English-speaking lands has been exemplary. I began my book with Maureen McLane's words on the Slavic writers who have become the emblem of poetic gravitas for their reluctantly sheltered Anglo-American confreres. As translator, proselytizer, and *éminence grise,* Miłosz presided over this phenomenon in recent decades. The last twenty-five years have seen his name take pride of place in an obligatory litany, a mantra that prefaces almost every recent discussion of poetry's function in the modern world. It runs, with variations, roughly as follows: Anna Akhmatova, Osip Mandelstam, Vasko Popa, Miroslav Holub, Joseph Brodsky, Czesław Miłosz, Zbigniew Herbert. Other Polish surnames—Szymborska, Różewicz, Zagajewski, Barańczak—sometimes surface on such lists. "The collective heart of the Swedish Academy still beats strongly for central Europe," one journalist observed when Wisława Szymborska's Nobel Prize in literature was announced in 1996. A glance at recent laureates seems to confirm the preeminence of Eastern Europe in modern poetry, with Miłosz (1980), Jaroslav Seifert (1984), Brodsky (1987), and Szymborska (1996) all receiving the prize in the last three decades.[8]

An expanded list of recent laureates in poetry further testifies to the influence that these poets and their Eastern European colleagues have exerted on writing in English generally. The two most recent recipients in English-language poetry, Derek Walcott (1992) and Seamus Heaney (1995), have been quick to acknowledge their debt to Eastern Europe. In "Polonaise," a poem later incorporated into his epic *Omeros* (1990), Walcott pays homage to a Poland besieged by its own rulers by invoking its poetry; the poem closes with three single, apparently self-explanatory names: "Zagajewski. Herbert. Miłosz." In his poetry and prose of the mid-eighties particularly, Seamus Heaney pays grateful tribute to the "heroic names" of Eastern European poetry: Mandelstam, Miłosz, Holub, Herbert. And Brodsky was typically hyperbolic—although not necessarily wrong—when he announced in 1988 that "if you know Polish (which would be to your great advantage, because the most extraordinary poetry of this century is written in that language)—I'd like to mention to you the names of Leopold Staff, Czesław Miłosz, Zbigniew Herbert and Wisława Szymborska." Recent American poet laureates include, moreover, both actual Eastern Europeans (Joseph Brodsky) and honorary ones (Miłosz's co-translators Robert Hass and Robert Pinsky). Yet another recent poet laureate, Billy Collins, has been known to begin his own readings by reciting the poems of Wisława Szymborska in English translation. Ted Hughes, who served as the British poet laureate from 1984 until his death in 1998, translated the Hungarian poet János Pilinszky and wrote admiringly of Miłosz, Herbert, Popa, and Holub. Through their poets, the countries of the former Soviet bloc finally appear to have avenged their betrayal at Yalta by way of this unexpected Eastern European invasion of Anglo-American poetry.[9]

Both British and American poets have fallen prey in recent decades to a surprising Polish complex, with Poland as a peculiarly inverted promised land: it serves as a kind of Slavic shorthand for "The Oppressed Nation Where Poetry Still Matters." Poland is not alone in this honor. The poets of Latin America and Eastern Europe alike are "in vogue for suspicious reasons," Helene J. F. de Aguilar complains in a singularly blinkered review of Miłosz's poetry in translation. But Polish poets, she continues, have a particularly unfair advantage due to the dazzling range of "demeaning possibilities," the spectacularly "variegated" "dire straits" that history has bestowed upon any poet fortunate enough to be born in twentieth-century Poland: "The national life against which they seem to contend is the aftermath of every sort of war and oppression."[10] The strength of De Guilar's *ressentiment* both demonstrates the power of the Polish influence on modern poetry and tells us something about its sources.

I have mentioned the troubles American poets have traditionally encountered in struggling to conflate their nation's life and destiny with their own. The geography that has largely shielded the United States from Europe's conflagrations plays a part in this, as does the programmatically antihistorical bent of a young nation committed to the possibility of new beginnings and endless self-reinvention. In this we are the antithesis of the country Miłosz describes in the preface to his *Postwar Polish Poetry,* a country plagued by history and geography alike. Polish poetry, he insists, is preoccupied "less with the ego than with the dramas of history." He gives a compelling reason for this peculiarity: "A historical steam-roller has gone several times through [this] country, whose geographical location, between Germany and Russia, is not particularly enviable."[11]

And yet some poets do envy it—and not Americans alone. For all its proximity to the continent, England's long history as an island-empire has left it relatively unscathed by Europe's greatest upheavals. "Contemporary English poetry," Seamus Heaney remarks, "has become aware of the insular and eccentric nature of English experience in all the literal and extended meanings of those adjectives": "England's island status, its off-centre European positioning, its history of non-defeat and non-invasion since 1066, these enviable and (as far as the English are concerned) normative conditions have ensured a protracted life within the English psyche for the assumption that a possible and desirable congruence exists between domestic and imagined reality."[12]

Heaney omits the high price paid at times to achieve this enviable history, a price to which any survivor of the Nazi blitz will testify. Still, England's centuries-long career as island-empire has not prevented the occasional English poet from claiming honorary status as a Polish-style victim of history. In an essay on Herbert, Donald Davie compares the plight of the modern Briton to the predicament of the Poles: "Whereas the chronically helpless or luckless Poles have found themselves in a situation of impotence through most of their history, the post-1945 British, living through a post-imperial twilight suddenly found their situation not very different. The USSR, the USA—there are great differences of course, but one or the other Big Brother limits the power of Poles and Britons alike."[13] Like their Romantic precursors, the poets of England apparently still must travel abroad, at least imaginatively, to seek out a more challenging relationship between poetry and society. And one of the more popular routes in recent years, Heaney notes, has been by way of Warsaw and Prague.

Warsaw, Krakow, Prague, and Petersburg: these are the chief cities of what many anglophone poets have come to see as "the republic of conscience," in Heaney's phrase. (This is, incidentally, the title of a poem from the mid-eighties that most strongly betrays the influence on Heaney's own work of what he calls Poland's "parable poetry.") And citizenship in this republic represents the apogee of "the unacknowledged legislator's dream." For such would-be martyrs, Poland must seem to represent a—somewhat perverse—poetic dream come true. Shelley and his fellow Romantics could not even get their dramas staged, let alone suppressed by the powers-that-be. Their plays were private affairs, closet dramas largely confined to the stage of their own creators' minds. Mickiewicz's *Forefathers' Eve* or Juliusz Słowacki's "Kordian" (1834) are no less unstageable than Byron's "Manfred" or Shelley's "Cenci"; indeed, Byron's play particularly was a major influence on the Poles. For all that, though, both Polish dramas have long, distinguished histories on Polish stages and in the Polish popular imagination alike. Indeed, even non-Poles could be granted de facto dissident status when it came to the banning of almost-unplayable verse dramas. Eliot's *Murder in the Cathedral*, with its priest slain by a criminal state, was apparently considered too volatile to be staged in a Poland under martial law, and authorities accordingly closed down a Polish production in 1982. It is not surprising that Shelley's twentieth-century descendants should find themselves drawn to Miłosz and other heirs of Eastern Europe's poet-bards as they searched for a way to engage with the politics and society of their own day.[14]

Miłosz among the Americans

I have felt that the problem of my time should be defined as Poetry and History.
　　　　—Czesław Miłosz, *"A Poet Between East and West"* (1977)

"The Polish poet Czesław Miłosz could hardly present a greater or more instructive contrast to . . . the great majority of contemporary American poets," Jonathan Galassi writes in a 1979 review of *Bells in Winter*. "Miłosz's work," he continues, challenges "American poetry to exit from the labyrinth of the self and begin to grapple again with the larger problems of being in the world." Such comments recur time and again in reviews of Miłosz's work. "The assumption that private life is embraced and controlled by history is rare among American poets," Marisha Chamberlain complains in an essay on Miłosz's collection *Rescue* (1945), written largely in wartime Warsaw. In another review, Terence des Pres explicitly contrasts "Miłosz's example with the Emersonian tradition in American poetry": "From Emerson and Dickinson onward, American poetry celebrates perception for perception's sake, it focuses on the interior drama of wholly isolated selfhood, it posits destiny in solely individual terms. For a poet like Miłosz, who saw Warsaw leveled and was among the handful to survive his generation's murder, such attitudes must not only sound out of place, but out of the world altogether." "People, places, things," he concludes, "everything for Miłosz is densely historical."[15]

Miłosz himself apparently concurs. In the recently translated *A Treatise on Poetry* (*Traktat poetycki,* 1957), America, predictably enough, plays Nature to Europe's History and Culture:

> America for me has the pelt of a raccoon,
> A chipmunk flickers in a litter of dry bark . . .
> America's wings are the color of a cardinal,
> Its beak is half-open and a mockingbird trills
> From a leafy bush in the sweat-bath of the air. (146)

In America, the works of "our gray-haired father Herodotus," the fore-bear of Western historiography, remain unread: "Herodotus will repose on his shelf, uncut" (144–147). In the *Treatise*'s conclusion, Miłosz's speaker exchanges comfortable exile in American "Natura" for Europe and history, just as Miłosz himself had done following his postwar years in the Polish diplomatic corps in New York and Washington.

In his influential *Witness of Poetry* (1983), Miłosz stresses the singular engagement with history that distinguishes modern Polish writing from its Western counterparts. In Polish poetry, he comments, "a peculiar fusion of the individual and the historical took place, which means that events burdening a whole community are perceived by a poet as touching him in a most personal manner." "The true home of the Polish poet," he insists, "is history."[16] The rootless, self-absorbed American and the Polish witness to history: these two poets would seem to be worlds apart in the quotes, both Polish and American, that I've assembled here. But the very works I've just cited—*A Treatise on Poetry* and *The Witness of Poetry*—hint at the complexities of Miłosz's engagement with Anglo-American writing, and with American poetry particularly, complexities to which his American audience, alert to his distinctive "Polishness," has remained surprisingly oblivious. And this in turn points to a far more complex relationship between private self and public history than Miłosz himself is sometimes willing to admit in his own writing—as well as his occasional complicity in the clichés of American rootlessness and Polish history that punctuate discussions of Polish poetry stateside.

Certainly Miłosz himself has made no effort to hide his indebtedness to American writing, and to one American author in particular. "I am a habitan of Vienna, St. Petersburg, Berlin," Walt Whitman boasts in "Salut au Monde!": "I belong in Moscow, Cracow, Warsaw." The prophet may go unnoticed in his own country. But Whitman proved prophetic at least in his hopes for a conquest of Europe's capitals, as I've noted elsewhere. Indeed, Whitman's name appears repeatedly not only in the *Treatise* and *The Witness of Poetry*, but throughout Miłosz's vast opus. The English translation of Miłosz's "Throughout Our Lands" (1961) begins by quoting his American master: "When I pass'd through a populous city / (as Walt Whitman says, in the Polish version)" (182). Polish has no definite or indefinite articles, and the translators' interpolation (the poem was translated by Miłosz with Peter Dale Scott) is misleading: the Polish Whitman was far too popular in the first part of the twentieth century to be served by one version alone. The Polish text is more specific: "When I pass'd through a populous city / (as Walt Whitman says in Alfred Tom's translation)." The scrupulous editor of

Miłosz's Polish *Collected Poems* (*Wiersze*) informs us, though, that Miłosz must have encountered this particular poem not in Tom's, but in Stefan Napierski's translation (2:316, 389). Miłosz himself refers to three separate translators, Tom, Napierski, and Stanisław Vincenz, in describing his first encounter with Whitman: "Immediately, revelation: to be able to write as he did."[17]

He was not alone in his enthusiasm: "What they really wanted was a new Whitman," Miłosz writes of Poland's interwar poets in *A Treatise on Poetry* (121). Whitman's song of himself was no stranger, then, to the young Miłosz. The biblical cadences and voracious, outsized speakers that mark Miłosz's own poetry clearly betray his debt, from his early lyrics on, to this particular exemplar of the "Emersonian tradition" that Des Pres and others oppose to his poetry and that of his fellow Poles. To read Miłosz, even in English translation, is to be reminded just how much Whitman's particular brand of egotistical sublimity has in common not only with Miłosz himself, but with the Eastern European bards whose impact on society Miłosz describes in *The Captive Mind* and elsewhere. Whitman's example also demonstrates, incidentally, that self-celebration and witness to history are not mutually exclusive categories. He served, we recall, as a nurse in Union hospitals during the Civil War: "From the stump of the arm, the amputated hand, / I undo the clotted lint, remove the slough, wash off the matter and blood," he notes in "The Wound-Dresser."[18]

Miłosz's catalyzing encounters with Whitman took place before he began to read English-language poetry in the original. But the Anglo-American influence on Miłosz's writing was not confined to Whitman alone. Many key works from the postwar years—"The Treatise on Morals" (1947), "Toast," "To Jonathan Swift," and others—defy translation, as Miłosz himself admits, due to the intricate verse forms that he found himself employing, to his own surprise, in his poetry of this period.[19] The titles of two untranslated poems remind us where Miłosz was and what he was doing when they were written: one is called "On a Bird's Song above the Banks of the Potomac," while the other is entitled "Central Park." In 1946, Miłosz was assigned to the Polish consulate in New York; and the following year he became the cultural attaché to the Polish embassy in Washington. (Still another poem of the period, "To Albert Einstein," commemorates Miłosz's visit to Einstein's Princeton home when he was seeking advice on whether or not to remain in the States.)[20]

I'm less concerned at this point with Miłosz's brief affiliation with the People's Republic and its aftermath than with the unofficial function Miłosz performed during these years, his work as a cultural attaché in a larger and more lasting sense. During his tour of duty stateside, Miłosz continued and intensified a campaign begun in wartime Warsaw to open Polish literature up to the riches of the English-language tradition. If in the States he is perceived as first bringing Polish poetry to the attention of an English-speaking audience, the inverse is true in Poland. Polish poets and critics alike credit him with singlehandedly shifting the cultural axis away from France, which had previously dominated Polish literary culture, and towards poetry written in English. The very verse forms that make the poems of *Daylight* (*Swiatło dzienne,* 1953) so resistant to translation are indebted to his voluminous readings in anglophone poetry. John Donne, W. H. Auden, Karl Shapiro, Robert Lowell, and Hart Crane all make appearances, inter alia, in the pages of his influential essay "An Introduction to the Americans," which appeared in Poland in 1947.[21] Miłosz himself cites Karl Shapiro's *Essay on Rime* (1945) as a prime inspiration for his own *A Treatise on Poetry.*[22]

"There are no direct lessons that American poets can learn from Miłosz," Helen Vendler declares in a controversial 1984 review. "Those who have never seen modern war on their own soil cannot adopt his tone; the sights that scarred his eyes cannot be seen by the children of a young provincial empire." Other critics point to Miłosz's wartime poetry as the marker of his distinctive, inimitable Polishness: Miłosz "found his voice and his subject during his years in Nazi-occupied Warsaw," Marisha Chamberlain comments.[23] These were also the years, though, when Miłosz first learned English and began his English-language translating career, modestly enough, with T. S. Eliot and Shakespeare. There are limits to what Americans can learn from a poet whose history, both personal and national, is so distant from their own, Vendler warns. Fair enough. Yet Miłosz himself drew poetic lessons in wartime Warsaw from a young American who had himself never witnessed war firsthand when he shaped his nightmare vision of a war-shattered Europe in *The Waste Land* (1921).

Miłosz's first version of "The Waste Land" dates from the war years—he revised it later—and Polish critics have been quick to see Eliot's influence in the poems most closely linked to the horrors Vendler evokes. I have in mind the poems of *Rescue* (*Ocalenie,* 1945), and particularly the "Voices of Poor People" and "Songs of Adrian Zielinski," in which Miłosz adapts Eliot's techniques, his impersonality (*pozaosobistość*) and personae, to horrific landscapes that far outstrip the parched plains and unreal cities of Eliot's famous poem-cum-apocalypse. The impact of Miłosz's translation, though, was such that his Polish critics routinely borrow the Polish title of *The Waste Land,* "jałowa ziemia," to describe not just Eliot's poem, but wartime Warsaw itself.[24]

Miłosz himself apparently concurs at times both with Vendler's warning and with the notion shared by poets like Forché and Des Pres that poetry written in extremis, poetry rooted in firsthand, horrific experience, is intrinsically more valid and valuable than any merely private poetic nightmares could ever hope to be. "A real 'wasteland' is much more terrible than any imaginary one," he insists in *The Captive Mind*. In the same book, Miłosz describes the rigorous standard for poetry he derived from his wartime experience: "A man is lying under machine-gun fire on a street in an embattled city. He looks up at the pavement and sees a very amusing sight: the cobblestones are standing upright like the quills of a porcupine. The bullets hitting against their edges displace and tilt them. Such moments in the consciousness of a man *judge* all poets and philosophers." "The vision of the cobblestones is unquestionably real, and poetry based on an equally *naked* experience could survive triumphantly that judgement day of man's illusions," he concludes. But one book that apparently passed his test does not meet the criterion he himself sets forth here.

> I was neither at the hot gates
> Nor fought in the warm rain
> Nor knee deep in the salt marsh, heaving a cutlass,
> Bitten by flies, fought.

So Eliot confesses by way of his aged speaker in "Gerontion." In *Native Realm*, Miłosz recalls clutching the Faber and Faber edition of Eliot's *Collected Poems* while crossing a potato field under Nazi fire: "Heavy fire broke loose at our every leap, nailing us to the potato fields. In spite of this I never let go of my book."[25]

What could an inhabitant of "imaginary waste lands" who had never witnessed war firsthand possibly have to offer a survivor of calamities unimaginable to his Anglo-American counterparts? Yet Eliot's famous lilacs bred from the dead land have clearly helped to pollinate the "spring flowers" that Adrian Zielinski watches being "pushed up by a subterranean hand" on the outskirts of war-ravaged Warsaw (67). And Polish critics have long since noticed Eliot's influence on the shattered landscapes—"A broken shadow of a chimney. Thin grass. / Farther on, the city torn into red brick. / Brown heaps, barbed wire tangled at stations. / Dry rib of a rusty automobile"— and mangled song fragments—"Heigh-ho. Fingers, strings. / So nice a song. / A barren field (*jałowe pole*)"—that make up a poem like "Outskirts" (65–66; 1:216–217). But Eliot's influence on Miłosz was not confined to the war years, and Miłosz did not restrict his reading in English to Eliot alone. I've already mentioned the voracious reading, writing, and translating that helped to transform the poetic landscape of postwar Poland. And it is his remarkable performance as a double agent infiltrating and altering two separate poetic cultures—both Polish and Anglo-American—that takes us to the heart of his paradoxical English-language reception.

"The English language is the language of poetry par excellence and every poet should be familiar with it," Miłosz insists in an essay of 1956. Elsewhere he suggests one reason for this dictum as he pits both American and Polish culture against a common enemy, France: "The fear of 'impurity'" that plagues French poetry, he comments, "is foreign" to Polish and American writers alike. The specific kind of impurity he has in mind here is poetic language expanded to include both prosaic, everyday speech and the discursive diction employed in other disciplines: philosophy, theology, history, and so on. But the implications of his linguistic cross-fertilization reach much farther. Miłosz's commitment to the creation of a "more spacious form" (240) is well-known: certainly poets writing in English have benefited from his poetic expansiveness. The poet Peter Filkins observes that Miłosz has "expanded poetry's reach to include philosophy, religion and even prose." In "The Impact of Translation," Seamus Heaney describes the "altogether thrilling" effect of hearing Miłosz's "Incantation" read for the first time: "We were enjoying a poem which did things forbidden within an old dispensation to which . . . I was subject," he recalls. "The poem was, for example, full of abstractions . . . [its] unabashed abstract nouns and conceptually aerated adjectives should have been altogether out of the question . . . and indeed the poem aspired to deliver what we had once long ago been assured it was not any poem's business to deliver: a message."[26]

These poets fail to realize that such gifts come to them in mediated form by way of their own precursors and contemporaries: Miłosz's expanded poetic diction was set in motion in key ways by his intensive postwar reading of American and English poetry. His essays of the period are peppered with comments on the brands of discursiveness he finds at work in Eliot, Auden, Shapiro, Merwin, Lowell, and others. Recent anglophone poetry, he remarks, does not shy away from "direct discourse, even using a multitude of words that have to be looked up in a philosophical dictionary." More than this—this same discursiveness is perceived by Polish critics to be Miłosz's distinctive contribution to his native Polish tradition by way of his English-language reading. The scholar Jerzy Kwiatkowski calls Miłosz an "amplifier" (*poszerzyciel*) of modern Polish culture. "He accomplished one of the most significant revolutions in Polish poetry of the twentieth century," Kwiatkowski writes, by "drawing upon the means of expression characteristic of all literature" and not just of poetry proper. And this "rehabilitation of discourse," he concludes, is due in large part to Miłosz's reading and translating of Anglo-American poetry.[27]

But this prompts still other questions. Why did Polish poetic discourse require rehabilitating? Why should the poets of postwar Poland, so rich in the historical experience that their Anglo-American counterparts envy, require this literary equivalent of the Marshall Plan? Why should Miłosz feel compelled to splice his native tradition with Anglo-American borrowings and why have these grafts proved so successful? "The unhistorical and the historical are equally necessary for the health of an individual, a people and a culture," Nietzsche insists in *On the Advantage and Disadvantage of History for Life*. Miłosz is no Nietzschean. His Polish experience has taught him, though, that too much history can be as great a burden as too little— though he is sometimes loathe to admit as much to American readers particularly. Unacknowledged legislators may be prophets with an audience of one. But poets forced by their unhappy nation's past to assume the mantle of poet-bard are faced by difficulties that their brethren in less embattled countries would find difficult to imagine. In "An Introduction to the Americans," Miłosz notes that Karl Shapiro was himself no stranger to war; the *Essay on Rime* that so influenced Miłosz was written while Shapiro was stationed in the Dutch Indies in 1944. "Instead of writing nostalgic patriotic poems as a Polish poet would certainly have done," Miłosz comments approvingly, "he wrote a verse treatise on contemporary poetics." Why should he approve of Shapiro's refusal to bear witness? And why should Miłosz himself be inspired by Shapiro's example in undertaking his own *Treatise on Poetry?*[28]

The *Treatise* itself, along with the commentary Miłosz provides in his English translation, suggests possible answers to such questions. The Polish poet's home is in history, Miłosz asserts in *The Witness of Poetry;* but this home in history can easily become a prison without constant rebuilding and renovation, or so he hints in the *Treatise on Poetry*. Modern Poland, he notes elsewhere, is rich "in defeats and lost illusions," in "the mythologies of the unlucky conquered nations." Such nations, comprised as they are of "the doomed, the deprived, the victimized, the underprivileged," provide fertile ground for the Romantic myth of the poet-prophet: martyrology is, of course, the Romantic poet's stock-in-trade. Hence the immense appeal of the Poles for their Anglo-American counterparts, as I've suggested here and elsewhere.[29]

But imported prophets and martyrs are a tricky business. In their eagerness to appropriate a vicarious "poetry of witness" for their own trauma-deprived homelands, English and American writers have too often reduced Miłosz's work to a single function and tonality—or so he himself insists in a famously furious response to a review of his *Collected Poems* (1987) in the *New York Review of Books*. A. Alvarez's essay, laudatory though it was, had the misfortune of being entitled "Witness," and in his letter, Miłosz attacked this reduction of his long and complex career to a single term: "Perhaps some Western writers are longing for subjects provided by spasms of historical violent change, but I can assure Mr. Alvarez that we, i.e. natives of hazy Eastern regions, perceive History as a curse and prefer to restore to literature its autonomy, dignity and independence from social pressures."[30] This response may seem disingenuous, to say the least, coming from the author of *The Witness of Poetry*: what's become of the much-touted home in history? We have only to return, though, to the English version of the *Treatise on Poetry* to sense the historically charged complexities that inform Miłosz's brand of poetic witness, complexities largely invisible to his American audience that are, for all that, key to his Polish reception.

In the *Treatise*, Miłosz takes to task some of the Romantic mythologies that have proven so attractive to the West. "A poet should not be a prisoner of national myths," Miłosz insists in his commentary—and the poets he has in mind here are "the twenty-year-old poets of Warsaw" who perished en masse on the battlefields and barricades of the doomed Uprising of 1944, a catastrophic enterprise that led to casualties counted in the hundreds of thousands, and that had been instigated, at least in part, by their own clandestine "propaganda poetry." Their writing, Miłosz remarks in his notes, "was a revival of Polish Romanticism, with its messianic overtones which stressed the redeeming value of selflessly sacrificing one's life for one's country." They "did not want to know that something in this century / Submits to thought, not to Davids with their slings," he charges in the poem proper—and the phrase is key in understanding his own turn to Anglo-American poetry in search of a creative counterpoise to a poetry determined to "feel too much" at the expense of the kind of considered discursiveness he finds at work in the Anglo-American tradition.[31]

Miłosz's commentary to the *Treatise* sheds light, in turn, on one of his best-known poems, "Dedication," which appears either at the beginning or the end of Miłosz's wartime collection *Rescue*, depending on which edition you consult.

> You whom I could not save
> Listen to me.
> Try to understand this simple speech as I would be ashamed of another.
> I swear, there is in me no wizardry of words.
> I speak to you with silence like a cloud or a tree.

What strengthened me, for you was lethal.
You mixed up farewell to an epoch with the beginning of a new one,
Inspiration of hatred with lyrical beauty,
Blind force with accomplished shape.

Here is the valley of shallow Polish rivers. And an immense bridge
going into white fog. Here is a broken city.
And the wind throws the screams of gulls on your grave
When I am talking with you.

What is poetry which does not save
Nations or people?
A connivance with official lies,
A song of drunkards whose throats will be cut in a moment,
Readings for sophomore girls.

That I wanted good poetry without knowing it,
That I discovered late, its salutary aim,
In this and only this I find salvation.

They used to pour millet on graves or poppy seeds
To feed the dead who would come disguised as birds.
I put this book here for you, who once lived
So that you should visit us no more.
                Warsaw, 1945 (77; 1:139–140)

Alvarez cites several stanzas of "Dedication" in his controversial review.
And the poem has since become a staple in English-language anthologies
of what Carolyn Forché has dubbed, partly under Miłosz's influence, "the
poetry of witness." Forché quotes the poem's opening lines in her introduc-
tion to her anthology *Against Forgetting* (1993) as she speaks of Miłosz's
efforts to "call up the departed only to banish *them* again" (my italics).
Miłosz's long-time collaborator Robert Hass describes the poem more
precisely as addressing "*the dead* of the Warsaw Uprising, which came
in August 1944" (my italics). And he's right—up to a point. Certainly the
time and place inscribed so carefully beneath the poem invite just such a
contextualization.[32]

But another kind of specificity is inevitably lost in the English transla-
tion. Forché and Hass are not alone in reading the poem as the voice of a
single poet speaking to the multitudes. In my experience, American readers
invariably see the poem this way, following the lead perhaps of the fourth
stanza's "people" and "nations" and the final stanza's "dead." The first line
of the Polish text tells us immediately and unambiguously, though, that
the addressee is a single person, a man whom the poet failed to save: "*Ty,*

którego nie mogłem ocalić." Both the singular, familiar "you" (*ty*) and the masculine pronoun "whom" (*którego*) vanish in the English text, and the poem's sense shifts as a result. The Polish lyric is clearly addressed to a single person who perished in the Uprising, a person with whom the speaker is on familiar terms.

Who is the friend to whom the poet speaks? The stanzas that follow suggest several possibilities. The speaker, the survivor, appears to be continuing a conversation or argument begun before his friend's untimely death. And this conversation returns relentlessly to art, or more precisely, to conflicting visions of poetry. "What is poetry?" the speaker asks, and his own self-proclaimed "simple speech" appears to oppose the "wizardry of words" that confuses the "inspiration of hate" with "lyrical beauty" and mistakes "blind force" for "accomplished shape." The dead man with whom the survivor speaks is, in other words, a poet; the poem is thus both a deeply ambivalent elegy and a debate with one poet whom another has outlived.

Miłosz gives us nothing more; but we do not have to look far to find plausible candidates for the part drawn from Miłosz's own wartime experience. Two brief biographical sketches in Miłosz's commentary to the *Treatise on Poetry* suggest possibilities: both Krzysztof Kamil Baczyński (1921–44) and Tadeusz Gajcy (1922–44) were gifted poets who died during the Uprising. We have met Baczyński before, in Szymborska's characteristically oblique critique of the Polish cult of martyred poets, "In Broad Daylight." The nationalistic "inspiration of hate" that Miłosz describes is more typical, though, of the group of talented young poets surrounding the underground publication *Art and Nation* (*Sztuka i naród*), whose writings helped to foment the Uprising. In Yeats's "Second Coming," the best lack all conviction, while the worst are full of passionate intensity. In wartime Warsaw, the best combined conviction with intensity, at least as Miłosz sees it, and the results were fatal not only for them, but also for the fellow citizens whom they spurred to action through their words. "Their verses and their deaths made them mythical figures, yet they built no bridge between past and future," Miłosz charges.[33]

"What strengthened me for you was lethal," the speaker mourns. And what he has in mind is poetry. The "good poetry" whose "salutary aim" he discovers late has been his salvation—I will return in a moment to what this "good poetry" might be—while the poetry of his dead friend, driven by social passions and national mythologies alone, proved to be his, and not only his, ruin. Both Forché and Des Pres celebrate a "poetry of extremity" "rooted in direct response to political pressure, which is to say in despair and resistance, in ruin and recovery"[34]; it sounds perilously close, at least potentially, to the "lethal" poetry that Miłosz describes in "Dedication."

Miłosz was no stranger to such longings—but he also knew their dangers. He fell prey at various points in his career to the temptations that the Polish tradition offers in abundance to the would-be poet-bard or poet-martyr. Indeed, his life's work might be seen as an oscillation between the demands and seductions of engagement, on the one hand, and the necessity for distance—be it aesthetic, ethical, or some combination of the two—on the other. Like his near-contemporary W. H. Auden, he began his inter-war career as a left-leaning political activist in verse. One of his first major publications, he recalls, was an anthology of "the so-called poetry of social protest" co-produced with a group of like-minded young writers, though he soon condemned this early work as "journalism . . . [that] had no connection with the living springs of art." He returned to such poetry once again during World War II, when he published an underground anthology of resistance poetry entitled *The Sovereign Song* (*Pieśń niepodległa*) in 1942. Yet he repudiated such patriotic poetic activism shortly afterwards. He not only refused to participate in the Warsaw Uprising himself; in "Dedication" and elsewhere, he rejects those poets who helped to foment the rebellion through their words and deeds.[35]

"I am Miłosz, I don't want to be Miłosz, being Miłosz, I must be Miłosz, I kill the Miłosz in myself in order, being Miłosz, to be more Miłosz": the perpetual self-contradiction Witold Gombrowicz captures in his aphoristic tongue-twister is nowhere more apparent than in Miłosz's attitude towards his inherited role as poet-prophet. "It makes me extremely uneasy to be turned into a patriot-poet, a bard," he insists in an interview with Aleksander Fiut. But he was hardly immune to the seductions of his national tradition. "Perhaps I was born so that the 'Eternal Slaves' might speak through my lips," the self-proclaimed "Promethean romantic" speculates in *The Captive Mind*: the comment would not be out of place in the writings of any of his great Romantic precursors, homegrown or foreign. His words would seem to have been borne out when his poem "You Who Wronged" was selected by workers for the Gdańsk monument to fallen strikers in 1981: "Do not feel safe. The poet remembers. / You can kill one, but another is born," the prophet thunders (103). At the same time, though, *The Captive Mind* also bears witness to Miłosz's recognition that this bardic tradition led in part to communism's early success in recruiting Polish writers, including Miłosz himself, to its cause. What would-be prophet would not feel tempted to become a priest of the "New Faith" that heralded the final coming of "the

Being which has taken the place of God in [the twentieth] century, i.e. history" in its fullest, Soviet Marxist incarnation?[36]

"A poet should not be a prisoner of national myths," Miłosz insists; and he took his own injunction quite seriously. He continued to enrage his Polish compatriots up to his death in 2004 and even beyond by challenging their continued allegiance to Polish Romantic messianism in its nationalist variant—in part by way of reminding them of Mickiewicz's and his own Lithuanian origins. "Send him back to Lithuania," outraged right-wingers cried as his family tried to make burial plans in the late summer of 2004. The sentiments are still alive today. "Why did he have to go on and on about Lithuania?" a teacher at a Krakow conference asked me recently. This points, incidentally, to yet another paradox in Miłosz's intercultural reputation: the self-proclaimed spokesman for what he dubbed the "Polish school of poetry" stateside stubbornly resisted the cult of Polishness at home that he himself had helped to export overseas, albeit in altered form.[37]

Mickiewicz has become a mere "patriotic prop (*rekwizyt patriotyzmu*) for educating youth," Miłosz charges in an untranslated line from the "Treatise on Theology" (*Traktat teologiczny,* 2002). "Dedication"'s final lines suggest another possibility derived from Poland's Romantic legacy. The "millet" or "poppy seed" scattered for the dead comes from Mickiewicz's poem "Forefathers' Eve, Part II." It thus takes us back to the Lithuanian folk rituals that Miłosz, like his great precursor, cherishes as part of his own childhood legacy. Time and again in his writing, Miłosz evokes a vanished multilingual, multiethnic Lithuania with its agrarian roots and pagan superstitions as a counterweight to Polish messianic nationalism. Mickiewicz's homely image serves just such a purpose here. Miłosz tacitly calls attention to a powerful counter-strain of the Polish Romantic tradition as a way of putting paid to the seductive myth of the poet-martyr that has taken the life not just of the unnamed poet he addresses, but of countless other victims who fell beneath his spell.[38]

This, at any rate, would explain the lines that have baffled some American readers; why should Miłosz, whose poems so lovingly resurrect the vanished dead of his and his country's past, seek to keep them from returning in "Dedication"'s closing?[39] In the Polish, it is clearly one single spirit whom he hopes to banish from his homeland, from the "us" that emerges in the poem's final line. I take this to mean that he seeks to bar the unnamed poet who embodies nationalist Romantic messianism from returning to haunt the inheritors of Poland's tragic legacy by way of the revised poetic tradition he himself hopes to create: "That I wanted good poetry without knowing it, / That I discovered late, its salutary aim, / In this and only this I find salvation." The poem invites, in other words, not emulation of Poland's poet-martyrs, but critical distance from them.

Witness and Distance

This is not to say that Miłosz abandons his Romantic roots in repudiating the martyr's calling. Far from it. In an essay of the early seventies, Barańczak observes that Herbert's characteristic "intellectual skepticism, irony, and critical perspective on tradition" mark him as a "dialectical Romantic." For all their differences, poetic and otherwise, Miłosz and Herbert share what Miłosz calls a "rebellious fidelity," made up in equal parts of attraction and resistance, to their nation's Romantic heritage. In this both differ from Szymborska, who keeps a consistently bemused distance throughout her work from any vision, native or foreign, that aims to transform mere poems into Poetry. Miłosz's insistence on his Lithuanianness serves not only to reproach his blinkered countrymen. It also becomes a way to establish his credentials as the true descendant of the master, who never set foot, after all, in Poland proper, and who conspicuously begins his epic poem *Pan Tadeusz* (1834), with a hymn to the wrong homeland: "Oh Lithuania! My fatherland! You are like health!" But this is not the only function of Miłosz's revisionary Romanticism. It also stems from a life story that conspicuously fails to fit the Polish model in one key respect. Like the autobiographical speaker in "Dedication," Miłosz was not a martyr, but a survivor, and a notably successful one at that: few martyrs end their careers tenured at major American universities with parking spaces marked "Nobel Laureate." How does the survivor lay claim to the mantle reserved for prophets slain in battle? The shape that survival takes in "Dedication" helps to illuminate both the nature of Miłosz's revised Romantic vocation and his complex relation to poetic engagement.[40]

Poetry both redeems and damns, the speaker tells us: "What strengthened me for you was lethal." His "salvation," as the English translation has it, has come by way of wanting "good poetry," just as surely as his compatriot's fate was sealed by his confusion of "hatred with lyrical beauty." And indeed, the goal of good poetry is precisely this, salvation. The English translation of the Polish *wybawczy,* "salutary," misleadingly points us in the direction of wholesomeness or health—though such associations are not out of place in a poem that relies so heavily on emblematic natural imagery, be it clouds, trees, gulls, or poppy seeds, to counteract the destruction unleashed by hatred's inspiration. But the Polish adjective has higher ambitions. It is linked to the root that generates Christ the Savior, "*Zbawiciel*," and its noun form, *wybawienie,* gives us an exact synonym not just for the poem's "salvation," but for the entire volume's title, *Rescue,* both of which are *ocalenie* in Polish. *Ocalenie* serves as the verbal noun, moreover, for two closely related verbs that are crucial to the poem's sense: *ocalić,* to save or rescue, and *ocaleć,* to survive. Forms of *ocalić* appear twice in the poem: first, in its opening line, "You, whom I could not save (*ocalić*)"; and once again in the fourth stanza's climactic question: "What is poetry which does not save (*ocala*) / Nations or people?"

"To survive," "*ocaleć*," on the other hand, surfaces only obliquely, through the verbal noun that does tacit double duty in the poem's penultimate stanza: "In this and only this I find salvation (*ocalenie*)," the English translation runs. The Polish original is more ambiguous, though, and not just because of the final word's double meaning. It is an impersonal construction whose subject is left unexpressed, and a more literal rendering would force a choice between two options: "This and only this is *survival,*" or "This and only this is *salvation.*" Which is it? And who will survive or be saved? The English version, translated by Miłosz himself, suggests that the poet alone has been redeemed. But the Polish requires no such decision, and the personalized meaning serves as a guarantor of the phrase's more general sense. The individual poet's survival, not his martyrdom, becomes the mark of his chosenness, of the bardic calling that will lead him in turn to rescue others.

The speaker survives, moreover, through a poetics derived, like Miłosz himself, from rural Lithuanian roots, as mediated in this case by Poland's great Romantic. The "you" to be banished in the poem's closing lines is singular, the same *ty* to whom he speaks from the poem's opening. For the first time, though, the poet-survivor speaks not for himself alone, but for "us," for the people to be saved by his "simple speech" from the evil spirit who preys on his unhappy nation's passions. And the book he uses to banish this spirit is presented as the life-giving equivalent of the seeds scattered to attract the beneficent dead disguised as birds whom Miłosz borrows from Mickiewicz. "There is in me no wizardry of words," the speaker vows. But the exorcism he performs by way of his book—presumably *Rescue* itself—rivals any of the magic spells cast in Mickiewicz's programmatically folkloric *Ballads and Romances* (1822), or for that matter, in "Forefathers' Eve, Part II," which takes its name from the Belorusian folk rituals it ostensibly reenacts.

The speaker would be ashamed, he insists, of anything but "simple speech." And the poem's unrhymed, end-stopped lines, its parallel constructions and declarative sentences—"Here is a valley . . . Here is a broken city"—seem to lend credence to his claim. For all its apparent directness, though, his speech is anything but straightforward: how does one speak in silence like a tree? We have seen "straight speaking" invoked as a social obligation among the poets of the Polish "Generation of '68." Miłosz's self-consciously "simple" language has, if anything, still broader ambitions, as the mute speech of his—deeply Romantic—clouds and trees suggests. English poets "beginning with Wordsworth seized so consciously on [plain English]," David Rosen remarks, "as an expression of their desires for both vatic authority and social participation."[41] Certainly that is the function of plain speaking in the powerful, programmatically straightforward "You Who Wronged." But the Mickiewiczean roots of "Dedication" suggest yet another dimension of Miłosz's poetic project.

He uses his Lithuanian past time and again, as I've mentioned, both to reproach his countrymen for their nationalist myopia and to establish his own link with Poland's greatest Romantic. For Miłosz, though, the two poets' Lithuanian origins become the mark not just of a common provinciality or even a shared variety of Polishness; they point to an even greater calling. "In the moment before his [prophetic] transformation," Lawrence Lipking observes, the "poet has seemed to be living in a backwater, a province or enclave that time has forgotten." At the moment of initiation, though, his obscure origins are transformed, Lipking continues, into "the focal point of all civilization." And this erstwhile provincial, the poet-initiate, shares Miłosz's larger ambition, which is not simply to restore an ideal, rural past, or to redeem a single people or nation, but to transform human nature as such, to turn mere "breadeaters into angels."[42]

"What if one were to study the antagonisms, the collaborations, the rivalries of the two chief callings of the modern era—the social prophet-revolutionary and the artist?" Miłosz's question illuminates the distinctive brand of rivalry at work in "Dedication." The false prophets of "Art and Nation," as Miłosz sees them, inflamed nationalist passions and spurred their people to a doomed revolt, for which they were rewarded with posthumous martyrdom, though "they built no bridge between past and future," he charges decades later. His phrase takes us back to "Dedication," with its "immense bridge" leading only into mist before a "broken city." This shattered city is, of course, Warsaw itself. But it is also akin to the composite collapsing city—"Jerusalem Athens Alexandria / Vienna London"—that marks the fall of civilization itself in *The Waste Land*.[43]

"Even the warfare that threatens [the initiate's] city becomes an emblem of the great eternal war—a conflict between secular and spiritual forces," Lipking remarks. The Uprising's poet-martyrs were not secular, in Miłosz's view. They were idolators, high priests celebrating the cult of the nation at the expense of its inhabitants, and of their own true mission. The genuine artist, though, builds bridges between pasts—his own, his nation's, and that of the human race as such—and a future in which not simply one poet or people alone will be redeemed. He seeks to change breadeaters into angels, to save the species itself and restore its true homeland, the fallen earth. Hence the blending in "Dedication" of rural Lithuania, in its Mickiewiczean redaction, and ruined Warsaw: these two loci represent not simply Miłosz's own past, or Poland's. They shape all of *Rescue,* with its bifurcated structure divided between the idealized, pastoral Lithuania of the cycle "The World," and the embattled capital in which the sequence "Voices of Poor People" and other key poems are set. In this larger context, their meanings extend far beyond modern Poland. They symbolize the earthly variants of the true Garden and the true City which are, Northrop Frye remarks, to be "brought into complete metaphorical identification in the book explicitly called the Apocalypse or Revelation"—or *Rescue,* or *Redemption,* or *Salvation.*[44]

Miłosz, Mickiewicz, and Eliot—cross-cultural influences make for strange bedfellows. The linkage points, of course, to the Romantic heritage that Eliot himself worked so hard to resist by way of his pointedly "impersonal" poetics. But it does more than this. The speaker of "Dedication" views his shattered city only from a distance: "Here is a valley of shallow Polish rivers . . . Here is a broken city." Miłosz himself likewise knew the disaster only from afar. He escaped from the city's outskirts as the hostilities began, and thus was not an "eyewitness to the Uprising," he explains in an interview with Renata Gorczyńska. His lack of "first-hand experience," he confesses, necessitated the "distance" that colors his description of the event in his novel *The Seizure of Power* (1952).[45]

This distanced description has a familiar ring to the reader of "Dedication": "Below, at the heart of the fire, the *great river* on which the city stood was a pink metallic ribbon. *Ruined bridges* lay in it like shipwrecked hulks." Other passages from the novel also apparently derive from Miłosz's own experience. "To the southwest, the city ended abruptly," the narrator records. "There, large modern apartment buildings bordered on fields of oats and potatoes. . . . A few tanks rolled slowly forward, churning up the dry soil of the potato fields. Taacoo—taccoo—taccoo—the echo answered their fire." These are surely the same bullet-riddled potato fields through which Miłosz himself fled the Uprising, fields located in Warsaw's outskirts, and thus already removed, as he recalls, from the heart of the action.[46]

In *Native Realm,* this flight begins accidentally. Miłosz is strolling with his wife and a friend as they discuss "something terribly important . . .

namely my new translation of an English poem." I suspect he has in mind *The Waste Land*, which, as he remarks a few pages earlier, "made somewhat weird reading as the glow from the burning ghetto illuminated the city skyline." Miłosz reads *The Waste Land* as the doomed Jewish Ghetto Uprising of 1943 goes up in flames; and he turns to Eliot once more at the outset of yet another ill-fated revolt. I have already cited Miłosz on the outcome of the seemingly innocent walk that leaves him clutching Eliot under gunfire. But it is worth noting the precise moment at which this incident occurs. It coincides with eruption of hostilities in the city's outskirts, and Miłosz's split-second decision to take flight. "In spite of this," he continues, "I never let go of my book—first of all out of respect for social ownership, since the book bore a call number of the University Library; secondly I needed it (although I could stop needing it). Its title: *The Collected Poems of T. S. Eliot*, in the Faber & Faber edition."[47]

Miłosz clings to Eliot's poems while escaping the devastation that claimed a quarter-million lives and left his nation's capital in rubble as it capitulated first to the Nazis and then to the Soviet forces. I have mentioned his desire for poetic distance from Polish Romantic nationalism in its virulent wartime variant. But clearly a more literal, far more urgent kind of distance is at stake in this passage. So why does he call our attention so pointedly to the book "[he] needed" just at a time when all reading would seem to be beside the point? This need extends, I suspect, beyond a corrective "impersonal poetics" and encompasses the life behind the scenes, both Miłosz's and Eliot's. The fleeing poet requires a counterbalance to the myth of the poet-martyr, the myth on which he has literally turned his back in leaving stricken Warsaw. Like Eliot before him, Miłosz chooses to keep his distance from the conflagration that would claim the lives of so many of his contemporaries in the hopes of living to give voice to a generation's and a culture's devastation.

Of course this comparison can only be taken so far. Miłosz's reputation in the West as exemplary poet-witness was hard-earned: the Polish poet experienced loss and destruction on a scale that Eliot could scarcely have imagined. But Miłosz is also an escape artist. And *Native Realm*, like so much of his work, is the story of one close call, one miraculous near-miss after another. It is also the story of the many choices, made often at great cost, that enabled him to keep writing what he saw not just as his own history, but the history of the modern age as embodied in one survivor's extraordinary life.

Miłosz may have needed the Anglo-American Eliot to help him gain distance on the Uprising in more ways than one. But an acknowledged bard closer to home had faced a similar dilemma over a century earlier. The poet Miłosz evokes in "Dedication"'s final lines also chose to sit out the traumatic event that had scarred a previous generation of Polish rebels. Mickiewicz was convinced that the Poles' 1830–31 insurrection against their Russian overlords could bear only "calamitous consequences." Still, as the "national poet he considered it his duty to join the movement," his friend S. Sobolevsky recalled.[48] Torn between these conflicting emotions, Mickiewicz traveled from his self-chosen exile in Rome not to Warsaw, but first to Paris and then to Dresden. From Dresden he made it as far as the Prussian-ruled province of Poznań—but he apparently never crossed the Prussian-Russian border to reach the embattled capital itself. It would be reading too much into Miłosz's Mickiewiczean millet to see this complex history at work in "Dedication" proper. Through this allusion, though, Miłosz summons up not just a single poem, but an entire Romantic tradition whose key works— *Pan Tadeusz, Forefathers' Eve, Part IV, The Books of the Polish Nation and Polish Pilgrimage*—were written far from the center of action in the years following a disastrous uprising in which their creator had notably failed to take part.

In a recent essay, the poet Geoffrey Hill takes Miłosz to task for the perverse snobbery he sees in *Captive Mind*'s call for a poetry based on the kind of "naked experience" Miłosz himself underwent in wartime Poland as he watched enemy bullets setting cobblestones on edge. Miłosz, Hill charges, espouses an "elitism of the man-of-the-moment," which "excludes from aesthetic regeneration those works unbaptised by an arbitrary experience of 'brutal, naked reality.'" There's some truth to this. Miłosz did not hesitate upon occasion to flaunt his hard-won credentials as poetic witness to history before his daunted Anglo-American admirers. But this image does not sit easily with the more complex notions of witness that underlie Miłosz's self-presentation elsewhere. I have mentioned the anthology of protest poetry Miłosz published in the early thirties, to his later chagrin. He gives a telling explanation in *Native Realm* for the anthology's emergence: he compiled it, he writes, "to *redeem* (*okupić*) my abstention from a violent workers' struggle with the police" (my italics). Revolt, abstention, salvation by way of poetry: the psychological dynamic at work here is familiar from "Dedication." And the Polish *okupić* adds yet another synonym to the verbs of rescue and redemption that shape both "Dedication" and the volume it prefaces or concludes in its various redactions.[49]

How do we reconcile the artist of the bullet-ridden streets with the poet who resists his nation's tradition of failed revolts by sitting out his own generation's moment of crisis? How does the poet-witness make peace with his refusal, on at least this occasion, to base his testimony upon the kind of first-hand experience he stresses in *The Captive Mind* and elsewhere? And what is the relation between this witness and the writer who claims, just a few years after the episode he describes in *Captive Mind,* that "poetry is 'recollection in tranquillity' (*przypominanie sobie w stanie spokoju*) and there's an end to it"?[50] In this chapter, I have emphasized Miłosz's attachment to Whitman and Eliot—though other anglophone poets, notably Blake, belong in any fuller discussion of his Anglo-American affinities and tastes. But it is peculiarly fitting to return here to an influence I mentioned in my introduction, one that is virtually invisible to those who know Miłosz only in English. This is of course William Wordsworth, whom he quotes in the passage above in a 1949 letter to Jarosław Iwaszkiewicz, at the time, that is, when he was serving as the cultural attaché at the Washington embassy of the newly formed People's Poland. Through the "Preface to *Lyrical Ballads*," the Polish poet working for a self-proclaimed revolutionary state seeks to disengage himself from the cause he had earlier embraced by way of a fellow renegade, an English poet in retreat from another radical upheaval some 150 years earlier. "And there's an end to it," Miłosz insists.

But the matter is rather less straightforward. "Without that detachment, that disinterestedness, you've got, and will get, nothing." Miłosz tells Iwaszkiewicz. What he derives, though, from his quasi-Wordsworthian detachment are not the introspective lyric musings one might expect. Not long after this letter was written, Miłosz's psychic retreat yielded one of the most potent and influential oppositional poems in the Polish tradition, "You Who Wronged," which bears the time and place of its composition in both its Polish and English versions, "Washington, D. C., 1950" (103; 2:128). The peculiar mixture of complicity, distance, and witness that produces this poem takes us to the heart of the paradoxes that shape his distinctive brand of poetic testimony.

The Washington-based Miłosz writes at a great physical remove from the "simple man" he defends in the poem—if we take that person to be a Pole in Poland, as Poles have often done (the poem itself does not specify). He finds himself, however, in close physical proximity to his foes, to the emissaries of the tyrant whom the poet addressed in the familiar, singular "ty" throughout the poem—if we see this poem, reasonably enough, as being inspired by the newly installed People's State in its postwar Stalinist incarnation. "Your deeds and words will be recorded" (*Spisane będą czyny i rozmowy*), the prophet warns. The disaffected insider at the Polish People's Embassy would have been privy to just such ominous conversations and acts. Indeed, Miłosz himself might easily be counted among those who "bowed down before you

. . . Glad to have survived (*przeżyli*) another day"—since the government employee who penned these lines surely kept his subversive sentiments to himself while on the job whose privileges he enjoyed.

Among these privileges was the intensive study of Anglo-American poetry that Miłosz used to distance himself psychically both from an increasingly repugnant state and from the Polish Romantic nationalism he mistrusted. His translations from the period include, among many other things, excerpts from "Song of Myself" and Whitman's "Dirge for Two Veterans," as well as a number of African-American spirituals and laments. Clearly he was drawn to forms of poetic witness far removed from his own tradition. His translation of Eliot's "Gerontion," which dates from about the same time, likewise hints at a continued interest in forms of poetic distance derived from foreign sources. (He had, we recall, translated "Tintern Abbey" just a few years earlier.)[51]

This ambiguous combination of distance and proximity ended up serving his fellow Poles very well. Not only was "You Who Wronged" chosen to commemorate Gdańsk's fallen workers in 1981. It also helped to shape a powerful postwar tradition, as Stanisław Barańczak notes in his preface to *The Poet Remembers: An Anthology of the Poetry of Witness and Opposition 1944–1984* (1984), a collection of Polish poems that appeared in London at the height of martial law. (It could not be published in Poland for obvious reasons.) Its very title derives from "You Who Wronged," a poem written, as Barańczak notes, "in the darkest moment of the Stalinist night and recalled at the height of Solidarity's hopes." "It has been on all our lips in recent years," he remarks. "'Your deeds and words will be recorded.' How often we've repeated that sentence, how often it has sustained poets' faith in the purpose of writing." The unacknowledged legislator's dream indeed. The poet as long-distance witness would seem to have amply fulfilled the demands that Eastern European history places upon its would-be bards, whose songs should "linger on many lips," and speak "of subjects of interest to all the citizens." Wordsworthian retreat—undertaken in admittedly singular circumstances—would seem to have produced its opposite here, truly effective poetic engagement.[52]

But are these really such opposites? Barańczak's introduction suggests otherwise. He rejects the "poetics of extremity" that American poets have often seen at work in his compatriots' writing, and dismisses the terms "political poetry," "engaged poetry," or "poetry of intervention" that pepper so many Anglo-American discussions of the Eastern Europeans. "'To record the deeds and words,' to bear witness to one's times—this would seem straightforward enough," Barańczak comments. His introduction, though, is meant to demonstrate otherwise. "I'll doubtless be criticized," he notes, "for seeing antitotalitarian protest at work in poets who appear to be more interested in their own imagination than in the objective social world." But "pure poetry," he concludes, "has never really existed," since lyric poetry generally consists of an ongoing negotiation between two mutable, mutually defining terms, "public" and "private." The argument with oneself is poetry, Yeats famously remarked, while the argument with others is mere rhetoric. For Barańczak, these two arguments cannot be kept apart. The poet's public voice is strengthened by the intensity of the individual viewpoint that informs it, while the privacy that fosters this viewpoint is challenged by the need to reach an audience, however large or small it might be. "To bear witness, to register protest at the age's lunacy or injustice," the lyric poet need only follow his or her chosen genre's own productively fraught proclivities, as Barańczak sees it.[53]

The tensions between private and public voices seems to be kept strictly behind the scenes in the case of "You Who Wronged." Miłosz the public servant performs his bureaucratic duties for a totalitarian state by day while insisting in personal letters on the retreat and tranquility he needs in order to sustain the private Miłosz, the writer. This second Miłosz produces a remarkably effective piece of public rhetoric in which the individual poet working for a particular state is replaced by the Poet-Prophet, the Poet-Martyr—"You can kill one [poet], but another will be born"—who defies the nameless Tyrant who wronged the Simple Man. But are these divisions really so airtight? "The words are written down, the deeds, the date," the poet warns in the English version. Its translator, Richard Lourie, has chosen to retain as much of the original's rhyme scheme as possible, and the last phrase is included exclusively for the sake of its rhyme-word, "weight"— there is no equivalent in Polish. There is a date to be found, though, in virtually every edition of the poem I have consulted, including the version in Barańczak's anthology. This is the date I mentioned earlier, the year which Miłosz himself scrupulously records alongside the place of the poem's composition beneath its final line.

This is Miłosz both keeping himself honest and alerting the reader to the compromising, "impure" situation that gave birth to his stirring poetic protest. The phrase "Washington, D.C., 1950" beneath a Polish poem of witness reads very differently, even to American eyes, than the "Warsaw, 1945" he inscribes beneath "Dedication." "The poet remembers," Miłosz announces in "You Who Wronged," and the dictator's words and actions are not the only thing he keeps before his reader's eyes, and his own. Does he produce this testament to poetic witness in spite of its complex autobiographical origins or because of them? My guess would be the latter. I have mentioned in my introduction Miłosz's remark, in *The Captive Mind*, on the subversive potentials "Tintern Abbey" presents to the totalitarian state. The call for lyric privacy Miłosz articulates by way of Wordsworth is no less subversive in the face of the enforced collectivization Socialist Realism imposes on its poet-subordinates. Yet it was precisely the temptation to lend his voice to the collective hymn of history in the making that drew him to state service to begin with, he suggests in *The Captive Mind*. This nexus of irreconcilable tensions seems to have provided Miłosz with the fuel he required to produce his poetic challenge to tyranny in "You Who Wronged."

Effective poetic witness grows in this instance from an unstable mixture of mediation and immediacy, distance and proximity, complicity and outrage. Another conflicted poet-witness, Seamus Heaney, locates a similar mixture in the poet from whom Miłosz himself drew unexpected inspiration in the early postwar years. The "essential" Wordsworth, Heaney writes, is torn between a "double necessity," "the double requirement of surrender and vigilance": "I am thinking of contradictory allegiances which his work displays to the numinous and to the matter-of-fact, his conflicting awareness of a necessity to attend to 'the calm that nature breathes' and a responsibility to confront the grievous facts of 'what man has made of man,' his double bind between politics and transcendence, morality and mysticism, suffering and song."[54] Is this the lesson Miłosz drew from Wordsworth? Or did Wordsworth simply reinforce an understanding that both Miłosz's own history and that of his nation had thrust upon him long since?

One passage in *Native Realm* lends credence to this second possibility. "I was stretched . . . between two poles," Miłosz writes of his life in interwar Poland, "[between] the contemplation of a motionless point and the command to participate actively in history." "I did not manage to bring these extremes into a unity," he confesses, "but I did not want to give either of them up."[55] The passage's opening will sound familiar to admirers of Heaney. It appears, unattributed, in "Away from It All," from *Station Island* (1985), whose central stanzas read as follows:

> . . . It was twilight, twilight, twilight
> as the questions hopped and rotted.
> It was oarsmen's backs and oars
> hauled against and lifting.
> And more power to us, my friend,
>
> hard at it over the dregs,
> laying in in earnest
> as the sea darkens

and whitens and darkens
and quotations start to rise

like rehearsed alibis:
I was stretched between contemplation
of a motionless point
and the command to participate
actively in history.

'Actively? What do you mean?'
The light at the rim of the sea
is rendered down to a fine
graduation, somewhere between
balance and inanition. . . . [56]

Participation versus contemplation, politics versus transcendence, suffer-ing versus song: it is a dilemma that Heaney himself knows all too well, coming as he does from a troubled land with its own rich tradition of poet-rebels and martyred bards. Even Poland's long history of partitions and poets-in-exile would be familiar territory to a Northern Irish poet long since resident in the less turbulent southern Republic. In *The Government of the Tongue* (1989), Heaney speaks modestly of the attraction that "poets from Eastern bloc countries" hold for "a reader whose formative experience has been largely Irish." And like many other anglophone poets I've cited, he reveres the great Eastern Europeans whose "tragic destiny" was to feel the "'call to witness' more extremely than most others."[57] Yet the Miłosz who appears in his own poem is not the poet in extremis, the witness to his-tory. Heaney evokes instead a typically Miłoszian moment of self-doubt and self-division, and then subjects this moment to further scrutiny. Does the speaker use Miłosz's words merely as a "rehearsed alibi," an excuse for his own inaction? And what shape should action take anyway? "*Actively?* What do you mean?" his friend inquires.

The quoted phrase does not conclude the poem or end the debate. It enters into the multiple vacillations—the hopping questions, the hauling oars, the waves shifting from light to darkness—that give the poem its shape. American poets can take no direct lessons from their Polish master, Vendler warns. But perhaps they can learn from a master of indirection, who learned to bear witness only by finding the proper distance, a distance he found partly through his immersion in the Americans.

Afterword: Martyrs, Survivors, and Success Stories, or the Postcommunist Prophet

I am ready for death.
> —*Osip Mandelstam, quoted by Anna Akhmatova,*
> *"Osip Mandelstam" (1964)*

Do not want to die for us,
do not want to live for us:

live with us.
> —*Ryszard Krynicki, "Do Not Want to Die for Us"*

My life story [is] the triumph of foolish Jan over his wiser brothers.
> —*Czesław Miłosz,* The Year of the Hunter
> *(Rok myśliwego, 1990)*

In the summer of 2002, I conducted a series of interviews with Miłosz in preparation for a biography I was just then beginning. Miłosz's attitude towards the project was, perhaps inevitably, mixed. He had given me his blessing, but was concerned nonetheless with the shape his life would take in another's hands. Sometimes this concern was expressed comically. "I have to convince you not to write the biography!" he exclaimed in one phone conversation. "But it's too late!" I said. "I've already spent the advance." (This was not entirely true, but I was not about to remove that particular line from my vita.) "Then you must make it a comedy," he responded. "It's the life of Forrest Gump." I'd handed him just the set-up he'd been looking for, and he roared at his own joke.[1]

At other times his worries took a darker turn. He knew I had written a book on Mandelstam, and he returned obsessively to the Russian poet in our conversations. "There's not enough about Stalin in your book," he complained. He meant, as it turned out, that I hadn't emphasized Mandelstam's conflicted loyalties, his waverings and vacillations. I'd overlooked, he felt, the poet's profoundly mixed feelings towards the leader who would give him the martyr's death he both courted and feared, the dictator whom he reviled in the "Stalin Epigram" (1933) and glorified in the "Stalin Ode" (1937). I pointed out the parts of my book that dealt with precisely these issues, and he ceded the point—for the moment. But my connection with Mandelstam led him back to the topic time and time again in our talks.[2]

Why should Miłosz have been so preoccupied with Mandelstam's posthumous reception as he neared the end of his own long, successful career? "Who is a poet?" Thomas Mann asks, and he answers his own question: "He whose life is symbolic." I have spoken of the prestige with which anglophone writers and readers have endowed Eastern Europe's poet-bards in recent decades. This points to yet another way in which the willfully context-free lyric poem castigated by modern critics shifts its meanings according to its setting: en route to its anglophone audience any lyric from Russia, Poland, Slovakia, or Slovenia becomes willy-nilly a "Poem from Eastern Europe," imbued with all the "world-historical seriousness" that poets in less tumultuous regions crave. This is not entirely a matter of misreading. The New Critics famously sought to erase all "biographical heresies" from considerations of the poet's art. They would have found few allies among the poets I've discussed in these pages, most of whom were avid "biographical heretics" of one stripe or another who labored to weave self and work together into the satisfyingly symbolic whole that Lawrence Lipking calls "the life of the poet." This symbolic life becomes in turn an analogue for the life of the people, the nation, even the species as such. One distinction between the poets of modern Russia and Poland and their Western counterparts, I've argued, is the seriousness with which their compatriots, be they friends or foes, take these far-reaching ambitions. Miłosz's concern with the martyred Mandelstam is a case in point.[3]

Miłosz's interest in Mandelstam and Stalin predated our conversations. In 1996, he published a essay entitled "Commentary on Osip Mandelstam's

'Stalin Ode'" in the journal *Na Głos*. The piece had been inspired, he notes, by the American Slavist Gregory Freidin's revisionary interpretation of the "Stalin Ode" as a sincere, sophisticated panegyric, and not as the last-ditch, failed lifesaving operation Nadezhda Mandelstam describes in her memoirs. An abridged version of Miłosz's essay appeared shortly afterwards in the weekend edition of one of Poland's two chief newspapers, *Gazeta wyborcza*, with a new title chosen by the editors, not by Miłosz himself, as he later protested. "Knowing Neither Shame Nor Measure" ran the controversial headline: both the title and the piece it prefaced sparked a firestorm in the Polish press.[4]

I do not exagerrate. It is difficult enough for Western readers to imagine one famous poet's account of another, long dead, writer's poetic politics occupying a full page in the front section of a major paper. That this essay would continue to stir controversy not just in the pages of *Gazeta wyborcza*, but in Poland's other major daily, *Rzeczpospolita*, for months to come defies comprehension. Miłosz's own interest in a great Eastern European precursor is not so surprising. Why, though, should the rest of his countrymen care? And care they did. Journalists and politicians, specialists and common readers alike entered into what *Rzeczpospolita* called the "Polemic with Miłosz." The implications of this debate extended far beyond its ostensible subject to encompass two identities, the poet's and his nation's. How was a newly freed Poland to see itself? Had it been tainted by long contact with its communist overlords? Or had the "Christ of Nations" survived unscathed? As usual this conflict involved the country's bards: "Milosz versus Herbert" ran the headline splashed in bold letters across the cover of a 1995 issue of the weekly *Polityka*. I cannot enter into all the details of this ongoing battle, in which Herbert plays the long-suffering patriot to Milosz's more dubious success story with the politically checkered past. The polemic about Mandelstam was a subplot in this far larger argument, though; hence the intensity of the reactions it provoked.[5]

Two pieces in this particular debate took their titles directly from Miłosz's own "You Who Wronged." "The Poet Doesn't Remember," the scholar Adam Pomorski charged in *Rzeczpospolita*'s weekend edition for December 28–29; "The Poet Remembers and Understands More than the Russianist," the critic Ryszard Matuszewski retorted in the same venue two weeks later.[6] Which is it? And what does the poet recall or forget? I won't enter into the questions of Russian and Polish history and cultural politics that Miłosz addresses in his essay, though these provoked many of the arguments that followed. Miłosz himself claims, in a response entitled "Why I wrote 'The Commentary on Mandelstam's 'Stalin Ode,'" that he took this particular example merely to indicate "what the state had meant to Russian poets" in modern history. But I suspect that his motivations are finally both more general and more personal. Miłosz applauds Freidin's efforts to replace the myth of Mandelstam the quasi-Christian martyr "who suffers for the sins of others" with a more complex understanding both of the poet's own political sympathies and of a Stalinist Russia in which "terror and ideological fervor went hand-in-hand" even for outcasts like Mandelstam. The editors took the title for the offending piece, though, from a paragraph in which Miłosz registers his differences with Freidin. Polish readers will not share Freidin's "high opinion of the 'Ode,'" Miłosz claims, since for them it can only be "a byzantine monstrosity, knowing neither shame nor measure in its flattery." Miłosz is careful to qualify his remark by describing the harrowing circumstances in which the poem was written: Mandelstam's sin, such as it was, lay simply in wanting to survive, he reminds us. Nevertheless, he cut the offending sentence from the version of the essay that appeared in book form a few years later.[7]

The piece's inflammatory opening, however, remains intact in all versions. "The Polish (and not just Polish) legend of Mandelstam as a martyr for spiritual freedom does not entirely answer the facts," Miłosz writes. Fair enough. Scholars such as Freidin and Mikhail Gasparov have labored in recent years to recuperate the complexities and contradictions of the life as lived, the work as written, from the obscuring myth of heroic martyrdom. "It's rather like finding a pagan among the Christian martyrs in ancient Rome, an unbeliever accused of disloyalty to Caesar by malicious rivals," Miłosz continues. Here he surely overshoots the mark, just as he does in dismissing the fatal "Epigram" as mere "satiric rhymes." Miłosz's imagery, though, with its intertwining of loyalty, politics, empire, and faith, will sound familiar to any reader of *The Captive Mind*. Indeed Miłosz himself makes the connection explicit in speaking of the "special social chemistry" created by the twentieth century's dictatorships: "One can [also] find examples of yielding to the communist hypnosis on a smaller scale in Poland, despite the argument that there were no Polish 'captive minds.'" Whose argument is this? And what does it have to do with Mandelstam?[8]

Adam Pomorski takes up these questions in "The Poet Doesn't Remember." He dismisses much of Miłosz's discussion as a mere "continuation of his ongoing quarrel with Gustaw Herling-Grudziński," and concludes that "attaching Mandelstam's tragedy to the argument about *The Captive Mind* is unseemly." Pomorski refers to the earlier, far more ferocious battle that followed the initial publication of *The Captive Mind* in Paris in 1953. The book outraged both supporters of People's Poland and its opponents, most notably the writer Gustaw Herling-Grudziński, who had gone into Western European exile following the war. All Miłosz's elaborate metaphors and subtle explanations served only to justify his own capitulation to Poland's communist rulers, Herling-Grudziński claimed. The true motivations for such behavior were far simpler, he argued, and consisted only of "fear and opportunism." It was clear which of the two had been the deciding factor for Miłosz himself in Herling-Grudziński's view. Similar charges followed Miłosz throughout his long life. He was merely "Moscow's dancing bear," a younger poet charged in one particularly vicious attack published shortly before Miłosz's death.[9]

It would be too easy to read Miłosz's "Commentary" as an unfortunate bit of schadenfreude, an uncharacteristically heavy-handed attempt to cut a poet-hero down to size. It was not simply Miłosz—or Szymborska, or Woroszylski, or Kołakowski, or Borowski, or so many other postwar artists and intellectuals—who fell under Soviet communism's spell at one point or another, Miłosz tacitly reminds his Polish audience. Even Mandelstam, the poet-martyr par excellence, turns out to have feet of clay. He too had been seduced not just by Marxism's utopian visions, but by their self-proclaimed inheritor and embodiment, Joseph Stalin. He too had been something of a captive mind, Miłosz insinuates. "In truth, [Mandelstam] *always* wanted to be a Bolshevik, it just didn't work out" (my italics), he claims in one of the essay's most contested sentences, and he takes his evidence from Mandelstam's late "Stanzas" (1935): "A damned seam, a silly whim / Has split us. Understand, / I must live on, *breathing and bolsheviz-ing* / Growing better before death / So as to stay and play with the people once again" (my italics).[10]

Miłosz far overstates his case. As he himself knew full well, a single line taken from a single poem, however striking, does not a lifetime make. Indeed, much of his essay is directed against the canonical posthumous reduction of Mandelstam's life to just such a static, unilateral affair. "A man who dies at the age of thirty-five," Walter Benjamin remarks, "is at every point of his life a man who dies at the age of thirty-five"—or at least so he will "appear to remembrance," since, as Benjamin adds, "the statement that makes no sense for real life becomes indisputable for remembered life." And yet Mandelstam's "remembered life"—the life of the poet-martyr who dies at the age of forty-six in the gulag—is exactly what Miłosz sought to redress.[11]

Mandelstam may have been ready for death—but he also wanted to live, and the months before his final arrest demonstrate "that human greatness and folly are close neighbors," Miłosz comments. The Russian poet did not know that his return to Moscow from exile was only a brief reprieve: "For a few months, it looked as though he'd be allowed to exist and publish." He also found time for a final romance, a love affair with a fervent young *stalinistka* named Liliia Popova. "And what of it?" Miłosz remarks. "We all know he was not the first master (*mistrz*) to be amorously inclined." More-over, Mandelstam wrote several more poems in praise of the Great Leader, perhaps under Popova's influence, before being sent to the transit camp that would mark the human being's end and the beginning of the legend.[12]

In the last of the "polemics with Miłosz," a piece entitled "Poet and Genius," the Russian poet Anatoly Naiman inadvertently demonstrates the tenacity of the myth that Miłosz seeks to debunk. "Mandelstam did not 'seek salvation' (*nie 'szukał ocalenia'*)" in writing the "Stalin Ode," he insists, since his path had been chosen for him long since. Mandelstam experienced "that fate and that death," Naiman concludes, "not because he wrote poems for or against, and not because it was a period of mass murders, but because as a seventeen-year-old boy, he began to write poetry": "You may write your poems in a café in Petersburg, Warsaw, or Paris, but sooner or later poetry guides its favorites to the stony road leading from kind Rome, gentle Flor-ence, vernal Moscow to wild Sarmatia, harsh Ravenna, to Kolyma." There is that pesky word again, *ocalenie,* "salvation" (or "rescue," or "survival"). True poets, like Mandelstam—and unlike Miłosz?—do not dream of it, since true poets know that all roads lead to Golgotha in the end.[13]

"Regardless of the length of life, a résumé is best kept short," Szymborska notes in "Writing a Résumé." Miłosz and Mandelstam come from tradi-tions in which the exemplary poet's life is "best kept short," kept in inverse proportion, that is, to the posthumous shadow it casts. The poet's quest for freedom—his own, his nation's, or that of oppressed peoples every-where—is invariably lopped off, ideally by one vengeful state or another. When Alexander Pushkin (1799–1837) had the misfortune to die in a singu-larly un-bardlike duel provoked by his foolish wife's high society flirtations, his self-designated successor Mikhail Lermontov (1814–41) taught his com-patriots to read his precursor's unseemly fate as a tacit form of christological martyrdom at the hands of a brutal state. "The executioners of Freedom, Genius, and Glory" who "stand around the throne" have replaced the poet's laurels with a "crown of thorns," he thunders in "The Poet's Death" (1837). The unpublished lyric not only reached a wide, receptive audience in hand-circulated form. It also helped to secure its young author's reputation as a worthy heir to the martyrological tradition that he himself had helped to identify—or initiate. Through his poem, moreover, he also—inadvertently, one assumes—provided future readers with a template for understanding his own dueling death four years later in the Caucasian resort of Piatigorsk.

This death was not simply the self-provoked outcome of a small-town society scandal: it was also the inevitable fate awaiting any "slave to honor" in a despotic state.[14]

Adam Mickiewicz lived far longer than his Russian coevals—he died at the relatively advanced age of fifty-seven. Still he overcame the misfortune of having missed the Uprising of 1830–31 by dedicating himself full-time in his final decades to freedom fighting in his various capacities as "a teacher, a prophet, a publicist, and an organizer." He abandoned poetry for action, and bequeathed his biography as "pilgrim, leader, and fighter" to generations yet to come, Miłosz notes. His quixotic death was no less exemplary. Mickiewicz died, like his beloved Byron, in the cause to which he had dedicated his life. He contracted typhus in Istanbul while forming a Jewish legion to fight against the Russian enemy in the Crimean War. His fellow poet and rival Juliusz Słowacki (1809–49) perished only slightly less gloriously. He died of tuberculosis not long after rushing to the Prussian-occupied part of Poland upon hearing of what proved to be an abortive revolution. In 1927, both he and Mickiewicz were disinterred from their resting places in Paris and brought back to Poland, where, as Tadeusz Komendant comments, "the necrophiliac Poles placed their earthly remains in a single crypt at Wawel Castle, where their spirits will squabble throughout eternity."[15]

What becomes in such traditions of the poet who is not only remarkably long-lived—Miłosz died at the age of ninety-three in 2004—but finds his final decades crowned with prizes and world renown? Modern poetry, Jean-Paul Sartre writes, "is the case of the loser winning. And the genuine poet chooses to lose, even if he has to go so far as to die, in order to win." Old legends die hard—or at least much harder than the short-lived poets they glorify. They are still more tenacious in cultures that respect poets enough to kill them, as Mandelstam remarks, or at least to send them to their deaths on one doomed barricade or another. In his famous essay, Jakobson condemns the postrevolutionary "generation that squandered its poets." Yet he himself recognizes—how could he miss it?—the role that Russia's sui generis Romantic tradition played in the creation and commemoration of these premature poetic casualties: "Ryleev was executed when he was thirty-one, Batjushkov went mad when he was thirty. Venevitinov died at the age of twenty-two, Delvig at thirty-two. Griboedev was killed when he was thirty-four, Pushkin when he was thirty-seven, Lermontov when he was twenty-six." One cannot escape, Jakobson concludes, "an oppressive sense of an evil destiny" afflicting Russia's poets. But this destiny was at least partly self-perpetuating. Mayakovsky, Jakobson notes, saw the battle with daily life that helped to precipitate his suicide as the metaphorical equivalent of Pushkin's and Lermontov's more literal, and no less deadly, duels.[16]

"Every time that he was accepted somewhere, I was cast out," Akhmatova remarks of her meeting with Frost in 1963. "When he was rewarded, I was disgraced. But the outcome is the same: we're both candidates for the Nobel Prize. Now that's food for philosophical reflections," she concludes. It is indeed. Even oppressed poets dream of success. Still, those who—by fate, or chance, or a dictator's whim—are granted long lives may still sustain their nation's martyrological traditions by exchanging, willy-nilly, the road to Golgotha for the more protracted Via Dolorosa of the poet-witness. Even success can turn to disaster under the right—that is to say, wrong—circumstances. Pasternak's personal life and poetic career were very nearly shattered by his receipt of the Nobel Prize in 1958, which he chose to decline for political reasons. Even so, the award was declared "an act of anti-Soviet political provocation" in the Soviet press, and he was expelled from the Soviet Writers' Union shortly thereafter.[17]

"No, without the hangman and the scaffold / The poet can't exist on earth," Akhmatova writes in one version of her poem "Dante" (1936). Her comment is only half-ironic at best—or so a later observation on her protégé Joseph Brodsky's fate suggests. When the future Nobel Laureate was exiled to the Soviet Far East in 1964 for the crime of "parasitism," she exclaimed, "What a biography they're making for our Ginger. As if he'd gone out and hired someone to do it." A strange form of PR indeed—the Soviet State as inadvertent poetic press agent—and a very successful one, to judge by the furor surrounding Brodsky's de facto expulsion from the Soviet Union in 1972.[18]

This is not to diminish the very real suffering and persecution experienced by Akhmatova, Brodsky, Pasternak, and so many of their fellow writers. Akhmatova's lines point, though, to the perversely symbiotic relationship I have explored in various forms throughout this book, the bond that exists between the oppressive state and the persecuted poet: "But he is a master?" Stalin asks the flabbergasted Pasternak in the famous phone call about Mandelstam. This bond is complicated, as Miłosz notes repeatedly, by the messianic Romanticism that gave birth to Marxist philosophy and modern poetry alike: "After all, Marx's philosophy took shape in the Age of Raptures," he remarks in *The Witness of Poetry*. The dream of the poet-prophet to overstep the limits of her or his small self and speak for the nation en masse may be realized, at least potentially, not just through resistance to one oppressive regime or another. It may also be achieved, again potentially, through collaboration with a state that has supplanted the messianic poet and his function, that claims, in other words, to have overthrown all past oppressors in the name of the people and their imminent liberation. Miłosz himself was drawn at different points to Romantic messianism in both its Marxist and its nationalist poetic modes. And true poetry remains in essence prophetic for Miłosz throughout his long career: it could scarcely be otherwise for a writer who claims Mickiewicz, Blake, and Whitman as his poetic ancestors. But it is the ways in which his life fails to fit either model completely that enables him to identify so astutely the dangers and the seductions of both. [19]

Brodsky died at the relatively young age of fifty-five after a life that seemed in many ways tailor-made for the prophetic model, as Akhmatova had foreseen. Still it was Brodsky who came up with a compelling template for the far longer and more controversial life of his friend and fellow exile. At the 1978 presentation of the Neustadt Prize, Brodsky spoke, in a much-quoted phrase, of the Polish author's "severe and relentless mind" for which the only parallel to be found "is that of the biblical characters—most likely Job." Miłosz was in fact translating the Book of Job from Hebrew to Polish at the time, and his activities may have suggested Brodsky's analogy. Certainly he felt affinities with Job's plight. "Poring over the Book of Job, I couldn't help but see the faces of those who entreated heaven in vain, the colors of the earth, nature's incomprehensible beauty with which my imagination still cannot make peace, just as it cannot make peace with Job's lament within myself," he explains in his translator's preface. [20]

But Miłosz would hardly have held himself up as Job's latter-day equivalent, the just and perfect man tormented through no fault of his own. "Why not concede," he admits in the "Treatise on Theology" (2002), "that I have not progressed, in my religion, past the Book of Job? / With the one difference that Job thought of himself as innocent . . . / I was not innocent; I wanted to be innocent, but I couldn't be." Shortly after the Polish translation of Job was published, moreover, his fate took a decidedly un-Jobian twist—or perhaps it came to resemble that of the aging patriarch whose ends are more blessed than his beginnings. After three decades of exile and isolation in the West, Miłosz received the news of his Nobel Prize. This is when the alternate life story emerges, a story not of undeserved torments, but unmerited rewards. Job's torments are unearned, while his final blessings are meant to compensate him for his long-suffering virtue. For "foolish Jan" and Forrest Gump, on the other hand, all triumphs are due to their blunders, not their virtues. This is the story of "fortune's favorite" and his "entanglement in the history / of the twentieth century, the absurdity of his actions, / the series of miraculous escapes" that are crowned in the end by fame and "honors." [21]

This last citation also derives from the "Treatise on Theology," in Miłosz's final collection, *Second Space* (*Druga przestrzeń*, 2002). Even in this last volume, he does not choose between Job and Forrest Gump. These two apparently contradictory tales coexist uncomfortably throughout his later work: human greatness and foolishness do indeed go hand in hand, the late writing suggests. Miłosz resisted what he saw as the temptations of nationalist mythologies by fleeing the Warsaw Uprising that produced poet-martyrs like Krzysztof Kamil Baczyński only to fall prey, however briefly, to the internationalist mythologies of the regime that had so recently added the latest chapters to the Russian Romantic tradition of bardic victims. Not only had he failed to fulfill the Polish poet-martyr's destiny during the war; he had joined forces afterwards with a state that had made a speciality of creating new martyrs on its home turf. This notably uncanonical life had led to both great anguish and finally, great fame. But perhaps it takes a poet who has experienced and rejected the two great competing ideologies of mid-twentieth-century Europe—the apotheosis of nation and the apotheosis of class—to perceive the limits of each as a means of healing the breach between the poet and the people for whom he longs to speak.

In "The Poet and the State," Miłosz speaks of "the myth of the poet's highest freedom, alongside which the might and glory of dictators is as nothing." This is the myth, he argues, to which Mandelstam has posthumously become a prime contributor. The truth, he insists, is more complex. His own emotional investment in debunking notions of unsullied martyrdom is evident in the essay's excesses. Still he is right to point out the conflicting impulses and tendencies that mark the modern poet's life and art alike. Dissidents' fates may become perversely intertwined with those of their oppressors, not least because both poetic dissenters and dictators may share the same Romantic dream of embodying the nation in their words. More than this—dissidents sometimes sit apart by necessity, not choice: "I offer the Revolution gifts for which it has no need," Mandelstam mourns in a 1928 questionnaire. Miłosz describes with great sympathy Mandelstam's grief at losing the "right to participate in the glorious, as he saw it, collective undertaking. [He bears] the mark of the pariah 'I' who is wracked with guilt, since the 'they,' the 'we' he wishes to join, all point at him accusingly."[22]

"The intellect of man is forced to choose / Perfection of the life, or of the work," Yeats famously proclaims. Miłosz rejects Yeats's ultimatum: his programmatically impure poetry is the product of a long, turbulent, and notably impure life, as he never allows us to forget. But readers prefer their prophet-heroes to be impeccably valiant, and not only in the lands of acknowledged legislation. The flap copy for Miłosz's *New and Collected*

Poems finds him heroically joining forces with the Polish resistance during the Second World War. Shortly before his death, though, Miłosz himself insisted on a correction for the English version of *Second Space,* which has him simply "surviv[ing] World War II in German-occupied Poland . . . [and] publishing his poetry in the underground press."[23]

Surviving and publishing: it should be enough. But resistance is the stuff of legends, and martyrdom is far more photogenic than mere endurance. What would have become of the martyred Baczyński had he survived? This is the question Szymborska asks in "In Broad Daylight":

> Goateed, balding,
> gray-haired, in glasses,
> with coarsened, weary features,
> with a wart on his cheek and a furrowed forehead,
> as if clay had covered up the angelic marble—he wouldn't
> know himself when it all happened.

"The price, after all, for not having died already / goes up not in leaps but step by step," Szymborska reminds us, "and he would / pay that price, too." What would that price have included? Might the "mountain boardinghouse" where he spends his vacations in the poem have been a state-run sanatorium for compliant writers? We'll never know.[24]

"Cast a cold eye on life, on death": Yeats remains imperiously bard-like to the end and beyond in his self-composed epitaph "Under Ben Bulben." But I will give the final word to one of modern poetry's most unprophetic success stories, Wisława Szymborska.

> Here lies, old-fashioned as parentheses,
> the authoress of verse. Eternal rest
> was granted her by earth, although the corpse
> had failed to join the avant-garde, of course.
> The plain grave? There's poetic justice in it,
> this ditty-dirge, the owl, the burdock. Passerby,
> take out your compact Compu-Brain and try
> to weigh Szymborska's fate for half a minute.[25]

Now that's food for philosophical reflections.

Notes

Introduction

1. Maureen McLane, "A Dirty Job" (review of William Logan, *The Undiscovered Country: Poetry in the Age of Tin*), *Chicago Tribune* (Dec. 11, 2005), Section 14:5. I am grateful to Michael Lopez for calling this essay to my attention. Nadezhda Mandelstam, *Vospominaniia: Kniga pervaia*, 3rd ed. (Paris: YMCA Press, 1982), 167.

2. Adam Zagajewski, "Kolce," *List: Oda do wielości* (Paris: Instytut literacki, 1983), 56; Zagajewski, "Gdyby Rosja," *Jechać do Lwowa* (London: Aneks, 1985), 50. All translations from Russian and Polish here and throughout the book are my own, unless otherwise noted. Seamus Heaney, "The Unacknowledged Legislator's Dream," *Poems 1965–1975* (New York: Farrar, Straus and Giroux, 1980), 211. Percy Bysshe Shelley, *A Defense of Poetry, Shelley's Poetry and Prose*, ed. Donald H. Reiman and Sharon B. Powers (New York: Norton, 1977), 478–510.

3. Czesław Miłosz, *The Captive Mind*, tr. Jane Zielonko (New York: Vintage, 1955), 175. W. H. Auden, *The Dyer's Hand and Other Essays* (New York: Vintage, 1968), 27. For a pathbreaking comparative study of poetry and responsibility on Russian and Polish soil, see Victor Erlich, *The Double Image: Concepts of the Poet in Slavic Literatures* (Baltimore: Johns Hopkins University Press, 1964). As my subtitle shows, I am also indebted to the work of another pioneering Slavist-comparatist, Wacław Lednicki, whose *Russia, Poland and the West* (London: Hutchinson, 1954) explores the relationship between Polish and Russian Romanticism and politics in its opening chapters.

4. Seamus Heaney, *The Government of the Tongue: Selected Prose 1978–1987* (New York: Farrar, Straus and Giroux, 1989), 107. Adam Zagajewski, "W dwadzieścia

lat później: Przedmowa 2002," *Solidarność i samotność* (Warsaw: Zeszyty Literackie, 2002), 7.

5. Zagajewski, "W dwadzieścia lat później," 7.

6. Piotr Chaadaev, "Letters on the Philosophy of History," *Russian Intellectual History*, ed. Marc Raeff (New York: Harcourt, Brace and World, 1966), 164. Słowacki is quoted in *Skrzydlate słowa*, ed. Henryk Markiewicz and Andrzej Romanowski (Warsaw: Państwowy Instytut Wydawniczy, 1990), 621.

7. Edward Said, *Culture and Imperialism* (New York: Vintage, 1994), 26, 108, 226, 162, xxi.

8. Joseph Conrad, *Heart of Darkness* (London: Penguin, 1995), 21. Fredric Jameson, "Modernism and Imperialism, "" *Nationalism, Colonialism, and Literature*, ed. Terry Eagleton, Fredric Jameson, and Edward Said, intro. Seamus Deane (Minneapolis: University of Minnesota Press, 1990), 47–48. For a more detailed discussion, see Clare Cavanagh, "Postcolonial Poland," *Common Knowledge*, vol. 10, no. 1 (Winter, 2004), 82–92.

9. Joseph Conrad, *Under Western Eyes* (New York: Modern Library, 2001), 20. Czesław Miłosz, *Beginning with My Streets*, tr. Madeline G. Levine (New York: Farrar, Straus and Giroux, 1991), 157. Octavio Paz, *Children of the Mire*, tr. Rachel Phillips (Cambridge, Mass.: Harvard University Press, 1991), v.

10. M. H. Abrams quotes Coleridge in "Structure and Style in the Greater Romantic Lyric," *Romanticism and Consciousness*, ed. Harold Bloom (New York: Norton, 1970), 206. Jerome McGann, *The Romantic Ideology* (Chicago: University of Chicago Press, 1983), 137. McGann, "Byron's Lyric Poetry," *The Cambridge Companion to Byron*, ed. Drummond Bone (Cambridge: Cambridge University Press, 2004), 211. Nicholas Roe, *The Politics of Nature: William Wordsworth and Some Contemporaries* (London: Palgrave, 2002), 7. Marjorie Levinson, *Wordsworth's Great Period Poems* (Cambridge: Cambridge University Press, 1986), 37–38. Sarah Zimmerman quotes Liu in *Romanticism, Lyricism, and History* (Albany: State University of New York Press, 1999), 27.

For recent accounts of the lyric under siege, see inter alia: Paul Breslin, "Shabine among the Fishmongers: Derek Walcott and the Suspicion of Essences" (unpublished talk, Northwestern University, 1997); Mark Edmundson, *Literature against Philosophy, Plato to Derrida: A Defense of Poetry* (Cambridge: Cambridge University Press, 1995); Eileen Gregory, *H.D. and Hellenism: Classical Lines* (Cambridge: Cambridge University Press, 1997), esp. 129–139; Mark Jeffreys, "Ideologies of Lyric: A Problem of Genre in Contemporary Anglophone Poetics," *PMLA*, vol. 110, no. 2 (March, 1995), 196–205; Susan J. Wolfson, "'Romantic Ideology' and the Values of Aesthetic Form," *Aesthetics and Ideology*, ed. George Levine (New Brunswick: Rutgers University Press, 1994), 188–218; Susan J. Wolfson, *Formal Charges: The Shaping of Poetry in British Romanticism* (Stanford: Stanford University Press, 1997), esp.1–30; Zimmerman, *Romanticism, Lyricism and History*, esp. ix-38.

Levinson, McGann, Cameron, and others I cite here may strike the Slavist as being as unexpected or even extraneous in this context as Tynianov, Gasparov, or Ginzburg might seem in a American discussion of the British Romantics. This is not to place an equal sign between the American critics and their Eastern European counterparts. I want merely to emphasize the ubiquity and influence of these critics in contemporary Anglo-American discussions of lyric poetry. And this in turn is my reason for examining these theories against a radically different cultural backdrop: Do they hold for modern poetry generally? Or can they be applied only to lyric poems produced in specific times and places? If so, then don't they leave key elements and possibilities of lyric poetry unexplained, even unrecognized?

11. Angus Fletcher, *A New Theory for American Poetry: Democracy, the Environment, and the Future of the Imagination* (Cambridge, Mass.: Harvard University Press, 2004), 91. Stephen Kotkin, *Magnetic Mountain: Stalinism as a Civilization* (Berkeley: University of California Press, 1995), 10.

12. Donald Davie, *Czesław Miłosz and the Insufficiency of Lyric* (Knoxville: University of Tennessee Press, 1986), 28. Aleksander Wat, *Poezje* (Warsaw: Czytelnik, 1997), 10. Max Eastman quotes Trotsky in *Artists in Uniform: A Study in Literature and Bureaucraticism* (London: Allen & Unwin, 1934), 52.

13. "Dedication," tr. Czesław Miłosz, *New and Collected Poems (1931–2001)* (New York: Ecco, 2001), 77. Wisława Szymborska, *Poems New and Collected 1957–1997*, tr. Stanisław Barańczak and Clare Cavanagh (New York: Harcourt Brace, 1998), 227. Roman Jakobson, *Language in Literature*, ed. Krystyna Pomorska and Stephen Rudy (Cambridge, Mass.: Harvard University Press, 1987), 368. Fletcher, *A New Theory*, 105. 127, 164, 83. Aleksander Wat, "Kilka uwag o związkach między literaturą a rzeczywistością sowiecką," *Świat na haku i pod kluczem* (London: Polonia, 1985), 114.

14. Fletcher, *A New Theory*, 176–177. MacLeish, "Ars Poetica," in *The Imagist Poem*, ed. William Pratt (New York: Dutton, 1963), 125. W. K. Wimsatt, *The Verbal Icon* (Lexington: University of Kentucky Press, 1954), 231.

15. Viktor Shklovsky, "Art as Technique," *Russian Formalist Criticism*, tr. and intro. Lee T. Lemon and Marion J. Reis (Lincoln: University of Nebraska Press, 1965), 12. Shklovsky, "Voskreshenie slova," *Texte der russischen Formalisten*, vol. 2, ed. Wolf-Dieter Stempel and Inge Paulmann (Munich: Wilhelm Fink Verlag, 1972), 3–4. Roman Jakobson, "Modern Russian Poetry: Velimir Khlebnikov," *Major Soviet Writers: Essays in Criticism*, ed. Edward J. Brown (London: Oxford University Press, 1973), 62. Jakobson, *Language in Literature*, 193, 215, 127.

16. Sharon Cameron, *Lyric Time: Dickinson and the Limits of Genre* (Baltimore: Johns Hopkins University Press, 1979), 88, 197, 71, 119.

17. Ibid., 23. Wolfson, *Formal Charges*, 12. Frank Lentricchia, *Criticism and Social Change* (Chicago: University of Chicago Press, 1983), 94. Terry Eagleton, *Literary Theory: An Introduction* (Minneapolis: University of Minnesota Press, 1983), 21.

Edmundson also comments on the New Historical resistance to form: "The proponent of historical criticism is likely to see the purveyors of close reading, whether they quest for organic form or the breaking of forms, as decadents, self-indulgently removed from real people and events" (*Literature against Philosophy*, 16).

18. David Bromwich, *Politics by Other Means* (New Haven: Yale University Press, 1992), 112. Roe, *Politics of Nature*, 8. Vincent B. Leitch, "Cultural Criticism," *The Johns Hopkins Guide to Literary Theory and Criticism*, ed. Michael Groden and Martin Kreiswirth (Baltimore: Johns Hopkins University Press, 1994), 181.

19. Terry Eagleton, *The Ideology of the Aesthetic* (Oxford: Blackwell, 1990), 3, 93–94. McGann, *Romantic Ideology*, 158.

20. Cameron, *Lyric Time*, 118–119.

21. Mikhail Bakhtin, "Discourse in the Novel," *The Dialogic Imagination*, ed. Michael Holquist, tr. Caryl Emerson and Michael Holquist (Austin: University of

Texas Press, 1981), 296–298, 216. "An Interview with Jerome McGann," McGann, *Byron and Romanticism,* ed. James Soderholm (Cambridge: Cambridge University Press, 2002), 257. Wolfson, *Formal Charges,* 19, 238. Charles Altieri bears witness to the centrality of Bakhtin's thought in recent theories of the lyric in his entry on "lyric autonomy" in *The New Princeton Encyclopedia of Poetry and Poetics,* ed. Alex Preminger and T. V. F. Brogan (Princeton: Princeton University Press, 1993), 113–114. "Claims for aesthetic autonomy may be little more than a defensive mechanism for idealizing artistic impotence," Altieri remarks, and he calls upon a familiar figure by way of explanation: "To Mikhail Bakhtin, the ideal of artistic purity becomes a 'monological' evasion of the dialogic play of languages that characterizes social life."

22. Osip Mandelstam, *Sobranie sochinenii,* ed. G. Struve and B. A. Filipoff, 4 vols. (vols. 1–3, Washington, D.C.: Interlanguage Library Associates, 1967–1971; vol. 4, Paris: YMCA Press, 1981), 2:334. Jurij Tynianov, "Promezhutok," *Arkhaisty i novatory* (Priboi, 1929; rpt. Ann Arbor: Ardis, 1985), 541–542.
This is not to say that either Mandelstam or Tynianov was entirely correct in his prognosis for poetry's downfall—lyric poetry continued and sometimes thrived long after the Bolshevik takeover. Their sense that a great age of poetry was past or passing, though, was shared by many of their contemporaries, including important party members and policy shapers.

23. Karl Marx, *The Eighteenth Brumaire of Louis Bonaparte* (New York: International Publishers, 1963), 18. Leon Trotsky, *Literature and Revolution,* tr. Rose Strunsky (Ann Arbor: University of Michigan Press, 1960), 98, 170. Nikolai Bukharin, "Poetry, Poetics and the Problems of Poetry in the U.S.S.R," *Problems of Soviet Literature: Reports and Speeches at the First Soviet Writers' Congress,* ed. H. G. Scott (Westport: Hyperion Press, 1980), 244–245, 254–255. Bukharin's speech was not based on his personal views, but was in fact a collectively composed "document submitted to the Politburo (Stalin) for approval and corrections prior to its public delivery—and then was subjected to extraordinarily fierce attacks at the Congress in what appears to be a carefully orchestrated campaign" (personal communication from Professor Lazar Fleishman, June 21, 2008). The views Bukharin articulated remained dominant during the relatively "liberal" period from 1934 to 1936. The very fact of these heated debates and fierce campaigns at the highest level of Soviet power indicates the remarkable significance the state attached to literature generally and poetry in particular.

24. Bukharin, "Poetry," 254. Mark D. Steinberg quotes Papernyi, René Fülöp-Miller, and Bogdanov in his illuminating discussion of "The Proletarian 'I'" in *Proletarian Imagination: Self, Modernity, and the Sacred in Russia, 1910–1925* (Ithaca: Cornell University Press, 2002), 102–146. Boris Eikhenbaum, "Konspekt rechi o Mandel'shtame," *O literature: Raboty raznykh let* (Moscow: Sovietskii pisatel', 1987), 447.

25. Bakhtin, "Discourse," 286–259, 331, 298. Levinson, *Wordsworth's Great Period Poems,* 37–38.
Levinson's book has become a touchstone for critical responses to New Historical readings of the Romantic lyric: see, inter alia, M. H. Abrams, "On Political Readings of *Lyrical Ballads,*" *Doing Things with Texts,* ed. Michael Fisher (New York: Norton, 1989), 364–392; David Bromwich, *Disowned by Memory: Wordsworth's Poetry of the '1790s* (Chicago: University of Chicago Press, 1998), 75–76; Edmundson, *Literature against Philosophy,* esp. 120–147; Thomas McFarland, *William Wordsworth:*

Intensity and Achievement (Oxford: Clarendon Press, 1992), esp. 1–35; and McFarland, *Romanticism and the Heritage of Rousseau* (Oxford: Clarendon Press, 1995), passim; Wolfson. *Formal Charges*, 14; Zimmerman, *Romanticism, Lyricism, and History*, passim.

26. Bakhtin, "Discourse," 296–298.

27. Ibid., 287, 273.

28. Mandelstam, *Sobranie sochinenii*, 1:202. On Bakhtin's more nuanced discussions of the lyric, see Caryl Emerson, "Prosaics and the Problem of Form," *Slavic and East European Journal*, vol. 41, no. 1 (Spring, 1997), 16–39.

29. Bromwich, *Disowned by Memory*, 110. Karl Radek, "Contemporary World Literature and the Tasks of Proletarian Art," *Problems of Soviet Literature*, 152. McGann, *Romantic Ideology*, 88.

30. Levinson, *Wordsworth's Great Period Poems*, 130, 103, 10. Frank Lentricchia, *Criticism and Social Change* (Chicago: University of Chicago, 1985), 76. Said, *Culture and Imperialism*, 283.

31. McGann, *Byron and Romanticism*, 11, 135. Nicholas Roe quotes Liu in *The Politics of Nature*, 5.

32. Mark Mazower, *Dark Continent: Europe's Twentieth Century* (New York: Vintage, 1998), 51, 376. Jameson, "Modernism and Imperialism," 29. Eagleton, "Introduction," *Marxist Literary Theory*, ed. Terry Eagleton and Drew Milne (Oxford: Blackwell, 1996), 1.

33. Roe, *Politics of Nature*, 5. McFarland, *Romanticism*, 267, 87. See also ibid., 133–34 for a brief, brilliant discussion of the persistence of Jacobinism of one stripe or another in twentieth-century Marxist practice. Edmundson, *Literature against Philosophy*, 119.

34. Eagleton, "Introduction," *Marxist Literary Theory*, 6. Miłosz, *Captive Mind*, 200–201. Aristotle, "Poetics," *Classic Writings on Poetry*, ed. William Harmon (New York: Columbia University Press, 2003), 41.

35. "Lecture IV," tr. Miłosz and Leonard Nathan, Miłosz, *New and Collected Poems (1931–2001)* (New York: Ecco, 2001), 497. *The Oxford Authors: William Wordsworth*, ed. Stephen Gill (Oxford: Oxford University Press, 1984), 133.

36. Miłosz, *The Captive Mind*, 74. On the projected anthology, see Miłosz, *Zaraz po wojnie: Korespondencja z pisarzami* (Krakow: Znak, 1998), 38. His translation appeared only several decades later in an anthology entitled *Mowa wiązana* (*A Fettered Speech*), ed. and tr. Czesław Miłosz (Warsaw: Państwowy Instytut Wydawniczy, 1986), 65–68. I'm grateful to Aleksander Fiut for making his copy of *Mowa wiązana* available to me. See also Miłosz, *Przekłady poetyckie*, ed. Magda Heydel (Krakow: Znak, 2005), 82–85.

37. Miłosz commented on his lack of sympathy for Wordsworth in a personal conversation of July, 2003: he had no interest, he said, in "excavating" at that late date the reasons that had led him to "Tintern Abbey" in the first place.

38. Miłosz, *Zaraz po wojnie*, 201. Wordsworth, "Preface to *Lyrical Ballads*," Gill, *William Wordsworth*, 611. Miłosz, *Captive Mind*, 56. "Mind-forged manacles" is Blake's phrase: *The Oxford Authors: William Blake*, ed. Michael Mason (Oxford: Oxford University Press, 1988), 276.

39. Aleksander Wat, *My Century: The Odyssey of a Polish Intellectual*, ed. and tr. Richard Lourie (New York: Norton, 1990), 92. I have adapted the translation slightly;

see Aleksander Wat, *Mój wiek,* 2 vols. (Warsaw: Czytelnik, 1998), 1:254. Levinson, *Wordsworth's Great Period Poems,* 34.

40. Tom Paulin, "Introduction," *The Faber Book of Political Verse* (London: Faber and Faber, 1986), 17, 52. Paulin clearly has in mind here not lyrics themselves, but misguided modes of reading; his anthology is dedicated to reclaiming the anglophone lyrical tradition from the hands of the "ahistoricists." His vision of the lyric is less nuanced elsewhere. "Social history and the lyric poem appear to be poles apart," he writes in an essay on Philip Larkin. "Politics and culture are always melting into different shapes, but the lyric speaks for unchanging human nature, that timeless essence beyond fashion and economics" (*Minotaur: Poetry and the Nation State* [Cambridge, Mass.: Harvard University Press, 1992], p. 233).

41. Paulin, "Introduction," 17, 51, 52. Miłosz, *Captive Mind,* 175. "Imperium" is Miłosz's term for the Soviet bloc throughout *The Captive Mind.*

42. Paulin, "Introduction," 48. Reginald Gibbons, "Political Poetry and the Example of Ernesto Cardinal," *Politics and Poetic Value,* ed. Robert von Hallberg (Chicago: University of Chicago Press, 1987), 293. Miłosz, *Captive Mind,* 56. Stanisław Barańczak, *Zaufać nieufności: Osiem rozmów o sensie poezji* (Krakow: Wydawnictwo M, 1993), 17.

43. Theodor Adorno, "On Lyric Poetry and Society," *Poetry in Theory: An Anthology 1900–2000,* ed. Jon Cook (Oxford: Blackwell Publishing, 2004), 344–345.

44. Kornei Chukovsky, "Akhmatova and Mayakovsky," tr. John Pearson, *Major Soviet Writers: Essays in Criticism,* ed. Edward J. Brown (Oxford: Oxford University Press, 1973), 51–52. Wiktor Woroszylski quotes *Pravda* in *The Life of Mayakovsky,* tr. Boleslaw Taborski (London: Victor Gollancz, 1972), 280. Lydia Chukovskaia quotes Akhmatova's critics in *Zapiski ob Anne Akhmatovoi 1952–1962* (Moscow: Soglasie, 1997), 77.

45. Amanda Haight quotes Mayakovsky and other Soviet critics on Akhmatova in *Anna Akhmatova: A Poetic Pilgrimage* (New York: Oxford University Press, 1976), 71–73. Trotsky, *Literature and Revolution,* 148–153. Woroszylski cites Mayakovsky in *The Life of Mayakovsky,* 347.

46. Adorno, "On Lyric Poetry," 346–347.

47. Bukharin, "Poetry," 233.

48. All references to Akhmatova's work derive from the following edition, unless otherwise noted: *Sochineniia,* 3 vols. (vols. 1 and 2, ed. Boris Filipoff and G. P. Struve, Munich: Interlanguage Literary Associates, 1967–68; vol. 3, ed. G. Struve, N. A. Struve, and B. A. Filippov, Paris: YMCA Press, 1983). *Requiem* appears in 1:359–370. For its troubled publication history, see the same volume, 422–423, and Susan Amert, *In a Shattered Mirror: The Later Poetry of Anna Akhmatova* (Stanford: Stanford University Press, 1992), 205. *From Six Books* was withdrawn from distribution shortly after its publication; see Roberta Reeder, *Anna Akhmatova: Poet and Prophet* (New York: St. Martin's Press, 1990), 229–230, 250–251.

49. V. Pertsov, "Chitaia Akhmatovu," Akhmatova, *Requiem,* ed. P.D. Timenchik (Moscow: Izd. MPI, 1989), 159–162.

50. "This box has a triple bottom," Akhmatova notes in the *Poem* (*Sochineniia,* 2:126).

51. Wat, *My Century,* 92; *Mój wiek,* 1:254.

52. Akhmatova, *Sochineniia,* 1:361, 369.

53. Bukharin, "Poetry," 223. Akhmatova, *Sochineniia*, 2:179.

54. James Longenbach, *The Resistance to Poetry* (Chicago: University of Chicago Press, 2004), 5.

55. Mandelstam, *Sobranie sochinenii*, 1:165–166. Osip Mandelstam, *The Complete Critical Prose and Letters*, ed. Jane Gary Harris, tr. Jane Gary Harris and Constance Link (Ann Arbor: Ardis, 1979), 478. On Mandelstam's lyrical "chamber music," see Roman Jakobson, "Noveishaia russkaia poeziia. Nabrosok pervyi: Viktor Khlebnikov, "*Texte der russischen Formalisten*, 140; Tynianov makes similar observations in "Promezhutok," 572–573. For a discussion of this poem in the context of Mandelstam's later work, see Clare Cavanagh, *Osip Mandelstam and the Modernist Creation of Tradition* (Princeton: Princeton University Press, 1995), esp. 247–250.

56. The editors quote Ilya Selvinsky on the infamous "mandelstamp" in *Sobranie sochinenii*, 1:489. Max Eastman quotes John Reed in *Artists in Uniform: A Study of Literature and Bureaucratism* (London: Allen & Unwin, 1934), 9. Aleksandr Zholkovsky cites A. Tarasenkov's entry "Mandel'shtam" (*Literaturnaia entsiklopediia*, vol. 6 (1932), 756–759) in his pithy analysis of Mandelstam's lyric, "Invarianty i struktura teksta. II. Mandel'shtam: 'Ia p'iu za voennye astry . . . '," *Slavica Hierosolymitana*, ed. L. Fleishman, O. Ronen, and D. Segal (Jerusalem: Magnes Press, 1979), 4:171.

57. The editors quote both Selivansky and Kovalenkov in *Sobranie sochinenii*, 1:494–495.

58. An excerpt from S. Malakhov, "Lirika kak orudie klassovoi bor'by" (*Zvezda*, 1931, no. 9) is reprinted in Timenchik's edition of *Requiem*, 91. Zholkovsky, "Invarianty," 176. The editors quote Chinnov in *Sobranie sochinenii*, 1:495.

59. Zagajewski's poem could not be published officially; Zagajewski himself had left Poland for exile in France the previous year. The poem made its way back to his compatriots by the two unofficial routes known in Russian as *tamizdat* and *samizdat*: Zagajewski, *List: Oda do wielości*, 12; and Zagajewski, *List: Oda do Wielości* (Krakow: Polka poetów, 1982), 9. I am grateful to Anna and Stanisław Barańczak for making the underground Polish edition available to me. For a slightly different English version of the poem, see Renata Gorczyński's translation in Adam Zagajewski, *Without End: New and Selected Poems*, tr. Clare Cavanagh, Renata Gorczyński, Benjamin Ivry, and C. K. Williams (New York: Farrar, Straus and Giroux, 2002), 101. I will discuss the trajectory of Zagajewski's career in more detail in Chapter 7.

60. Zbigniew Herbert, *Report from the Besieged City*, tr. John and Bogdana Carpenter (New York: Ecco, 1985), 69–70.

61. Herbert, "To Ryszard Krynicki—A Letter," ibid., 21–22.

62. *King Lear*, 2.4.264–265. Mandelstam, "Stikhi o neizvestnom soldate," *Sobranie sochinenii*, 1:244–249.
See M. L. Gasparov, "Stikhi o neizvestnom soldate: apokalipsis i/ili agitka" (The verses on the unknown soldier: apocalypse and/or agitational poem"), *O. Mandel'shtam: Grazhdanskaia lirika 1937* (Moscow: Rossiiskii gosudarstvennyi universitet, 1996), 6–77, for a compelling rebuttal to earlier readings that followed Nadezhda Mandelstam's lead in interpreting the poem as an anti-Stalinist apocalypse. On Mandelstam's purported "attachment to parasitical ideology and culture," see Zholkovsky, "Invarianty," 171.

63. Nadezhda Mandelstam records her husband's remarks in *Kniga tret'ia* (Paris: YMCA Press, 1987), 154. Heaney, *Government of the Tongue*, xviii–xix.

64. Heaney, *Government of the Tongue*, xvi, xix.

65. Ibid., 39, 99, 135. Eastman, *Artists in Uniform*, 45. Richard Poirier, *Poetry and Pragmatism* (Cambridge, Mass.: Harvard University Press, 1992), 37, 54.

66. Poirier quotes Emerson in *Poetry and Pragmatism*, 156. Heaney, *Government of the Tongue*, 128.

67. Mandelstam, *Sobranie sochinenii*, 1:23, 202. The "prophet's staff and ribbons" comes from Szymborska's "Soliloquy for Cassandra," *Poems New and Collected*, 83.

68. *Collected Works of Velimir Khlebnikov: Letters and Theoretical Writings*, tr. Paul Schmidt, ed. Charlotte Douglas (Cambridge, Mass.: Harvard University Press, 1987), 333. James Longenback quotes Pound in *Stone Cottage: Pound, Yeats, and Modernism* (Oxford: Oxford University Press, 1988), 74.

69. Lucy McDiarmid, *Saving Civilization: Yeats, Eliot, and Auden between the Wars* (Cambridge: Cambridge University Press, 1984), 68. Benedikt Sarnov, *Zalozhnik vechnosti: Sluchai Mandel'shtama* (Moscow: Izd. "Knizhnaia palata," 1990), 10, 24. On Marx's and Engel's early poetic proclivities, see *Marxism and Art: Essays Classic and Contemporary*, ed. with commentary by Maynard Solomon (Detroit: Wayne State University Press, 1979), 3–5; and Horst Höhne, "Shelley's 'Socialism' Revisited," *Shelley: Poet and Legislator of the World*, ed. Betty T. Bennett and Stuart Curran (Baltimore: Johns Hopkins University Press, 1996), 201–212. "According to his biographer, Gustav Mayer," Solomon reports, Engels dreamed of "'preaching through poetry the new ideas which were revolutionizing his inner world.' He wrote poetic cycles devoted to humanity in the style of Shelley, and he began a translation of *Queen Mab*" (4–5). On Stalin as Romantic writer-prophet, see Jeffrey Brooks, *Thank You, Comrade Stalin! Soviet Public Culture from Revolution to Cold War* (Princeton: Princeton University Press, 2000), esp. 54–82.

70. Isaiah Berlin, *Karl Marx* (Oxford: Oxford University Press, 1996), 24, 5. Karl Marx, "Manifesto of the Communist Party," *The Portable Karl Marx*, ed. Eugene Kamenka (New York: Penguin, 1983), 203. Adam Mickiewicz, *Dzieła* (Warsaw: Czytelnik, 1999), 5:15, 19–20; I have taken my translation from Norman Davies, *God's Playground: A History of Poland*, 2 vols. (New York: Columbia University Press, 1982), 2:9.

71. Roman Jakobson, "Shifters, Verbal Categories, and the Russian Verb," *Selected Writings*, vol. 2: *Word and Language* (The Hague: Mouton, 1971), 132.

72. Adam Mickiewicz, *Dziady* (Warsaw: Czytelnik, 1974), 168. Aleksandr Blok, *Sochineniia v dvukh tomakh* (Moscow: Khudozhestvennaia literatura, 1955), 1:453. Vladimir Mayakovsky, *Sochineniia v trekh tomakh* (Moscow: Khudozhestvennaia literatura, 1978), 3:91. Akhmatova, *Sochineniia*, 1:369. Zagajewski, "W liczbie mnogiej," *List: Oda do wielości*, 49. I have borrowed the term "lyric strategies" from Edward Balcerzan, *Poezja polska w latach 1939–1965*, pt. 1: *Strategie liryczne* (Warsaw: Wydawnictwo Szkolne i Pedagogiczne, 1982).

73. Mandelstam, *Sobranie sochinenii*, 2:334, 217.

74. McGann, "Byron's Lyric Poetry," 210–211. Levinson, *Wordsworth's Great Period Poems*, 43. Miłosz, *New and Collected Poems*, 81–82. Zbigniew Herbert, *Barbarian in the Garden*, tr. Michael March and Jaroslaw Anders (New York: Harcourt Brace Jovanovich, 1985), 101. For a more detailed discussion of Miłosz's poem, see Clare Cavanagh, "Poetry and History: Poland's Acknowledged Legislators," *Common Knowledge*, vol. 11, no. 2 (Spring, 2005): 185–197.

75. Miłosz, "You Who Wronged," tr. Richard Lourie, *New and Collected Poems*, 103. Miłosz, "Prywatne obowiązki wobec polskiej literatury," *Prywatne obowiązki* (Krakow: Wydawnictwo Literackie, 2001), 95–135. Bromwich, *Disowned by Memory*, 156, 139. Andrzej Zawada, *Miłosz* (Wrocław: Wydawnictwo dolnoślaskie, 1997), 147. For Miłosz on mass culture and "high art," see "Pytania do dyskusji," in *Kultura masowa*, ed. and tr. Czesław Miłosz (Paris: Instytut literacki, 1959; rpt. Krakow: Wydawnictwo Literackie, 2002), 150–169.

76. Mandelstam, *Sobranie sochinenii*, 2:253. Wisława Szymborska, *Nonrequired Reading*, tr. Clare Cavanagh (New York: Harcourt, 2002), 104.

77. Miłosz, "Bobo's Metamorphoses," tr. Czesław Miłosz and Richard Lourie, *New and Collected Poems*, 193–197. Levinson, *Wordsworth's Great Period Poems*, 32. "Tintern Abbey," in Gill, *William Wordsworth*, 131–135. Heaney discusses the derivation of "verse" in *Preoccupations: Selected Prose 1968–1978* (New York: Farrar Straus Giroux, 1980), 65.

78. Edmundson, *Literature Against Philosophy*, 134. See Roe for a similar argument (*Politics of Nature*, 169). Szymborska, *Poems New and Collected*, 148. Fletcher, *A New Theory*, 105.

79. Davie, *Czesław Miłosz and the Insufficiency of Lyric*, 71. Christopher Ricks, *Reviewery* (New York: Handsel Books, 2002), 284–285. Helen Vendler, *Seamus Heaney* (Cambridge, Mass.: Harvard University Press, 1998), 5–7.

80. Cameron, *Lyric Time*, 71. Szymborska, *Poems New and Collected*, 245.

81. Hans Robert Jauss, "Literary History as a Challenge to Literary Theory," in Jauss, *Toward an Aesthetic of Reception*, tr. Timothy Bahti (Minneapolis: University of Minnesota Press, 1982), 44.

82. Mandelstam, *Vospominaniia: Kniga pervaia*, 200.

83. Miłosz, *The Year of the Hunter*, tr. Madeline Levine (New York: Farrar, Straus and Giroux, 1994), 119. Miłosz, *New and Collected Poems*, 497–498. Mason, *William Blake*, 395.

84. Fletcher, *A New Theory*, 29, 14. Robert Pinsky, "The Idiom of a Self: Elizabeth Bishop and Wordsworth," *Elizabeth Bishop and Her Art*, ed. Lloyd Schwartz and Sybil P. Estess (Ann Arbor: University of Michigan Press, 1983), 49. Szymborska, *Poems New and Collected*, 122, 135, 196, 265. Szymborska, *Monologue of a Dog*, tr. Clare Cavanagh and Stanisław Barańczak (New York: Harcourt, 2006), 69.

85. Szymborska, *Monologue of a Dog*, 69.

86. W.H. Auden, *Collected Poems*, ed. Edward Mendelson (New York: Vintage, 1991), 141. Szymborska, *Monologue of a Dog*, 69. Szymborska, *Poems New and Collected*, 67, 232, 263, 42.

Chapter 1. Courting Disaster

1. Thomas Kilroy, "*The Seagull*: An Adaptation," *The Cambridge Companion to Chekhov*, ed. Vera Gottlieb and Paul Allain (Cambridge: Cambridge University Press, 2000), 80–82.

2. Laura Engelstein, *The Keys to Happiness: Sex and the Search for Modernity in Fin-de-Siècle Russia* (Ithaca: Cornell University Press, 1992), 96–97. R. F. Foster, *W. B. Yeats: A Life*, vol. 1: *The Apprentice Mage, 1865–1914* (Oxford: Oxford University Press, 1997), 254.

3. Aleksandr Blok, "Vozmezdie," *Sochineniia v dvukh tomakh* (Moscow: Khu-dozhestvennaia literatura, 1955), 1:476–522, esp. 492–497. Further references to this edition will appear in the text with volume and page. Kornei Chukovsky, *Aleksander Blok as Man and Poet*, tr. and ed. Diana Burgin and Katherine O'Connor (Ann Arbor: Ardis, 1982), 5. Avril Pyman quotes Blok on his fears and Kluyev's dismissive assessment in *The Life of Aleksandr Blok: The Release of Harmony 1908–1921* (Oxford: Oxford University Press, 1980), 139, 21.

4. Pyman quotes Blok in *Alexander Blok: Selected Poems*, ed. and intro. Avril Pyman (Oxford: Pergamon Press, 1972), 282. Chukovsky, *Blok*, 4.

5. For an overview on Symbolist "life-creation" in its cultural context see *Creating Life: The Aesthetic Utopia of Russian Modernism*, ed. Irina Paperno and Joan Delaney Grossman (Stanford: Stanford University Press, 1994). Olga Matich's *Erotic Utopia: The Decadent Imagination in Russia's Fin de Siècle* (Madison: University of Wisconsin Press, 2005) provides a richly detailed portrait of Symbolist philosophy and practice. For an innovative discussion of life-creation and gender in Blok specifically, see Jenifer Presto, *Beyond the Flesh: Russian Symbolism and the Sublimation of Sex* (Madison: University of Wisconsin Press, 2008), esp. 19–133.

6. Declan Kiberd, *Inventing Ireland: The Literature of the Modern Nation* (Cambridge, Mass.: Harvard University Press, 1996), 119. T. S. Eliot, "Tradition and the Individual Talent," *Selected Prose of T. S. Eliot*, ed. Frank Kermode (New York: Harcourt Brace Jovanovich, 1975), 40. Yeats, "Modern Poetry," *Essays and Introductions* (New York: Collier Books, 1986), 506–510.

7. Marjorie Howes quotes Yeats in *Yeats's Nations: Gender, Class and Irishness* (Cambridge: Cambridge University Press, 1996), 161, 164. "To try to understand what has come upon us," Auden proclaims in 1940, may be "the most heroic of the tasks required to save civilization" (quoted in Lucy McDiarmid, *Saving Civilization: Yeats, Eliot, and Auden between the Wars* [Cambridge: Cambridge University Press, 1984], 9).

8. Sigmund Freud, *Civilization and Its Discontents*, tr. James Strachey (New York: Norton, 1961), 57. Mario Praz, *The Romantic Agony*, tr. Angus Davidson (New York: Meridian Books, 1961), vii. Howes quotes Yeats in *Yeats's Nations*, 110.

9. W. B. Yeats, *The Poems*, ed. Richard J. Finneran (New York: Scribner, 1997), 27. Further references to this edition will be given in the text.

10. Osip Mandelstam, "On the Nature of the Word," *Complete Critical Prose and Letters*, ed. Jane Gary Harris, tr. Jane Gary Harris and Constance Link (Ann Arbor: Ardis, 1979), 128. I am drawing upon James Pethica's annotation in *Yeats's Poetry, Drama, and Prose*, ed. James Pethica (New York: Norton, 2000), 12. On Yeats's involvement in the Golden Dawn, see Alex Owen's *The Place of Enchantment: British Occultism and the Culture of the Modern* (Chicago: University of Chicago Press, 2004), esp. 51–84.

11. Pyman, *The Life of Aleksandr Blok: The Distant Thunder 1880–1908* (Oxford: Oxford University Press, 1979), 67. The literature on Soloviev's Divine Sophia and her followers is vast; see, inter alia, Z. G. Mints, "K genezisy kosmicheskogo u Bloka (Vl. Soloviev i A. Blok)," *Aleksandr Blok i russkie pisateli* (St. Petersburg: Iskusstvo-SPB, 2000), 389–442; D. Maksimov, "O mifopoeticheskom nachale v lirike Bloka," Maksimov, *Russkie poety nachala veka* (Leningrad: Sovetskii pisatel', 1986), 199–239; Avril Pyman, *A History of Russian Symbolism* (Cambridge: Cambridge University

Press, 1994), 226–242; Olga Matich, "The Symbolist Meaning of Love: Theory and Practice," *Creating Life*, 24–50.

12. Fyodor Tiutchev, *Sochineniia v dvukh tomakh* (Moscow: Khudozhevstvennaia literatura, 1984), 1:212. My interpretation of "Predchustvuiu Tebia" is indebted both to Presto's astute reading of the poem (*Beyond the Flesh*, 91–94), and to the splendid work done by participants in a 2005 seminar I taught on Blok and Yeats at Northwestern University: Katia Bowers, Jan Peters, Nina Tyurina, and Lisa Yountchi. Their energetic, imaginative discussions of both poets make themselves felt throughout this chapter.

13. Presto, *Beyond the Flesh*, 91–94.

14. Kiberd, *Inventing Ireland*, 99. On Yeats and the late nineteenth-century attempts to revive Irish Gaelic, see ibid., 133–154.

15. Pyman, *The Distant Thunder*, 68.

16. Howes, *Yeats's Nations*, 72. Pethica, *Yeats's Poetry*, 21. For Mangan, Ferguson, and Davis in the development of modern Irish writing and identity, see Seamus Deane, *A Short History of Irish Literature* (Notre Dame: University of Notre Dame Press, 1986), 60–89.

17. On the ancient folkloric traditions of Russia as what G. Fedotov calls a "great divine female power," see Joanna Hubbs, *Mother Russia: The Feminine Myth in Russian Culture* (Bloomington: Indiana University Press, 1988), 3. Marjorie Howes discusses the colonial vision of Ireland as woman in *Yeats's Nations*, esp. 1–43.

18. D. Maksimov quotes Blok in "O mifopoeticheskom nachale," 211. His comment on Blok's metahistoricism derives from the same essay (205). Yeats, "Ireland and the Arts," *Essays and Introductions*, 203–210. Yeats's Slavic peasants appear in "The Message of the Folklorist," Pethica, *Yeats's Poetry*, 262–263.

19. F. S. L. Lyons quotes Joyce in *Culture and Anarchy in Ireland 1890–1939: From the Fall of Parnell to the Death of W. B. Yeats* (Oxford: Oxford University Press, 1979), 65. Seamus Deane, "Yeats and the Idea of Revolution," *Celtic Revivals* (Winston-Salem: Wake Forest University Press, 1985), 40. Yeats, *Essays and Introductions*, 210–249.

20. Deane, "Yeats and the Idea of Revolution," 46. Pyman quotes Blok on Europe in *The Release of Harmony*, 245. The notion of Russia's barbaric boundlessness as the shape of the future has a distinguished nineteenth-century Russian pedigree, as Blok himself well knew; see his essays "Narod i intelligentsia" and "Ditia Gogolia" for his eccentric celebration of Gogol's "unborn" Russia (2:85–91, 107–110).

21. Edward Said paraphrases Spencer in "Yeats and Decolonization," *Culture and Imperialism* (New York: Vintage, 1994), 222. Friedrich Nietzsche, *The Antichrist*, *The Portable Nietzsche*, ed. and tr. Walter Kaufmann (New York: Viking Penguin, 1982), 652. Yeats records Lady Gregory's remark in *Autobiographies: Memories and Reflections* (London: Macmillan, 1955), 400. Foster comments on the Anglo-Irish fascination with the occult in *The Apprentice Mage*, 50.

22. On the early twentieth-century Russian fascination with the occult, see Maria Carlson, "Fashionable Occultism: Spiritualism, Theosophy, Freemasonry, and Hermeticism in Fin-de-Siècle Russia," *The Occult in Russian and Soviet Culture*, ed. Bernice Glatzer Rosenthal (Ithaca: Cornell University Press, 1997), 135–152. Alex Owen notes the affinities between the English (and Anglo-Irish) and Russian esoteric fascinations, which were linked by the figure of Madame Blavatsky, in *The Place of Enchantment*, 45. Pyman, *The Distant Thunder*, 198.

23. The rose upon the cross in Yeats's poem is of course the emblem of Rosicrucianism; Blok draws upon the same imagery in his play "The Rose and the Cross" (*Roza i krest*, 1912). Yeats, *Essays and Introductions*, 246.

24. The photographs can be found in Pyman, *The Distant Thunder*, 176–177 and 112–113. Mendeleeva-Blok, "Facts and Myths about Blok and Myself," *Blok: An Anthology of Essays and Memoirs*, ed. and tr. Lucy Vogel (Ann Arbor: Ardis, 1982), 54. Pyman quotes Blok on his wife in *The Distant Thunder*, 149. Konstantin Mochulsky cites his letter in *Aleksandr Blok*, tr. Doris V. Johnson (Detroit: Wayne State University Press, 1983), 64.

25. Pyman quotes Blok's letter in *The Distant Thunder*, 127. On the popularity of such "white marriages" in Symbolist circles, see Presto, *Beyond the Flesh*, Matich, "The Symbolist Meaning of Love," and Matich, *Erotic Utopia*, esp. 212–235.

26. Mendeleeva-Blok, "Facts and Myths," 38–39. Pyman quotes Blok's journal in *The Release of Harmony*, 232.

27. On Aphrodite's dual nature, see Sir William Smith, *Smaller Classical Dictionary* (New York: Dutton, 1958), 307, and I. Aghion, C. Barbillon, and F. Lissarrague, *Gods and Heroes of Classical Antiquity* (Paris: Flammarion, 1996), 294–299. Pyman quotes Blok on his love for the motherland in *The Release of Harmony*, 25.

28. Deane, "Yeats and the Idea of Revolution," 44. Blok, "Avtobiografiia," *Polnoe sobranie stikhotvorenii v dvukh tomakh*, ed. Vl. Orlov (Moscow: Sovetskii pisatel', 1946), 11. On the wedding's consummation, see Matich, *Erotic Utopia*, p. 107; Pyman also discusses the consummation and Mendeleeva-Blok's symbolic fall from grace in *The Distant Thunder*, 175–176.

29. See Presto, *Beyond the Flesh*, for a discussion of mythic femininity in Blok's work generally, esp. 41–70. Engelstein, *Keys to Happiness*, 301. Kristi Groberg describes the 1905 representations of Mother Russia as sexual victim in ""'The Shade of Lucifer's Dark Wing': Satanism in Silver Age Russia," *The Occult in Russian and Soviet Culture*, 104. Pyman mentions the poetic postcards in *The Release of Harmony*, 22. She records Blok's comments from his notebooks and mentions Petersburg's Blokian streetwalkers in *Alexander Blok: Selected Poems*, 240, 218.

30. See Presto, "Poetry against Progeny: Blok and the Problem of Poetic Reproduction," *Beyond the Flesh*, 19–133: Presto quotes Blok's notebooks ibid., 29, 125. Matich quotes Soloviev and Gippius in "The Symbolist Meaning of Love," 31.

31. Said, *The World, the Text, and the Critic* (Cambridge, Mass.: Harvard University Press, 1983), 16–17. Foster describes the "ex-debutante" turned seductress in *The Apprentice Mage*, 87.

32. Foster, *The Apprentice Mage*, 87. Yeats, *Autobiographies*, 364. Said mentions Yeats's "super-terrestrial idea of revolution" in *Culture and Imperialism*, 227.

33. On Yeats's courtship of both mother and daughter, see Foster, *The Apprentice Mage*, esp. 116–123, 391–396, and Foster, *W. B. Yeats: A Life*, vol. 2: *The Arch-Poet Life: II* (Oxford: Oxford University Press, 2003), 55–56, 90–92. Brenda Maddox discusses this literal family romance in *Yeats's Ghosts: The Secret Life of W. B. Yeats* (New York: Harper Collins, 1999), 41–54.

34. "Eros and mystical love": the phrase is Pyman's (*The Distant Thunder*, 105). Yeats contrasts himself with Gonne in *Autobiographies*, 363. Foster, *The Apprentice Mage*, 114, 122–123.

35. Kilroy, "*The Seagull*," 31. Pyman mentions the casting of "Neznakomka" in *The Release of Harmony*, 198.

36. Yeats, "*Cathleen Ni Hoolihan*," *Eleven Plays of William Butler Yeats*, ed. A. Norman Jeffares (New York: Collier, 1964), 221–232.

37. Foster quotes Stephen Gwynne on "Cathleen" in *The Apprentice Mage*, 262.

38. Presto quotes Blok in her discussion of *Retribution* and disrupted lines of descent in *Beyond the Flesh*, 242–243. Maddox, *Yeats's Ghosts*, 23.

39. Lyons, *Culture and Anarchy in Ireland*, 1. Sheila Fitzpatrick discusses the various ways of dating Russia's revolution in *The Russian Revolution 1917–1932* (Oxford: Oxford University Press, 1982), 1–10.

40. Yeats, *A Vision* (New York: Collier Books, 1966), 26.

41. James Longenbach, *Stone Cottage: Pound, Yeats and Modernism* (Oxford: Oxford University Press, 1988), 131. Kiberd, *Inventing Ireland*, 315. Pound and Eliot likewise made use of what Pound called the "bolcheviki" and their "rheffolution" in their poetry: Eliot refers the reader to the "present decay in Eastern Europe" as a key to the imagery in *The Waste Land* (*The Complete Poems and Plays 1909–1950* [New York: Harcourt, Brace & World, 1971], 53–54; Pound, *The Cantos* [New York: New Directions, 1975], 74). All three poets see the revolution as the most egregious example of the cultural mayhem that their poetry is intended to combat.

42. Longenbach quotes the early version of Yeats's poem in *Stone Cottage*, 131. Maddox, *Yeats's Ghosts*, 234; this is also the source for Yeats's comment on history's cycles. Foster quotes Yeats's letter in *The Apprentice Mage*, 282.

43. Yeats, *Autobiographies*, 164; *A Vision*, 268.

44. Kiberd, *Inventing Ireland*, 318. Yeats, *A Vision*, 9. Maddox, *Yeats's Ghosts*, 9.

45. See Pethica's commentary on the probable meaning of the poem's "bays," *Yeats's Poetry, Drama, and Prose*, 95.

46. Kiberd, *Inventing Ireland*, 449. Yeats, "Irish Language and Irish Literature," Pethica, *Yeats's Poetry, Drama, and Prose*, 271.

47. Howes, *Yeats's Nations*, 105. I'm indebted to Howes's splendid book throughout my discussion of Yeats, and I've drawn here particularly upon her fourth chapter, "In the Bedroom of the Big House: Kindred, Crisis, and Anglo-Irish nationality," 102–130. Yeats, *Essays and Introductions*, 231.

48. On Blok and Nietzsche, see Evelyn Bristol, "Blok between Nietzsche and Soloviev," *Nietzsche in Russia*, ed. Bernice Glatzer Rosenthal (Princeton: Princeton University Press, 1986), 149–160. On affinities between Yeats's and Khlebnikov's elaborate geometries of history, see Marjorie Perloff, "The Pursuit of Number: Yeats, Khlebnikov, and the Mathematics of Modernism," *Poetic License: Essays on Modernist and Post-Modernist Lyric* (Evanston: Northwestern University Press, 1990), 71–97.

49. For a discussion of Blok's "Polish poem" and his unexpected debt to Polish Romantic messianism, see Wacław Lednicki, *Russia, Poland and the West: Essays in Literary and Cultural History* (London: Hutchinson, 1954), 349–399.

50. Chukovsky, *Aleksander Blok*, 15, 18. Presto, *Beyond the Flesh*, 197.

51. See Pyman, *Alexander Blok: Selected Poems*, 271–275, for an excellent synthesis of both contemporary responses to "The Twelve" and Blok's own notes and comments on the poem and its reception. "Anathema or hosanna" is Chukovsky's phrase (*Alexander Blok*, 140). For a sampling of conflicting contemporary reactions, see ibid., 25, 34, 132–140, and Leon Trotsky, "Alexander Blok," *Literature and Revolution*, tr. Rose Strunsky (Ann Arbor: University of Michigan Press, 1960), 116–125.

52. Chukovsky, *Alexander Blok*, 132.

53. Trotsky, *Literature and Revolution*, 122.

54. For more on the parallelism between Katka and Mother Russia and the effeminacy of the Old World's representatives in the poem generally, see Irene Masing-Delic, *Abolishing Death: A Salvation Myth of Russian Twentieth-Century Literature* (Stanford: Stanford University Press, 1992), 198–209. Boris Gasparov also notes the parallel between Katka and Russia in "Poema A. Bloka 'Dvenadtsat'" i nekotorye problemy karnavalizatsii v iskusstve nachala XX veka," *Slavica Hierosolymitana*, vol. 1 (1977), 125. Eliot Borenstein, *Men without Women: Masculinity and Revolution in Russian Fiction, 1917–1929* (Durham: Duke University Press, 2000), 17. I'm indebted to Borenstein's discussion of masculine collectivity in the early years of the revolution throughout this portion of my discussion.

55. Ezra Pound, *Selected Poems* (New York: New Directions, 1957), 64.

56. Howes, *Yeats's Nations*, 82.

57. Pyman quotes Blok on the "feminine phantom" in *Selected Poems*, 273. The second quote is taken from Chukovsky, *Alexander Blok*, 25.

58. Engelstein quotes Rozanov in *The Keys to Happiness*, 327. For more on Rozanov's anti-Christian vision of Christ, see Anna Lisa Crone, "Nietzschean, All Too Nietzschean? Rozanov's Anti-Christian Critique," *Nietzsche in Russia*, 95–112. Pyman quotes Blok in *The Release of Harmony*, 152.

59. On Yeats's death, burial, and reburial, see Foster, *The Arch-Poet*, 651–659.

60. Pyman quotes Blok on his attempted suicide in *The Distant Thunder*, 118. Chukovsky, *Aleksander Blok as Man and Poet*, 20.

61. Osip Mandelstam, "Barsuch'ia nora," *Sobranie sochinenii*, ed. G. Struve and B. A. Filipoff (vols. 1–3, Washington, D.C.: Interlanguage Library Associates, 1967–1971; vol. 4, Paris: YMCA Press, 1981), 2:270–275. Boris Eikhenbaum, "Blok's Fate," *Blok: An Anthology of Essays and Memoirs*, 134. Trotsky, "Alexander Blok," *Literature and Revolution*, 116–125,

62. Anatoly Lunacharsky, "Aleksander Blok," *On Literature and Art*, ed. A. Lebedev (Moscow: Progress Publishers, 1965), 159–213.

63. Trotsky, "Alexander Blok," Lunacharsky, "Aleksander Blok," *passim*.

64. Eikhenbaum, "Blok's Fate," 132.

65. Lunacharsky, "Aleksander Blok," 212, 160.

66. Ibid., 239.

Chapter 2. Whitman, Mayakovsky, and the Body Politic

1. Guillaume Apollinaire, *The Cubist Painters* (1913) quoted in Betsy Erkilla, *Whitman among the French: Poet and Myth* (Princeton: Princeton University Press, 1980), 199; and Roger Shattuck, *The Banquet Years: The Origins of the Avant-garde in France 1885 to World War I* (New York: Vintage Books, 1968), 284–285, 322. Walt Whitman, "Ages and Ages Returning at Intervals," *Complete Poetry and Collected Prose* (New York: Library of America, 1982), 264. All subsequent citations of Whitman's work in the text will refer to this edition, unless otherwise noted. For accounts of Whitman's influence on European and American avant-garde writing, see *Walt Whitman Abroad*, ed. Gay Wilson Allen (Syracuse: Syracuse University Press, 1955); and James E. Miller, Jr., *The American Quest for a Supreme Fiction: Whitman's Legacy in the Personal Epic* (Chicago: University of Chicago Press, 1979).

2. Czesław Miłosz, *Miłosz's ABC's,* tr. Madeline Levine (New York: Farrar, Straus and Giroux, 2001), 299.

3. For Whitman's fate on Russian and Soviet soil, see Kornei Chukovsky, "Uitmen v russkoi literature," Chukovsky, ed. and tr., *Uolt Uitmen: Poeziia griadushchei demokratii,* 6th ed. (Moscow: Gosudarstvennoe izdatel'stvo, 1923), 143–165; Chukovsky, "Uolt Uitmen v Rossii," Chukovsky, ed. and tr., *Moi Uitman* (Moscow: Progress, 1966), 241–268; Stepan Stepanchev, "Whitman in Russia," *Whitman Abroad,* 144–155; Yassen Zassourskii, "Whitman's Reception and Influence in the Soviet Union," in *Walt Whitman of Mickle Street: A Centennial Collection,* ed. Geoffrey M. Sill (Knoxville: University of Tennessee Press, 1994), 283–290; Thomas Eekman, "Walt Whitman's Role in Slavic Poetry," *American Contributions to the Eighth International Congress of Slavists,* ed. Victor Terras, 2 vols., (Columbus: Slavica, 1978), 2:166–190. On Balmont and Whitman see Martin Bidney, "Leviathan, Yggdrasil, Earth-Titan, Eagle: Bal'mont's Reimagining of Walt Whitman," *Slavic and East European Journal,* vol. 34, no. 2 (Summer 1990), 176–191. For a summary of Chukovsky's work on Whitman, see Gay Wilson Allen, "Kornei Chukovsky, Whitman's Russian Translator," *Walt Whitman of Mickle Street,* 276–282. Chukovsky, *Moi Uitman,* 251.

4. On Whitman's careful structuring of his image, see Betsy Erkilla, *Whitman: The Political Poet* (Oxford: Oxford University Press, 1989), esp. 3–6; Donald Pease, "Walt Whitman's Revisionary Democracy," *The Columbia History of American Poetry,* ed. Jay Parini (New York: Columbia University Press, 1993), 148–171; Ed Folsom, "Whitman and the 'Visual Democracy of Photography,'" *Walt Whitman of Mickle Street,* 80–93.

5. Erkilla, *Whitman,* 3–5. On Mayakovsky's yellow blouse, see Svetlana Boym, *Death in Quotation Marks: Cultural Myths of the Modern Poet* (Cambridge, Mass.: Harvard University Press, 1991), 137–147. On Symbolist "life-creation," see *Creating Life: The Aesthetic Utopia of Russian Modernism,* ed. Irina Paperno and Joan Delaney Grossman (Stanford: Stanford University Press, 1994).

6. Chukovsky, "Maiakovskii," 349–352.

7. Chukovsky, *Ego-futuristy i kubo-futuristy* (Petersburg, 1914; rpt. London: Prideaux Press, 1976), 42–43; Chukovsky, "Uitmen v russkoi literature," 161; Chukovsky, "Maiakovskii," 349.

8. Mayakovsky, "150,000,000," Vladimir Mayakovsky, *Sochineniia,* 3 vols. (Moscow: Khudozhestvennaia literatura, 1978), 3:108–9. All references in the text to Mayakovsky's work will be taken from this edition, unless otherwise noted.

9. Chukovsky, *Dnevnik 1901–1929,* ed. E. Ts. Chukovskaia (Moscow: Sovetskii pisatel', 1991), 195. On Whitman and the Proletkult, see also Victor Erlich, *Modernism and Revolution: Russian Literature in Transition* (Cambridge, Mass.: Harvard University Press, 1994), 86.

10. Chukovsky gave his 1923 edition of Whitman's poetry the subtitle "The Poetry of the Coming Democracy." Chukovsky's "democracy" had a distinctly radical flavor in tsarist and revolutionary Russia alike. The Social Democrats, or SD's, comprised one of the largest Marxist parties of prerevolutionary Russia; they were tolerated for a time following the revolution as well. The Bolsheviks also preempted the use of the term "democratic" for their own experiments in constructing a socialist society.

11. Chukovsky, "Maiakovskii," 162. See also Edward Brown, *Mayakovsky: A Poet in the Revolution* (Princeton: Princeton University Press, 1973), 89, 115, 171, 177,

182–183; Victor Terras, *Vladimir Mayakovsky* (Boston: Twayne, 1983), 47–48, 79, 129.

12. Whitman continued to revise and expand *Leaves of Grass* throughout his life; editions of the book appeared in 1855, 1856, 1860, 1867, 1871–72, 1876, 1881, 1889, 1891–92 (Miller, *Supreme Fiction*, 40). On the significance of this ceaseless revision, see Lawrence Lipking, *The Life of the Poet: Beginning and Ending Poetic Careers* (Chicago: University of Chicago Press, 1981), 114–129; and Michael Moon, *Disseminating Whitman: Revision and Corporeality in Leaves of Grass* (Cambridge, Mass.: Harvard University Press, 1991).

13. Miller, Jr., *Supreme Fiction*, 44. Louis Simpson quotes Lawrence in "Strategies of Sex in Whitman's Poetry," *Walt Whitman of Mickle Street*, 33). Erkilla, *Whitman*, 282.

14. Roman Jakobson, "On a Generation that Squandered Its Poets," tr. Edward J. Brown, *Twentieth-Century Russian Literary Criticism*, ed. Victor Erlich (New Haven: Yale University Press, 1975), 139.

15. Anatoly Lunacharsky, *On Art and Literature* (Moscow: Progress Publishers, 1965), 233.

16. Erlich, *Modernism and Revolution*, 263. Leon Trotsky, "Futurism," *Literature and Revolution*, tr. Rose Strunsky (Ann Arbor: University of Michigan Press, 1960), 146–149.

17. Chukovsky, *Ego-futuristy*, 43.

18. Vladimir Mayakovsky, "Piatyi International," *Polnoe sobranie sochinenii*, 13 vols. (Moscow: Khudozhestvennaia literatura, 1955–61), 4:127.

19. M. H. Abrams, *Natural Supernaturalism* (New York: Norton, 1971), 31, 12. Northrop Frye, *Anatomy of Criticism* (Princeton: Princeton University Press, 1957), 141–142.

20. On Mayakovsky's "sado-masochistic" poetics, see Yuri Karabchievsky, *Voskresenie Maiakovskogo* (Munich: Strana i mir, 1985), esp. 51–78; and Aleksandr Zholkovsky, "O genii i zlodeistve, o babe i vserossiiskom masshtabe (Progulki po Maiakovskomu)," A. K. Zholkovsky and Iu. K. Shcheglov, *Mir avtora i struktura teksta* (Tenafly: Hermitage, 1986), 255–278.

21. Chukovsky, "Maiakovskii," 349. On this incident of "misreading," see Karabchievsky, *Voskresenie*, 76–78.

22. Harold Bloom, *The Anxiety of Influence* (Oxford: Oxford University Press, 1973).

23. Frye, *Anatomy of Criticism*, 143–147.

24. Ibid., 148. "Meat," Karabchievsky notes, with all its "anatomo-gastronomical associations," is Mayakovsky's "favorite poetic dish" (*Voskresenie*, 77–78).

25. Viktor Shklovsky, "Voskreshenie slova" (leaflet, 1914); reprinted in *Texte der russischen Formalisten*, ed. Jurij Striedter (Munich: Fink Verlag, 1969–72), 2:2–17.

26. Galina Patterson quotes Lenin in "Reimaging Majakovskij: Another Viewpoint on '150,000,000'" (unpublished essay). Patterson is excellent on the ambivalence that permeates Mayakovsky's text and the critical reaction it provoked.

27. On Mandelstam's poetic body, see Clare Cavanagh, *Osip Mandelstam and the Modernist Creation of Tradition* (Princeton: Princeton University Press, 1995), esp. 66–102.

28. Trotsky, "Futurism," 148; Karabchievsky, *Voskresenie*, 48.

29. Quoted in Erkilla, *Whitman*, 198. I am drawing upon Erkilla's fine analysis of Whitman's Civil War poetry in my discussion here (ibid., 190–225).

30. Karabchievsky, *Voskresenie*, 20–23.

31. "In Majakovskij's spiritual world," Jakobson notes, "an abstract faith in the coming transformation of the world is joined . . . with hatred for the evil continuum of specific tomorrows that only prolong today . . . and with undying hostility to that 'broody-hen' love that serves only to reproduce the present way of life" ("Generation," 153–54).

32. Mayakovsky, *Polnoe sobranie sochinenii*, 4:127–134.

33. For a critique of Mayakovskian misogyny, see Zholkovsky, "O genii i zlodeistvii."

34. Like many of his revolutionary brethren, Mayakovsky was strongly under the influence of Nikolai Fedorov (1828–1903), whose ideas on physical resurrection of the dead apparently presented Mayakovsky with what he saw as a plausible alternative to outmoded bourgeois procreation. On Mayakovsky and Fedorov, see Jakobson, "Generation," 151; Svetlana Semenova, *Preodolenie tragedii: "Vechnye voprosy" v literature* (Moscow: Sovetskii pisatel', 1989), esp. 262–284; and Irene Masing-Delic, *Abolishing Death: A Salvation Myth of Russian Twentieth-Century Literature* (Stanford: Stanford University Press, 1992).

35. Terras, *Mayakovsky*, 47–48; Brown, *Mayakovsky*, 115.

36. Trotsky, *Literature and Revolution*, 155. N. Aseev, B. Arvatov, et al., "Za chto boretsia Lef?" *Lef*, vol. 1 (1923), 1; I. Zdanevich, A Kruchenykh, et al., "Manifest '41°,'" *41°* (Tiflis, 1919). Both translations are taken from *Russian Futurism through Its Manifestoes, 1912–1928*, ed. and tr. Anna Lawton and Herbert Eagle (Ithaca: Cornell University Press, 1988), 194, 177.

37. Erkilla, *Whitman*, 146. M. Mendel'son both summarizes and continues the Soviet tradition of reading Whitman as spurned socialist in his *Zhizn' i tvorchestvo Uitmena* (Moscow: Nauka, l965), passim. Jean-Paul Sartre, *"What Is Literature?" and Other Essays*, tr. Bernard Frechtman et al. (Cambridge, Mass.: Harvard University Press, 1988), 334.

38. Trotsky, *Literature and Revolution*, 150.

39. Ibid., 254–257.

40. Richard Stites quotes Alexei Gastev in his discussion of "Man the Machine," in Stites, *Revolutionary Dreams: Utopian Vision and Experimental Life in the Russian Revolution* (Oxford: Oxford University Press, 1989), 145–164. Trotsky, *Literature and Revolution*, 170–171.

41. Ritualistic commemoration of Lenin's "sacred" corpse began almost immediately after his death. Indeed, one Soviet elegist chose to model his dirge on Whitman's commemoration of Lincoln's death in "O Captain! My Captain!"—yet another testament to Whitman's pervasive presence in early Soviet poetry (Nina Tumarkin, *Lenin Lives! The Lenin Cult in Soviet Russia* [Cambridge, Mass.: Harvard University Press, 1983], 99).

42. Boris Pasternak, "Okhrannaia gramota," *Vozdushnye puti* (Moscow: Sovetskii pisatel', 1982), 282.

43. Jakobson, "Generation," 161, 163.

44. Mandelstam, *Sobranie sochinenii*, ed. G. Struve and B. A. Filipoff, 4 vols. (vols. 1–3, Washington, D.C.: Interlanguage Library Associates, 1967–1971; vol. 4, Paris: YMCA Press, 1981), 2:334.

45. Wiktor Woroszylski quotes Lunacharsky's attack in *The Life of Mayakovsky,* tr. Boleslaw Taborski (London: Victor Gollancz Ltd., 1972), 250. Lunacharsky, *On Art and Literature,* 239, 234, 245, 240.

46. Lunacharsky, *On Art and Literature,* 250.

47. Ibid., 252–253.

Chapter 3. The Death of the Book à la russe

1. Jacques Derrida, *Of Grammatology,* tr. Gayatri Chakravorty Spivak (Baltimore: Johns Hopkins University Press, 1976), 8, 18; Michel Foucault, "What Is an Author?" *Language, Countermemory, Practice: Selected Essays and Interviews,* ed. Donald F. Bouchard, tr. Donald F. Bouchard and Sherry Simon (Ithaca: Cornell University Press, 1977), 113–139, esp. 117; Roland Barthes, "The Death of the Author," *Image—Music—Text,* ed. and tr. Stephen Heath (New York: Hill and Wang, 1977), 142–143.

2. Roman Jakobson, "On a Generation That Squandered Its Poets," tr. Edward J. Brown, *Twentieth-Century Russian Literary Criticism,* ed. Victor Erlich (New Haven: Yale University Press, 1975), 164. Barthes, "The Death of the Author," 143. For a provocative discussion of the notion of the "death of the author" in modern French and Russian poetry, see Svetlana Boym, *Death in Quotation Marks: Cultural Myths of the Modern Poet* (Cambridge, Mass.: Harvard University Press, 1991).

3. Derrida, *Of Grammatology,* 15. Allan Megill, *Prophets of Extremity: Nietzsche, Heidegger, Foucault, Derrida* (Berkeley: University of California Press, 1985), 340, 347, 351. Friedrich Nietzsche, *The Will to Power,* ed. Walter Kaufmann, trans. Walter Kaufmann and R. G. Hollingdale (New York: Vintage Books, 1968), 396.

4. Miłosz, *The Witness of Poetry* (Cambridge, Mass.: Harvard University Press, 1983), 66.

5. "What Is an Author?" 124. For a succinct discussion of the limits of Foucauldian theory on Stalinist soil, see Beth Holmgren, *Women's Works in Stalin's Time: On Lidiia Chukovskaia and Nadezhda Mandelstam* (Bloomington: Indiana University Press, 1993), 7–9. Vitaly Shentalinsky quotes Mandelstam's guard in *Arrested Voices: Resurrecting the Disappeared Writers of the Soviet Regime* (New York: The Free Press, 1996), 182. Nadezhda Mandelstam, *Vospominaniia: Kniga pervaia,* 3rd ed. (Paris: YMCA Press, 1982), 178. On martyrological readings of Mandelstam's own life and work, see Clare Cavanagh, "Rereading the Poet's Ending: Mandelstam, Chaplin and Stalin," *PMLA,* vol. 109, no. 1 (January, 1994), 71–86.

6. Mandelstam, *Vospominaniia: Kniga pervaia,* 200. "Believe me, I've had it up to here/ With the triumphs of a civic death," Akhmatova complains in one late lyric ("Torzhestvami grazhdanskoi smerti," *Sochineniia,* 3 vols. [vols. 1 and 2, ed. Boris Filipoff and G. P. Struve, Washington, D.C.: Interlanguage Library Associates, 1967–1968; vol. 3, ed. G. Struve, N. A. Struve, and B. A. Filippov, Paris: YMCA Press, 1983], 3:502). She explains the nature of her premature burial and "posthumous existence" in her essay on Georgii Ivanov's *Peterburgskie zimy* (1961): "They stopped publishing me altogether from 1925 to 1939. . . . I was witness to my civic death for the first time then. I was thirty-five years old . . ." ("On Petersburg Winters," in Anna Akhmatova, *My Half Century: Selected Prose,* ed. Ronald Meyer [Ann Arbor: Ardis, 1992], 57). Leon Trotsky, *Literature and Revolution,* tr. Rose Strunsky (Ann Arbor: University of Michigan Press, 1960), 171.

Mandelstam refers to "Stalin's book" in his last lyrics, written in Moscow before his final arrest. The phrase itself is taken from his chilling "Stanzas" (*Stansy*), written in July 1937, as printed in Osip Mandelstam, *Sochineniia v dvukh tomakh*, ed. P. M. Nerler (Moscow: Khudozhestvennaia literatura, 1990), 1:316–317. On Stalin as the master artist who fulfills avant-garde dreams of fusing life and art, see Andrei Sinyavsky, *Soviet Civilization: A Cultural History*, tr. Joanne Turnbull (New York: Little, Brown, 1990), 93–113; and Boris Groys, *The Total Art of Stalinism: Avant-Garde, Aesthetic Dictatorship, and Beyond*, tr. Charles Rougle (Princeton: Princeton University Press, 1992).

7. Anna Akhmatova, "Mandelstam (Listki iz dnevnika)," *Sochineniia*, 2:181. Anatoly Naiman quotes the Soviet critics on Acmeist "chamber music" in *Remembering Anna Akhmatova*, tr. Wendy Rosslyn (New York: Henry Holt, 1991), 128. Osip Mandelstam, "Literary Moscow: The Birth of Plot," *The Complete Critical Prose and Letters*, ed. Jane Gary Harris, tr. Jane Gary Harris, and Constance Link (Ann Arbor: Ardis, 1979), 152. All further translations of Mandelstam's prose will be taken, with slight modifications, from this edition. Akhmatova, "Poema bez geroia," *Sochineniia*, 2:125.

8. Osip Mandelstam, *Sobranie sochinenii*, ed. G.P. Struve and B.A. Filipoff, 4 vols. (vols. 1–3, Washington, D.C.: Interlanguage Library Associates, 1967–1971; vol. 4, Paris: YMCA Press, 1981), 1:202.

9. Quoted in Lazar Fleishman, *Boris Pasternak: The Poet and His Politics* (Cambridge. Mass.: Harvard University Press, 1990), 176. Shetalinsky records the transcripts of Mandelstam's interrogation in *Arrested Voices*, 172–181. Polianovsky and Nadezhda Mandelstam also report the interrogator's reactions in E. Polianovsky, "Smert' Osipa Mandelstama I," *Izvestiia* (May 23–28, 1992); and Mandelstam, *Vospominaniia: Kniga pervaia*, esp. 88, 96–98, 165–170.

10. A. S. Pushkin, *Sobranie sochinenii*, ed. D. Blagoi, vol. 2 (Moscow, Khudozhestvennaia literatura, 1970), 84. Mandelstam, *Sobranie sochinenii*, 3:147.

11. On Mandelstam's recitations of the epigram, see Polianovsky, "Smert' Osipa Mandelstama I," 23–28; and Mandelstam, *Vospominaniia: Kniga pervaia*, 88, 96–98, 165–170.

12. Shentalinsky, *Arrested Voices*, 184.

13. Mandelstam, *Complete Critical Prose*, 438, 317.

14. Ibid., 316–317, 314; Mandelstam, *Sobranie sochinenii*, 1:157–158.

15. Akhmatova, *Sochineniia*, 1:361; translation taken from Susan Amert, *In a Shattered Mirror: The Later Poetry of Anna Akhmatova* (Stanford: Stanford University Press, 1992), 32.

16. Boris Eikhenbaum, *Anna Akhmatova* (Izd. Lev, 1923; rpt. Paris: Lev, 1980), 86–87. "Journey to Armenia" (1933), Mandelstam, *Complete Critical Prose*, 372. Mandelstam, *Sobranie sochinenii*, 1:170, 214, 169. On the role of articulation in Akhmatova's late poetry, see Amert, *Shattered Mirror*, 32–34.

17. Andrei Sinyavsky quotes Voloshin in *Soviet Civilization*, 233.

18. "Poema bez geroia," Akhmatova, *Sochineniia*, 2:101.

19. Bulgakov's famous phrase derives from *The Master and Margarita* (*Master i Margarita*).

20. "And now I'm writing, just as before, without corrections/ My verses in a burnt notebook," Akhmatova notes in a poem of 1956 ("Son," *Sochineniia*, 1:291). I am

indebted to Amert's discussions of Akhmatova's "burnt notebooks" and "poems written for the ashtray," *Shattered Mirror*, 143–151.

21. Akhmatova quotes Mandelstam in her recollections of the poet (*Sochineniia*, 2:185).

Chapter 4. Akhmatova and the Forms of Responsibility

1. I first learned of the so-called Mystery House through childhood visits. The quotes and factual data on Sarah Winchester's mansion derive from "The Winchester Mystery House: The History of One of America's Most Haunted Houses," by Troy Taylor (www.prairieghosts.com/ winchester.html), 1–7); and "Winchester Mystery House: Amazing Facts" (no author) (www.winchestermysteryhouse.com/ facts.html), 1–2.

2. Ibid.

3. I draw my chief version of the *Poem* from Anna Akhmatova, *Sochineniia*, 3 vols. (vols. 1 and 2, ed. Boris Filipoff and G. P. Struve, Munich: Interlanguage Literary Associates, 1967–68; vol. 3, ed. G. Struve, N. A. Struve, and B. A. Filippov, Paris: YMCA Press, 1983). All further citations from these volumes will be indicated in the text. I have also consulted D. Timenchik's edition of the *Poem* in Anna Akhmatova, *Poema bez geroia* (Moscow: MPU, 1989), 30–61. All translations from the poetry are my own, unless otherwise noted. Akhmatova comments on the *Poem* in its introductory texts; Anna Akhmatova, *My Half Century: Selected Prose*, ed. Ronald Meyer (Ann Arbor: Ardis, 1992), 130.

4. Quoted in Timenchik, *Poema*, 67.

5. I have taken my translation here, with slight modifications, from Akhmatova, *My Half Century*, 136 (*Sochineniia*, 3:156).

6. Roberta Reeder quotes Solzhenitsyn in *Anna Akhmatova: Poet and Prophet* (New York: St. Martin's Press, 1994), 373. For Amert's splendid discussion of *Requiem*'s "framing texts" and their function, see *In a Shattered Mirror: The Later Poetry of Anna Akhmatova* (Stanford: Stanford University Press, 1992), 30–59.

7. Lydia Chukovskaya, *Zapiski ob Anne Akhmatovoi*, 3 vols. (Moscow: Soglasie, 1997), 2:123. I follow Milena Michalski and Sylva Rubashova's lead in my term for the volumes collectively in the text: see Lydia Chukovskaya, *The Akhmatova Journals*, vol. 1: *1938–1941*, tr. Milena Michalski and Sylva Rubashova (New York: Farrar, Straus and Giroux, 1994). Untranslated volumes will appear as Chukovskaya, *Zapiski* in the notes.

8. Akhmatova, *My Half Century*, 53, 57.

9. Chukovskaya includes Akhmatova's poem in *Zapiski*, 2:260. Akhmatova's comments on *Requiem*'s auditors are quoted in Anna Akhmatova, *The Word that Causes Death's Defeat: Poems of Memory*, tr. and ed. Nancy K. Anderson (New Haven: Yale University Press, 2004), 83. On Mandelstam's reading of the Stalin epigram, see E. Polianovsky, "Smert' Osipa Mandel'shtama I," *Izvestiia* (May 23–28, 1992); and Nadezhda Mandelstam, *Hope Against Hope*, tr. Max Hayward (New York: Atheneum, 1976), 83.

10. Kees Verheul, "Public Themes in the Poetry of Anna Axmatova," *Tale Without a Hero and Twenty-Two Poems by Anna Axmatova*, ed. Jeanne van der Eng-Liedmeier and Kees Verheul (The Hague: Mouton, 1973), 21. Anderson, *The Word*, 185.

11. Stephany Gould, *"Requiem* as Revised Epic," unpublished essay (Madison, Wis., 1993). Chukovskaya mentions reading the novella to Akhmatova in *The Akhmatova Journals,* 58–60. Lydia Chukovskaya, *Sofia Petrovna,* tr. Aline Werth (Evanston: Northwestern University Press,1988), 60.

12. Catherine Merridale, *Night of Stone: Death and Memory in Twentieth-Century Russia* (New York: Viking, 2000), 308. She mentions the Bolshevik resistance to mourning in the same work, 129. "Muse of weeping" derives from Tsvetaeva's cycle on Akhmatova: Marina Tsvetaeva, *Stikhotvoreniia i poemy,* 5 vols. (New York: Russica Publishers, 1980), 1:232.

13. His purported attachment to "formalism" in art and his popularity among his university students were also contributing factors (private communication from Lazar Fleishman).

14. On Stalin's order to "isolate but preserve," see Nadezhda Mandelstam, *Hope against Hope,* 32. For the *Poem*'s omitted stanzas see Timenchik, *Poema,* 64. Amert, *Shattered Mirror,* 124.

15. Timenchik, *Poema,* 23. Chukovskaya, *Zapiski,* 2:130.

16. Mayakovsky, *Sochineniia,* 3 vols. (Moscow: Khudozhestvennaia literatura, 1978), 3:91. Anatoly Naiman, *Remembering Anna Akhmatova,* tr. Wendy Rosslyn (New York: Henry Holt, 1991), 127. Lev Loseff, "Who Is the Hero of the Poem without One?" *Essays in Poetics,* vol. 2 (Spring, 1986), 91–105. Osip Mandelstam, *Sobranie sochinenii,* ed. G. Struve and B. A. Filipoff, 4 vols. (vols. 1–3, Washington, D.C.: Interlanguage Library Associates, 1967–1971; vol. 4, Paris: YMCA Press, 1981), 1:106.

17. Kees Verheul, *The Theme of Time in the Poetry of Anna Akhmatova* (The Hague: Mouton, 1971), 217.

18. The lines I attribute to each speaker are provisional; one voice frequently blurs into the next.

19. Akhmatova, *My Half Century,* 128–133.

20. Amert, *Shattered Mirror,* 34–35. Akhmatova, *My Half Century,* 130, 132.

21. Amert, *Shattered Mirror,* 36–48.

22. This is also Akhmatova's friend Olga Glebova-Sudeikina, as Akhmatova herself indicates.

23. Emily Dickinson, *Final Harvest: Emily Dickinson's Poems,* ed. Thomas H. Johnson (Boston: Little, Brown, 1961), 55. Chukovskaya records that Akhmatova claimed to have read *Ulysses* six times by 1940 (*The Akhmatova Journals,* 168), and she read Eliot's *Quartets* with great interest after the war; I will return to this later in my discussion.

24. Chukovskaya, *Zapiski,* 2:325, 123. Akhmatova, *My Half Century,* 132.

25. Ezra Pound, *Selected Poems* (New York: New Directions, 1957), 15. For the dates of Akhmatova's stay in the House on the Fontanka, see Akhmatova and Ronald Meyer's commentary in *My Half-Century,* 100, 354.

26. Chukovskaya, *Zapiski,* 2:185. Verheul, *Theme of Time,* 204.

27. Pavlovsky is quoted in Akhmatova, *Sochineniia,* 2:368. Naiman, *Remembering Anna Akhmatova,* 120. Akhmatova, *My Half Century,* 14. Lawrence Lipking, *The Life of the Poet: Beginning and Ending Poetic Careers* (Chicago: University of Chicago Press, 1981), 65–137; his comment on Virgil can be found on 77. On Akhmatova and Eliot, see Reeder, *Anna Akhmatova,* 389, V. N. Toporov, "K otzvukam

zapadnoevropeiskoi poezii u Akhmatovoi (T. S. Eliot)," *International Journal of Slavic Linguistics and Poetics*, vol.16 (1973), 157–176.

28. Akhmatova, *My Half Century*, 301. T. S. Eliot, *The Complete Poems and Plays 1909–1950* (New York: Harcourt, Brace & World, 1971), 140.

29. Toporov, "K otzvukam," passim. Lipking, *Life*, 65–66, 75. Eliot, *Complete Poems*, 117, 144–145.

30. Akhmatova, *My Half Century*, 1. The phrase "counterrevolutionary poetess" is quoted in Chukovskaya, *Zapiski*, 2:106.

31. "The accursed tsarist past" is Chukovskaya's phrase (*Zapiski*, 2:285). Anderson quotes Akhmatova in *The Word*, 68.

32. Lipking, *Life*, 67. Akhmatova, *My Half Century*, 58, 15. Chukovskaya quotes Tvardovsky in *Zapiski*, 2:370. The "Royal Court" appears in Chukovskaya, *The Akhmatova Journals*, 107.

33. Akhmatova has in mind particularly the memoirs of the poet Georgii Ivanov and the ostensibly scholarly study of Leonid Strakhovsky, *Craftsmen of the Word: Three Poets of Modern Russia* (1949). The quotes and references to Strakhovsky and Ivanov are taken from Chukovskaya, *Zapiski*, 2:623, 225, 348, 675.

34. Eliot, *Collected Poems*, 144. Nadezhda Mandelstam refers to the Stalinist "pre-Gutenberg era" in *Hope against Hope*, 192.

35. Caryl Emerson, "The Tolstoy Connection in Bakhtin," *Rethinking Bakhtin: Extensions and Challenges*, ed. Gary Saul Morson and Caryl Emerson (Evanston: Northwestern University Press, 1989), 163.

36. Akhmatova recalls Tsvetaeva's reaction in Timenchik, *Poema*, 353. On Blok, Akhmatova, and the *Poem* see, inter alia, V. M. Zhirmunsky, "Anna Akhmatova i Aleksandr Blok," *Russkaia literatura*, vol. 3 (1970), 57–82; Sam Driver, "Axmatova's *Poema bez geroja* and Blok's *Vozmezdie*," *Aleksandr Blok Centennial Conference*, ed. Walter N. Vickery (Columbus: Slavica, 1984), 89–99; Michael Wachtel, "Poeticheskaia perepiska Bloka s Akhmatovoi; Vzgliad na pervuiu publikatsiiu," *Stikh, iazyk, poeziia: Pamiati Mikhaila Leonovicha Gasparova* (Moscow: RGGU, 2006), 154–166. On the *Poem*'s self-conscious theatricality, see Wendy Rosslyn, "Theatre, theatricality and Akhmatova's *Poema bez geroya*," *Essays in Poetics*, vol. 13, no. 1 (1988), 89–108.

37. Driver quotes Akhmatova in "Axmatova's *Poema*," 89. Rosslyn quotes the critic A. A. Mgebrov on the Silver Age's ubiquitous Pierrots in "Theatre and Theatricality," 96.

38. V. F. Khodasevich, "Konets Renaty," *Nekropol'* (Brussels: Les Editions Petropolis, 1939; rpt. Paris: YMCA Press, 1976), 7–60.

39. Ibid., 23.

40. Akhmatova's comments on Glebova-Sudeikina are quoted in Timenchik, *Poema*, 212. Khodasevich quotes Blok in "Konets Renaty," 22; the other citations from "Konets Renaty" may be found on 8, 12, 14–15.

41. For Akhmatova on Glebova-Sudeikina, see Timenchik, *Poema*, 212. Ronald Meyer quotes Ginzburg in *My Half Century*, xx. Mandelstam, *Sobranie sochineniia*, 1:37.

42. See for example Chukovskaya, *Zapiski*, 2:238.

43. Khodasevich, "Konets Renaty," 14. On Mandelstam in the *Poem*'s opening texts, see Rory Childers and Anna Lisa Crone, "The Mandel'shtam Presence in the

Dedications of *Poema bez geroja,*" *Russian Literature,* vol. 15, no. 1 (1984), 51–84. Akhmatova quotes Mandelstam in *My Half Century,* 99.

44. Ian Balfour, *The Rhetoric of Romantic Prophecy* (Stanford: Stanford University Press, 2002), 32.

45. Isaiah Berlin, "Meetings with Russian Writers in 1945 and 1956," *Personal Impressions,* ed. Henry Hardy (New York: Penguin, 1982), 190, 199. The phrase "genius for self-dramatization" comes from Michael Ignatieff, *Isaiah Berlin: A Life* (New York: Henry Holt, 1998), 156. For accounts of Berlin's encounters with Akhmatova and their aftermath, see: Gyorgy Dalos, *The Guest from the Future: Anna Akhmatova and Isaiah Berlin,* tr. Antony Wood (New York: Farrar, Straus and Giroux, 1996); Ignatieff, *Isaiah Berlin,* esp. 150–172, 232–233; Reeder, *Anna Akhmatova,* esp. 286–288, 324–326, 458–460.

46. Berlin, *Personal Impressions,* 192.

47. Ibid., 202, 190. Eliot, *Collected Poems,* 48. Akhmatova speaks of the *Poem*'s doppelgänger in *My Half Century,* 136.

48. Carl Woodring quotes Auden in *Politics in English Romantic Poetry* (Cambridge, Mass.: Harvard University Press, 1970), 47. For Stalin's phone call to Pasternak, see Nadezhda Mandelstam, *Hope against Hope,* 145–149. I have altered the translation to reflect the Russian original, *master,* as opposed to Hayward's "genius." Reeder quotes Stalin on Akhmatova in *Anna Akhmatova,* 229. Michael Ignatieff cites the informer's report on Akhmatova on the basis of a lecture on the "Akhmatova file" given by a KGB operative in Berlin in 1993 (*Isaiah Berlin,* 165, 168). Berlin quotes Akhmatova on Stalin's alleged response to their meeting in *Personal Impressions,* 201–202.

49. Berlin, *Personal Impressions,* 202.

50. Timenchik, *Poema,* 61; it also appears in a footnote to the Struve/ Filipoff text (2:132).

51. Balfour, *Rhetoric,* 70–71. Berlin, *Personal Impressions,* 205, 203.

52. For Akhmatova's response to Frost, see Naiman, *Remembering Anna Akhmatova,* 111. Her comment to Chukovskaya is quoted in *Zapiski,* 2:509.

53. James Longenbach, *Modern Poetry after Modernism* (Oxford: Oxford University Press, 1997), 77. Frost, *Collected Poems, Prose, and Plays* (New York: Library of America, 1995), 739–740. F. D. Reeve quotes Frost in Reeve, *Robert Frost in Russia* (Boston: Little, Brown, 1964), 105, 132, 112, 126–127. Tom Paulin, *Minotaur: Poetry and the Nation State* (Cambridge, Mass.: Harvard University Press, 1992), 185.

54. Chukovskaya, *Zapiski,* 2:509. Berlin, *Personal Impressions,* 181, 184–186.

55. Berlin, *Personal Impressions,* 195. Ryszard Krynicki, "Do Not Want to Die for Us," *Spoiling Cannibals' Fun: Polish Poetry of the Last Two Decades of Communist Rule,* ed. and tr. Stanisław Barańczak and Clare Cavanagh (Evanston: Northwestern University Press, 1991), 142. Szymborska, *Poems New and Collected 1957–1997,* tr. Stanisław Barańczak and Clare Cavanagh (New York: Harcourt Brace, 1998), 83.

Chapter 5. Avant-garde Again

1. I'm grateful to friends who made the research for this chapter possible by generously providing me with key texts concerning the Mayakovsky cult and its aftermath in postwar Poland: Anna and Stanisław Barańczak, Ryszard Krynicki, and especially

Michał Rusinek, who, as always, exceeded the call of Socialist Realist duty by tracking down and xeroxing virtually all of Wiktor Woroszylski's early poetry for me.
My quotes are taken from Jacek Łukasiewicz, "Wiersz wewnątrz gazety," *Teksty drugie*, vol. 4, no. 10 (1991), 25–26. See also Tadeusz Nyczek, *22 × Szymborska* (Poznań: Wydawnictwo a5, 1997), 19–20.

2. Quoted in Łukasiewicz, "*Wiersz*," 26. Wisława Szymborska, *Dlatego żyjemy* (Warsaw: Czytelnik, 1954).

3. Wiktor Woroszylski quotes Mayakovsky and his critics in *Życie Majakowskiego* (Warsaw: Państwowy Instytut Wydawniczy, 1965). Woroszylski's biography appeared in English, in (unacknowledged) abridged form, as *The Life of Mayakovsky*, tr. Boleslaw Taborski (London: Victor Gollancz, 1972), 510, 427, 483. Trotsky attacks Mayakovsky's "Bohemianism" in *Literature and Revolution*, tr. Rose Strunsky (Ann Arbor: University of Michigan Press, 1960). 131.

4. Edward Brown quotes Stalin in *Mayakovsky: A Poet in the Revolution* (Princeton: Princeton University Press, 1973), 370. I quote Lazar Fleishman from a private communication. He continues: "A few years before that, on January 21, 1931 Lily Brik sent a letter to Stalin asking him to write an introduction for the Collected Works of Mayakovsky and to give his political and artistic evaluation of Mayakovsky's epic 'Lenin.' Stalin left this letter unanswered." Boris Pasternak, "Liudi i polozheniia," *Vozdushnye puti: Proza raznykh let* (Moscow: Sovetskii pisatel', 1982), 458.

5. On Mayakovsky's visits to Poland, see Aleksander Wat, *My Century: The Odyssey of a Polish Intellectual*, tr. Richard Lourie (New York: Norton, 1988), esp. 25, 43–48; Tomas Venclova, *Aleksander Wat: Life and Art of an Iconoclast* (New Haven: Yale University Press, 1996); Marcy Shore, *Caviar and Ashes: A Warsaw Generation's Life and Death in Marxism, 1918–1968* (New Haven: Yale University Press, 2006), 52–69; and Wiktor Woroszylski, "W Polsce," *Życie Majakowskiego*, 605–624. This chapter was omitted from the English translation, which also contains a number of less substantive omissions, none of which are identified in the English text. On Wat's political beliefs and activities in the twenties, see Venclova, *Aleksander Wat*, 69–83; and Shore, *Caviar and Ashes*, 10–78.

6. Wat, *My Century*, 44, 24. Woroszylski quotes Tuwim in *Życie Majakowskiego*, 608–609. Edward Balcerzan, *Poezja polska w latach 1918–1939* (Warsaw: Wydawnictwa Szkolne i Pedagogiczne, 1996), 32, 138. Tuwim passed through a brief infatuation with Futurism himself—"I'll be the first Polish Futurist," he crowed in 1918—but his love for Mayakovsky survived his short-lived fascination with Futurist aesthetics (ibid., 32).

7. Woroszylski records the responses of Polish witnesses to the visit in *Życie Majakowskiego*, 610–621. Mayakovsky himself wrote the introduction to his selected poems in Polish translation that appeared in 1927. See Leonid Katsis, "Vladimir Maiakovskii v Varshave v 1927 (russkii literaturnyi kontekst)," *Włodzimierz Majakowski i jego czasy*, ed. Wiesława Olbrzych and Jerzy Szokalski (Warsaw: SOW, 1995), 29–42.

8. See Boym, *Death in Quotation Marks: Cultural Myths of the Modern Poet* (Cambridge, Mass.: Harvard University Press, 1991), esp. 119–190, for an account of the often contradictory interpretations of Mayakovsky's death generated by his French and Russian contemporaries. Trotsky quotes the official report on Mayakovsky's suicide in *Leon Trotsky on Literature and Art*, ed. Paul N. Siegel (New York: Pathfinder Press, 1970), 175.

9. On the issue of *Miesięcznik literacki* devoted to Mayakovsky, see Wat, *My Century*, 56; and Krystyna Sierocka, "Miesięcznik literacki (1929–1931)," *Słownik literatury polskiej XX wieku*, ed. Alina Brodzka, Mirosława Puchalska, et al. (Wrocław: Zakład Narodowy im. Ossolińskich, 1992), 619–622. Balcerzan comments on Broniewski's poem in *Poezja polska*, 143–144, and gives the poem in its entirety in *Włodzimierz Majakowski* (Warsaw: Czytelnik, 1984), 159.

10. Mayakovsky, *Sochineniia*, 3 vols. (Moscow: Khudozhestvennaia literatura, 1978), 2:31. For a more detailed discussion of the poet's death and its Polish repercussions, see Shore, *Caviar and Ashes*, 79–81.

11. On the "Batalia o Majakowskiego" and the postwar Polish "majakowszczyzna," see Edward Balcerzan, *Poezja polska w latach 1939–1965*, 2 vols. (Warsaw: Wydawnictwa Szkolne i Pedagogiczne, 1988), 2:43–46; Stanisław Stabro, *Poezja i historia: Od Żagarów do Nowej Fali* (Krakow: Universitas, 2001), 181; Leszek Szaruga, *Walka o godność: Polska poezja w latach 1939–1988* (Wrocław: Wiedza o kulturze, 1993), 43–49. For Trotsky's critique of Mayakovsky, see *Literature and Revolution*, 126–161. On "Mayakovshchina" in Soviet Russia of the twenties, see my introduction, and Woroszylski, *Life of Mayakovsky*, 274, 280–281, 419. Woroszylski's remark is taken from his *Powrót do kraju* (London: Polonia, 1979), 47.

12. Mayakovsky, *Sochineniia*, 3:178. On the origins of the group's derogatory nickname, see Jacek Bocheński, "Moje przygody z Wiktorem, jak je pamiętam," *Woroszylski*, ed. Iwona Smolka (Krakow: Wydawnictwo Baran i Suszczyński, 1997), 5–12. Balcerzan quotes from "The Battle for Mayakovsky" in *Poezja polska w latach 1939–1965*, 2:45. Woroszylski, *Poezje wybrane* (Warsaw: Ludowa Spółdzielnia Wydawnicza, 1982), 6.

13. Alicja Lisiecka, *Pokolenie 'pryszczatych'* (Warsaw, 1964), 4. Quoted in Stabro, *Poezja i historia*, 181.

14. Woroszylski, "Od autora," *Poezje wybrane*, 6. Woroszylski, *Powrót do kraju*, 38. Mayakovsky, *Sochineniia*, 1:146–147.

15. Even a change of style was not enough to save Jasieński, who wrote a prototypical Socialist Realist novel—appropriately entitled *Man Changes His Skin* (*Chelovek meniaet kozhu*, 1932)—but perished just the same in a transit camp en route to Kolyma in 1939. Broniewski's poetics had always been more conservative than his politics, making him a far more likely candidate for successful Sovietization. He not only survived his stint in the dreaded Lubianka prison, but went on to become the official "national poet" of postwar Poland. Wandurski died in a Soviet prison sometime after 1934 and was posthumously rehabilitated in 1956. On these poets' fates see Czesław Miłosz, *The History of Polish Literature* (Berkeley: University of California Press, 1983), 398–400. For Wat's far more complex biography, see Venclova, *Aleksander Wat*, and Wat, *My Century*.

16. Max Eastman quotes Trotsky on the lyric in *Artists in Uniform: A Study in Literature and Bureaucratism* (London: George Allen & Unwin, 1934), 52. *Literature and Revolution*, 150. Woroszylski quotes Mayakovsky's Soviet critics and the poet himself on his deplorable lyric tendencies in *The Life of Mayakovsky*, 250, 340, 346, 431. Mayakovsky, "Vo ves' golos," *Sochineniia*, 3:334.

17. *Literature and Revolution*, 170–171. Szaruga quotes Ważyk in *Walka o godność*, 64–65. Wojciech Ligeza quotes the Socialist Realist critic L. Flaszen in *O poezji Wisławy Szymborskiej: Świat w stanie korekty* (Krakow: Wydawnictwo

Literackie, 2001), 45. See Jacek Łukasiewicz, "Poezja," for a more detailed description of the antilyrical bent of Polish Socialist Realism: "The individual 'I,' whether agitator or cult functionary, was irrelevant," he explains (*Słownik realizmu socjalistycznego*, ed. Zdzisław Łapinski, Wojciech Tomasik [Krakow: Universitas, 2005], 206–210).

18. Szaruga quotes Ważyk in *Walka o godność*, 64–65. Woroszylski, "O miłości—gawęda chaotyczna," *Śmierci nie ma! Poezje 1945–1948* (Warsaw: Ksiązka i wiedza, 1949), 41–44.

19. Woroszylski, "Rosa Lee," *Śmierci nie ma!* 45–50.

20. Szaruga quotes from Woroszylski's essay in *Walka o godność*, 47; Woroszylski himself began his writing career as a state journalist, and continued his journalistic work for many years both within Poland and in other eastern bloc countries. I have tried to make my translation as infelicitous as Woroszylski's clunky parody, which labors to reproduce even Poe's well-known rhyme scheme; see Poe, "Annabel Lee," *American Poetry: The Nineteenth Century*, ed. John Hollander, vol. 1 (New York: Library of America, 1993), 550–551. Mayakovsky, "Bruklinskii most," *Sochineniia*, 1:519–523.

21. Woroszylski describes the master key that was to be his generation's point of entry into universal history in *Powrót do kraju*, 37.

22. Mayakovsky, "Domoi," *Sochineniia*, 1:528–532, "Pro eto," ibid., 3:142–185.

23. On Soviet schoolchildren's mandatory Mayakovsky, see Boym, *Death in Quotation Marks*, 183. Woroszylski, *Powrót do kraju*, 11. Balcerzan, *Poezja polska w latach 1939–1965: Część II* (Warsaw: Wydawnictwa Szkolne i Pedagogiczne, 1988), 43. Woroszylski, "O miłości—gawęda chaotyczna," *Śmierci nie ma!* 43.

24. Woroszylski, *Powrót do kraju*, 10, 60–61. I have drawn additional information on Woroszylski's life and later work on Mayakovsky from Boleslaw Taborski's "About the Author" in *The Life of Mayakovsky*, 561–562. For a more detailed discussion of Woroszylski's engagement with, and disengagement from, People's Poland, see Anna Bikont and Joanna Szczęsna, *Ławina i kamienie: Pisarze wobec komunizmu* (Warsaw: Proszyński i S-ka, 2006), esp. 56–67, 284–295.

25. Irene Masing-Delic, *Abolishing Death: A Salvation Myth of Russian Twentieth-Century Literature* (Stanford: Stanford University Press, 1992), 5. Mayakovsky, *Sochineniia*, 3:337, 1:66.

26. Woroszylski, *Śmierci nie ma!* 8–9, 54.

27. Mayakovsky, *Sochineniia*, 3:7–36.

28. Woroszylski, *Śmierci nie ma!* 2–8. Mayakovsky, *Sochineniia*, 1:16–35. Roman Jakobson, "On the Generation That Squandered Its Poets," tr. Edward J Brown, *Twentieth-Century Russian Literary Criticism*, ed. Victor Erlich (New Haven: Yale University Press, 1975), 138–168.

29. Woroszylski, "Niech się męcza," *W dżungli wolności* (Warsaw: Biblioteka 'Więzi,' 1996), 246.

30. On this production, see Balcerzan, "Włodzimierz Majakowski i nasze czasy," *Włodzimerz Majakowski i jego czasy*, 10; Stabro, *Poezja i historia*, 344.

31. "Od autora," *Poezje wybrane* (Warsaw: Ludów Spółdzielnia Wydawnicza, 1982), 5–6.

32. Woroszylski, *Powrót do kraju*, 45. *The Life of Mayakovsky*, 530. I have amended Taborski's translation slightly to bring it closer to Pasternak's original Russian. For a discussion of Mayakovsky's and Esenin's suicides, see Boym, *Death in Quotation Marks*, 119–190, 222–224.

33. Woroszylski, *Śmierci nie ma!* 6–7, 55.

34. Ibid., 11, 39–40.

35. Ibid., 40–44. Mayakovsky, *Sochineniia*, 3:11–17.

36. Ibid. Mayakovsky, *Sochineniia*, 2:13.

37. *Śmierci nie ma!* 41–44.

38. Ibid., 54. Jan Kott, "Introduction," Borowski, *This Way to the Gas, Ladies and Gentlemen,* tr. Barbara Vedder (New York: Penguin, 1976), 12 .

39. Balcerzan quotes Borowski on Mayakovsky in *Poezja polska w latach 1939– 1965,* 2:44. Milosz, *The Captive Mind,* tr. Jane Zielonko (New York: Vintage, 1955), 134. Wat, *My Age,* 47. Woroszylski, "Nowotko," *Ojczyzna* (Warsaw: Państwowy Instytut Wydawniczy, 1953), 8.

40. *Poezja Polski Ludowej,* ed. Ryszard Matuszewski and Seweryn Pollack (Warsaw: Czytelnik, 1955), 567–575. Woroszylski, *Ojczyzna,* 5–6, 46. 71–74. Woroszylski, *Z podróży, ze snu, z umierania: Wiersze 1951–1990* (Poznań: Wydawnictwo a5, 1992), 11.

41. Woroszylski, "O sobie i o wierszach," *Z podróży,* 243–246. Szaruga, *Poezja polska,* 84.

42. Woroszylski, *Poezje wybrane,* 9.

43. Woroszylski, *Życie Majakowskiego,* 5–6.

44. Walt Whitman, *Poetry and Prose,* ed. Justin Kaplan (New York: Library of America, 1982), 87. Mayakovsky, *Sochineniia,* 3:91. Balcerzan describes the fate of Broniewski's translations, *Poezja polska w latach 1939–1965,* 2:38. Jacek Bocheński, "Moje przygody z Wiktorem, jak je pamiętam," *Woroszylski,* ed. Iwona Smolka (Krakow: Wydawnictwo Baran i Suszczyński, 1997), 8. Woroszylski, "Od autora," 11. Woroszylski, *Powrót do kraju,* 29.

45. Woroszylski, *Powrót do kraju,* 28. Łukasiewicz mentions Woroszylski's *Historie* in "Wspomnienia," Smolka, *Woroszylski,* 33–36.

46. The censorship was never as strict in People's Poland as it was in the Soviet Union proper. Joseph Brodsky was only the most visible of the many Russian intellectuals who learned to read Polish so as to gain access to literary texts, including contemporary Western works in translation, that could not be printed in Poland's neighbor to the east.

47. Andrei Sinyavsky, *Soviet Civilization: A Cultural History* (New York: Little, Brown, 1990), 232. Two recent volumes bear tribute to Mayakovsky's continuing popularity among Polish and anglophone artists. A 1996 issue of the prominent Polish journal *Literatura na świecie* dedicated some sixty pages to Mayakovsky's work, including translations by Tuwim, Jastun, and others alongside comments by recent poets on Mayakovsky's continued influence (*Literatura na świecie,* no. 7 [1996], 195–260). *Night Wraps the Sky: Writings by and about Mayakovsky,* ed. Michael Almereyda (New York: Farrar Straus and Giroux, 2008) incorporates the comments of American filmmakers, poets, and critics among Mayakovsky's own writings and Russian reactions to the poet.

Chapter 6. Bringing Up the Rear

1. Anna Bikont and Joanna Szczęsna, *Pamiątkowe rupiecie, przyjaciele i sny Wisławy Szymborskiej* (Warsaw: Proszyński i S-ka, 1997), 143. Wojciech Ligęza,

"Przepustowość owiec: Rozmowa z Wisławą Szymborską," *Teksty drugie*, vol. 10, no. 4 (1991), 153. Edward Balcerzan, "Laudatio," *Wokół Szymborskiej: Poznańskie studia polonistyczne*, Seria literacka 2.22 (Poznań, 1995), 26. Wisława Szymborska, *Poems New and Collected: 1957–1997*, tr. Stanisław Baranczak and Clare Cavanagh (New York: Harcourt Brace, 1998), 205. Further references to this volume will appear in the text.

2. Bikont, Szczęszna, *Pamiątkowe rupiecie*, 73,103.

3. Fredric Jameson, "Foreword," in Jean-François Lyotard, *The Postmodern Condition: A Report on Knowledge*, tr. Geoff Bennington and Brian Massumi (Minneapolis: University of Minnesota Press, 1984), xiv. "Grand narratives" is Lyotard's term (*Postmodern Condition*, 15).

4. Tomashevsky, "Literature and Biography," *Readings in Russian Poetics: Formalist and Structuralist Views*, ed. Ladislav Matejka and Krystyna Pomorska (Ann Arbor: Michigan Slavic Publications, 1978), 47–55. Jacek Łukasiewicz, ""Poezja," *Słownik realizmu socjalistycznego*, ed. Zdzisław Lapiński and Wojciech Tomasik (Warsaw: Universitas, 2004), 206–210. Wisława Szymborska, *Dlatego żyjemy* (Warsaw: Czytelnik, 1954), 4, 9, 13.

5. Bikont, Szczęszna, 112.

6. Wojciech Ligęza quotes L. Flaszen in *O poezji Wisławy Szymborskiej: Świat w stanie korekty* (Krakow: Wydawnictwo Literackie, 2001), 45.

7. Tadeusz Nyczek comments on its popularity in *22 × Szymborska* (Poznań: Wydawnictwo a5), 133.

8. Bikont and Szczęszna quote both Nyczek and Szymborska in *Pamiątkowe rupiecie*, 106, 137, 162, 172, 161. Wisława Szymborska, "Bringing Up the Rear," *Nonrequired Reading*, tr. Clare Cavanagh (New York: Harcourt, 2002), 104.

9. Jerzy Smulski, "Konwencje i gatunki literackie," *Słownik realizmu socjalistycznego*, 108–112. Bikont and Szczęszna quote Szymborska in *Pamiątkowe rupiecie*, 107.

10. Walter Benjamin, "The Storyteller," *Illuminations*, ed. Hannah Arendt, tr. Harry Zohn (New York: Schocken Books, 1969), 100. Julia Hartwig, "In Your Eyes," *Spoiling Cannibals' Fun: Polish Poetry of the Last Two Decades of Communist Rule*, ed. and tr. Stanisław Baranczak and Clare Cavanagh (Evanston: Northwestern University Press, 1991), 48.

11. Tadeusz Nyczek, "Bach na dachu Lubianki (Aleksander Wat)," *Emigranci* (London: Aneks, 1988), 28.

12. Szymborska, "Nicość przenicowała się także i dla mnie," *Wiersze wybrane* (Krakow: Wydawnictwo a5, 2000), 194.

13. The term is Katherine Verdery's, from *What Was Socialism and What Comes Next* (Princeton: Princeton University Press, 1996), passim.

14. Czesław Miłosz, "On Pasternak Soberly," *Emperor of the Earth: Modes of Eccentric Vision* (Berkeley: University of California Press, 1981), 73.

15. "Linguistics and Poetics," *Language in Literature*, ed. Krystyna Pomorska and Stephen Rudy (Cambridge, Mass.: Harvard University Press, 1987), 71.

16. Michael André Bernstein, *Foregone Conclusions: Against Apocalyptic History* (Berkeley: University of California Press, 1994), passim. Frank Kermode, *The Sense of an Ending: Studies in the Theory of Fiction* (Oxford: Oxford University Press, 1966), 164.

17. Zbigniew Herbert, *Mr. Cogito*, tr. John Carpenter and Bogdana Carpenter (New York: Ecco Press, 1993), 30.

18. Quoted in Richard Stites, *Revolutionary Dreams: Utopian Vision and Experimental Life in the Russian Revolution* (New York: Oxford University Press, 1989), 42.

19. Szymborska, "Z elementarza," *Dlatego żyjemy*, 38.

20. Quoted in Bikont and Szczęsna, *Pamiątkowe rupiecie*, 177.

21. Szymborska, "Close Calls," *Nonrequired Reading*, 121. Bernstein *Foregone Conclusions*, 19.

22. I'm indebted in this portion of my discussion particularly not just to Bernstein's book, but to years of wonderfully productive arguments with my friend and colleague, Gary Saul Morson, whose ideas on what he calls "prosaic" history may be found, inter alia, in Morson, *Narrative and Freedom: The Shadows of Time* (New Haven: Yale University Press, 1995).

23. Jameson, "Marxism and Historicism," *New Literary History*, vol. 11, no. 1 (Autumn, 1979), 41–74.

24. Leszek Szaruga, *Walka o godność: Poezja polska w latach 1939–1988* (Wrocław: Wiedza o kulturze, 1993), 67.

25. Sheila Fitzpatrick, *The Russian Revolution 1917–1932* (New York: Oxford University Press, 1982), 149.

26. Zbigniew Herbert, *Still Life with a Bridle: Essays and Apocrypha*, tr. Michael March (New York: Ecco Press, 1991), 60.

27. Anna Akhmatova, "Lotova zhena," *Sochineniia*, 3 vols. (vols. 1 and 2, ed. Boris Filipoff and G. P. Struve, Munich: Interlanguage Literary Associates, 1967–68); vol. 3, ed. G. Struve, N. A. Struve, and B. A. Filippov, Paris: YMCA Press, 1983), 1:222. Szymborska, *Nonrequired Reading*, 104.

28. Jacek Łukasiewicz, "Wiersz wewnątrz gazety," *Teksty drugie*, v. 4/ 10 (1991), 29, 27.

29. Zagajewski, *List: Oda do wielości* (Paris: Instytut literacki, 1983), 49.

30. Zagajewski, "Poezja swobody," Barańczak, "Posążek z soli," Kornhauser, "Czarodziejstwo," *Radość czytania Szymborskiej*, ed. Jerzy Illg (Krakow: Znak, 1996), 255–276.

Chapter 7. Counterrevolution in Poetic Language

1. Adam Michnik, "Anti-authoritarian Revolt: A Conversation with Daniel Cohn-Bendit," *Letters from Freedom: Post–Cold War Realities and Perspectives*, ed. Irena Grudzinska Gross (Berkeley: University of California Press, 1998), 37. "The unrepresented world" is Julian Kornhauser's and Adam Zagajewski's phrase, from their book by that name (*Świat nie przedstawiony* [Krakow: Wydawnictwo Literackie, 1974]).

2. Denis Hollier, "May, 1968: Actions, No! Words, Yes!" *A New History of French Literature*, ed. Denis Hollier (Cambridge, Mass.: Harvard University Press, 1989), 1037. Yve-Alain Bois, "1973: French Lib," ibid., 1041. On the legacy of 1968 in modern French thought, see Luc Ferry and Alain Renaut, *French Philosophy of the Sixties: An Essay on Antihumanism*, tr. Mary H. S. Cattani (Amherst: University of Massachusetts Press, 1990) and Danielle Marx-Scouras, *The Cultural Politics of Tel Quel: Literature and the Left in the Wake of Engagement* (University Park: Pennsylvania State University Press, 1996).

3. Hollier, "May, 1968," 1034. Michnik, "Anti-authoritarian Revolt," 37.

4. Neal Ascherson, *The Polish August* (New York: Penguin Books), 93. Michnik, "Anti-authoritarian Revolt," 42–45. Tony Judt quotes polemicists of the Parti Socialiste Unifié in *Past Imperfect: French Intellectuals, 1944–1956* (Berkeley: University of California Press, 1992), 281.

5. Michnik, "Anti-authoritarian Revolt," 36, 47. Michnik comments on the Polish press coverage of May, 1968 ibid., 46.

6. Jacques Derrida was at the same time, incidentally, busily forging the beginnings of what would prove to be a spectacular international career by lecturing American academics on the significance, inter alia, of Vietnam and Martin Luther King's assassination. He reminded them, too, that his own talk had been written under duress: "The universities of Paris were being invaded by the forces of order" at the very moment that he was preparing his lecture, he informed his audience (Hollier, "May, 1968," 1039).

7. On the omission of Poland from postcolonial criticism generally, see Clare Cavanagh, "Postcolonial Poland," *Common Knowledge*, vol. 10, no. 1 (Winter, 2004), 82–92.

8. Michnik, "Anti-authoritarian Revolt," 42. Ascherson, *Polish August*, 91–92. Tadeusz Nyczek, "The Poetry of the '68 Generation," *Humps & Wings: Polish Poetry Since '68*, ed. Tadeusz Nyczek, tr. Bogusław Rostworowski (San Francisco: Invisible City, 1982), 7. On the Romantics and Solidarity, see Timothy Garton-Ash, *The Polish Revolution: Solidarity* (New York: Vintage, 1985), 44–45; and Norman Davies, *Heart of Europe: A Short History of Poland* (Oxford: Oxford University Press, 1986), 382.

9. Julia Kristeva, *Revolution in Poetic Language*, tr. Margaret Waller (New York: Columbia University Press, 1974). Kristeva, "How Does One Speak to Literature?", *Desire in Language: A Semiotic Approach to Literature and Art* (New York: Columbia University Press, 1980), 123.

10. Tel Quel, "Division of the Assembly," *The Tel Quel Reader*, ed. Patrick ffrench and Roland-François Lack (New York: Routledge, 1998), 21–24.

11. Suleiman paraphrases Pleynet and quotes Sollers in "1960: As Is," 1011–1018. Matei Calinescu describes Tel Quel's members as "monomaniacs of the idea of Revolution" in *Five Faces of Modernity: Modernism, Avant-Garde, Decadence, Kitsch* (Durham: Duke University Press, 1987), 144–145.

12. Kristeva, "The Ethics of Linguistics," *Desire in Language*, 27, 31. On Tel Quel's fascination with Futurism and Formalism, see Marx-Scouras, *The Cultural Politics of Tel Quel*, 115–134. On Kristeva and the Russian avant-garde, see Clare Cavanagh, "Pseudo-revolution in Poetic Language: Julia Kristeva and the Russian Avant-garde," *Slavic Review*, vol. 52, no. 2 (Summer, 1993), 283–297.

13. Tadeusz Nyczek quotes Karasek in his introduction to *Określona epoka: Nowa Fala 1968–1993*, ed. with commentary by Tadeusz Nyczek (Krakow: Oficyna Literacka, 1994), 7. Ryszard Krynicki, "Obywatele Fantasmagorii," *Magnetyczny punkt: Wybrane wiersze i przekłady* (Warsaw: Wydawnictwo CiS, 1996), 90. Nyczek, *Określona epoka*, 3, 7.

14. Wit Jaworski, "Maj 68 (Image)," Nyczek, *Określona epoka*, 67.

15. Zagajewski, "Rzeczywistość nie przedstawiona w powojennej literaturze," *Świat nie przedstawiony*, 36. Miłosz, *Nobel Lecture* (New York: Farrar, Straus and Giroux, 1980), 13.

16. Jean-Joseph Goux, "Marx and the Inscription of Labour," Marx-Scouras, *The Tel Quel Reader*, 53. Ibid., 78. This is also the source of Foucault's remark.

17. Hollier, "1968, May," 1037.

18. Leszek Szaruga discusses Socialist Realist "hermetic poetics" in *Walka o godność: Poezja polska w latach 1939–1988* (Wrocław: Wiedza o kulturze, 1993), 67. François Furet, *The Passing of an Illusion: The Idea of Communism in the Twentieth Century*, tr. Deborah Furet (Chicago: University of Chicago Press, 1999), 139.

19. Velimir Khlebnikov, *Collected Works*, ed. Charlotte Douglas and Ronald Vroon, tr. Paul Schmidt (Cambridge, Mass.: Harvard University Press, 1987–89), I: 321. Lenin comments on art in "Partiinaia organizatsiia i partiinaia literatura," *Sochineniia*, vol. 10 (Moscow: Ogiz, 1947), 27.

20. Aileen Kelly quotes Malia in "The Secret Sharer," *New York Review of Books*, vol. 47, no. 4 (March 9, 2000), 33.

21. "The unrepresented world" is the title of Kornhauser and Zagajewski's programmatic study, as cited above. "The unfalsified world" comes from Barańczak's essay "Parę przypuszczeń na temat poezji współczesnej" (1970), *Etyka i poetyka* (Paris: Instytut Literacki, 1979), 263. Jacek Kuron, and Jacek Zakowski, *PRL dla początkujących* (Wrocław: Wydawnictwo dolnośląskie, 1998), 230.

22. Michnik, *Letters from Freedom*, 287. Michnik, "Biały gołąb szeptu," *Wyznania nawróconego dysydenta* (Warsaw: Zeszyty literackie, 2003), 62. Nyczek, *Określona epoka*, 9.

23. Miłosz, *The Captive Mind*, tr. Jane Zielonko (New York: Vintage, 1981), 75. Zagajewski, "New World," *Without End: New and Selected Poems*, tr. Clare Cavanagh, Renata Gorczynski, Benjamin Ivry, and C. K. Williams (New York: Farrar, Straus and Giroux, 2002), 67. Nyczek, *Powiedz tylko słowo* (London: Polonia, 1985), 20. Romanticism figures even in the subtitle of Barańczak's influential *Nieufni i zadufani: Romantyzm i klasycyzm w młodej poezji lat sześćdziesiątych* (Wrocław: Zakład Narodowy im. Ossolińskich, 1971), in which he describes the recent development of what he calls "dialectical Romanticism" among younger poets (passim). Zagajewski discusses the "plain speaking" of the poetic group "NOW" (TERAZ) as a form of "populist Romanticism" in *Świat nie przedstawiony* (150).

24. Nadeau quotes Breton in *Five Faces of Modernity*, 117, 248; his own comments can be found ibid., 223. Sinyavsky, *Soviet Civilization: A Cultural History*, tr. Joanne Turnbull (New York: Arcade, 1988), 210.

25. Kristeva, "From One Identity to An Other," *Desire in Language*, 132.

26. Kornhauser and Zagajewski, *Świat nie przedstawiony*, 43–44. Barańczak, *Neufni i zadufani*, 31.

27. Nyczek, *Powiedz tylko słowo*, 16. Barańczak, "Parę przypuszczeń," *Etyka i poetyka*, 264. Krynicki, "Podróż pośmiertna II," *Magnetyczny punkt*, 56.

28. Krynicki, "Akt urodzenia," *Magnetyczny punkt*, 28.

29. Krynicki, "Podróż pośmiertna (III)," *Magnetyczny punkt*, 88.

30. Ibid., 87. Krynicki, "Świat nie istnieje," *Magnetyczny punkt*, 92.

31. Kornhauser and Zagajewski, *Świat nie przedstawiony*, 43; Krynicki, "Świat nie istnieje," 92.

32. Krynicki, *Organizm zbiorowy* (Krakow: Wydawnictwo Literackie, 1975), 89.

33. Barańczak, "Określona epoka," *Wybór wierszy i przekładów* (Warsaw: Państwowy Instytut Wydawniczy, 1997), 140. For a more extensive discussion of

Barańczak's poetics, see Clare Cavanagh, "Setting the Handbrake: Barańczak's Poetics of Displacement," *Living in Translation: Polish Writers in America,* ed. Halina Stephan (New York: Rodopi Press, 2003), 77–96.

34. Seamus Heaney, *The Government of the Tongue: Selected Prose 1978–1987* (New York: Farrar, Straus and Giroux, 1989). On the complex relationship to the censor that shaped the generation's work, see Joanna Hobot, *Gra z cenzurą w poezji nowej fali (1968–1976)* (Krakow: Wydawnictwo Literackie, 2000).

35. Quoted in Ferry and Renaut, *French Philosophy of the Sixties,* 98.

36. Barańczak, "8.2.80: I nikt mnie nieuprzedził," *Wybór wierszy,* 212.

37. William Carlos Williams, "This Is Just to Say," *Selected Poems* (New York: New Directions, 1969), 55.

38. Akhmatova, "Mne ni k chemu odicheskie rati," *Sochineniia,* 3 vols. (vols. 1 and 2, ed. Boris Filipoff and G. P. Struve, Munich: Interlanguage Literary Associates, 1967–68); vol. 3, ed. G. Struve, N. A. Struve, and B. A. Filippov (Paris: YMCA Press, 1983), 1:251.

39. Osip Mandelstam, *Sobranie sochinenii,* ed. G. Struve and B. A. Filipoff (vols. 1–3, Washington, D.C,: Interlanguage Library Associates, 1967–1971; vol. 4; Paris: YMCA Press, 1981), I:221. Zagajewski, "Antennas in the Rain," *Eternal Enemies,* tr. Clare Cavanagh (New York: Farrar, Straus and Giroux, 2008), 111. On the "game with the censorship," see Hobot, *Gra z cenzurą, passim.*

40. Mark Edmundson, *Literature against Philosophy, Plato to Derrida* (Cambridge: Cambridge University Press, 1995), 220. Dickinson, *Final Harvest: Emily Dickinson's Poems,* ed. Thomas H. Johnson (Boston: Little, Brown, 1961), 55. Barańczak, *Wybór wierszy i przekładów,* 69. Christopher Benfey quotes Mill in *Emily Dickinson and the Problem of Others* (Amherst: University of Massachusetts Press, 1984), 53. Mandelstam, *Sobranie sochinenii,* 1:196–197. Eliot, "The Three Voices of Poetry," *On Poetry and Poets* (New York: Farrar, Straus and Giroux, 1961), 96. Szymborska, *Poems New and Collected, 1957–1997),* tr. Stanisław Barańczak and Clare Cavanagh (New York: Harcourt Brace, 1998), 205.

41. Barańczak, "Pokolenie 68," *Etyka i poetyka,* 195.

42. All quotes are taken from Nyczek, *Określona epoka,* 224, 204, 43.

43. Zagajewski, "W pierwszej osobie liczby mnogiej," *Komunikat* (Krakow: Wydawnictwo Literackie, 1972), 14. Zagajewski, "Sklepy mięsne," *Sklepy mięsne* (Krakow: Wydawnictwo Literackie, 1975), 25. I'm drawing here on Nyczek's comments in "Komunikaty, listy, wyznania," in *Powiedz tylko słowo,* 47–56.

44. Zagajewski, *Sklepy mięsne,* 13.

45. Hobot, "Rozmowa z Adamem Zagajewskim," *Gra z cenzurą,* esp. 335, 337. Zagajewski, "New World," *Without End,* 70.

46. T. S. Eliot, *After Strange Gods* (New York: Harcourt, Brace, 1934), 30. Hobot, "Rozmowa z Adamem Zagajewskim," 336.

47. Barańczak, "Spójrzmy prawdzie w oczy," *Wybór wierszy,* 70.

48. Zagajewski, "Filosofowie," *Sklepy mięsne,* 46. The translation is mine (*Without End,* 74).

49. All quotations come from Ferry and Renaut, *French Philosophy of the Sixties,* 24–25.

50. Ibid., 26.

51. Barańczak, *Wybór wierszy*, 183–184.

52. Ibid., 149.

53. Nyczek, *Określona epoka*, 279–280. Zagajewski's "Mysticism for Beginners" gave its name to one collection in English; Zagajewski, *Mysticism for Beginners*, tr. Clare Cavanagh (New York: Farrar, Straus and Giroux, 1997), 7.

54. Miłosz, *Captive Mind*, 29.

55. Herbst, "Zapis VIII," Nyczek, *Określona epoka*, 253. Barańczak, "Pokolenie '68," *Etyka i poetyka*, 195–196. Ferry and Renaut quote Engels and Foucault's student, M. Clavel, in *French Philosophy of the Sixties*, 8, 106.

56. Barańczak, "Drobnomieszczańskie snoty," *Wybór wierszy*, 295–296. Zagajewski, "Fire," tr. Renata Gorczynski, *Without End*, 101. For a more detailed discussion of Zagajewski's poetic trajectory, see Clare Cavanagh, "Lyrical Ethics: The Poetry of Adam Zagajewski," *Slavic Review*, vol. 59, no. 1 (Spring, 2000), 2–15.

57. Adorno, "Lyric Poetry and Society," *Telos*, vol. 20 (1974), 52–71. Barańczak, "Parę przypuszczeń," *Etyka i poetyka*, 264.

58. Kornhauser, "Życie wewnętrzne," *Międzyepoka* (Krakow: Wydawnictwo Baran i Suszczyński, 1995), 147. Zagajewski, *Solidarity, Solitude*, tr. Lillian Vallee (New York: Farrar, Straus and Giroux, 1990), 114, 71. Nyczek, "Bach na dachu Lubianki (Aleksander Wat)," *Emigranci* (London: Anyks, 1988), 28.

59. Kornhauser, "Lwów jest wszędzie," *Międzyepoka*, 100. Zagajewski, "Rzeczywistość nie przedstawiona w powojennej literaturze polskiej," *Świat nie przedstawiony*, 36.

60. Zagajewski, "O tym jak 27 marca 1972 roku 19 studentów pod kierunkiem doktora Prokopa analizowało mój wiersz Miasto," *Sklepy mięsne*, 33. "W liczbie mnogiej," *List: Oda do wielości* (Paris: Instytut literackie, 1983), 49. "Fire," tr. Renata Gorczynski, *Without End*, 101.

61. Adam Zagajewski, "Try to Praise the Mutilated World," tr. Clare Cavanagh, *New Yorker* (September 24, 2001), 96. The poem appears in a slightly different version in *Without End*, 60.

62. Czesław Miłosz, *Postwar Polish Poetry* (Berkeley: University of California Press, 1983), xi–xii. Miłosz, *The Witness of Poetry* (Cambridge, Mass.: Harvard University Press, 1983), 111.

63. Wisława Szymborska, *Poems New and Collected 1957–1997*, tr. Stanisław Barańczak and Clare Cavanagh (New York: Harcourt Brace, 1998), 42, 145. Zbigniew Herbert, "Mr. Cogito Reads the Newspaper," *Mr. Cogito*, tr. John Carpenter and Bogdana Carpenter (Hopewell: Ecco Press, 1993), 16.

64. Adam Zagajewski, *Two Cities: On Exile, History, and the Imagination*, tr. Lillian Vallee (New York: Farrar, Straus and Giroux, 1995), 260.

Chapter 8. The Unacknowledged Legislator's Dream

1. "Among School Children," *The Collected Poems of W. B. Yeats* (New York: Macmillan, 1974), 212–214.

2. Miłosz, "To Robinson Jeffers," *New and Collected Poems (1931–2001)* (New York; Ecco/Harper Collins, 2001), 252. Future references to this edition will appear in the text; references to the Polish texts are taken from Czesław Miłosz, *Wiersze*, ed. Aleksandr Fiut, 4 vols. (Krakow: Znak, 2001–2004), unless otherwise noted. Seamus

Heaney, "The Impact of Translation," *The Government of the Tongue: Selected Prose 1978–1987* (New York: Farrar, Straus and Giroux, 1989), 36–44. Joseph Brodsky, "How to Read a Book," *On Grief and Reason: Essays* (New York: Noonday/Farrar, Straus and Giroux, 1995), 96–103.

3. *Postwar Polish Poetry*, ed. Czesław Miłosz (Berkeley: University of California Press, 1983). Zbigniew Herbert, *Selected Poems*, trans. Czesław Miłosz and Peter Dale Scott (Harmondsworth: Penguin Books, 1968).
Shelley did have a political afterlife, abroad and at home, that would have gratified at least some of his legislative ambitions. Not only did he inspire Marx and Engels, who relished his revolutionary sentiments. He posthumously influenced the politics of the future prime minister William Gladstone, and his "Song to the Men of England" inspired the Chartist poets, and became in time a "classic working-class song," as Lawrence Lipking has informed me (unpublished correspondence). See also Bouthaina Shaaban, "Shelley and the Chartists," and Andrew Bennett, "Shelley in Posterity," *Shelley: Poet and Legislator of the World*, ed. Betty T. Bennett and Stuart Curran (Baltimore: Johns Hopkins University Press, 1996), 114–128, 215–223.
On American poetry and radical politics in the sixties, see Paul Breslin, *The Psycho-Political Muse: American Poetry since the Fifties* (Chicago: University of Chicago Press, 1987); and Robert von Hallberg, *American Poetry and Culture 1945–1980* (Cambridge, Mass.: Harvard University Press, 1985), esp. 111–147.

4. Sven Birkerts, *The Electric Life: Essays on Modern Poetry* (New York: William Morrow, 1989), 84, 29. Pearce quotes and discusses Tocqueville in *The Continuity of American Poetry* (Princeton: Princeton University Press, 1961), 137–141.

5. Lawrence Lipking, *The Life of the Poet: Beginning and Ending Poetic Careers* (Chicago: University of Chicago Press, 1981), 18. A. Alvarez, "Introduction to the Poetry of Zbigniew Herbert," *Selected Poems*, 9.

6. Jonathan Aaron, "Without Boundaries" (review of recent Polish poetry in translation), *Parnassus: Poetry in Review* (Spring/Summer, 1981), 124, 128.

7. Zbigniew Herbert, "Prayer of Mr. Cogito-Traveler," *Report from the Besieged City and Other Poems*, tr. John and Bogdana Carpenter (New York: Ecco Press, 1985), 12–13. Carl Woodring quotes Byron in *Politics in English Romantic Poetry* (Cambridge, Mass.: Harvard University Press, 1970), 173–174.

8. Robert Boyes, "Irony of a Poetic Soul Wins Nobel for Pole," *The Times* (London, Oct. 4, 1996), 1.

9. Derek Walcott, "Polonaise," *New Yorker* (Oct. 9, 1989), 52; *Omeros* (New York: Farrar, Straus and Giroux, 1990), 210–212. Seamus Heaney, "The Impact of Translation," 39. Brodsky, "How to Read a Book," 102. A number of younger Irish poets have been so strongly influenced by "European [and] Eastern European poets," Dillon Johnston notes, "that they are undervalued by Irish readers . . . looking for 'Irish poetry'" (*Irish Poetry after Joyce* [Syracuse: Syracuse University Press, 1997], xvii).
On Hughes and Eastern European writing, see Michael Parker, "Hughes and the Poets of Eastern Europe," *The Achievement of Ted Hughes*, ed. Keith Sagar (Manchester: Manchester University Press, 1983), 37–51; and Hughes's introduction to Vasko Popa, *Collected Poems*, tr. Anne Pennington and Francis R. Jones, ed. Francis R. Jones (London: Anvil Press, 1997), xxi–xxx.

10. Helene J. F. de Aguilar, "'A Prince Out of Thy Star': The Place of Czesław Miłosz," *Parnassus: Poetry in Review* (Fall/Winter, 1983; Spring/Summer, 1984), 138, 142.

11. Miłosz, *Postwar Polish Poetry*, xi–xii.

12. Heaney, "The Impact of Translation," 41.

13. Donald Davie, *Slavic Excursions: Essays on Russian and Polish Literature* (Chicago: University of Chicago Press, 1990), 290.

14. Heaney, "From the Republic of Conscience," *The Haw Lantern* (New York: Farrar, Straus and Giroux, 1980), 211; "Sounding Auden," *Government of the Tongue*, 127; "The Unacknowledged Legislator's Dream," *Poems: 1965–1975* (New York: Farrar, Straus and Giroux, 1980), 211.

By the early 1840's, "Manfredism" had already become a dramatic cliché in Polish writing: "You stand like Manfred, with your face paler than the moon," one character tells the Romantic poseur-hero of Słowacki's play "Fantazy" (Juliusz Słowacki, *Dramaty* [Warsaw: Państwowy Instytut Wydawniczy, 1972], 2:58).
On the fate of Eliot's play in Poland, see Norman Davies, *Heart of Europe: The Past in Poland's Present* (Oxford: Oxford University Press, 2001), 394.

15. Jonathan Galassi, "The Horses of Fantasy and Reality," *New York Times Book Review* (March 11, 1979), 14, 25; Marisha Chamberlain, "The Voice of the Orphan: Czesław Miłosz's Warsaw Poems," *Ironwood*, vol. 18 (1981), 28–35; Terence Des Pres, "Czesław Miłosz: The Poetry of Aftermath," *The Nation* (Dec. 30, 1978), 741–743. For an English-language overview of Miłosz's influence on American poetry, see Bogdana Carpenter, "The Gift Returned: Czesław Miłosz and American Poetry," *Living in Translation: Polish Writers in America*, ed. Halina Stephan (Amsterdam: Rodopi Press, 2003), 45–76.

16. Miłosz, *The Witness of Poetry* (Cambridge, Mass.: Harvard University Press, 1983), 94–95, 111.

17. Whitman, *Complete Poetry and Collected Prose* (New York: Library of America, 1982), 264. Miłosz, *Miłosz's ABC's*, tr. Madeline Levine (New York: Farrar, Straus and Giroux, 2001), 299–300.

18. Whitman, *Complete Poetry*, 444–445.

19. Quoted in Czesław Miłosz and Renata Gorczyńska, *Rozmowy: "Podróżny świata"* (Krakow: Wydawnictwo Literackie, 2002), 101–102.

20. Miłosz, "Na śpiew ptaka nad brzegami Potomaku," "Central Park," "Do Alberta Einsteina," *Wiersze*, 2:32, 48, 147.

21. Miłosz, "Wprowadzenie w Amerykanów," *Kontinenty* (Krakow: Znak, 1999), 91–137.

22. Miłosz, *Miłosz's ABC's*, 30.

23. Helen Vendler, "Czesław Miłosz," *The Music of What Happens: Poems, Poets, Critics* (Cambridge, Mass.: Harvard University Press, 1988), 223. Chamberlain, "Voice of the Orphan," 28.

24. Miłosz, "Wprowadzenie w Amerykanów," 91. See, for example, Marian Stala's afterword to Miłosz, *Poezje* (Krakow: Wydawnictwo Literackie, 1999), in which he refers more than once to the wartime Miłosz as "an inhabitant of the waste land" (*mieszkaniec jałowej ziemi*), 460–462.

25. Miłosz, *The Captive Mind*, tr. Jane Zielonko (New York: Vintage, 1981), 216, 41. Miłosz, *Native Realm*, tr. Catherine S. Leach (New York: Doubleday, 1968), 249. T. S. Eliot, *The Complete Poems and Plays 1909–1950* (New York: Harcourt, Brace & World, 1971), 21.

26. Miłosz, "Próba porozumienia" (1956), "Poezja amerykańska" (1956), *Kontinenty*, 432, 414. Filkins, "The Poetry and Anti-Poetry of Czesław Miłosz," *Iowa*

Review, vol. 19, no. 2 (Spring/Summer, 1989), 190. Heaney, "The Impact of Translation," 37.

27. Miłosz, "Proba porózumienia," 442. Jerzy Kwiatkowski, "Miejsce Miłosza w poezji polskiej," *Magia poezji: O poetach polskich XX wieku* (Krakow: Wydawnictwo Literackie, 1995), 21–22.

28. On Eliot's influence in Poland, see Jean Ward, *T. S. Eliot w oczach trzech polskich pisarzy* (Krakow: Universitas, 2001); and Magdalena Heydl, *Obecność T. S. Eliota w literaturze polskiej* (Wrocław: Wydawnictwo Uniwersytetu Wrocławskiego, 2002). Friedrich Nietzsche, *On the Advantage and Disadvantage of History for Life*, tr. Peter Preuss (Indianapolis, 1980), 10. "Wprowadzenie w Amerykanów," 121.

29. Miłosz, *Witness of Poetry*, 112–113; Miłosz, *Unattainable Earth*, tr. Miłosz and Robert Hass (New York: Ecco Press, 1986), 69; Heaney, "The Interesting Case of Nero, Chekhov's Cognac and a Knocker," *Government of the Tongue*, xx.

30. A. Alvarez, "Witness," *New York Review of Books* (June 2, 1988), 21–22. Czesław Miłosz, letter to the editor, *New York Review of Books* (July 21, 1988), 46.

31. Czesław Miłosz, *A Treatise on Poetry*, tr. Miłosz and Robert Hass (New York: Ecco Press, 2001), 33, 100, 103–104.

32. Carolyn Forché, "Introduction," *Against Forgetting: Twentieth-Century Poetry of Witness*, ed. Carolyn Forché (New York: Norton, 1993), 40. Robert Hass, "Reading Miłosz," *Ironwood*, vol. 18 (1981), 49.

33. Miłosz, *Treatise*, 103–106. Miłosz himself mentions the poets associated with *Art and Nation* in his commentary (104). I'm indebted to Michał Markowski for his comments on this section of this chapter particularly.

34. Forché, "Introduction," 36; Des Pres, "Czesław Miłosz," 743.

35. Miłosz, *Native Realm*, 121. On Auden's early political poetry, see Samuel Hynes, *The Auden Generation: Literature and Politics in England in the 1930's* (Princeton: Princeton University Press, 1976). *Pieśń niepodległa*, ed. Czesław Miłosz (Warsaw, 1942; rpt. Ann Arbor: Michigan Slavic Publications, 1981).

36. Miłosz quotes Gombrowicz in *Rozmowy*, 152–153. Miłosz, *The Year of the Hunter*, tr. Madeline Levine (New York: Farrar, Straus and Giroux, 1994), 119. Ewa Czarnecka and Aleksander Fiut, *Conversations with Czesław Miłosz*, tr. Richard Lourie (New York: Harcourt Brace Jovanovich, 1987), 321. Miłosz, *Captive Mind*, 175, 250, 31.

37. Miłosz, *Treatise*, p. 100. On the controversies surrounding Miłosz's funeral, see Clare Cavanagh, "Chaplain of Shades: The Ending of Czesław Miłosz," *Poetry*, vol. 185, no. 5 (February, 2005), 378–386.

38. Czesław Miłosz, *Druga przestrzeń* (Krakow: Znak, 2002), 67. An English translation of the poem, minus this line, may be found in Miłosz, *Second Space*, tr. Miłosz and Robert Hass (New York: Ecco, 2004), 47–66.

39. "In contradistinction to Miłosz's later work, however, these dead are not desired. They are a burden," Forché comments ("Introduction," 40).

40. Barańczak, *Neufni i zadufani: Romantyzm i klasycyzm w młodej poezji lat sześćdziesiątych* (Wrocław: Ossolineum, 1971), 12. Lidia Banowska quotes Miłosz in *Miłosz i Mickiewicz: Poezja wobec tradycji* (Poznań: Wyd. Naukowe UAM, 2005), 9. Miłosz stands proudly before his parking space in a Polish documentary on his life in the States, *Czarodziejska góra* (*A Magic Mountain;* Telewizja Polska, 2000). I'm grateful to Jerzy Illg, one of the film's producers, and his wife Joanna for showing me the film in their home.

41. David Rosen, *Power, Plain English, and the Rise of Modern Poetry* (New Haven: Yale University Press, 2006), 3.

42. Lawrence Lipking, *The Life of the Poet: Beginning and Ending Poetic Careers* (Chicago: University of Chicago Press, 1981), 19. Miłosz, *Year of the Hunter*, 119.

43. Miłosz, *Year of the Hunter*, 208. Eliot, *Collected Poems*, 48.

44. Lipking, *Life*, 19. Northrop Frye, *Anatomy of Criticism* (Princeton: Princeton University Press, 1957), 141.

45. Miłosz and Gorczyńska, *Rozmowy*, 113–114.

46. Miłosz, *The Seizure of Power*, tr. Celina Wieniewska (New York: Farrar, Straus and Giroux, 1982), 34–35.

47. Miłosz, *Native Realm*, 238, 249.

48. Wiktor Weintraub quotes Sobolevsky in *The Poetry of Adam Mickiewicz* (The Hague: Mouton, 1954), 148–149.

49. Geoffrey Hill, "Language, Suffering, and Silence," *Literary Imagination*, vol. 1, no. 2 (Fall, 1999), 251. Miłosz, *Native Realm*, 121. I have adapted the English translation here; see Miłosz, *Rodzinna Europa* (Krakow: Wydawnictwo Literackie, 2001), 139.

50. Miłosz quotes Wordsworth in *Zaraz po wojnie: Korespondencja z pisarzami* (Krakow: Znak, 1998), 221.

51. See Miłosz, *Przekłady poetyckie* (Krakow: Znak, 2005), 88–91, 122–128, 277–279.

52. *Poeta pamięta: Antologia poezji świadectwa i sprzeciwu 1944–1984*, ed. Stanisław Barańczak (London: Puls Publications, 1984), 5. Miłosz, *Captive Mind*, 175.

53. Barańczak, *Poeta pamięta*, 5–9.

54. Heaney, "Introduction," *The Essential Wordsworth* (New York: Ecco, 1988), 9.

55. Miłosz, *Native Realm*, 125.

56. Heaney, *Station Island* (New York: Farrar, Straus and Giroux, 1984), 16–17.

57. Heaney, *Government of the Tongue*, xx, xvi.

Afterword

1. Conversation with Czesław Miłosz, 2002. Miłosz was not above using the same joke more than once; see Anna Bikont and Joanna Szczęsna, *Lawina i kamienie: Pisarze wobec komunizmu* (Warsaw: Proszyński i S-ka, 2006), 189.

2. Conversations with Miłosz, 2003. Miłosz apparently didn't engage other interlocutors on this topic with such frequency, to judge by what two of his long-time friends and colleagues, Adam Michnik and Irena Grudzińska-Gross, told me in another private conversation (Boston, 2005).

3. Lawrence Lipking, *The Life of the Poet: Beginning and Ending Poetic Careers* (Chicago: University of Chicago Press, 1981), passim. Lipking quotes Mann, 113. "World-historical seriousness" is Maureen McLane's phrase, from "A Dirty Job" (review of William Logan, *The Undiscovered Country: Poetry in the Age of Tin*), *Chicago Tribune* [Dec. 11, 2005), Section 14:5. See the introduction, 1).

4. Czesław Miłosz, "Komentarz do Ody do Stalina Osipa Mandelsztama," *Na Głos*, no. 22 (1996). The abridged, retitled text appeared as "Nie znając wstydu ni miary," *Gazeta wyborcza* (Nov. 23–24, 1996), 12. Yet another version, abridged this time by the author himself, was published in Miłosz, *Eseje*, ed. Marek Zaleski

(Warsaw: Świat Książki, 2000), 278–285. Miłosz was so concerned that I understand his position that he personally made sure that I obtained a copy of this version. For Freidin's interpretation of the ode, see *A Coat of Many Colors: Osip Mandelstam and His Mythologies of Self-Presentation* (Berkeley: University of California Press, 1987), 222–272.

5. To judge by the state-sponsored "Year of Zbigniew Herbert," commemorating ten years since the poet's death in 1998, Herbert seems to have won a posthumous victory in this particular wrestling match: see Barbara Zukowski, "Battling Bard: The Politics of Zbigniew Herbert" (honors thesis, Northwestern University, 2008).

6. The responses to Miłosz's article run as follows: Fazil Iskander, "W nadziei na zmiłowanie," *Gazeta wyborcza* (Nov. 23–24, 1996), 13; Jerzy Pomianowski, "Tematy nie do odstąpienia," ibid., (Nov. 30–Dec. 1, 1996), 16–17; Zbigniew Dmitroca, "Kiedy w miescie panuje dżuma," ibid., (Dec. 7–8, 1996), 22; Miłosz, "Poeta i państwo," *Rzeczpospolita, Plus-Minus* (magazine section, Dec. 7–8, 1996), 1; Adam Pomorski, "Poeta nie pamięta," ibid., (Dec. 28–29, 1996), 4; Ryszard Matuszewski, "Poeta pamięta i rozumie więcej niż rusycista," ibid., (Jan. 11–12, 1997), 6; Anatolii Naiman, "Geniusz i poeta," *Gazeta wyborcza* (March 22–23, 1997), 18. I am grateful to Piotr Sommer for passing on the entire sequence to me shortly after it appeared.

7. Miłosz, "Nie znając wstydu," 12. Miłosz, *Eseje*, 278.

8. See Freidin, *Coat of Many Colors*; Mikhail Gasparov, O. *Mandel'shtam: Grazhdanskaia lirika 1937 goda* (Moscow: Rossiiskii gosudarstvennyi universitet, 1996); and my own "Rereading the Poet's Ending: Mandelstam, Chaplin and Stalin," *PMLA*, vol. 109, no. 1 (Jan. 1994), 71–86, and *Osip Mandelstam and the Modernist Creation of Tradition*, esp. 279–304. Miłosz, "Nie znając wstydu," 12.

9. Pomorski, "Poeta nie pamięta," 4. Jerzy Giedroyc paraphrases Herling-Grudziński in Andrzej Zawada, *Miłosz* (Wrocław: Wyd. Dolnośląskie, 1997), 132. I am grateful to Anna Barańczak for illuminating this debate for me.
Miłosz himself was very upset by the young poet's charges and mentioned them to me repeatedly in our talks of summer, 2002. I no longer recall which poet made the accusations, but they were the subject of much discussion among Miłosz's friends that summer.

10. Miłosz, "Nie znając wstydu," 12. Osip Mandelstam, *Sobranie sochinenii*, ed. G. P. Struve and B. A. Filipoff (vols. 1–3, Washington, D.C,: Interlanguage Library Associates, 1967–1971; vol. 4; Paris: YMCA Press, 1981), 1:217.

11. Walter Benjamin, "The Storyteller," *Illuminations* (New York: Schocken, 1978), 100.

12. Miłosz, "Nie znając wstydu," 12. On Liliia Popova and the late poems, see Clare Cavanagh, *Osip Mandelstam and the Modernist Creation of Tradition* (Princeton: Princeton University Press, 1995), 357; and S. S. Averintsev, "Sud'ba i vest' Osipa Mandel'shtama," Mandelstam, *Sochineniia v dvukh tomakh* (Moscow: Khudozhestvennaia literatura, 1990), 1:62.

13. Anatolii Naiman, "Geniusz," 18.

14. Wisława Szymborska, *Poems New and Collected 1957–1997*, tr. Stanislaw Baranczak and Clare Cavanagh (New York: Harcourt Brace, 1998), 205. M. Iu. Lermontov, *Sobranie sochinenii*, 4 vols., ed. G. Makogonenko (Moscow: Pravda, 1986), 1:41–42.

15. Czesław Miłosz, *The History of Polish Literature* (Berkeley: University of California Press, 1983), 231–232. Tadeusz Komendant, "Między wieszczami," *Polityka*, no. 3 (Feb. 25, 1995), 4.

16. Jean-Paul Sartre, *"What Is Literature?" and Other Essays*, tr. Bernard Frechtman et al. (Cambridge, Mass.: Harvard University Press, 1988), 334. Roman Jakobson, "On a Generation That Squandered Its Poets," tr. Edward J. Brown, *Twentieth-Century Russian Literary Criticism*, ed. Victor Erlich (New Haven: Yale University Press, l975), 163.

17. Lydia Chukovskaia quotes Akhmatova in *Zapiski ob Anne Akhmatovoi*, vol. 2 (Moscow: Soglasie, 1997), 509. Lazar Fleishman, *Boris Pasternak: The Poet and His Politics* (Cambridge, Mass.: Harvard University Press, 1990), 289–290.

18. Brodsky was directed by Soviet authorities to accept an invitation to Israel—as a Jew he was eligible for "repatriation" under Soviet law—that he had not sought. He complied only to avoid yet another extended stay in prison or exile. See Lev Losev, *Iosif Brodskii: Opyt literaturnoi biografii* (Moscow: Molodaia gvardiia, 2006), 146–148. Anna Akhmatova, *Sochineniia*, 3 vols. (vols. 1 and 2, ed. Boris Filipoff and G. P. Struve, Munich: Interlanguage Literary Associates, 1967–68; vol. 3, ed. G. Struve, N. A. Struve, and B. A. Filippov, Paris: YMCA Press, 1983), 1:236. Anatoly Naiman quotes Akhmatova in *Remembering Anna Akhmatova*, tr. Wendy Rosslyn (New York: Henry Holt, 1991), 5.

19. Benedikt Sarnov describes Stalin's phone call to Pasternak in *Zalozhnik vechnosti: Sluchai Mandel'shtama* (Moscow: Knizhnaia palata, 1990), 30. Czesław Miłosz, *The Witness of Poetry* (Cambridge, Mass.: Harvard University Press, 1983), 36.

20. For Brodsky's comment, see *Czesław Miłosz: Conversations*, ed. Cynthia Haven (Jackson: University Press of Missouri, 2006), 188. His remarks also appear in abbreviated form on the jackets of many of Miłosz's English-language translation. Czesław Miłosz, *Księgi biblijne* (Krakow: Wydawnictwo Literackie, 2003), 286.

21. Czesław Miłosz, *Second Space*, tr. Miłosz and Robert Hass (New York: Ecco, 2004), 59, 62. I have adapted the translation somewhat; see *Druga przestrzeń* (Krakow: Znak, 2002), 80, 84.

22. Miłosz, "Poeta i państwo," 1, "Nie znając wstydu," 11. Mandelstam, *Sobranie sochinenii*, 2:217.

23. W. B. Yeats, *The Poems*, ed. Richard J. Finneran (New York: Scribner, 1997), 251.

I discussed the changes to *Second Space*'s flap copy in phone conversations with his son Antoni Miłosz, who was assisting his ailing father with the volume's preparation at the time (July, 2004).

24. Szymborska, *Poems*, 192–193.

25. Yeats, *Poems*, 336; Szymborska, *Poems*, 52.

Credits

Index

Titles of works follow other subentries under authors' names.

Lyric Poetry and Modern Politics